Guy Walters is the author of several books on the
Second World War, including *Hunting Evil*. A former

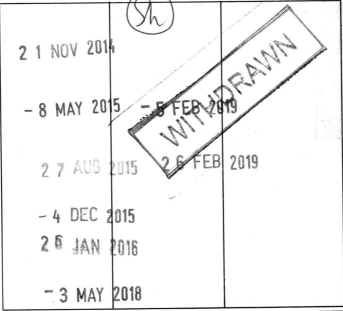

THE REAL GREAT ESCAPE

GUY WALTERS

BANTAM BOOKS

LONDON • TORONTO • SYDNEY • AUCKLAND • JOHANNESBURG

TRANSWORLD PUBLISHERS
61–63 Uxbridge Road, London W5 5SA
A Random House Group Company
www.transworldbooks.co.uk

THE REAL GREAT ESCAPE
A BANTAM BOOK: 9780553826111

First published in Great Britain
in 2013 by Bantam Press
an imprint of Transworld Publishers
Bantam edition published 2014

The Random House Group Limited supports the Forest Stewardship
Council® (FSC®), the leading international forest-certification
organisation. Our books carrying the FSC label are printed on
FSC®-certified paper. FSC is the only forest-certification scheme
supported by the leading environmental organisations, including
Greenpeace. Our paper procurement policy can be found at
www.randomhouse.co.uk/environment

Typeset in 11/14pt Sabon by Falcon Oast Graphic Art Ltd.
Printed and bound by CPI Group (UK) Ltd, Croydon. CR0 4YY.

2 4 6 8 10 9 7 5 3 1

MIX
Paper from
responsible sources
FSC® C016897

This book is for
Richard and Venetia Venning

Contents

THE REAL
GREAT
ESCAPE

GUY WALTERS

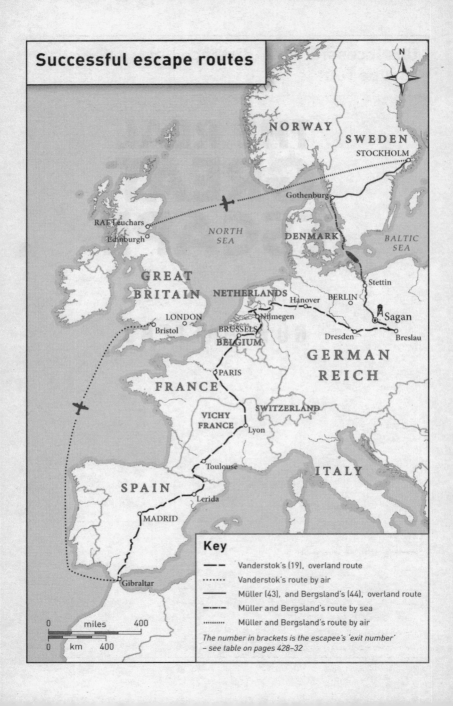

Successful escape routes

Key

— — —	Vanderstok's (19), overland route
·········	Vanderstok's route by air
——	Müller (43), and Bergsland's (44), overland route
—·—·—	Müller and Bergsland's route by sea
··········	Müller and Bergsland's route by air

The number in brackets is the escapee's 'exit number' – see table on pages 428–32

Unsuccessful long-distance escape routes

Key

—— Bushell (4), Scheidhauer (5)	––– Kirby-Green (17), Kidder (18)
—— Catanach (23), Christensen (24), Fugelsang (8), Espelid (9)	xxxxxxx Marcinkus (10), Walenn (11), Picard (15), Brettell (16)
— — Cochran (27)	xxxxxxx Neely (28)
·········· Day (36), Tobolski (37)	ooooooo Plunkett (13), Dvorak (14)
–·–·– Gouws (6), Stevens (7)	······· Van Wymeersch (20)
·········· Hayter (58)	

The number in brackets is the escapee's 'exit number' – see table on pages 428-32

Unsuccessful short-distance escape routes

Cottbus

Long (61) Bethell (65)

Gmina Żary

Sagan

Thompson (42)
Churchill (48) Evans (59)

Birkland (51)
Brodrick (52) Street (53)

GERMAN
REICH

Tiefenfurt

Kohlfurt

Bunzlau

Liegnitz

Bautzen

Görlitz

Shand
(78)

Marshall (2)
Valenta (3)

Armstrong (47)
Humphreys (49)
Royle (50)

Bull (1) Williams (32)
Mondschein (30)
Kierath (35) Green (38)

Boberrohrsdorf
Hirschberg

Tonder (25)
Stower (26)

Poynter (31)

Dodge (29)
Wernham (34)

Pawluk (33)
Kiewnarski (41)
James (39)
Skanziklas (40)

Reichenberg

OCCUPIED
CZECHOSLOVAKIA

N

miles
0   20

0   km   20

OCCUPIED
POLAND

Dowse (21)
Krol (22)

Kempen

Oels

Breslau

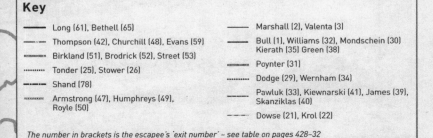

Key

——— Long (61), Bethell (65)	——— Marshall (2), Valenta (3)
—·—· Thompson (42), Churchill (48), Evans (59)	━━━ Bull (1), Williams (32), Mondschein (30) Kierath (35) Green (38)
▪▪▪▪▪ Birkland (51), Brodrick (52), Street (53)	⋈⋈⋈⋈ Poynter (31)
·········· Tonder (25), Stower (26)	·········· Dodge (29), Wernham (34)
——— Shand (78)	——— Pawluk (33), Kiewnarski (41), James (39), Skanziklas (40)
⋈⋈⋈⋈ Armstrong (47), Humphreys (49), Royle (50)	—·—· Dowse (21), Krol (22)

The number in brackets is the escapee's 'exit number' – see table on pages 428–32

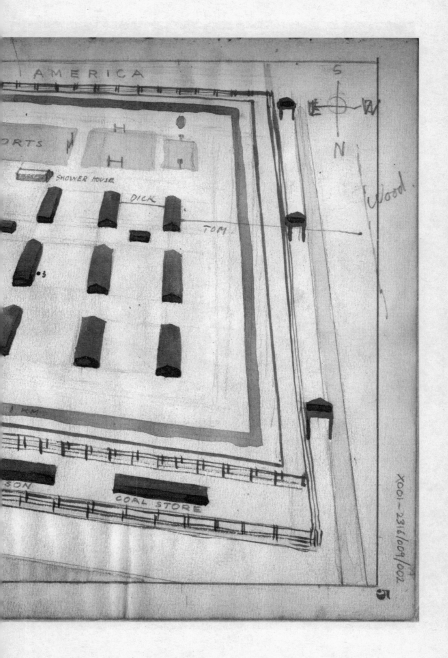

AMERICA

RTS

SHOWER HOUSE

DICK

TOM

KW

SON

COAL STORE

S

N

Wood

X001-2316/009/002

5

76 OFFICERS ESCAPED Breaking two [...]
   Longest tunnel (320 feet in len[...]
   and greatest number of men [...]
50 Officers were shot by the Germa[...]
   or attempting to re-escape.

...ds for both World Wars.
...) breaking German record in Canada
... escape at one time.
...whilst attempting to evade recapture

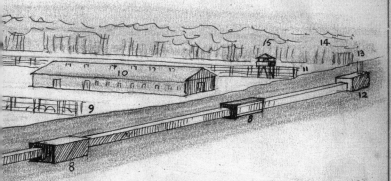

1. Block No 104. Stalag Luft III Sagan.
2. 30 ft deep shaft.
3. Air pump Chamber (pump bellows - 2 Kit bags)
4. Assembly Chamber (wood & metal work)
5. Entrance to shaft under corner fireplace
6. Tunnel - 2'6" square with wooden rail
   track & hand car pulled by ropes for
   displaced sand & human transit.
7. Warning Rail round camp.
8. 2 Half way chambers for pulling Cars.
9. Barbed wire round camp (Sound detectors)
10. Luftwaffe Prison building.
11. Outer barbed wire.
12. Assembly Chamber.
13. Exit shaft. (Exit 20 feet inside)
14. Pine Woods.
15. Observation box on Road passing Camp.

Introduction

THE NARRATIVE of the Great Escape resonates through our culture as persistently as the score of the film. Just as most can complete Elmer Bernstein's entire tune if they merely hear its opening B flat and E flat, many of us can relate the tale denoted by simply the two words 'great' and 'escape'. The story of the film, for those who missed it last Christmas, is that of a group of Allied prisoners of war imprisoned in a German camp set deep in a forest in occupied Lower Silesia. Hungry to get back to the fight and eager to prove as much of an annoyance to their captors as possible, the POWs mount an audacious plan to tunnel out of the camp in order to secure the escape of some two hundred prisoners. Led by an ambitious RAF officer called 'Roger Bartlett', himself a veteran escaper and a survivor of torture by the Gestapo, the prisoners execute their plan with the utmost ingenuity, not only building three tunnels, but also producing perfectly forged passes and brilliantly tailored civilian clothes. Finally, the night of the escape arrives, and when the tunnel is broken, the POWs are shocked to find that it falls some 50 feet short of woods. Because of this, and other mishaps, fewer than eighty manage to break free from the camp, which is nevertheless a brilliant achievement. However, of these, only three manage to make it home, and the remaining escapers are recaptured as they flee through various parts of the Third Reich. At the end of the film, as fifty of the POWs are supposedly being driven back to the camp, they are invited to stretch their legs in a field, whereupon they are all shot dead on the order of a vengeful Adolf Hitler.

As films based on actual events go, the outline of *The Great Escape* is reasonably faithful to the true story of the mass breakout of prisoners from Stalag Luft III in what is now Poland in March 1944. Although a few of the *dramatis personae* are drawn on real personalities, many are necessary composites in order not to over-burden the movie with characters. 'Roger Bartlett', as played by Richard Attenborough, is perhaps the most accurately drawn, based on a Squadron Leader Roger Bushell, who did indeed play the leading role in organising the escape. Many of the details of how the civilian clothes and documents were produced are reasonably accurate, although the results in the film are distinctly more accomplished than their real counter-parts. The relationship between the Germans and their captives is also well observed, and rings true to the reminiscences of the men who were there. However, as is to be expected, there is much in the film that is either sensational (a certain motorcycle chase comes immedi-ately to mind) or simply wrong: the weather is exceptionally fine in the film, whereas at the time it was freezing and thick snow lay around.

From a historical point of view, the film contains two great failings. The first is tone. Much of the movie is comic, and although it is this quality that helps to make the film a classic, it does a disservice to the grimness of the real tale. It is in that depiction of the grimness that the second fault lies: the film places too little emphasis on the murders. Not only does it portray the men's executions incorrectly, but *The Great Escape* – quite necessarily for a jaunty blockbuster – fails to dwell on these killings. This ignores the fundamental fact that it is the execution of 'the Fifty' that distinguishes the real story of the Great Escape from the numerous other mass breakouts conducted by Allied POWs from German camps. Ultimately, this is a story as much about a terrible crime as it is about heroism and ingenuity. If this seems wilfully mawkish, then it is worth noting that the other mass breakouts – no less great, no less ingenious – have all been forgotten. It is undoubtedly the murders that set this story apart.

The purpose of this book is to ascertain the real story behind the escape. Of course, there have been other books about it, not least those by Paul Brickhill, himself a former 'Kriegie' – the POW slang for POW, derived from the German for 'prisoner of war' – at Stalag Luft III, who wrote two accounts of the breakout: *Escape to Danger* in 1946, and *The Great Escape* in 1951. Both are suitably exciting, but what they lack is objectivity and analysis. Furthermore, as he wrote them shortly after the war, Brickhill was not able to draw upon the vast amount of material contained in archives in Britain, Germany and the United States. As a result, his books contain many errors, many of which are forgivable, but some of which are clearly the result of needing to make the story commercially appealing. Many of the histories that followed Brickhill's have built upon his somewhat shaky foundations and, as a result, the errors have been magnified, and many new ones have been inserted. Previous historians of the escape have relied far too heavily on the book that came before, and, with two exceptions, very little attention has been paid to the wealth of primary sources. Not one of these books offers a fresh perspective, or even raises any pertinent questions. As a result of the clumsy application of too much varnish, the true story of the Great Escape has been almost totally obscured.

Historians always like to claim that their work is a 'new history', and I do not claim to be exceptional. This *is* a new history because I have attempted to strip back all those layers of varnish. The best tool for that process is archival work, and I have been surprised – but not shocked – at the enormous disparities between the documents and the histories. What has also raised my eyebrows is the ubiquity of downright fabrication in the memoirs of some of the escapers themselves, which cannot be explained away as the product of faltering memories. Trying to resolve the differences between those memoirs, histories, interviews and wartime files has nevertheless proved to be an enjoyable task, not least because that is the job of the historian.

After removing the varnish, the next task is the restoration, and it is during this process that big questions need to be asked. In the case of the Great Escape, there are several. What was the real purpose of the breakout? What did it achieve? What was Roger Bushell's motivation? What warnings did the POWs receive before they broke out? Was it really the duty of an officer to escape? How many men actually wanted to escape? How much assistance did the POWs receive from their German captors? Who were the men who carried out the executions of the fifty escapers? Was it right that these men were hanged after the war? Does the escape really deserve a place in our national consciousness? In short, was the Great Escape really that great?

Such questions may make some suppose I have approached this subject with a preformed iconoclastic agenda, but they should be assured that I did not. My only object was simply to tell the story from scratch, as if the film and all those other books had never been released. This history, therefore, is based as much as possible on primary sources, and what those sources reveal is a very different tale to the one that we are used to. In addition, as well as presenting a narrative of the escape itself and examining the life of Roger Bushell, these pages tell the story of the murders that followed, and scrutinise the decisions taken by the men who pulled the triggers. After all, the story of the Great Escape is as much theirs as it is that of the escapers. Some of the conclusions I draw will doubtless cause discomfort, but my findings are based on evidence and not prejudice. Readers should also be aware that my approach emphatically does not make me a killjoy. The real Great Escape you hold in your hands is just as exciting and absorbing as the almost fictional version you currently have in your head. The only bad news is that nobody escaped on a motorbike, but then you probably already suspected as much.

Guy Walters
Mead End
January 2013

Chapter One

'A man of fate'

WITHOUT ROGER BUSHELL there would have been no Great Escape. Certainly, tunnels would have been dug, wires would have been cut, passes would have been forged and all manner of escape activities would have taken place, but what Bushell provided was truly dynamic leadership, organisational genius and vaulting ambition – an ambition that ultimately over-leaped itself. Bushell was a giant personality – a combination of charm, egotism, humour, recklessness, intelligence, devilry, arrogance, softness and magnetism. His story and that of the Great Escape are entwined so securely that it would be foolhardy to attempt to separate them. To reach an understanding of why the escape took place, one has to examine Bushell's motivation, and to do that, one needs to learn about the man.

Bushell was born on 30 August 1910 near the mining town of Springs, some 30 miles east of Johannesburg in the Gauteng province of South Africa. Coal had been found in the area in 1887, although it was the subsequent discovery of gold that would secure the town's expansion and enrichment. The first gold mine was established just two years before Bushell's birth, and by the late 1930s, the area would become the largest gold-producing area in the world, boasting eight working mines.[1] Bushell's father, Benjamin, was a mine manager, and he had migrated with his wife Dorothy from Britain to South Africa to take advantage of the prospects offered by Springs. At the time of Bushell's birth, the family was living very comfortably, and Dorothy had given birth to a daughter called Rosemary.

Shortly after his birth, Bushell fell sick and was close to death. For a week he lost much weight, and the nursing sister, who was a Roman Catholic, insisted on holding an impromptu christening in the Bushells' home. Either through divine intervention or nature Bushell recovered, and soon developed into an affectionate and wilful child, who delighted in being able to spit vast distances, burning his sister's dolls, and playing with a mongrel called Rubbish that had been found on a tip.

Roger did, however, have a softer side, which was hardened at the age of eight and a half when he was sent to board at Park Town prep school on Mountain View hillside to the northeast of Johannesburg. Park Town was a turn-of-the-century mansion originally built for a mining engineer, and it had more than forty rooms, including a huge entrance hall and a minstrels' gallery.

As well as participating in the normal prep-school activities, Bushell might have taken part in something more extracurricular: tunnelling. Running inside an upstairs wall that spanned the length of the school was a tunnel that the boys used for holding secret midnight feasts. It must have come as a shock when, on one occasion, they found that a master had left a bin inside the tunnel with a sign asking the tunnellers to use it for their litter. The Park Town tunnel would certainly not be the last that would feature in Bushell's life.[2]

After prep school, Bushell's parents sent him to Wellington College in Berkshire in southeast England at the beginning of 1923, where he joined a house called The Wellesley. Dorothy took him over to Britain, and although Roger would have been accustomed to being away, the thought of boarding nearly 6,000 miles from home must have been tough to bear for both son and mother. Dorothy was no doubt partially satisfied by the letter she received from his housemaster two weeks after his arrival. 'Don't worry about him any more,' he wrote. 'He has already organised the new boys in the House and is very fit and full of himself. I know the type well. He will be beaten fairly often; but he will be much liked and perfectly happy.'[3] The housemaster's words were prescient, and accurately captured much of Bushell's character, not only as a schoolboy, but also as an adult. Throughout his life, Bushell certainly attracted punishment, but it never seemed to undermine his like-ability. It is a measure of his charisma that both schoolmasters and Germans alike were usually minded to forgive him any transgressions.

As his teenage years passed, Bushell would start to

reveal the strength of personality that would later see him establish one of the most redoubtable escape organisations of the Second World War, or indeed of any war. Like many strong-minded and headstrong teenagers, Bushell was something of a rebel, and he was no respecter of authority or regulations. Furthermore, he also had a good imagination, and he was inclined to express his ideas rather firmly. Although he could be arrogant and tiresome, he seems to have remained reasonably well liked and was no bully. One housemate, two years Bushell's junior, recalled how he once cut in front of Bushell in order to get to the entrance of The Wellesley. 'I remember particularly his reaction,' the boy would recall six decades later. 'A good-natured grin and "Good God. What ignominy. Beaten by a squealer!"'[4]

By all accounts, Bushell had a satisfactory school career. Regarded as being 'vigorous and well known', he became a house prefect, played rugby for the First XV and was an adept Scout. However, he did apparently 'detest' cross-country running, which hardly made him exceptional. After passing his School Certificate A in English, History and Physics-and-Chemistry, Bushell briefly studied at Grenoble University on the advice of a master, where he learned to speak French. According to one report, Bushell had an 'amazing capacity as a linguist', and as we shall see, his facility with languages would be of immense use in his career as an escaper; but at the time, there was no obvious application for his talent.[5]

Unsurprisingly, Bushell's father wanted his son to join him in the lucrative mining industry, and, in November 1926, Roger had applied for a place at Pembroke

College, Cambridge, to read for an Engineering Honours degree.[6] However, Bushell was not keen to follow in his father's footsteps down the mines for the simple reason that he was claustrophobic. The fact that Bushell suffered from this anxiety disorder seems extraordinary when one considers the nature of the escape by which he would make his name.

As we shall see, claustrophobia stopped many men from escaping under the ground, and the fear of confinement in the narrow, dangerous tunnels built for the Great Escape was even felt by those who did not suffer from such anxieties. But for claustrophobes, going down the tunnels was an especially terrifying experience, and for Bushell to have overcome this fear shows a remarkable strength of character and will. As Dorothy had observed, Bushell was not a person who felt no fear, but he would force himself to face it and to overcome it. That is surely the hallmark of courage.

In 1929, Bushell went up to Cambridge, where, instead of reading engineering, he decided to study law with a view to becoming a barrister. Such a choice of career was appropriate, as Bushell possessed a forceful nature, an analytical mind, a theatrical bent and plenty of charm. Now aged nineteen, he also cut an impressive physical figure. He stood at a burly 5 feet 10 inches, boasted a head of thick black hair, had an easy smile and, most notably, arrestingly light-blue eyes. Although not conventionally handsome – Bushell would never be a beauty – women certainly found him attractive. Thanks to the lucrative mines of Springs, he was well heeled, and was able to indulge in the then glamorous sport of skiing, which he had discovered at the age of fifteen when he went to Mürren in Switzerland with a group of school friends. Today, we would call Bushell an alpha male, and, like many such characters, he enjoyed the company of women. He had many girl-friends, most of whom were wealthy, and some of whom were married. Either up at Cambridge, or up on the slopes, Bushell found himself a world away from the relative hickdom of Springs. He drove in the same manner in which he skied – recklessly – and would incur huge bills at his tailor's, which would be passed on to his father. The difference between the two men started to yawn, and father and son would often argue.

While Benjamin Bushell was a no-nonsense, largely self-made man who had worked hard for his fortune, his son was turning into what might have looked a somewhat reckless and spendthrift boulevardier. Wellington, Cambridge and his father's wealth had enabled Roger to run – and, indeed, ski – in faster and more socially elevated circles than those inhabited by his own family, and Bushell might have regarded his father as being less sophisticated than his smart new friends. Although it would be unfair to label Bushell a snob, he was perfectly capable of looking down his nose, a trait that was perhaps inherited from his mother.

Bushell's upward social mobility was exemplified by his taste for skiing, a sport which was largely reserved for those with capacious wallets. Throughout the early 1930s, Bushell was a dominant figure amongst the Alpine fraternity, his position secured by a combination of sporting and social prowess. 'He was one of the great characters of St Moritz,' wrote the famous skier and mountaineer Arnold Lunn, 'and uncrowned king of the fashionable Italian skiing centre, Sestrières, within a fortnight of his arrival, not because he broke the record on the most popular of the Sestrières runs, but because the cosmopolitan clientèle of Sestrières were captivated by his boisterous charm.' Lunn, who did not particularly like Bushell, acknowledged that the word 'charm' was too 'weak a word to describe Roger's magnetism'. Lunn ascribed his appeal to the fact that Bushell expressed himself in forthright terms. 'I remember once hearing (from a distance) Roger describing to a sympathetic group in the Palace lounge the precise nature of the "lousy skiing" which had lost him an important slalom,' he recalled. Lunn approached Bushell and suggested that he might adopt a 'slightly less robust turn of speech', whereupon Bushell exclaimed, 'Christ, Arni! I *never* swear!'[7] In fact, Bushell loved swearing, and was famous for it. But despite Lunn's misgivings, he had to admire the young man's social chutzpah. Lunn recalled one Anglo-Swiss post-race dinner in which the Swiss captain, Victor Streiff, paralysed by shyness, was unable to make a speech. He was heckled to speak, but he remained silent. 'Then Roger arose,' Lunn later wrote, 'and standing just behind Victor, made the speech which Victor should have made, in Bernese-German as accurate and far more fluent than Victor's. He condoled with the British team on their narrow defeat and in a few well-chosen words congratulated their team captain, Roger Bushell, on a fine performance.'[8]

However, Bushell was much more than a charming blue-tongued lounge lizard: he was in fact a superb skier. In 1931, he won the long-distance race at the

British Ski Championship meeting at Wengen in Switzerland.[9] In 1932, he won the Varsity Slalom.[10] In 1935, in St Moritz, Bushell came fifteenth in the World University Ski Championship, a ranking that he might have found disappointing. According to most accounts, Bushell's skiing style was not unlike his driving – fast and reckless. 'He used to take one course straight down at uniform, maximum speed, swearing like a trooper,' wrote one observer.[11] Predictably, Bushell's daredevilry on the slopes would result in injury. In a cross-country race in Canada in 1932, he suffered a bad fall and the tip of one of his skis tore open a gash in his right cheek and injured his right eye. For reasons that are unclear, Bushell refused to have the wound dealt with in Montreal, and he returned to Britain with half his face in bandages. He was finally operated on back in London, where the surgeon found that the gash had become infected. Although the operation had been a success, for the rest of his life his eye permanently drooped in a somewhat sinister fashion.

Bushell graduated from Cambridge in 1932 with a third-class degree, which is perhaps indicative that he put pleasure before study. Furthermore, he had missed the Lent term of 1931 for reasons that are unknown, and the skiing accident had seen him miss the Lent term of 1932.[12] Nevertheless, this poor result did not stymie his chances of becoming a barrister, and he joined the chambers of G. D. Roberts, KC, from where he was called to the Bar in 1934. Bushell quickly established a reputation as an able criminal barrister. Over the next five years, he both defended and prosecuted fraudsters, murderers, thieves and sexual offenders, including a soldier accused of molesting a 14-year-old girl.[13] In one of his last cases before the war, in July 1939, Bushell prosecuted an autogiro test pilot for flying dangerously low over houses in Hanworth to the west of London.[14] Acting for the prosecution in such a case must have been anathema to Bushell, who maintained his love of motorised daredevilry. Ironically, he once had to prosecute a young music teacher called Marion Cunningham, who was accused of refusing to stop for a police car, and was chased 9 miles from Hendon Central to South Mimms. Cunningham covered the distance in eleven minutes, during which for half of the time she had not put on her headlights. Bushell described the chase in court as 'remarkable', although he must have said the word with an inner grin, as such driving was very much his own style.[15]

Had it not been for the war, there can be little doubt that Bushell would have risen to the top of the profession. In December 1937, the *Empire News* marked him down as a 'fledgling to watch' after he had made an 'eloquent and successful plea at the Old Bailey'.[16] Bushell's style of advocacy appeared to be as aggressive as his driving and skiing. Although such a style can alienate juries, it seemed to do Bushell no professional harm. It showed that beneath his charm lay an acidulous nature, which he did not hesitate to display. At the resolution of one case, in which he had successfully defended a London gangster on a murder charge, the defendant wished to shake hands. 'I don't shake hands with murderers,' Bushell replied. 'I only do what I'm paid to do.'[17] By the outbreak of war, Bushell was regarded, according to his head of chambers,

G. D. Roberts, as a 'familiar and popular figure in the Criminal Courts', for whom 'nothing was too much trouble'. Roberts also noted that Bushell had 'every desirable quality' to make a success at the Bar, and he managed not to allow any of his 'manifold outside interests to interfere with his steady determination to make good'.[18]

As well as skiing, one of those interests was flying. In 1932, Bushell joined the RAF Auxiliary and Reserve Volunteers, and was assigned to 601 Squadron, which had been dubbed the 'Millionaires' Squadron' owing to its formation in October 1925 by a group of wealthy young amateur aviators. Bushell was invited to join the squadron by Lord Knebworth, with whom he had made friends while skiing.[19] Bushell would have felt at home amongst his fellow pilots, many of whom had modified their RAF uniforms with red silk linings and had a penchant for motorcycle polo. The squadron car park in Northolt, west London, featured some of the finest sports cars of the day, which were mostly used to get their owners back to White's club after a hard Saturday in a Hawker Hart. Although Bushell was not a member of the exclusive White's,[20] being a member of 601 carried a similarly weighty social cachet, and Bushell's fellow pilots included the likes of Max Aitken, the son of Lord Beaverbrook; Sir Philip Sassoon; fellow skiing fanatic William Rhodes-Moorhouse; the Conservative MP Loel Guinness; Brian Thynne, whose great-grandfather was the 3rd Marquess of Bath; Rupert Bellville, reputedly the first Briton to practise as a bull-fighter and who would later fly with Franco's air force;[21] Bushell's flatmate Michael Peacock; and Anthony 'Rex'

Hayter, who would be a fellow Great Escaper. Photographs taken of the squadron are pure Bertie Wooster, depicting dashing young men variously nick-named 'Boylo', 'Reggie', 'Jacko', 'The Doc', 'Hobbie', 'Bobbie', 'Nono', 'Parko' and 'Gillo' flying in a variety of aircraft, such as Avro 504s and Westland Wapitis. Sometimes, the photographs show the pilots with their canine companions, and in one shot from 1934, a black West Highland terrier perches on Bushell's lap. The presence of the likes of Noël Coward and David Niven in some of the pictures only adds to the sense of high society.[22] The 601 'breed' was summed up well by Max Aitken. 'They were the sort of young men who had not quite been expelled from their schools,' he wrote, 'whom mothers warned their daughters against – in vain – who stayed up far too late at parties and then, when everyone else was half dead with fatigue, went on to other parties.'[23] Perhaps predictably, many of the members of 601 married each other's sisters, which caused Bushell to observe drily, 'If this sort of thing goes on much longer, this squadron will be as in-bred as an Austrian village.'[24]

Pictured wearing dark glasses, and holding either a cigarette or a pipe or even a rifle, Bushell fitted in with the 'Millionaires', combining Old-World polish with just the right measure of New-World roughness. 'With engaging eloquence to suit the occasion he could charm a jury or outclass a sailor in profanity,' observed Tom Moulson, a fellow member of 601. As well as being renowned for being able to 'spit an incredible distance', Bushell's charisma soon acquired him celebrity status throughout the Royal Air Force. By all accounts, the young barrister-cum-pilot revelled in his fame. 'The trouble with Bushell is he's always hiding his light under himself,' one senior officer punned. Bushell's capacity to hold his drink also drew some comment. 'He looks the sort of chap who, if you turned a tap on, would run out.'[25] As well as roister-doistering, Bushell also appeared to enjoy dallying with the opposite sex. On one occasion an earring was found in his plane, which caused much mirth among his fellow pilots. However, it was Bushell's facility with the bluest of language that really earned him his reputation. Fellow pilots would be ordered about over the air with the foulest of terms, which burned the ears of those hearing the transmissions on the ground. Among them was a radio amateur, who wrote to the squadron that although he enjoyed listening in when it was airborne, 'I am sorry to say that when Red Leader [Bushell] comes on the air I have to send the children out of the room.'[26]

Bushell was undoubtedly a more than competent airman, but he would also take the kind of risks that saw him entered into squadron legend. During the weekend of 15 August 1936, 601 Squadron was holding its summer camp at Lympne Aerodrome above Romney Marsh in Kent. Although it was only 2 miles away, Bushell and his fellow pilots often flew down to the nearest pub, the Botolph's Bridge Inn, where they would land on a small field nearby. That evening, an 'eager and thirsty' Bushell was heading down to the pub in a single-seater Aeronca C-3 owned by Max Aitken. Just as he was about to land, Bushell had to swerve to avoid a sheep, and he overshot the field. The Aeronca, which only weighed 569 pounds, careered through a hedge, knocked the head off a signpost that read 'To Dymchurch', and smashed into pieces on the road directly in front of the pub. 'Bushell stepped unscratched from the wreckage,' recalled Tom Moulson, 'apologised to Aitken with a deep bow, and began immediately to auction off the Aeronca's remains to the gathering crowd of spectators.'[27] The Aeronca – or what was left of it – was won by a Mrs Ann Davis, who composed a poem based on the plane's registration.

> G one is Max's aeroplane
> A rtful Roger is to blame
> D own at Botolph's Bridge one night
> Z ero was his cruising height
> Z oomed too low – out went the light!

Bushell's crash even made the pages of the *Daily Mirror* the following Monday, although the report merely stated that Bushell had overshot the airfield.[28] Unsurprisingly, the 'To Dymchurch' sign was claimed as a prized trophy, and was shown with the squadron's silverware.[29]

As such a giant character, Bushell was undoubtedly a member of London society, which was exemplified in July 1935 by his being made godfather to the daughter of his fellow pilot, Peter Clive. The christening took place at St Peter's in Eaton Square, and attending the service was Lady Georgiana Mary Curzon.[30] Although it is not clear whether this was the first time Bushell and 'Georgie' had met – it is more likely that they had done so at the Clives' wedding in May 1934[31] – it was around this time that the two became lovers. The story of their relationship is a tragic one, and it shows that the South African-born Bushell – with a father who managed mines – was never wholly accepted by some members of the aristocratic set with whom he associated.

Georgie was quite a catch – tall, willowy, with dark hair and ivory skin, she was beautiful, and, furthermore, extremely aristocratic. Eight months older than Bushell, she was the daughter of Francis Curzon, the 5th Earl Howe. Educated at Eton and Christ Church, Oxford, Curzon had seen action at Gallipoli during the First World War, and in the 1918 General Election he successfully stood as the Conservative candidate for Battersea South, a seat he held until 1929, when he succeeded to his father's peerage. His great passion was motor racing, and while he was an MP, he founded the British Racing Drivers' Club and spent much of the 1930s racing. His greatest sporting achievement was winning the 24 Hours of Le Mans in 1931, a race in which he participated six times.[32] Between 1935 and 1938, Curzon was aide-de-camp to George V, an office that exemplifies the height of the family's social elevation.[33] If further proof of Georgie's place in society were required, one only has to consult the guest list of a dance hosted for her by her parents in London in July 1928, which included at least one duke, four duchesses, three marquesses, three marchionesses, thirteen earls, fifteen countesses, and ten viscounts.[34]

Like many attractive women from her background, Georgie was recruited by the cosmetics firm Pond's to advertise its famous cold cream and tissues. The combination of lineage and beauty was considered irresistible to potential customers, especially those in the United States. By the time Bushell met her, Georgie had featured in several magazines, including *Picturegoer* in 1932, in which 'the charming debutante, Lady Georgiana Curzon . . . guards her youthful loveliness with Pond's two creams'.[35] In the *New Yorker* magazine in September 1931, she appeared alongside her mother to promote Pond's Tissues, which were, the pair claimed, 'the best way to remove cold cream we ever found'.[36] In February of that year, Georgie was accompanied by Lady Alexandra Haig, Lady Louis Mountbatten and various other aristocratic beauties in a full-page advertisement in several American newspapers to sell the Pond's range. 'If debutantes had time to write up diaries,' Georgie is quoted as saying, 'the name of Pond's would certainly occur in every page . . . Pond's Method is a blessing! It is so quick and simple it makes it easy always to look your best.'[37]

Doubtless Georgie did not take the copywriters' gush seriously, but the advertisements do capture how she was perceived. 'Her flower-like face, her charm, have made her one of the most popular members of the aristocratic younger set,' read the copy in an advertisement placed in the *Straits Times* of Singapore. Describing her as 'gay . . . glamorous . . . lovely', Pond's naturally attributed her 'flawless complexion' to the 'faithful use' of Pond's Two Creams.[38] It is a measure of Georgie's success as a model that she featured in advertisements for products other than cosmetics and in countries other than Britain and the United States. Magazine readers in Poland were able to see her promoting a Cadillac, in which it was claimed that Georgie was 'one of many Cadillac owners among the aristocratic spheres', along with luminaries such as the Emperor of Japan, the Shah of Persia and the unlikely figure of the 'Prince of Bedford'.[39]

Although little is known of the relationship between Bushell and Georgie, it seems that the two were much in love. A photograph shows them sitting on a lawn, arms around each other and beaming at the camera. They made a good-looking couple. However, it appears that the union may have been kept secret, with Bushell telling neither his parents nor his close friends.[40] Secret or not, the relationship did not end in marriage, possibly because Georgie's father supposed that Bushell's background was not suitably grand to allow him to be his son-in-law. On 28 October 1935, *The Times* announced that Georgie was engaged to be married to Lieutenant Home Kidston of the Royal Navy, whose late brother, Glen, was a motor-racing friend of Earl Howe. The couple had only met two years before, during which Kidston had spent much of his time in New Zealand. Kidston and Georgie had written to each other frequently, and, in Kidston's words, 'got to love each other to the extent I wanted to come home to England to be with you again'.[41] Georgie's father evidently thought Kidston a suitable match, and pressured him to return from the southern hemisphere to marry his daughter. However, it appears that some of Georgie's friends were wary of Kidston, with at least one doing all he could to prevent Kidston from coming home. Nevertheless, at some point in 1935, Kidston did return and proposed to Georgie. 'I did not feel that I could do anything other than carry out what was expected of me and get married,' Kidston later wrote. Just a few days before the wedding, Kidston shared his anxieties about his forthcoming marriage with a friend, telling him 'that I thought that perhaps I was making an awful mistake about the whole thing and that it would be better to call it off'.[42] However, as Kidston observed, 'things had gone so far that this course seemed impossible' and the couple married on 27 November at Holy Trinity Church in Penn Street, near Amersham in Buckinghamshire. The wedding, which was attended by numerous aristocrats and racing drivers – including Raymond Mays, who had competed in that year's German Grand Prix – was filmed by Gaumont British Newsreels, and a picture of the seemingly happy couple appeared in *The Times* the following day.[43] On 17 April 1937, Georgie gave birth to their only son, Glen, but, predictably perhaps, the marriage was to be a failure. As we shall see, Kidston may have come from the right stock, but he was a poor husband. It is also possible that he knew where his wife's real affections lay.

It is not known how Bushell felt about not being able to marry Georgie, and we can only assume that he was saddened. Perhaps acting on the rebound Bushell himself got engaged to Marguerite 'Peggy' Hamilton, who was an old friend who lived in Wellesley House on Sloane Square, just half a mile from Bushell's flat in Tite Street. Peggy was a member of 'Cochran's Young Ladies', a group of women who sang and danced in revues put on by the celebrated impresario C. B. Cochran. With her smouldering glamour, she was an obvious catch for the charming young barrister-about-town.

However, as with so many men of his generation, the war stymied Bushell's plans, whether they were romantic or professional. Nevertheless, the conflict also brought opportunity, especially to those, like Bushell, who were felt to have a destiny. His mother Dorothy identified that as well as having both a 'joie de vivre' and a 'joie de vice', her son also had a strong sense of purpose, and that he was fated for some sort of greatness.

For his part, it was evident to Bushell that war was coming. Visits to the Alps had put him in contact with Germans and Austrians, and he had witnessed an unpleasant eager martiality, which, according to Tom Moulson, aroused a strong anti-Germanism in Bushell. No appeaser, Bushell became 'increasingly incensed by what he judged to be culpable myopia on the government's part', Moulson later wrote.[44] Nevertheless, the partying continued. Shortly after Neville Chamberlain returned from Munich in September 1938, Janet Aitken, the daughter of Max, hosted a party in Belgrave Square with her friend Sibell Lygon for the pilots of 601 Squadron. The cellar was raided for 'vast quantities of champagne, claret and burgundy', much of which was no doubt drunk by Bushell, the contents of whose glass would appear ceaselessly to evaporate. 'The laughter, drinking and dancing continued far into the night,' Janet Aitken recalled. 'It was the party to end all parties, and in a way that's exactly what it turned out to be.'[45]

Chapter Two

'I'd left the camp without asking'

ON 25 AUGUST 1939, Bushell's parents received a telegram from their son, informing them that he was returning from the south of France to join up with 601 Squadron. Bushell had been mobilised, and with it came an end to glamorous days of flying boats and the Riviera. Like most, Bushell was hopeful that the declaration of war the following week would be nothing more than just that.

For the time being, however, the RAF had more call upon Bushell's legal acumen than his skill as a pilot. Ever since he had joined 601 Squadron, Bushell had been willing to lend freely his services to any fellow pilot up in front of an RAF court for some airborne misdemeanour. Along with Michael Peacock, Bushell managed to get many of his friends out of trouble, which, according to Tom Moulson, was not entirely appreciated by the RAF. 'They won more than their fair share of cases and became something of a legend,' he recalled. 'The authorities were continually embarrassed.'[1] Bushell would often fly to the RAF courts in his uniform, and then change into his wig and gown when he arrived in the court. Peacock would go one stage further: when taxiing his aircraft, he would swap his flying helmet for his wig, which startled the ground crew.[2] However, in September 1939, Bushell found himself defending two fellow pilots for a more serious offence than buzzing vicarage tea parties – they were being court-martialled for a friendly-fire incident. On the morning of 6 September, just three days after the declaration of war, Spitfires of 74 Squadron at Hornchurch in Essex were scrambled to intercept a flight of unidentified aircraft heading for London. Led by Adolph 'Sailor' Malan, the Spitfires soon spotted the aircraft and Malan called out 'Tally-ho!' which was taken as an order to attack. A few seconds later, Malan saw that the aircraft were in fact Hurricanes, and he ordered his men to break off. Two of the pilots, Paddy Byrne – who was a friend of Bushell – and John Freeborn, appeared not to hear his words, and they shot down two of the Hurricanes, which resulted in the death of one of the pilots. Byrne and Freeborn were arrested as soon as they returned to Hornchurch, and the ensuing court martial was a bitter affair. The defence was led by Sir Patrick Hastings, KC, with Bushell as his deputy. Malan appeared as a witness for the prosecution, and accused Freeborn of being irresponsible, while Hastings accused Malan of being a liar. Thanks to the advocacy of Hastings and Bushell, the two pilots were acquitted.[3] It is perhaps worth noting that because of the 'Battle of Barking Creek', the first plane ever shot down by a Spitfire was a Hurricane.[4]

During the court martial, Bushell was still a flight lieutenant, but his superiors, recognising his organisational and leadership skills, promoted him to squadron leader and, on 12 October 1939, ordered him to reform 92 Squadron based at RAF Tangmere near Chichester in West Sussex. It is a measure of the high regard in which he was held that Bushell was the first auxiliary officer asked to raise a squadron. He was only twenty-nine, and he had no experience of regular military service. On paper, the appointment looked fantastic, but when Bushell arrived at Tangmere a few days later, he found a skeleton ground crew, no officers and no equipment. Nevertheless, he was heartily welcomed by the officers of 43 Squadron who were also using the base, and on his first night, according to 92 Squadron's diary, the clubbable Bushell 'went to his bed at a late hour, feeling that Tangmere was the best station to be found in the country in the best of all possible wars'.[5] Although the squadron was initially equipped with Bristol Blenheim night fighters, by the beginning of March 1940 it had been issued with Spitfires, which would have been far more to Bushell's liking.

Bushell appeared to be an autocratic squadron leader, to the extent that he was even nicknamed 'the Führer' by his junior officers. Certainly he had high standards, and any pilots – such as one of his night commanders – who did not measure up were swiftly purged.[6] However, Bushell was no mere martinet, and the reason for his toughness lay in a deep compassion for his pilots. 'He's quite a bloke to serve under,' one of Bushell's officers told a new recruit. 'Don't be put off by his manner. To him his squadron and his pilots are everything. Once you are accepted into the squadron you will never find yourself alone. He'll bollock you from arsehole to breakfast time but he'll support you up to the hilt if necessary and you won't know a thing about it.'[7]

On 23 May 1940, Bushell flew out on what would be his only day of aerial combat operations, leading twelve of his squadron's Spitfires. Bushell's orders were to patrol the French coastline between Boulogne and Dunkirk to help cover the retreat of the British Expeditionary Force (BEF). At 11.45 a.m., as the Spitfires passed over Cap Gris Nez, a flight of eight Messerschmitt 109s bore down on them. In the ensuing dogfight, the squadron managed to down two Messerschmitt 109s, but one Spitfire was also destroyed. By some accounts, the engagement had been an ill-disciplined affair, with the nervous chatter of the young and inexperienced RAF pilots clogging up the airwaves.[8]

After returning home, the squadron was sent back across the Channel at 5.20 that afternoon, and on this occasion Bushell and his men ran into a much larger formation of enemy aircraft – an estimated twenty Messerschmitt 110s, fifteen Heinkel 111s and, above them, a pack of 109s. 'I don't know how Roger proposed to attack the Armada,' wrote Tony Bartley, one of the Spitfire pilots, 'and I thought of Henry V at Agincourt, perhaps because it was not far from us.'[9] Despite being outnumbered, Bushell was indeed not the type of man to shirk a fight, and he ordered his squadron to attack. 'Paddy, your flight take on the top cover,' he said. 'The rest stick with me, and we'll take on the bombers.' As soon as the battle started, Bushell was set upon by nearly half a dozen aircraft. In the ensuing mêlée, Bushell claimed to shoot down two Messerschmitt 110s. Bushell then put his Spitfire into a spin, with two enemy planes firing at him from his aft quarter. After a single rotation, he pulled up to the left and saw a Messerschmitt coming at him from below. The two planes flew head first at each other, both firing. Bushell's shots hit first, and he killed the pilot. The Messerschmitt missed him by inches, and Bushell turned to see the plane rear up in a stall and then plummet down with its engine smoking.

However, with the odds against him, it was not long before Bushell's plane was hit. His engine received numerous rounds, and soon the Spitfire was on fire, with coolant gushing out everywhere. Finally, at around 5,000 feet, he levelled the plane, started her up again, and tried to make for the airstrip at Saint-Inglevert, about 8 miles southwest of Calais. The engine soon packed up, and the cockpit filled with smoke. He resolved to bale out, but just as he was undoing his harness, the fire went out, so he decided to try a belly landing. He was successful, and the only injury that he suffered was a blow to the nose. With the plane on fire, Bushell scrambled out of the cockpit, and then sat down with a cigarette to watch it go up in flames. A few minutes later, a motorcycle appeared, the rider of which he assumed to be French, as he had landed just east of Boulogne, which he thought was in friendly territory. As the bike drew near, he realised that the man's helmet was of a rather more German variety, a suspicion soon confirmed by the simple fact of having a pistol pointed at his chest. Bushell raised his arms.

Bushell's war, as the cliché would have it, was over, and he had only experienced a few minutes of combat. His squadron may have claimed five kills, but they had come at a price: four aircraft and pilots had been lost, with another aircraft badly damaged and its pilot wounded.[10] Although Bushell was not to know these tallies, he would have been – like any other pilot in his circumstances – disappointed not only at the prospect of captivity, but also at the brevity of his war. Furthermore, although he claimed to have shot down two aircraft, these kills would never be confirmed, and officially, Bushell would always have a clean 'score-card'. For a personality such as his, the blow must have been especially punitive; this was, after all, a man who was used to winning. For the rest of the war, Bushell would vigorously attempt to get his own back at the Germans, and it is reasonable to assume that part of what motivated him was a strong desire to eradicate a sense of failure. More than most, what Bushell really wanted was a good war.

When the surviving members of his squadron returned to England, they reported that Bushell had, in all likelihood, been killed. The following day, his parents received a telegram from the Under Secretary of State at the Admiralty that Bushell was 'reported missing and believed to have lost his life as a result of air operations'. On 28 May, a telegram from the Air Ministry conveyed a similar message. Doubtless, Bushell's parents would have clung to the belief that their son was alive, but they must have known it was unlikely. It was not until 14 June that the best news of all arrived, contained in a telegram from the Under Secretary of Air, which stated that Bushell was a prisoner of war in Germany.

Like many downed airmen, Bushell was sent to Dulag Luft transit camp at Oberursel, north of Frankfurt. With the Germans almost unable to cope with the thousands of Allied combatants they had captured, POWs such as Bushell had to walk to their camps. It is not known whether Bushell walked all 350 miles from Boulogne to Oberursel but he certainly had some weight to lose. When he was shot down, he weighed over fourteen stone, and was regarded by one pilot as 'a pretty hefty chap and . . . just plain ugly in a pleasant sort of way'.[11]

Shortly after his arrival, Bushell wrote to both his family and G. D. Roberts, the head of his chambers. The letters, which were censored, suggest that Bushell was trying to come to terms with his captivity, and to make the best of his situation. Bushell asked Roberts to send him some standard law books, such as those by John Salmond, as well as all the quarterlies so he could stay abreast of developments in the legal world. To Roberts, Bushell also broke the terrible news that his flatmate, fellow barrister and 'Millionaire', Michael Peacock, had been shot down and killed while ground strafing near Arras on 20 May, on the very day that he had taken command of 85 Squadron.[12]

Bushell's letters belied his real intentions, as he was emphatically not the type of man who wished to sit out the war reading *Salmond on Jurisprudence*. It was in Bushell's nature to escape, and, unsurprisingly, he was far from alone. In fact, Dulag Luft was where he was to forge relationships that would be crucial to the planning and execution of the Great Escape. Among those he befriended was Wing Commander Harry 'Wings' Day, who was the camp's Senior British Officer (SBO). Born in August 1898, Day was considerably older than most of his fellow officers, and he was referred to as 'Uncle'. Tall, slim and balding with a beaky nose, Day possessed an enormous amount of charisma, which made him a natural leader. 'Wings Day could charm the birds out of the trees,' recalled one POW. '[He was a] man for whom one had enormous respect. If Day had said, "Well, I'm afraid we're going to have heavy casualties from this idea, but I'm asking for volunteers to storm the wire to get a few people out," he would probably have had a lot of volunteers.'[13] Another remembered Day as being a 'good character, a jolly chap, a bit hairy-scary, a bit keen on escaping, active, intelligent, very popular'.[14] He was also undeniably brave. In January 1919, when a lieutenant in the Royal Marines, Day had been awarded the Albert Medal for repeatedly returning below the decks of the torpedoed *Britannia* to rescue two trapped and injured sailors. 'The cordite fumes were very strong,' read his medal citation, 'and his life was in danger throughout. His courage and resource were beyond praise.'[15] Later, when the Albert Medal was discontinued, Day's award was exchanged for a George Cross, which indicates how highly his actions had been regarded. As well as being courageous, it was often recalled that Day had a fondness for the bottle. 'He was notorious for his drinking bouts,' another POW observed. 'He would drink people under the table. His life had been saved by being shot down, because he didn't have access to alcohol.'[16]

Shot down just five weeks after the war had started, it was Day, along with Dulag Luft's Commandant Theo Rumpel, who formulated an arrangement by which the captors and captives would coexist. Day quickly realised that it would be as well to observe the Geneva Convention, and to maintain an air of military courtesy towards the Germans. Although that might have raised the eyebrows of a few officers, Day's decision to breach military regulations by allowing officers to be granted parole in order to take exercise outside the camp's cramped confines was more controversial still. Day correctly appreciated that the men's physical and mental fitness would be better served by allowing them to enjoy a feeling of space, even if it did mean having to give one's word of honour to the enemy.[17] Rumpel, who was later described by one POW as 'not a Nazi – pro-German – clever, diplomatic – soldier and gentleman', reciprocated this air of gentlemanliness by inviting Day and some of his officers to dine with him in his own private mess.[18] For the prisoners, such dinners must have seemed the height of luxury: sauerkraut, smoked eel, thick soup, ham and wine were most certainly not features of camp rations.[19] When Bushell wrote to tell his parents that in July 1940 he and his fellow POWs were being well treated, he was not just pleasing the censor. For his thirtieth birthday party in August, the Commandant sent him a bottle of whisky, and even joined the subsequent party.

The cooperative attitude exhibited by Bushell and Day masked a desire to escape that was more than a 'bit keen'. Day's adjutant was Lieutenant Commander

Jimmy Buckley, a Fleet Air Arm pilot who had been shot down in May 1940. Small, tough and wiry, Buckley was appointed by Day to be the first chairman of the escape committee, which was soon given the more mysterious appellation of the X Organisation.[20] Also part of the organisation was Major Johnny Dodge, a 46-year-old American by birth, who was related by marriage to Winston Churchill. After becoming a British subject in 1915, Dodge had served in the British army, winning both a DSO and a DSC.[21] Between the wars, Dodge had become a stockbroker and contested the Mile End constituency for the Conservatives in the General Elections of 1924 and 1929, although he lost both times to the Labour candidate, John Scurr.[22] Dodge rejoined the army with the outbreak of war, and he attached himself to the Middlesex Regiment, with which he went to France as part of the BEF. Like so many others, Dodge was captured at Dunkirk, despite a valiant attempt to swim out to sea under an artillery barrage to catch a steamer.[23] Another significant member of the X Organisation was Pilot Officer Bertram 'Jimmy' James, who would prove to be one of the keenest escapers of the war. A Wellington bomber pilot, James was shot down over the Dutch coast on the night of 5 June, and he managed to evade capture until he was handed to the Germans by a Dutch family with whom he had sought shelter.[24]

These, then, were some of the men whom Bushell befriended at Dulag Luft. Recognising his talents, Buckley appointed him as the X Organisation's head of intelligence.[25] Although such positions were in their infancy, Bushell's role was a vital one, as he was in effect the spymaster of the camp. It was his job to gather as much intelligence as possible, and to pass it back to Britain via coded letter to MI9, a newly formed agency that was tasked with communicating with POWs, and assisting them with escaping and evading capture. One of Bushell's first tasks involved handling his friend and former client at the court martial for the Battle of Barking Creek, Paddy Byrne. Like Bushell, Byrne had been taken prisoner on 23 May, and had arrived at Dulag Luft on 1 June. At some point after arriving at the camp, Byrne received a coded message from MI9 instructing him to convince the Germans that he was anti-British: 'Byrne – double-cross the Germans – any length – great possibilities, but very dangerous.'[26] Coded messages confirming the instructions were sent to Bushell, Day and a Squadron Leader Turner. Byrne was indeed being asked to play a dangerous game, as he was required to become extremely friendly with the Germans in order to extract intelligence, which meant that he risked being branded a traitor by his comrades. In fact, Byrne's orders were an extreme version of what all the POWs had been ordered to do. According to one former prisoner, Day, Bushell and Buckley had told the prisoners that they 'were to adopt a policy of friendship with the Germans in order to allay their suspicions concerning our escape activities and also in order to get certain information from the Germans which we required'.[27]

However, there were some among the POW population who appeared to be more than willing to befriend the Germans, for reasons that were rooted more in politics than patriotism. Among them was Pilot Officer

Railton Freeman, a 36-year-old landowner from Gloucestershire who had been recommissioned into the RAF in January 1940, and had been shot down on 23 May by two Messerschmitt 109s.[28] Compared to the overwhelming majority of his fellow POWs, Freeman's political views were beyond the pale. A member of Oswald Mosley's British Union, Freeman regarded Nazism as the 'one apparently solid barrier' to what he saw as the 'Asiatic doctrine' of communism.[29] Although membership of the British Union was by no means exceptional among the POW population, Freeman was singularly open about his adherence to fascism. Wings Day once cautioned Freeman that it was 'unnecessary for him to express his views so forcibly and openly', although Day never ordered Freeman to be silent, because Day had no wish to restrict free speech, as that 'would be behaving exactly the same as the Germans'.[30] One person who got to know Freeman well was Paddy Byrne, who decided to pretend to befriend him as he regarded Freeman as a threat 'from the camp security point of view'.[31] The deception appeared to work, as Freeman gave Byrne full exposure to his views, not least those concerning the Jews, who he claimed had organised a 'financial clique' that was running the British Empire.[32] Freeman's politics soon came to the attention of the Germans, to whom Freeman, in his own words, 'made no secret of the fact' that he was a member of the British Union, and that he wished peace to be made with Germany.[33] Over the course of several months, Freeman and various members of the German camp staff took part in tentative negotiations regarding how Freeman might help the German war effort. These discussions would bear fruit in the form of Freeman's eventual agreement to broadcast for the Germans, and his subsequent joining of the Waffen-SS in October 1944.[34]

As well as trying to learn as much as he could about enemies both within and without, there was also much Bushell needed to learn about the methods of escaping. It did not take long for many to realise that there are only four ways to escape from a POW camp: under, through, over, or by dying. As going over required some form of aircraft, this was deemed unfeasible. Going through the wire or the gate was highly risky, and required the type of expertise that was not yet in abundance. With dying not looking attractive, that left under, which meant digging. Although midnight feasts down tunnels at prep schools were the limit of his subterranean experiences, the claustrophobic Bushell swiftly realised that tunnelling was the most likely way of getting out.

That summer saw the first attempts made by Bushell and his comrades to escape. The first tunnel started beneath the bed of Paddy Byrne, under which the tunnellers worked in complete darkness, and wore long-johns in order not to dirty their uniforms.[35] Their intended exit point was underneath a bridge that crossed over a dry ditch, and after a few weeks, the tunnel was within 8 feet of its target. As well as worrying about being detected by the Germans, Bushell was concerned that Railton Freeman might learn about the tunnel and reveal it to the enemy. As Freeman's room was just across the passage from Byrne's, and with Freeman frequently dropping by, it seemed likely that the Nazi sympathiser might curry favour with the

Germans by betraying its existence.[36] Nevertheless, the tunnellers managed to keep their activities secret from both Freeman and the Germans. Then disaster struck, as it often would with tunnels. The aridity of the ditch was deceptive, because near it was an underground spring which flooded the tunnel.[37] The only consolation for the officers was that their efforts had not been stymied by the Germans, or indeed by a fellow POW. Undeterred, they started a new tunnel, this time from under the bed of Day himself. However, this was discovered by their captors, and as winter approached, escape attempts were put on hold.

While Bushell waited, his thoughts often returned to his fiancée, Peggy Hamilton. Although he clearly wanted to do his best for her, an insistence in his letters concerning her suitability suggests he may have felt some doubts. In late 1940, he wrote to his uncle, Harry North Lewis, asking him to instruct Bushell's bank, Cox & Kings, to have his pay made over to Peggy. Bushell's finances were hardly in a healthy enough shape for such an act of generosity, as the account, typically, was overdrawn and he was also behind with his rent on the flat in Tite Street. Bushell told his uncle that his life insurance would cover the overdraft, although he still wished to keep paying the premiums.

Perhaps as a way of coming to terms with his captivity, Bushell wrote to his parents telling them that he was certain that he had some sort of destiny, and that all his energy was being reserved for something in the future. This attitude is crucial to an appreciation of what motivated Bushell, and therefore how the Great Escape came into existence. Although it can be construed simply as the wishful thinking of a caged lion trying to justify its captivity, it is clear that Bushell shared with his mother the idea that he was fated to do something great. Although such monumentally high self-regard is often delusional, Bushell had the ability, charisma, leadership, willpower and ego to fulfil his own prophecy. If he had lacked this sense of fate and calling, then it is highly likely that the Great Escape would never have taken place.

With the arrival of spring, the escapers decided to resurrect the first tunnel. Drainage holes were sunk along its length to draw off the water, but the conditions were still tough. The tunnellers had to work in cold mud, and the going was slow.[38] As well as the damp, the tunnellers faced another problem – Railton Freeman. Although Freeman had not discovered the tunnel during its first incarnation, Bushell, Day and Byrne knew that their luck was unlikely to hold. It was Byrne who came up with the radical solution of simply telling Freeman. 'As he was always coming into my room,' Byrne recalled, 'and he was bound to sooner or later find somebody of the three of us – one of the three of us – coming out from under my bed, and the risk was too dangerous, I decided that we should trust Freeman.'[39] Byrne consulted with, among others, Bushell, and they agreed to Byrne's idea. Although, on the surface, the notion of telling a potential traitor about the tunnel looked inadvisable, the idea was sound, as Freeman realised that if the tunnel was discovered, then he would naturally be suspected as the culprit. Furthermore, although Freeman admired Nazism, he was not anti-British, and indeed, he attempted to affect the persona

of the English squire. In fact, Freeman would later claim
to find the whole business of the tunnel a bore. 'I was
also kept annoyingly well posted with all the latest news
and plans about this confounded tunnel by [. . .] Byrne,'
he recalled. 'I did not actually assist in this affair, was
not asked to, and frankly I was not interested.'[40]

Somewhat bizarrely, it appears that Bushell himself
actually consulted Freeman as to the direction and the
construction of the tunnel. 'He would see me and discuss details,' Freeman said, 'as he stated he would like
my opinion. I criticised the direction of his tunnel and
the final tunnel that was built was made in exactly the
direction I said I would dig a tunnel.'[41] Although it
would be easy to dismiss the words of a man like
Freeman, it appears that Bushell really did consult him,
as Paddy Byrne would later confirm it.[42] Bushell's
decision to do so is curious, as Bushell loathed Freeman.
According to Freeman, Bushell 'and his crowd put out
that I was the danger man of the camp and much care
was to be taken'.[43]

Ironically, on one occasion, it was Freeman who
actually saved the tunnel from being detected. At some
point in or around April 1941, Paddy Byrne and a
Flight Lieutenant Gould were making their way out of
the tunnel, with Gould leading. Just before Gould was
about to emerge into the room, Byrne heard the sound
of two voices in his room, although the only voice he
could identify was that of Freeman. Byrne tried to tell
Gould not to go up, but he was unable to, and Gould
removed two of the boards that made up the trap
underneath Byrne's bed. Byrne was right to be concerned, as the other voice belonged to a German officer,

who was standing in the entrance to the room. Freeman, who was sitting near to the bed, spotted the boards being moved, and had the presence of mind to stretch his legs across the gap to stop the officer from seeing it. He also appeared to tread on Gould's fingers as a warning. There can be no doubt that Freeman's actions saved the tunnel. 'If Gould had come up,' Byrne recalled, 'then the tunnel would have been discovered and the people concerned with the tunnel would have been discovered, and all the equipment, such as clothes and money, would have been downstairs.'[44] In addition, Byrne had also left half a coded message in the entrance to the tunnel, and had that been found, then the code would have been compromised.[45] No doubt through gritted teeth, Bushell had no option but to praise Freeman.[46] Nevertheless, despite Freeman's actions, Bushell maintained his animus towards Freeman, who in turn, according to Paddy Byrne, 'had taken a distinct disliking to Bushell'.[47] Matters came to a head a few weeks later, when Bushell and Freeman had a huge row, which was witnessed by Byrne and two other officers. Bushell told Freeman that when he got back to Britain, he would have Freeman court-martialled.[48]

By May, the tunnel had reached the bridge, and the X Organisation selected nineteen men to escape on the first weekend in June, when the moon was not due to rise until after midnight.[49] Among the nineteen were Bushell, Day, Byrne, Buckley and Dodge, all of whom were equipped with basic false papers. However, with just a week to go, Bushell decided that he wished to go it alone twenty-four hours before the main escape. Of all the escapers, he told Day, it was he who had the best chance of making a 'home run'. He spoke both French and German fluently, and he also knew the area around the Swiss-German border at Schaffhausen, which lay around 220 miles exactly due south. Bushell had also worked out an alternative method by which he could escape. In the corner of a field outside the camp in which the prisoners exercised stood a near-derelict shed, which was inhabited by a goat. Bushell suggested that he would hide under the goat's straw, and that he would stay there when the prisoners returned to the camp. If Buckley was able to arrange for a miscount at that evening's *Appell* – roll-call – then he would have a clear twenty-four hours before the main break and the ensuing alert to get down to the Swiss border by train, posing as a Swiss ski instructor. Day put Bushell's plan to the X Organisation, and he found that there were more than a few dissenting voices. Some were concerned that if Bushell were caught, the inevitable tightening of security was likely to jeopardise the main escape attempt. The decision lay with Day, and he found in favour of Bushell.[50]

Bushell's desire to go it alone raises the question of whether his individualism conflicted with the needs of the team. His character certainly featured a confidence that spilled into arrogance, and those who spoke against his proposed solo effort did so for sensible reasons. From a numerical point of view, it made little sense to risk the potential liberty of eighteen men just so that Bushell could have a better chance. After all, in terms of the war effort, it would be hard to quantify one man, even one such as Bushell, as being worth eighteen others. But Bushell's confidence lay on good grounds. He was an extremely capable linguist, he knew the territory and its people, and he had boundless chutzpah. Of all those imprisoned at Dulag Luft, Bushell was in a different league. Many of his fellow Kriegies were considerably younger and less worldly, and also lacked Bushell's undoubted qualifications as an escaper. It may have been arrogant to have wanted to go solo, but it was also merited. It was to be a pattern of behaviour that would remain constant for the next three years.

Bushell's plan did in fact work, although it was nearly blown by none other than Railton Freeman, who was still piqued by his row with Bushell. Freeman had learned of Bushell's plan, and had threatened to tell the Germans about it. It fell to Byrne to stop Freeman from informing. 'It was with the utmost difficulty and persuasion that I eventually stopped Freeman from reporting this to the guard,' Byrne recalled. 'This would have led to Bushell's discovery.'[51] Freeman would get his revenge on Bushell, although, as we shall see, it came many years later.

On the late afternoon of Thursday 5 June, Bushell burrowed under a mixture of straw and goat dung while his fellow prisoners were ushered back to the camp. After enduring the smell of the animal and its excrement until nightfall at around 10 p.m., Bushell crept out of the hut, slipped through a simple barbed-wire fence, and made his way to a station, which may have been that at Niedernhausen.[52] He caught a train to Tuttlingen, which lies about 15 miles north of the Swiss border, from where he took a branch line 30 miles southwest to Bonndorf, which is just 8 miles from the frontier. He arrived on Friday afternoon, and decided to walk to the border, posing as a tipsy Swiss ski instructor who had started the weekend a little too early. If anybody could have pulled off such a deception, it was Bushell. A few hours later, he reached the village of Stühlingen, which sits on the Wutach river which marks the Swiss-German frontier. Just twenty-four hours after leaving Dulag Luft, he was almost a free man. Bushell now had to decide whether to wait until nightfall to make his crossing, or simply go across during daylight, maintaining his pose as a drunk Swiss on his way home. He opted for the latter, but as he walked through the village, a local came out from his house and challenged him. Bushell chatted easily to the man, but the local was unconvinced, and suggested that he should be checked out at the local police station. At this, Bushell bolted and ran – straight into a dead end with high walls. With the man raising the alarm, Bushell knew his escape was over. 'I could have taken a girls' school across if I'd chosen a spot a few hundred yards to the west,' he later recalled.[53] To a colleague at the Bar, Bushell later laconically observed, 'I missed my Swiss by a few yards.'[54]

While Bushell was being taken into custody, over 200 miles north, his fellow escapers were emerging into the darkness from the tunnel exit. Unfortunately, all were captured within forty-eight hours, although none made it as far as Bushell. Day had headed north in order to reach the Mosel Valley and make his way into France. However, he soon got lost, and after two nights of roughing it, he was apprehended by two axe-wielding forestry workers.[55] Others were captured simply because they did things the wrong way – Dodge and his escape partner, for example, drew much attention for walking down an autobahn.[56] One of the greatest problems was the lack of accurate papers, which saw the downfall of many. Within a few days, all the escapers, including Bushell, were returned to Dulag Luft.

After his capture, Bushell had been locked up in a gaol in Frankfurt, from where he was fetched and taken back to Dulag Luft by a man who would do him many favours: Lieutenant Günther von Massow, who was one of the camp's security officers. Von Massow treated Bushell to dinner at a restaurant in Frankfurt, and complimented Bushell on his escape attempt. Von Massow was well connected – his brother, Gerd, was a colonel in the Luftwaffe and was the Higher Commander of the Fighter Schools, and would be promoted to Major General in April 1943.[57] As we shall see, von Massow would prove to be more than just a friendly face.

Back at Dulag Luft, the 'black sheep' were greeted by Rumpel, who managed to maintain his cordiality despite the fact that the escape had cost him his job. When Day apologised to Rumpel for causing him so much bother, the Commandant is reputed to have replied, 'I would have done the same if the positions had been reversed. To escape is a prisoner's job.' When Day wished him goodbye, Rumpel said, 'Better luck next time, even if I'm not supposed to say that.' Within a few weeks, the 'naughty boys' were transferred to Stalag Luft I, which lay near the town of Barth on the Baltic Coast. Apparently, Rumpel even provided them with a case of champagne for the 500-mile journey.[58] From Barth, Bushell wrote to his parents towards the end of June, and he supplied them with a censor-friendly account of his first escape attempt, in which he mischievously said that he had 'left the camp without asking'.

In October, the entire population of the camp was entrained to Oflag VIB, which was situated on an isolated plateau 3 miles from the railway station at Warburg, some 130 miles north of Frankfurt.[59] Bushell, however, was never to get there. A train journey was too good an escape opportunity to miss, and he paired up with a 24-year-old Czech, Pilot Officer Jaroslav 'Jack' Zafouk, who had been shot down in a Wellington bomber over Holland in July.[60] Bushell managed to obtain some German money, and, through bribing a German guard with cigarettes, some food coupons. The two men then made some civilian clothes out of blankets and a modified naval uniform. Their plan was equally rough and ready, and involved making their way to Prague, via Zafouk's brother who lived on the Czech border, in order to contact the Czech Underground, which would, they hoped, spirit them to Switzerland or another neutral country.

At around nine o'clock one evening, Bushell and Zafouk were herded with twenty-eight other POWs into a cattle truck for the 300-mile journey southwest to Warburg. As soon as the train started, Bushell and his fellow prisoners cut away at the floor of their truck with a table knife, and, after one and a half hours, they had made a hole large enough to squeeze through. At 11 p.m., the first two escapers lowered themselves on to the tracks when the train came to a halt. Bushell and Zafouk followed an hour later, as the train was slowing down at a large goods station.

After jumping, the two men got to their feet, ran

across the railway lines, and crouched underneath a stationary train. They paused for a while in the darkness, before running back across the rails, over a fence, on to a road, and then lying down in a field. There, they changed into their quasi-civilian clothes and buried their uniforms, and waited a few hours until daybreak. Bushell and Zafouk walked to the nearest station, where Bushell bought two tickets for Dresden. 'Everything went according to plan,' Zafouk recalled, and after an uneventful journey, they arrived in Prague two days later. Zafouk immediately went to find a friend, who agreed to put them up for four days, before finding them an apartment consisting of a single room with its own entrance.

Anticipating a wait of no more than several days or a few weeks, the two men found themselves stranded in the city for over eight months. Zafouk tried to contact the Underground through the husband of a cousin, who promised to help them, but who was promptly arrested by the Gestapo. After a month, the friend said that the owner of the single-room apartment needed it back, and so they had to move back in with the friend for a few days.

Eventually, a solution to their accommodation problem was provided by an old friend of Zafouk called Otokar Zeithammel, a 24-year-old police sergeant, who told the men that they could move in with him and his family.[61] The Zeithammel family consisted of Otokar's 59-year-old father, Otto, who was a technician, and his 27-year-old sister, Blažena, who was a sculptor who had studied from 1936 to 1939 at the Academy of Fine Arts in Prague under the tutelage of Professor O. Španiel.[62]

As well as taking a great risk, the family members were severely hampering their domestic life. The Zeithammels lived in flat number 23 in a large and austere block at 1564 Strakonická, which lies about a mile south of the city centre on the left bank of the Vltava river.[63] With just two rooms and a kitchen, there was hardly space for five people. Bushell and Zafouk initially stayed in the flat for three months. They repeatedly offered to leave, saying that they were putting the family in too much danger, but the Zeithammels insisted that they stay, and said that the flat was quite safe.

At some point, contact was made with the Underground, and just before Christmas, arrangements were made to smuggle the two escapers to Turkey. Bushell and Zafouk managed to reach what had been the border with Slovakia, but the organisation helping them was broken by the Gestapo, and they had to flee back to Prague.[64] Bushell and Zafouk returned to the flat, where they waited for the next word to go, but that word never came. For the next five to six months, they were forced to stay in the flat, with Zafouk unable to go out for fear of being recognised, and Bushell because he did not speak any Czech. All the two men could do was read, and discuss the war and their own situation. Their sojourn in Prague came to an abrupt end one morning in the middle of May 1942. At around 9 a.m., the doorbell was rung very violently. Bushell and Zafouk sat still, and after a short while, the door was forced open. It was the Gestapo.

The question of who informed on Bushell and Zafouk has still not been resolved. According to Zafouk's widow, the men were betrayed by Blažena to a former boyfriend, who then sold the information to the Gestapo. Blažena had apparently been angered by the fact that Bushell had rejected her advances, and had presumably acted in a fit of pique.[65] This seems unlikely, as Blažena would have been aware that she and her family would face the death penalty for sheltering escapers, and indeed, that was exactly how the Zeithammels were punished, for they were shot in the suburb of Kobylisy to the north of Prague the following month.[66] Another account suggests that the two men were betrayed by the porter of the apartment block, which seems more plausible.[67]

The two men were handcuffed and taken by car to the headquarters of the Gestapo, where they were separated and interrogated for an entire month. The Germans came to suspect the two men were involved in the assassination of Reinhard Heydrich, the acting Reichsprotektor of Bohemia and Moravia, who had been attacked by SOE at the end of May 1942, and had died on 4 June. The wave of recriminations across the former Czechoslovakia was typically brutal, with some 13,000 arrested or killed. It was therefore not unreasonable for the Gestapo to suspect the two men of having a hand in the assassination, that they were saboteurs rather than escapers. Bushell and Zafouk had been in hiding for several months, and an interrogator might have assumed that their agenda was rather more destructive than fugitive. The Gestapo believed Bushell was a secret service agent, and that since his escape and arrest he had managed to return to London, and had been parachuted back into Czechoslovakia to help foment an insurrection.

While Bushell was being held, it appears that he made

contact with a fellow RAF officer called Marshall, who was being detained in a nearby cell. The two men managed to snatch a few seconds of conversation whenever they passed each other's cells, and Bushell revealed that he was deeply worried by what would happen to Blažena and her family. Initially, Bushell was reluctant to reveal his name to 'Marshall', but eventually he left a note behind the lavatory cistern, which gave his name and service number. 'They are going to shoot me,' he wrote. 'Please pass full particulars to the Red Cross.'[68]

It is not possible to know precisely what happened next to Bushell. Although Zafouk was sent straight to Colditz, the Germans appeared to despatch Bushell to a military gaol in Berlin, where he was to be interrogated for a further three months. At some point in June, Bushell was sent to Berlin, where, it is often said, he was tortured. This is impossible to confirm, as Bushell, for obvious reasons of censorship and a desire to avoid parental anxiety, would never tell his family about his time there.

Whether he was tortured or not, Bushell still seemed to enjoy some rights as a POW while he was being held in Berlin, and he was able to send and receive post. In July, he received a letter that would have given him pause. It was from Georgie, and she told Bushell that she and Home Kidston – whom Bushell detested – were separating.

Bushell's dislike of Kidston appears to have been justified, as Georgie was suing for divorce on the grounds that her husband had committed adultery with, of all people, her stepmother, Joyce, Countess Howe. According to one family member, Georgie had actually caught the two *in flagrante delicto*.[69] In her petition for divorce, Georgie cited two occasions in late October 1941 in which her husband had slept with Joyce at their home, Southover House, near Tolpuddle in Dorset.[70] It appears that an irate Georgie had confronted her stepmother, who informed her that Kidston was in love with her, and was no longer in love with Georgie. On 29 October, Kidston, who was serving on the destroyer *Highlander*, received a telegram from Georgie asking if Joyce's words were true. Kidston admitted that they were, but tried to exculpate himself in the time-stained manner typical of so many adulterers, by stressing that he 'couldn't help this happening any more than can Joyce'.[71] At the end of the following month, Kidston wrote from the *Highlander* to tell Georgie that he had spent too long trying to cover up a 'mistake' and that he 'should never have been married to you in the first place'. Refusing a request by Georgie for him not to see her stepmother, Kidston wrote that he was in love with Joyce, 'and it will always be so whatever I might have to promise to anyone under duress'.[72]

On 16 July, Georgie and her father were both granted decrees nisi by Mr Justice Henn Collins, who pronounced that Kidston should pay his father-in-law £5,000 in damages – worth some £182,000 at the time of writing.[73]

Even though he was able to correspond while he was held in Berlin, Bushell was certainly in danger. His incarceration came to the knowledge of Günther von Massow, who was now the censor officer at the new camp of Stalag Luft III, which contained many RAF officers, including Wings Day. Despite the risk of being arrested, von Massow was determined for Bushell not to be held by the Gestapo, and he asked his brother and the Commandant of Stalag Luft III to do all they could to intervene. It appears that these combined efforts paid off reasonably quickly, because Bushell was sent to the camp in September 1942, although he was initially placed in solitary confinement. Before the Gestapo released him, he was told that if he tried to escape again, he would be shot.

Bushell finally walked into Stalag Luft III in the middle of September 1942. 'The news of Squadron Leader Bushell's return to Stalag Luft III soon spread through the compound,' recalled Flight Lieutenant N. Flekser. 'Excited groups gathered, delighted that this legendary mastermind of escapes was back, after a long and ominous absence.'[74] Although Flekser was of course wrong when he wrote these words, as Bushell had never set foot in Stalag Luft III, it is a measure of Bushell's reputation that his arrival was treated as if it were a return. Although he had not made a 'home run', his escape achievements were impressive. He had reached as far as the Swiss border, and shown that he could spend an extended time in the new Greater Germany without being detected. In a letter home to a friend, Bushell reflected ruefully that he had had 'an eight months' run for my money, and now am back, alas, behind the wire'.[75] The only benefit of the escape was an ability to now speak 'tolerable Czechish', but for Bushell, these achievements were not enough.

When he arrived at his new camp, it was clear to old friends and first acquaintances that, if anything, he was more determined to escape than anyone else. Some found that he was a changed man. His weight loss had made his cheeks hollow and his drooping eye 'more foreboding'.[76] The psychological alterations appeared to match this new somewhat sinister presence. An American POW recalled:

> I never found out what the Gestapo had done to him . . . but whatever it was, they had turned him into a vengeful, bitter man who was out to do in all Germans by any means possible. Actually, underneath his forbidding exterior, Roger was a charming, cultivated gentleman, but nature had bestowed on him a visage that can only be described as sinister . . . The Germans would soon learn it had been a black day for them when they had captured him.[77]

This description may be exaggerated, but there was no doubt that Bushell had become a somewhat bitter man. By the end of the month, he had received a letter from Peggy telling him that she had married someone else. He did his best to remain phlegmatic, and claimed not to care. Despite his stated indifference, Bushell wanted his money back from Peggy, and he asked his uncle to try to recover it, although he acknowledged that legally there was little that could be done. As it turned out, Peggy had played Bushell for a fool, and had in fact married Joseph, the 17th Baron Petre, on 25 October 1941. Nevertheless, the contents of the mail were not all bad. Georgie had made contact with Roger, which clearly cheered him up. The correspondence from her, coupled with the escape opportunities offered by the new camp, started to give Bushell a sense of optimism.

Chapter Three

Surrounded by Pines

WHEN BUSHELL STEPPED through the gate of Stalag Luft III, smoking a cigar and with a civilian suit bundled under his arm, the camp had only been open for around six months.[1] The head of the Luftwaffe, Hermann Göring, had ordered the establishment of the camp in October 1941, which he wanted to be a *Musterlager* – a 'warehouse' – into which all captured Allied air force officers would be gradually collected.[2] Previously, most air force prisoners had been sent to Barth, but that had become overcrowded, owing to the increasing number of captured airmen.[3] The new camp was opened the following March, and it lay in a thick pine forest on the outskirts of the Silesian town of Sagan, some 100 miles northwest of Breslau.[4] Sitting just three-quarters of a mile from the junction of six railway lines, Stalag Luft III made an ideal location to which prisoners could be brought, although such excellent transportation links would also prove to be a boon for escapers.[5]

What was less useful for the POWs was the camp's extremely sandy soil, which made tunnelling hazardous. Furthermore, the Germans, after over two years' experience of 'looking after' Allied prisoners, had designed a camp from which escape seemed impossible. Separated into two compounds, east compound and centre compound, the prisoners were surrounded by two 2.5-metre barbed-wire fences placed 1.5 metres apart. The gap – called the *Loewengang* (the 'lion walk') – was filled with concertina wire. Inside each compound, at a distance of some 10 to 20 metres, a warning line was placed, which consisted of thin wooden planks supported, at a height of 50 centimetres, by wooden posts placed at 2-metre intervals. Prisoners who stepped outside the warning line were liable to be shot unless they stopped and raised their arms.[6] Along the fence were placed watchtowers at 150-metre intervals, each of which was manned by a guard equipped with a searchlight, a rifle, a machine pistol and a light machine gun.[7] During daylight, the space between each tower was patrolled by a guard, and during the night, this patrol was doubled. Accompanying the nocturnal patrols were some twenty to twenty-five dogs, which were employed alongside the outer fence to each compound, as well as inside the compound.[8]

Despite the sandy soil, the Germans were still worried about tunnelling, so each of the barrack blocks was raised about 3 feet off the ground on brick pillars, which created a space into which the Germans could crawl and inspect for any suspicious activities. The blocks themselves were essentially large wooden huts, each of which was to house over one hundred officers. The huts were divided into twelve to eighteen rooms of about 15 feet square, each of which slept eight to twelve officers on bunk beds. The rooms also functioned as dining rooms and living rooms, and the furniture consisted of little more than a table and stools. Although the huts had plenty of large windows, at night these were covered by shutters, and the air in each room therefore became thick with the smell of body odour and tobacco smoke. Before the camp became crowded, two rooms were usually reserved as a library and a reading room, and each hut also featured a washroom, a lavatory and a kitchen.[9] The provision of just one kitchen for around a hundred men was completely inadequate. Although each compound had a separate cookhouse, this was used for little more than boiling up water for ersatz coffee and tea, and the small kitchens in the huts became bottlenecks. It seems that most huts organised strict rotas for mess times, and prisoners took it in turns to do the cooking. Many dreaded being the 'chef', as the kitchen stoves were extremely unreliable, and food could either be burned to cinders within seconds, or never get more than lukewarm.[10]

The range of ingredients was also somewhat limited. The staple ration provided by the Germans was a huge 5-pound loaf of rye meal bread that contained potatoes, acorns and quite possibly some sawdust. 'It was often mouldy,' recalled American POW Major Jerry Sage. 'We usually cut the bread into thin slices and toasted it thoroughly to dissipate the mouldy taste.'[11] The bread was supplemented with margarine and jam made from sugar beets, which just about made it palatable. The quality of the meat was little better, and it was often unclear which animal it was from. 'We sometimes saw some unusual-looking animal heads in the disposal area,' wrote Sage.[12] Foodstuffs that were really beyond the pale were *Blutwurst* – blood sausage – and *Fischkäse* – 'fish cheese' – the provenance of which was never authoritatively determined. 'It was made of those parts of a fish that would be best kept to itself,' observed RCAF Spitfire pilot William Ash. 'Though it started out looking like sawdust, it had to be soaked in water for about a week, and by that time it developed both the consistency and smell of wet dog hair, but tasted much worse. The next step was to cut it into slabs, fry it and then, in most cases, hurl it out of the hut door in disgust.'[13] It is hardly surprising that nobody got fat at Sagan. In fact, the diet was barely adequate, and was just enough to sustain a life of physical indolence. Jimmy James recalled how he once ran a mile in the camp's summer sports, and the exertion left him weak for days.[14] According to Lieutenant Charles Woehrle of the US Eighth Air Force, all the Kriegies could talk about was 'food, food, food'. 'There'd be fellas going round making recipe books,' Woehrle said, 'and they'd ask you if you could remember a recipe your grandmother or your mother had made that was especially good.'[15] The only supplement to the rations was the comparative delicacies to be found in the Red Cross parcels, which included chocolate, tins of powdered milk called Klim, Spam, bully beef, crackers and, most essential of all, cigarettes.

When Bushell arrived at the camp, the British officers

were housed in the east compound, which contained just six huts, a bathhouse, a cookhouse and a latrine block.[16] For young men who had been accustomed to the freedom of flying, this small 'rectangle of desert' was a depressing place to call home.[17] Moreover, it was the encircling forest, more than the barbed wire and the watchtowers, that reminded the men of their captivity. As Flight Lieutenant Flekser recalled:

> I grew to hate the pine tree forest which surrounded us, denying me even a glimpse of anything which would link me, no matter how tenuously, with the world I used to know – a woman, a child, a horse, anything. The closely planted pine trees stood there, dark and brooding, forming an impenetrable, menacing wall which seemed to advance, intent on smothering me.[18]

Australian Spitfire pilot Paul Brickhill felt a similar contempt for the forest. 'Woods completely encircled the compound,' he later wrote, 'not pleasant green woods but gaunt pines packed close together in the dry, grey earth. They were everywhere you looked, monotonous barriers that shut out the world and increased the sense of Godforsaken isolation.'[19] That sense of isolation and distance from home was expressed poetically by C. G. King, a gunner who acted as an officers' orderly in the camp.

'Surrey Sun'

From where I lie
below two stunted pines

The Silesian sun shines
boldly
   In an October sky.
A long long way from here
   Lies a sheltered mossy glade
    Silent in leafy gloom
Where the Surrey sun peeps
   gently down.
Flecking the leaf laden
  shade
   The Sun,
   People say is the same
anywhere
   Fools
   I know the difference for one[20]

Flight Sergeant Alfie 'Bill' Fripp – who had been shot down in October 1939 – recalled how he and his fellow Kriegies would seek some form of escapism by lying on the ground looking at the clouds. 'We would say to ourselves, "Well, that cloud should reach Bournemouth in two days' time."'[21]

It is hard to overstate the strong feeling of alienation felt by Kriegies such as King and Fripp, many of whom had spent years away from the comforting and gentle leafy lanes of places such as Surrey. Furthermore, they had no way of knowing how much longer they would spend their lives surrounded by the looming Silesian pines. The desire just to see what lay beyond them was immense, and often men yearned to escape not because they thought they had a genuine chance of securing their liberty, but more for a simple change of scene. It is easy to forget that prisoners of war are in fact prisoners, and the psychological burdens are similar to, and perhaps worse than, those carried by incarcerated criminals, who at least know the length of their sentences and have an opportunity to earn early release. RAF pilot Stephen Johnson wrote:

> The most trying part of all was undoubtedly not knowing how long we were there for. If the authorities want to half empty the prisons in this country there is a simple way of so doing. When sentencing a criminal to a prison sentence all they need to do is just to say, 'You are going to prison. We will not tell you for how long but you will be let out at the appointed time.' Believe me that six months under those conditions would hold far more terror than two years under the present system of knowing when you are going to get out.[22]

In addition, convicted criminals may also draw some succour from the fact that their imprisonment is the result of deliberate transgression rather than forgetting to check whether a Messerschmitt was on their tail.

Faced with the depressing prospect of an undetermined length of time in a small space, many POWs realised that they had to occupy themselves in order to maintain their mental health. Flying Officer Leonard Hall observed:

> My philosophy, and it was most people's philosophy, was that you had to keep busy. Whether you were going to lectures, playing football, giving lectures, digging tunnels, performing on the stage, or whatever you were doing, you had to look at your diary and say, 'Sorry, I

can't do that on Friday, I have a prior engagement'. If you were in that situation you were all right, because the morale in the camp was very good and very high.

However, Hall identified that some lacked the psychological robustness to deal with captivity. 'There were just a few people, who lay on their bunks waiting for the war to end, who deteriorated,' he recalled.[23] Some of them turned, in the words of Pathfinder pilot Robert Lamb, into 'cabbages'. 'You got the other people who were tragic and got completely introspective,' he said. 'They did nothing except ate and slept . . . They were in a state of mental atrophy. They used to sit around, even stop reading.'[24]

Stephen Johnson ascribed this wallowing to sexual abstinence:

Complete sexual stagnation and segregation makes Kriegies want to lie back on their beds with all the apathy of neuter cats. It is remarkable how quickly new prisoners adapt themselves to this life. They do quite often pass through a productive stage . . . before apathy engulfs their initiative and they pass into a state of oblivion for the duration.[25]

Surprisingly, many Kriegies found a life without the complications of female company relatively easy to bear, if somewhat dull. 'I should say it's like sailing on a sea without waves or tides,' one Kriegie observed. 'Navigation is too simple; you always know where you are.'[26] Some felt the loss more keenly, and were wistful about how they were missing out. 'Being a prisoner of war for two and a half years had been a highly educational experience,' wrote Leonard Hall, 'from which I claim to have emerged knowing all there was to know about men, and nothing at all about women.'[27] Nevertheless, many grew accustomed to the lack of sex and female company, mainly because, in the words of one, 'after the first six months the only appetites left are for food and freedom'.[28] 'There was nothing about pin-up girls,' recalled Charles Woehrle, 'or anything erotic at all among those young men – [just] food, food, food.'[29]

The German staff certainly did not ignore the issue of keeping the prisoners occupied. 'Only waiting for victory and for the end of the war could not fill up the long days, months and even years,' wrote Major Gustav Simoleit, the Deputy Commandant. 'The boredom of camp life resulted in several cases of depression and even mental disease.'[30] Simoleit, who had been a professor of history, geography and ethnology before the war, saw POW life as being an excellent opportunity for the young officers to improve themselves. Many teams, groups and classes flourished, and Simoleit himself even gave German classes, for which examinations were taken in the camp and sent back to English universities to be marked. It is unclear quite how many of Simoleit's students studied the language purely for the intellectual challenge rather than for the purposes of escaping. Other activities were perhaps of less value, but were a great deal more entertaining than learning German. Small offcuts of wood were transformed into functioning clocks; model sailing boats were built and launched on to ponds; and a miniature working steamship was even constructed, its engine made out of melted copper coins.[31] To the enormous delight of the onlooking Kriegies, the steamship, after darting across the pond several times, exploded.[32]

Sports were naturally an extremely popular diversion, and the British and Commonwealth officers played rugby, cricket and football. During the winter, the Canadians even made an ice rink and played hockey, although the Germans were concerned that the skating blades could be modified into wire cutters. In the American compound, softball and American football were popular, but one game that was common to all compounds was golf, which was more of the crazy variety than St Andrews.[33]

Gardening was another activity that was taken up by many, although the poor soil made horticulture a challenge. The earth was supplemented by composted potato peelings, and one gardener formulated a noxious mixture of German blood sausage and horse manure that did wonders for his tomatoes. Horse manure was particularly sought after, and whenever a horse entered the camp, it found itself followed by POWs holding out boxes beneath its rear end, 'all eager to stake their claim'.[34] 'It was a serious business,' remembered Flight Lieutenant Martin Smith, 'and once or twice I witnessed quite heated arguments over who had reached the prize first. For some POWs it was quite unseemly to be seen shovelling up horse manure but I noticed nobody ever refused the bits of veg we managed to grow.'[35]

As the camp grew throughout the war, so did the facilities. Theatres were built, for which the Germans procured the finest historical costumes from major theatres in Dresden and Berlin.[36] As is to be expected when Englishmen of a certain background are forced into lengthy cohabitation, a certain propensity for theatrical transvestism soon became evident. 'We had little difficulty finding people to play the feminine roles,' wrote Blenheim telegraphist and air gunner Richard Passmore, 'but the producer was often reduced to near-despair by the difficulty of getting a ten-stone healthy male to walk on the stage as convincingly as a woman would.'[37] Most plays heavily featured such 'actresses', and some of the players found themselves to be the objects of some considerable lust. Fleet Air Arm observer Maurice Driver recalled:

> To our women-starved lives, they looked absolutely great. They were wonderful. There was one of them, Michael Ormond, a New Zealander, and he played women most attractively, and there was a Belgian pilot called Bobby Laumans who was very very similar, and between the two of them, they excited the hearts . . . We had the same reaction to them as in normal civilian life, and we were quite prepared to treat these men as women . . . I was ripe, if you like, for getting into the show.[38]

Some POWs, such as the orderly C. G. King, seemed to be unaware that the women were in fact men. After one show in September 1943, King wrote home to tell his wife Peggy:

> Last night we saw our first show in the new theatre – how we enjoyed it! Everything was perfect & you should just have seen those girls! I'm not kidding when

I say that no boy would have thought twice about escorting at least 4 of them to any dance.[39]

Quite how Peggy reacted to her husband's apparently unironic appreciation is not recorded. Had any of the Kriegies become sufficiently 'ripe' so as to wish to take things further with a member of the chorus line, they would have found it difficult, even if both parties were willing. The opportunity to practise homosexuality discreetly was non-existent. As one POW commented on a rather effeminate fellow officer: 'If he is queer, I feel sorry for him. Here he is, surrounded by desirable men, often naked, and there is nothing that he or anyone else can do about it – we are never alone.'[40]

Homosexuality and drag aside, not all the theatrical productions were of the bawdy variety. Professor Simoleit found that some of the productions, such as *Macbeth*, *Hamlet*, *A Midsummer Night's Dream*, *Arsenic and Old Lace*, *Blithe Spirit* and *The Man Who Came to Dinner*, were highly sophisticated.[41] 'Never in my life I saw [*sic*] so many of Shakespeare's dramas on the stage as in the camp of Sagan,' he wrote. 'The performances were very good. Among the many thousands of prisoners there were excellent sportsmen, musicians and actors. In such hours we were really guests, not jailers.'[42] One of the leading lights was Bushell, who took readily to the stage. Bushell appeared in a 'playlet' called *Apprehensions* in which he took on the role of a fat and worried old stockbroker. Other roles included Malcolm in Gerald Savory's *George and Margaret*, and, in general, Bushell appeared to be a natural on the boards.

Of course, such hours in which the dynamic between

jailers and captives was forgotten were infrequent. Even during the theatrical performances, to which the Germans were extended the courtesy of an invitation, the players and the audience were always aware that they were separated by more than just a stage. During a performance of *The Merchant of Venice*, the Kriegies decided not to play Shylock as a hackneyed conniving Jewish figure. 'We played him so he was a hero,' recalled Bill Fripp. 'And so all the Germans got up and marched out. They realised what we were doing.'[43] The relationship that emerged, as it would in so many other POW camps in which the majority of the prisoner population consisted of young officers, was similar to that between boys and masters at a British public school.[44] As one American-born POW observed, 'the atmosphere in the camp was a bizarre mix of prison and British boarding school'. It would be wrong to labour the analogy, but many of the RAF officers were not long out of such schools, and many of the officers among the camp staff were of a similar age to those who had taught them. Indeed, some such as Simoleit were educators themselves, and regarded the prisoners with a benevolent schoolmasterly attitude.[45] Some of the Kriegies openly acknowledged that they were little more than schoolboys. One wrote:

> We're all quite young people and so have a lot in common. It reminds one of school, in fact, with members from nearly all parts of the world . . . We live rather like school-boys in other ways. The similarity is remarkable. There's a great interest taken in the various sports, for instance, and constant matches are organised.[46]

The 'headmaster' figure was naturally the Commandant, Colonel von Lindeiner, who was universally respected by both his staff and the POWs. Often described as being 'an officer of the old school', von Lindeiner was sixty-one when the camp had opened, and he had enjoyed an illustrious military career. Posted to German East Africa in 1902, von Lindeiner won the Pour Le Mérite medal – better known as the 'Blue Max' – and the Prussian Order of the Crown for his role in helping to put down the Maji Maji Rebellion against the German colonialists. At the outbreak of the First World War, he commanded the 1st Foot Guards, a regiment renowned for its aristocratic membership. Wounded three times between November 1914 and December 1915, von Lindeiner finished the war as Adjutant of the 4th Army, and he retired in September 1919. After marrying a Dutch baroness, he spent several years in business, and travelled extensively around Europe and the Americas.

As he was based in the Netherlands, von Lindeiner was able to watch the growth of Nazism from afar, and he had little time for it. When he and his wife moved to Germany in 1932, they refused to join the Nazi Party, despite the deleterious effect this had on his business and social connections. Nevertheless, despite his manifest anti-Nazism, von Lindeiner felt obliged to accept a position in the Luftwaffe on the personal staff of Hermann Göring – the Füstab – a position from which he unsuccessfully tried to retire on the grounds of ill health. His appointment to command Stalag Luft III in the spring of 1942 therefore represented an opportunity to serve his country without directly serving the regime he so despised.[47]

After installing himself and his family at the Jeschkendorf Manor, some 3 miles west of Sagan, there were some in von Lindeiner's position who would have seen the appointment as a *de facto* retirement, but, judging by the praise he would often receive, the old colonel regarded the job as anything but. His deputy, Gustav Simoleit, saw him as an 'honest, open-minded, liberal man [who] influenced and formed with his plans, ideas and orders the whole spirit in the relations between the prisoners and the German personnel'. According to Simoleit, von Lindeiner did what he could 'to make the hard lot of the thousands of prisoners endurable, and, to reach his aim [to establish] a coexistence and cooperation based on mutual understanding and estimation'.[48] In the main, it appears that the POWs respected the efforts made by von Lindeiner – 'He was a gent, an absolute gent,' recalled Bill Fripp[49] – although some were sceptical of his motives. 'Lindeiner knew that our escape record could be his undoing,' noted American Spitfire pilot Albert P. Clark. 'He operated on the assumption that if he treated us well enough, our escape efforts would diminish. He was tragically wrong.'[50]

Von Lindeiner oversaw a camp that would grow to hold some 12,600 prisoners and many hundreds of German personnel – a community as large as a medium-sized German town.[51] In order to make things run smoothly, the administration was split into several *Abteilungen* – departments: Department I was the Commandant and his office, which ran the company of guards; II was the office of the Adjutant or Deputy Commandant, Major Simoleit; III was 'counter intelligence', which spied and snooped on the prisoners; IV was concerned with financial matters as well as the construction of new barracks and the supply of food; V was the camp's organisation, run by Simoleit; VI was mail censoring; VII was the hospital.

As is apparent, Simoleit was one of the hardest-working figures in the camp. It was his job to liaise with the senior Allied officers in each compound, and also to maintain a vast index of all the POWs. Most stressful of all, however, was having to conduct the daily *Appell*. The roll-calls often took hours, and much paperwork was involved in establishing how many prisoners were in hospital, in solitary confinement, or had business in some other part of the camp. Often, the Kriegies would deliberately force a miscount to waste time, and the whole process would have to be started again to ensure that there had been no escapes. 'For me, the roll-call with the following examination, calculation and evaluation was a real nerve-strain every day,' Simoleit wrote. 'I could not relax before I handed my report to the Commandant.'[52] In fact, Simoleit found his job so stressful that he suffered from sleeplessness, and had to take sleeping pills almost every night.[53] Simoleit's insomnia may have also been a product of his pastoral – and perhaps unrealistic – approach towards his job. When he had been appointed to his first POW camp in August 1940, Simoleit saw the camps as being places in which officers and men from both sides could meet and establish personal contacts and learn from each other. 'A faint hope began to grow in my heart that perhaps I could help a little to pave the way for a better understanding in and after the time of war,' he recalled.[54]

Simoleit certainly acted upon his principles. At Stalag Luft III, when he discovered that the Polish POWs were not receiving any letters and books because Department VI lacked a Polish-speaking censor, he spent his free evenings doing the work himself. Simoleit performed the same service for the Czechs, although for that he had to teach himself the language. Such selflessness was rare among the staff at POW camps, although it is hard to establish what effect Simoleit's charitable disposition had on the culture of the camp as a whole. What is apparent is that the two most senior members of the camp staff regarded incarceration as being an opportunity for international understanding rather than merely something to be endured. Both men were sophisticated and cosmopolitan, and were as distrustful of the Nazis as any POW. Although the scepticism of those such as Albert Clark and Jimmy James is understandable – there was, after all, a war on – it is evident that von Lindeiner and Simoleit wished to promote an atmosphere of cooperation and mutual appreciation that went well beyond the demands of any convention or the mutual respect shown between officers. The two Germans naturally did not wish their prisoners to escape, but they certainly wished the best for them, to the extent that Simoleit worried that his attitude might see him shot for treason.

This sympathy was also shared by another key figure on the camp staff: Captain Hans Pieber. Like Simoleit, Pieber had also been involved in education, and a caricature drawn by one of the Kriegies certainly gives Pieber a schoolmasterly air, with pebble glasses, sticking-out ears, and the invocation, 'Pleese Gentlemen

– Don't Sit on Ze Varning Vire!'[55] Although he was only in his forties, to the majority of Kriegies, that made him an old man. 'It was hard to imagine anyone who looked less like a soldier,' wrote Flight Lieutenant Flekser. 'He was thin, weedy, and stoop shouldered. His myopic watery blue eyes were magnified by the thick lenses of his glasses.'[56] The fact that Pieber himself signed the caricature reveals that he was able to laugh at himself, and his sense of humour was perhaps his most marked characteristic. Pieber referred to prisoners who had played female roles on stage forever after by their female names, and whenever misbehaviour was detected or escape attempts foiled, he could usually be relied upon to provide some levity.[57] On one occasion, when two POWs had been caught on the run while wearing fake German uniforms, Pieber had to officiate at the taking of photographs for the camp records. As the photographer trained his lens on the two prisoners, Walter Morison and Lorne Welch, they looked understandably surly. 'Come along now, gentlemen, why are you looking so miserable?' Pieber queried with a twinkle in his eye. 'Look a little cheerful, please.' Welch's reply displayed the type of banter upon which Pieber thrived. 'We *should* look miserable – we're supposed to be Germans, aren't we?'[58]

Morison's view of Pieber was universally shared. '[He] understood the handling of prisoners,' he wrote. 'Even when tempers were at their hottest he never lost his own, but always had a joke ready, often against himself, which pacified an angry crowd when military discipline might have provoked real trouble.'[59] Pieber displayed his trademark humour whenever much-despised late-night searches were carried out. 'Ach! Don't worry gentlemen!' he would say. 'It's only your old friend Hans Pieber come to count you little chickens in their nests. *Eins, zwei, drei, vier, fünf, sechs* . . . All right gentlemans!'[60] Although Pieber's sense of humour was appreciated, some felt that the friendly demeanour was merely a way of exerting his will and ensuring his long-term self-preservation. Morison ominously observed that Pieber would have made similar wisecracks had he been commanding a firing squad rather than a photography shoot.[61] Others, such as Paul Brickhill, shared Morison's cynicism: 'If he'd been a *Lageroffizier* in hell and had seen you brought in screaming he'd have blinked tenderly behind his glasses and wished you a felicitous sojourn.'[62]

Such suspicion was probably engendered by the widespread knowledge of Pieber's Nazi past. An Austrian, Pieber was reputed to hold the Nazi Party's forty-ninth membership card, and was believed to be a recipient of the Blood Order, which was awarded to Austrians who had participated in the 1934 February Uprising or the failed July Putsch of that same year. Pieber's Nazism appeared to have waned after the annexation of Austria to Germany in 1938, after which he reportedly refused to wear the Blood Order.[63] As well as his political beliefs, Pieber appeared to be keeping another part of his personality in abeyance: his sexuality. Some of the POWs strongly suspected that Pieber, although he was married, fancied a young RAF officer called Peter Gates. 'He was slim and long brown hair flowed down to his shoulders,' Flekser recalled. 'Peter's large hazel eyes were ringed by long curled eyelashes.' Gates and Pieber struck up a friendship, which was highly unlikely to have been sexually consummated. Nevertheless, Pieber was so entranced by Gates's 'fluttering eyelashes, pretty face and effeminate gestures' that he was to help the POWs in a way that was vital to the Great Escape.[64]

Another prominent figure known to many was Sergeant Major Hermann Glemnitz, who worked for Department III of the camp administration, which spied on the prisoners and attempted to curtail their escaping activities, and was staffed by soldiers from the Abwehr.[65] Glemnitz and his men were known as 'ferrets' because the nature of their work called for them to creep around and underneath huts wearing dark blue overalls as they made their searches for tunnels and contraband. Like the animals after which they were named, the ferrets were intelligent, and indulged in what Simoleit regarded as a 'war of brains' with the equally resourceful POW population. 'Both sides tried to surpass each other in inventive faculty,' Simoleit wrote. 'This was performed in a sportlike [sic] spirit.'[66] As part of this 'war', the prisoners naturally resorted to giving the ferrets unflattering nicknames, with Glemnitz often referred to as 'Dimwitz', although the man was anything but dim.

Born on 29 November 1898 in the nearby town of Breslau, Glemnitz, like Pieber, Simoleit and von Lindeiner, had a more worldly outlook than the average German NCO. After working as a blacksmith, Glemnitz had been called to the Western Front in October 1916, where he served as a rifleman before volunteering as a pilot. The war ended before he finished his training, and

Glemnitz returned to Breslau briefly before taking up a succession of jobs as a ship's machinist and a field technician for a steam plough company that took him to Peru, Chile, the United States, Mexico, Spain and Tunisia. He returned to Breslau in 1937 with a wife and two children, and in August 1939, at the age of forty, he was once more called up for service, and was sent to Poland and France as part of a Luftwaffe anti-aircraft battery. After falling sick, Glemnitz was posted away from the front to Berlin, where he answered a call for interpreters to work in POW camps. As Glemnitz spoke English, Spanish and French, he was, in his own words, 'an ideal volunteer' and he was sent to Stalag Luft I, before transferring to Sagan in April 1942.[67]

Reporting to Major Peschl and Captain Broili, Glemnitz found that he had to organise Department III's ferreting activities on a virtually improvised basis. His men – who numbered around twenty – were not trained, and Glemnitz had to rely on his common sense to try to outwit the prisoners.[68] As with Pieber, the POWs liked and respected Glemnitz. '[He was] a jovial giant of a man,' recalled one, '[who] managed in an extraordinary way to combine exemplary duty to his own Service with treatment of his prisoners as though they were his own men. His behaviour was impeccable and his good humour infectious.'[69] 'He was a fair, honest and trustworthy opponent,' said another POW.[70] Bill Fripp regarded him similarly. 'Within his duties, he was very German,' he recalled. 'But outside of that, if there was anything he could do for us to make life pleasant, he would do it. He was very fair in all his doings.'[71] Most saw him in the same light as Bob

Vanderstok, a Dutch RAF Spitfire pilot, did: 'Like the Commandant of Stalag Luft III and several officers, Glemnitz was regarded as a gentleman and a very good soldier, but one who was just on the wrong side.'[72] He also appeared to have a sense of humour, and whenever he was receiving new arrivals, he would say, 'Welcome to Stalag Luft III. Here, you will find the beer is pisspoor but the gin is shit hot.'[73] 'He was a droll fellow in a sardonic way,' remembered Paul Brickhill, 'with a leathery face you could crack rocks on.'[74]

Although Glemnitz may have been wily, he was aware that some of his junior ferrets were less so. Many of the Germans, as we shall see in chapter seven, were susceptible to bribery. 'There were times when I had to tell my men, "Stay away from him, he is too clever for you,"' Glemnitz recalled, who was himself in-corruptible.[75] '[He was] one of the very few we could not bribe at all,' said Bomber Command pilot Geoffrey Cornish. 'He would accept a cigarette from us, and we would say, "Have another one, Glemnitz." "No," he said, "I know you buggers are digging a tunnel some-where and I've got to find it," and off he would stomp.'[76]

If Glemnitz publicly denied knowing the location of the latest tunnel, then it is likely he was dissembling. 'I knew that pilots are different from infantry men who were happy to be out of that shit,' he said. 'Pilots always wanted to be airborne and to escape so we had to keep them busy to keep them from going mad or killing themselves. We let them dig.'[77] It is hardly surprising that von Lindeiner regarded Glemnitz most highly. 'Most outstanding of all was Glemnitz,' he wrote, 'with a hardcore, strong personality, devoted to duty, solidly reliable, and resistant to some very tempting bribes. He also knew how to skilfully apply, if necessary, an appearance of bonhomie.'[78]

The Commandant also respected the work of two of Glemnitz's juniors: Corporals Griese and Pilz. Nicknamed 'Charlie' by the British POWs, Pilz was also respected by the inmates for his ability to sniff out tunnels. 'He was not very intelligent but he had a good nose,' Glemnitz said. Although it was Pilz who would often report something suspicious occurring in the huts and thereby cause a highly disruptive search, Glemnitz suspected that his junior had been bribed, as 'he seemed always to report the little things and left the big things running'.[79] As there is no evidence that Pilz was ever bribed, Glemnitz's suspicions may well have been incorrect. One figure who, like Glemnitz, was unsusceptible to corruption was Corporal Griese, who was nicknamed 'Rubberneck' because of his habit of always looking over his shoulders and searching everywhere.[80] Of all the personalities on the German side of the camp, Griese attracted a seemingly unique level of opprobrium. 'He was just nasty,' remembered one POW. 'He was vindictive and cold.'[81] 'He was a nasty piece of work,' said Bill Fripp, 'and everybody shied away from him when he came in the compound.'[82] His unpleasant nature was augmented by a hugely despised ability to detect POW misbehaviour. 'He was overly conscientious,' said another prisoner. 'He would appear in the wrong place, and make a thorough nuisance of himself, which was his job after all. He was a nasty piece of work.'[83] Alan Bryett, a bomb aimer on a

Halifax, recalled how the Kriegies watched Griese 'with great care, because if there was anything subversive to be spotted in the camp, Rubberneck was going to be the one to do it'.[84]

Nevertheless, the Kriegies did try to get their own back on the hated Griese. Whenever he entered a hut, the POWs would volubly moan about his body odour, and offer him a piece of much-treasured soap, which Griese had to refuse in case he was accused of theft or accepting a bribe. In return Griese would hit the prisoners with the butt of his Luger if they did not move fast enough, and others were made to strip in the cold corridor for no good reason. 'He became', in the words of Bob Vanderstok, 'one of the few real enemies, while many of the other guards were just strict but not truly hateful.'[85]

This, then, was the environment in which Roger Bushell found himself when he entered the camp in the autumn of 1942. His presence sent a charge around the camp that heralded what many correctly anticipated would be an exciting new page in its hitherto short history. Until Bushell's arrival, escape attempts had been haphazard and ill-disciplined affairs; their organisation was poor, and made more in the amateur spirit of Park Town prep than that of a professional military operation. As a result, the camp was settling into a kind of routine that presented little threat to the Germans. Bushell's presence would transform the camp, and turn it from what approximated an uprooted and spartan British public school into a new theatre of war.

Chapter Four

'Escaping was a real objective'

WHEN BUSHELL ARRIVED at the east compound of Stalag Luft III he found many familiar faces from Barth and Dulag Luft. Among them were those of Harry 'Wings' Day, Jimmy Buckley, Johnny Dodge and Jimmy James, all of whom were members of the X Organisation, which had now been reborn at Sagan. Once again, Day had appointed Buckley as its head, although Day himself was not the compound's Senior British Officer; that post was filled by a Group Captain Kellett.[1] Under the stewardship of Buckley and Day, the X Organisation had launched many valiant attempts to get out of the camp, but none had ultimately been successful. In the 'war of brains', Glemnitz and his ferrets most certainly constituted the winning side as they fought against the Kriegies' subterranean activities. Lorries were driven around the compound to cause tunnels to cave in; fire engines were brought in to flood the ground under the barrack blocks; and an 8-foot trench was dug between the warning line and the fence.[2] Tunnelling in the already treacherous sand became an increasingly dangerous occupation, and it was extremely fortunate that no prisoners were killed by one of the frequent collapses. During that summer, around forty tunnels were started, of which all but one were discovered by the Germans. Glemnitz was understandably cock-a-hoop, and whenever an escaper was caught, he would roar with laughter and say, 'Ha ha! Now we have caught you again!'[3]

The only successful tunnel was that devised by Bill Goldfinch, Jack Best and Henry Lamond, who managed to convince the Germans that the drainage system in the wash hut was ineffective by secretly and repeatedly flooding it. Fearing an outbreak of typhus, the Commandant gave the POWs permission to dig a large drainage ditch, out of which the three men dug a tunnel towards the wire. After several days, they were within striking distance, and on the evening of 21 June, the three men were sealed into the tunnel so that they could 'mole' their way out that night. With Goldfinch digging at the front, the men passed through and then packed the sand behind them as they advanced, occasionally boring holes to the surface to provide an air supply. Their progress was slow, and they only managed to burrow some 25 feet to the warning line before they had to stop, worried that they might be heard. The three men then spent the entire following day – right in the middle of summer – lying still and silent in the excruciatingly cramped confines of the tunnel. Once night fell, the men continued, with those above such as Day measuring their progress by observing the small wisps of condensing breath emanating from the air holes. After a few hours, the trio reckoned they were safely beyond the wire and they successfully surfaced into moonlight and freedom. The men made their way to the Oder river where they stole a boat and headed north to the Baltic. Unfortunately, the theft was reported to the police, and the three men were arrested after some ten days on the run.[4]

Tunnelling was by no means the only method of escape. Not long after the 'mole' tunnel, Flight Lieutenant Ken Toft and Flying Officer William Nichols cut through the wire fence in broad daylight at a blind spot they had discovered between two watchtowers. While other Kriegies diverted the guards' attention with a boxing match, the two men scarpered towards the woods. Just as they were about to reach cover, a guard noticed them and immediately raised his rifle. One of those watching was Day, who started towards the tower until, to his great surprise, he found Buckley restraining him. The guard did not pull his trigger, and he allowed Toft and Nichols to flee. Day started to remonstrate with Buckley, but the head of the X Organisation had correctly assumed that the guard would be unwilling to shoot, as it would reveal that he had been slack in not spotting the escapers sooner – far better simply to let them get away and deny all knowledge. The luck of Toft and Nichols ran out shortly afterwards, and after they had been recaptured and returned to the camp, an impressed von Lindeiner presented them with a bottle of whisky.[5]

Despite the chivalrous presentation of such tokens, the Commandant was becoming increasingly concerned at the level of escape activity. Von Lindeiner finally snapped in September when the ferrets discovered a tunnel some 300 feet long leading from the barrack hut in which Day and Buckley were quartered. Of all the tunnels dug before those of the Great Escape, this was easily the most impressive. When judged by later standards, its methods of excavation were primitive, though none the less effective. The spoil was removed in a metal sink pulled by a piece of string, and ventilation was provided by air holes pushed 20 feet up to the surface. The men worked naked in near darkness, and after two hours at the face, they would crawl out, suffering from headaches and often vomiting. Collapses were frequent and, at one point, Flight Lieutenant Wally Floody, a Canadian fighter pilot, was buried under half a ton of sand. It took a whole hour to dig him out, with the Kriegies expecting to find a corpse. Luckily, his face had been exposed, and he had been able to breathe.[6] Such an experience was clearly disquieting. 'It was a horrifying feeling,' wrote Flight Lieutenant Ivo Tonder, an RAF Spitfire pilot with the 312 (Czech) Squadron. 'At that moment you could do nothing. Nothing at all. One false move would be enough to bring on another collapse.' Tonder recalled that it took him a week to get over the experience, but one of the Norwegians who had endured similarly vowed never to go down a tunnel again.[7] The tunnel's undoing lay in the problem of sand dispersal. Griese had once taunted the prisoners, 'You will never build a tunnel, unless you can make sand disappear,' and those words had proved apposite.[8] The sand was simply dumped under a nearby hut, and eventually, Glemnitz found it and concentrated his search nearby.[9]

One morning, the ferrets raided the hut and, after nearly dismantling the building, they discovered the tunnel and then flooded it.[10] The Commandant was livid, and told Day that had a mass breakout occurred, then he would have lost his job and been incarcerated in a fortress.[11] Von Lindeiner took swift action, and in October, he purged the camp of around one hundred of its 'naughtiest boys', who included Day, Buckley and Dodge. The men were sent some 150 miles northeast to a camp in Szubin, and en route, true to his indefatigable form, Johnny Dodge prised up the floorboards in his cattle truck and jumped out, but was almost immediately caught. A photograph of a smirking Dodge walking along the railway track with his hands aloft, followed by a group of stern pistol-toting German officers and NCOs, captures the essence not just of Dodge's personality, but also of the levity that was attached to such escape attempts by the Kriegies.[12] Dodge and his fellow prisoners knew that he had no hope of getting back to Britain from deepest occupied Poland dressed in the uniform of a British major, but the important thing was to try, and what was more, such attempts were seen as good sport. These attitudes would soon change.

From the German standpoint, von Lindeiner could not have chosen the subjects of his purge better. For the Kriegies it was a real blow – both the head and heart of the X Organisation had been removed. However, to one man, the absence of men such as Day and Buckley represented an opportunity to mould the X

Organisation in his own image. Ever since he had arrived, Bushell had kept quiet, knowing that he was a marked man, but now was his chance, and he was swiftly appointed by the SBO as 'Big X'. Although he was eager to start putting his designs into practice, there were two elements that held him up: the imminent harsh Polish winter, and the fact that many of the Kriegies in the east compound were to be moved in the spring to the new north compound that was currently being constructed by Russian POWs. There was clearly little point in attempting anything significant, but what Bushell could do was muster his team and finesse his plans so that the X Organisation could leap into action as soon as the move took place.

The men that Bushell drew together during that winter of 1942 to 1943 must be considered to constitute one of the most talented escape organisations that has ever existed. 'Very soon the air force prisoners became famous all over Germany to be the most skilful and dangerous escapers,' observed Gustav Simoleit. 'It was no wonder that this was really true. They were selected people with outstanding bodily and spiritual abilities and with excellent technical training. Their inventive genius was astonishing.'[13] Simoleit's appreciation, although not specifically applied to those on the escape committee, is nevertheless an apt description of its twenty members. One of Bushell's most crucial appointments was that of head of compound security, and for that role – known as 'Big S' – he chose Lieutenant Colonel Albert P. Clark, the second in command of the 1st US Fighter Group until he had been shot down in his Spitfire on 26 July 1942. As Big S, Clark's job was to ensure that all escape activities were kept secret from Glemnitz and his ferrets. This involved monitoring the movements of every German who entered the compound – in effect, guarding the guards. A 'Duty Pilot' was posted to the gate, who kept a roster of which Germans were in the compound, and while the Germans were present, they were tailed by a series of 'stooges', who would relay, through a system of innocent signals, in which direction a specific ferret was heading. Clandestine activities, such as forging and tailoring, could therefore be quickly halted or packed away before discovery. Keeping watch on the Germans was a full-time job, and with the stooges working in shifts, Clark later estimated that several hundred men were involved.[14] Of course, the Germans were aware that they were under surveillance, and Glemnitz would even approach the Duty Pilot as he sat in his armchair fashioned from plywood tea chests and Red Cross parcels to ask the whereabouts of his own men.[15]

Another key post on the committee was that of tunnel security, and it too was allocated to another North American, Flight Lieutenant George Harsh of the Royal Canadian Air Force. Harsh's background was singularly unconventional. The spoiled son of a wealthy family, in 1929 Harsh had shot and killed a grocery store clerk in a botched hold-up he and four friends had staged 'for kicks' in his native Atlanta. Although he was sentenced to death, his family's financial clout paid for a series of expensive legal challenges that reduced his sentence to life. At the age of eighteen, Harsh found himself working on a Georgia chain gang, shovelling for fourteen hours a day, sleeping in a stinking cage and fending off the sexual attacks of other prisoners. 'The idea of rehabilitation had no place in the Georgia penal system in those days,' Harsh wrote. 'Punishment in the Old Testament sense was the only concept even remotely considered.'[16] Within a few years, Harsh was transferred to become an orderly in a prison hospital, and there he might have stayed for life had it not been for his performance of an urgent and improvised appendectomy on a 61-year-old black prisoner. After steadying his nerves with a tumbler of ginger ale heavily laced with medicinal alcohol, Harsh made his incision and worked his finger around the intestine and drew the pus-swollen appendix to the surface. 'I don't think I breathed as I tied this off,' he recalled, 'excised it, sutured it, and carefully worked the intestine back into place.'[17] Harsh's actions had saved the man's life, and as a result he was pardoned. Nevertheless, with the murder of the store clerk still weighing on his conscience, Harsh decided that his crime required more expiation, and the fight against Nazism provided him with an opportunity. Like many Americans, he enlisted in the RCAF, which required him to change his nationality, and after surviving two years of operations, he and his Halifax bomber were shot down over Cologne in October 1942.[18] Harsh's experiences as a convict not only made it comparatively easy for him to adjust to POW life, but also made him suitable to mastermind tunnel security. Like Clark, he was tasked with establishing a system of stooges who would warn of approaching guards by using secret signals, many of which were appropriated from the world of major-league baseball.[19]

Harsh had been approached to join the committee by

Wally Floody, who was one of three tunnellers on the escape committee, and in charge of all digging. Standing at 6 feet 6 inches, Floody made an unlikely candidate for working in cramped subterranean conditions, but his experience as a mining engineer in Northern Ontario before the war outweighed any drawbacks engendered by his bulk.[20] Universally regarded as a 'very capable and likeable chap', Floody's abilities would earn him the label of the 'genius of the Great Escape', bestowed on him by Clark.[21] His two fellow tunnellers on the escape committee were Flight Lieutenants Johnny Marshall and Robert 'Crump' Ker-Ramsay, both of whom were equally popular figures around the camp.

Of course, tunnelling and providing security represented only a fraction – albeit a significant one – of any escape attempt. Kriegies also had to be provided with civilian clothing, and the responsibility for the 'tailoring department' lay with Flight Lieutenant Tommy Guest. Flight Lieutenant Desmond Plunkett, who had flown in Stirling bombers for 218 Squadron, was placed in charge of drawing up maps, although his appearance belied the meticulousness required for such a task. 'He was a bit untidy,' remembered one Kriegie. 'His bed was always known as the "lair of the troglodyte".'[22] Another job that required neatness was forgery, an activity for which Flight Lieutenant Gilbert 'Tim' Walenn was eminently suitable: before joining the RAF, he had designed wallpapers and fabrics for his uncle's design studio. One of his co-forgers, Alex Cassie, recalled how Walenn was a shy man, with gentle manners. 'He was impeccably polite, always,' said Cassie. 'He never seemed to lose his temper. He didn't smoke himself, but he always made sure that if anyone came into our room there was a box of cigarettes available and he would immediately offer them a cigarette.'[23] Good-looking and sporting a great bushy moustache, Walenn was always well dressed and somewhat resembled the British comic actor Jimmy Edwards, who was himself a wartime RAF pilot. 'He was extremely well liked,' Cassie remembered, 'and it was well known that he was one of the people engaged in forging documents and very capable of doing it.'[24] Walenn's looks, talent and manners did, however, hide a personal tragedy. On 24 May 1940, he had been involved in a car crash in Marlborough in Wiltshire with his fiancée, Mary Beauport, and she had been killed.[25] 'He never mentioned that,' said Cassie, 'and I was told that he never liked talking about it.'[26]

Over the winter, Bushell briefed the X Organisation on the contents of his plan. Its scope was highly ambitious, something which came as a surprise even to those who knew its progenitor. Bushell wished to strike a grand coup, something that would really hit back hard against the Germans. George Harsh recalled a meeting in which Bushell outlined his plan to the committee. After snapping at the Canadian for being late, Bushell announced:

I've decided on three tunnels, because I like the asymmetry of the figure three. The Germans will probably find one of these tunnels – maybe even two – but the third gives us a light break. When they find one of these elaborate tunnels they'll think we've put everything we've got into it. And if they find the second, they'll know damn well we have. And that's just what I want 'em to think.[27]

Furthermore, Bushell wanted no fewer than two hundred to escape on the first night alone. 'Then,' he added, 'we can close up the hole, and if it survives the searches, we can send out another lot later.'[28] In total, Bushell wanted at least six hundred to escape.

What became clear to those attending the meeting was that Bushell was not only advocating a more ambitious approach to escaping, but also one that was far more professional. Bushell insisted that the Kriegies now had to think like the Germans. 'We've got to get inside their minds and stay one jump ahead of 'em.'[29] All ideas for escape attempts would now have to be approved by the committee, which would decide whether they merited an allocation of clothing and forged paperwork. 'Gone were the days of private enterprise schemes competing higgledy-piggledy and falling over one another in the process,' wrote Walter Morison.[30] Construction techniques needed to be dramatically improved in order to make tunnels safer and capable of withstanding repeated use. Spoil needed to be dispersed far more effectively – the existence of too many tunnels had been revealed to the ferrets by telltale deposits of sand casually dumped under huts. In short, Bushell was trying to make the business of escape a military exercise, with himself as the sole commander.

There can be no doubt that Bushell's autocratic manner provoked some resentment amongst the Kriegie population at large. Bushell was known to walk into a room and, without any ceremony, point at each man in turn and curtly tell him that he was to be a stooge or perform some other function. When Bushell had turned his back, some Kriegies would regard such orders as being 'bullshit'.[31] Bomb aimer Alan Bryett recalled:

> He was a very taciturn man. A man who said very little, who always looked rather grumpy and irritable and didn't communicate with anyone at all unless he was directly talking to them, and then he was just asking questions to which he wanted the answers and that was the end of it.[32]

Flight Lieutenant Flekser thought him 'stern, cold, aloof', a man with whom it was hard to make friends.[33] Others were less flattering still. Fleet Air Arm observer Maurice Driver said:

> His manner was one that one rather tends to associate with lawyers. Rather legalistic minds, I suppose, people who had very strong opinions about things, people who were not all backward in expressing them. Whatever you felt about the opinions and what effect they had on you meant nothing to him at all. I didn't find him an agreeable character. I didn't find him likeable. He must have got things done but I had nothing to do with him. He didn't inspire me with anything except distaste.[34]

Some Kriegies acknowledged that Bushell's abrasive personality was nevertheless appropriate for the task he had set himself. Although Jack Rae, a Kiwi Spitfire pilot, regarded Bushell as being 'dispassionate', he also saw him as a 'great leader' and 'well suited for the operation he took on'.[35] Flight Lieutenant Lorne Welch thought that Bushell was a 'strange character', who was extremely quick to make judgements and assessments. 'A maddening habit if you're wrong,' Welch observed, 'but he wasn't wrong, he was practically always right.'[36]

There were plenty, however, who did like Bushell. Richard Churchill, a Handley Page Hampden pilot, had an enormous amount of respect for the man. '[He] stood out when you were speaking to him or listening to him,' said Churchill. 'In a group of people, he certainly had what one would describe as charisma, as well as being highly intelligent, and the two don't necessarily always go together. He had a great deal of natural authority.'[37] Sydney Dowse, a Spitfire reconnaissance pilot who lived in the room next to Bushell, regarded him as a 'very good friend', and remembered him as 'always at the forefront because he was the sort of chap who would take over doing this and doing that'.[38] Dowse recalled how Bushell did not shy from exerting his natural authority over the Germans. On one occasion, Bushell took them to task for constantly waking Dowse throughout the night, to check that he had not escaped. 'He gave absolute hell to the Germans, and went, "Look you can't go on stopping this man from sleeping every night . . . You bloody well can't do this, we're not going to let you." And then it stopped, and I managed to get some sleep.'[39] The Germans certainly respected Bushell, and many decades after the war, Glemnitz said that he was 'the finest man I ever knew'.[40]

It appears that those who liked Bushell were men who shared his strong desire to escape. Perhaps surprisingly, the majority of Kriegies had little or no interest in escaping, and regarded escape activities with wariness. This widespread lack of appetite for breaking free is certainly at odds with the received wisdom transmitted by many films and books, which portray POWs – and especially those at Stalag Luft III – as a homogeneous bunch of heroic, escape-hungry men. Perhaps the primary reason for not wishing to escape was rooted in the manner in which most at Stalag Luft III had lost their liberty: they had been shot down. Nearly every Kriegie had suffered a terrifying experience in which he had witnessed comrades being burned to death, or seen them plummeting towards the ground trapped inside a doomed aircraft. For those shot down over water, the experience was rendered doubly horrific. One Sagan Kriegie, Squadron Leader Denys Maw, recalled a bomber crew who had survived eleven days floating in the Mediterranean, and had endured the last two or three days in the blazing hot sun with no water. One of Maw's roommates in the camp was the first pilot to have ditched a Bristol Beaufighter and to have lived. He had hit the water at 216 knots and had been flung through the windscreen. The pilot and his navigator managed to climb aboard their inflatable dinghy, but before they landed in Holland three days later, the navigator had died. Even when the Germans captured the pilot, half dead with cold exposure, they refused to give him a ride in their sidecar and made him walk.[41]

Many Kriegies had similar stories to tell, and because each of them knew that they had been immensely fortunate, the notion of voluntarily rejoining operations was anathema to many. 'As a result of their experiences of crash and capture,' wrote William Ash, 'most prisoners were understandably not overly keen on pushing the odds even further by escaping in the heart of

Germany.'[42] Many suffered from burns, others from nightmares. Such physical and psychological scars were as much barriers to escape as the fence that surrounded them. The wire may have deprived the men of their liberty, but it also protected them. 'One could well understand the attitude of many prisoners,' wrote Wellington pilot Ken Rees, 'who, after such traumatic experiences, felt that they were exceptionally lucky to be alive and simply wanted to make the best of a boring but relatively safe existence.'[43] However, for men such as Bushell, the fact of survival was emphatically not a reason for sitting it out. According to George Harsh, Bushell saw all the Kriegies as living on borrowed time, as each of them should really have been dead. 'The only reason why the good Lord preserved us', Bushell declared, 'is so we can give these blasted Huns as much hell as we can.'[44] Such an attitude – suggesting as it does a divinely inspired mission – was not shared by most of the POWs. Some were happy simply to thank the Lord for having survived and were unwilling to roll the dice once again. 'There was quite a strong religious content in our outlook,' wrote one POW. 'Most of us had escaped death by a matter of inches or seconds, and it occurred to some of us that we ought to consider what the alternative might have been.'[45]

Fear of death was not the only reason why many chose not to try to escape. Although most were keen after they had arrived at Sagan, it swiftly became apparent that escaping was an extremely difficult business that required quite exceptional talents. At some point during their captivity, the vast proportion of prisoners came to the uncomfortable realisation that they did not possess the necessary skills. 'After a while most of us came to the conclusion that the chances of getting out were slim . . . ,' admitted Stephen Johnson, who nevertheless helped others as much as he could, 'but my hope of getting home myself gradually evaporated.'[46] Johnson's willingness to assist those who felt they could escape was almost ubiquitous. Albert Clark – 'Big S' – realised that while 'not everyone in the camp was fired up over the idea of escape', every POW was prepared to do his bit, no matter how modest. Furthermore, 'everyone clearly understood the need for security, which meant no curiosity or loose talk about activities related to escape'.[47] Some Kriegies, such as 7 Squadron bomb aimer George Atkinson, were self-avowedly most unfired up about the business of escaping. 'Personally, I had no ambition to go, frankly,' he said. 'I can't say that I felt particularly enthusiastic about it because I think the problems that had to be overcome to get away were very elaborate and considerable.'[48]

In the claustrophobic confines of a prison camp, the relationship between the escapers and the stayers would sometimes become strained. The latter somewhat derisively referred to the former as 'Tally-Ho', regarding them as 'cloak-and-dagger boys' who were treating the whole thing as a game.[49] Some stayers even regarded the escapers as ruining the relative comforts of camp life. 'There was quite a bit of feeling that way,' said James 'Dixie' Deans, an NCO pilot with 102 Squadron. 'They were a damn nuisance at times. That feeling was expressed. They upset the whole routine of the camp, because obviously when an escape attempt was made the Germans immediately clamped down and took away certain privileges.'[50] Such irritation was not often vocalised, however, and many stayers guarded their tongues. 'I think there were those [who were opposed to escape],' said George Atkinson, 'but I don't think they got much of a platform on which to oppose it. I don't remember personally having any discussions with any POWs who positively and actively opposed it.'[51] The silence of the stayers, who, according to Jimmy James, accounted for around two-thirds of the camp,[52] was also ensured by Roger Bushell himself. 'This was a game that he was determined to win,' wrote Flight Lieutenant Flekser, 'even to the extent of threatening to court martial recalcitrant critics.'[53] The fact that Bushell had to make such a threat is indicative of a bolshie element that held escaping in low regard. In some camps, that element would even resort to treason in order to ensure that its peace was not disturbed. In Oflag VIIB at Eichstätt, for example, one escape attempt was stymied when a POW threw a tin over the wire that contained a note informing the Germans that there was a tunnel being built from block two.[54]

Upon initial consideration, the motive for those who wished to escape would appear to be quite simple: they just wanted to get out. However, there were more subtle reasons, which formed part of what one Kriegie referred to as 'occupational therapy'.[55] For many, the very act of trying to escape was regarded as an end in itself. Walter Morison said:

We were young men, and by and large wanted to do something that had some purpose to it. Otherwise it was pointless waiting for the end of the war. Escaping was a real objective . . . Of course, it was such fun. It was a game, a sport. Maybe it was more like a traditional English field sport in its way.[56]

Such a view was echoed by Squadron Leader Denys Maw, who regarded Bushell's plan as 'a rather exciting game with a spice of danger to it'.[57] The notion that escaping was a sport was widely held, and many acknowledged that the taking part in this particular sport was more important than the winning, which every Kriegie knew to be an unlikely result. One POW observed:

> Very few anticipated they would ever make it home, but the opportunity of getting out and getting a breath of fresh air and a different environment was such, that to get over the boredom and monotony of just walking around the camp was a goal which most people were anxious to achieve even if it was only for a day or two.[58]

The notion of escape almost being seen as an excursion was somewhat prevalent. 'There were an awful lot of people who didn't bother to escape,' said Sydney Dowse. '[But] there were others like myself who just wanted the freedom to wander around and see the towns of Germany – with the view of getting back to England of course.'[59]

Common to all prisoners, whether they wanted to escape or not, was the understanding that there was a duty to escape. In nearly every memoir by, or interview with, former RAF officer POWs, there will invariably be a statement that asserts this as fact. One Kriegie recalled

Wings Day telling the prisoners that 'it's your duty to escape if you can', although another did not remember it being 'emphasised in any way'.[60] Most prisoners seemed to assume that it was indeed their duty, with some even believing that there was a 'Red Cross Convention' in which it was enshrined.[61] There were Germans who apparently thought that British POWs were ordered to make at least three escape attempts or they would face a court martial, while some British understood that German officer POWs shared a similar obligation.[62] 'Whether you were English or German, technically it was your duty to escape,' claimed Arthur Cole.[63] Only a handful doubted it. 'We used to say to the Goons that it was our duty to escape,' said Walter Morison. 'I'm not quite sure that was strictly true, maybe it was.'[64] In fact, Morison's doubts were correct – he and his fellow officers were under no duty to escape whatsoever. There was no requirement in the King's Regulations, or in any form of international convention. One official document that might possibly have stipulated a duty to escape was the booklet issued to all RAF aircrew in the European Theatre entitled *The Responsibilities of a Prisoner of War*. However, that mainly concerns itself with how POWs should behave when dealing with the enemy, and does not once mention an obligation to get away from his clutches.[65] Even after the war, when British military courts conducted war crimes trials against defendants accused of murdering POWs who were attempting to escape, not one of the courts identified the source of any legal duty to do so. Under law, a POW was simply entitled – but not obliged – to try to escape, with the corollary being that his captors were then perfectly entitled to shoot him to prevent him from doing so successfully.[66]

However, it would be wrong to excoriate Kriegies for their ignorance of legal matters. If any duty did exist, then it was more as George Atkinson described it:

There was a kind of corporate policy of intent that it was part of our duty to play a part in escape arrangements. And I think, by and large, as loyal members of the Royal Air Force, most of us accepted this principle, whether we felt particularly enthusiastic about escape ourselves or not.[67]

What is clear is that the duty was born more out of a social obligation than a legal one. After all, a sense of duty to one's comrades is often stronger than any obligation stipulated by a state. Peer pressure, precedent, circumstances and mores all combined to make the duty feel as if it really was included in the King's Regulations. The fact that no legally mandated duty existed may well have been because RAF officers simply assumed, as a point of honour, that they should try to escape, just as they should try to be brave or to fight well. 'You just did it,' said Paul Royle. 'If you wanted to, you did it.'[68]

There was one final reason for escaping, which, like the notion of a duty to do so, was commonly held to be true by nearly every Kriegie. Knowing that nearly all escape attempts ended in failure, the POWs would draw consolation from the fact that they had nevertheless 'kept the Germans busy', and that by escaping, they were in some way tying up enemy personnel who could more usefully be deployed on the front line. The thinking behind Bushell's plan to launch a mass break-out had essentially evolved from this idea. If two people broke out, that caused the Germans a lot of fuss, but imagine, so the reasoning went, the hue and cry if a few hundred managed to escape. It would be like opening another front, right inside the heart of Germany. 'There will be a massive flap,' Bushell predicted. 'Even if no one gets clean away, this escape will put a dent in their war effort.'[69] For those deprived of their liberty, sitting frustrated in a camp in the middle of a Silesian forest while their comrades carried on with the fighting, earning medals and promotion, the idea that escaping was another way of doing one's bit understandably appealed. On the surface, the notion seems reasonable, but the idea of a mass breakout had particular flaws so serious that the Great Escape ended up being more beneficial to the Germans than it was to the Allies. Hermann Glemnitz said many years after the war that 'the big tunnel was a silly idea', and, as we shall see, he was right.[70]

Chapter Five

Tom, Dick and Harry

ON THURSDAY 1 APRIL 1943, around 850 Kriegies were transferred to the newly constructed north compound. The Germans saw the move as an ideal opportunity to search every POW and, in the process, many compasses and maps were discovered and confiscated. However, to the delight of many, equipment used for distilling managed to make it past Glemnitz and his men. 'This small victory over the ferrets made us buzz like excited schoolboys,' wrote Ken Rees.[1] In comparison to the tired and dirty east compound, the new compound was a large improvement. A new latrine pit emptied by a workman the POWs described as the 'Scheisse Führer' was a significant boon, as were the fifteen huts, which smelled of fresh pine.[2] In addition, the south of the compound featured a large recreation ground, although as it was still studded with tree stumps, it could not immediately be used for sports. Their new home may well have been basic, but compared to their fellow officers at other camps, the prisoners at Stalag Luft III had it good. One POW who had been moved from Stalag VIIIB at Lamsdorf (today called Łambinowice) thought 'it was like moving off the gutter into a luxurious hotel'.[3] In fact, this was no exaggeration – Lamsdorf was a real hellhole, and regarded as the worst POW camp in Germany. Intended as a transit camp, its barracks were dirty, their windows broken and the concrete walls leaking. Fuel was so short that Kriegies had to burn their own bunks and then sleep on the concrete floor. In the summer, the coldness was replaced by a plague of flies. The latrines were rat-infested: the lids covering the holes were not there for neatness or cleanliness, but simply to stop the rodents climbing out.[4] In comparison to these conditions, Sagan's new north compound was indeed more five star than frightful.

That Thursday did not mark the first day in which the POWs had set foot in their new home. Thanks to a seeming cessation in escape activity, von Lindeiner had allowed the prisoners to enter the compound in order ostensibly to help build a theatre.[5] Of course, the real purpose of such visits was twofold: first, to smuggle in escape equipment; and second, to make a thorough survey in order to establish the location of the tunnels. The recces were carried out by Floody, Ker-Ramsay and Marshall, and they reported back to the escape committee that the best locations were from huts 122, 123 and 104. The three tunnels were codenamed by Bushell as 'Tom', 'Dick' and 'Harry', with Tom running from hut 123, which lay close to the western part of the perimeter and at the far south of the compound. Dick would run from hut 122, which was immediately east of hut 123. Both of these huts were as far as possible from the *Vorlager* – the German part of the camp – and therefore likely to be subject to less scrutiny. Harry in hut 104, however, was to be deliberately located as close to the *Vorlager* as possible, in the belief that the Germans would never suspect such a location, particularly as it also required a tunnel well over 100 feet longer than any other that could be built in the compound. Each tunnel was then assigned a chief engineer, with Marshall in charge of Tom; Ker-Ramsay, Dick; and Floody, Harry.

As soon as the transfer was made, Bushell ordered the team to begin work. The first task was to establish the precise locations of the tunnels' entrances – their traps – which took until the end of the following week. As the Germans had elevated the huts well off the ground with thin brick columns, the only places in which tunnels could be successfully concealed were the large pillars of concrete that contained the huts' drains. All three traps were made by three Polish RAF Flight Lieutenants – E. Gotowski, L. Kozlowski and 'Dick' Mickiewicz – and their ingenuity was astonishing. In hut 123, the trap for Tom was made in the concrete floor of a small annexe to one of the rooms. Surrounded by two walls and a chimney, the trap took up an area of 2 square feet. Slowly, the concrete was chipped out, and replaced by a slab made from some cement that had been left lying around by some German workmen. When the first tunnellers turned up for duty on

15 April, they were unable to find the trap until they were shown exactly where it was.[6] The trap for Dick in hut 122 was even more ingenious. In the floor of the washroom was an iron grating covering a concrete drain 18 inches square and 2 feet deep. Water ran into the drain from the north and south sides, and the drain-pipe was on the west side. The grating was removed by Mickiewicz, the water baled out, and the east side of the drain chipped away to reveal earth. A concrete slab was then set in place on the east side, which could be slid up and down, and sealed with soap and sand. What was particularly ingenious was that the water could be replaced in the drain, and work on the tunnel could continue while it was still there.[7] In hut 104, the trap for Harry was located under a stove standing on top of a grid of a hundred tiles. These were taken up and then reset on a wooden frame, which could be lifted with two strips of sheet metal which folded down sideways and could be hooked up with a knife.[8] The join was then filled with cement paste and covered with dirt.[9]

After the traps were made, the next stage was to construct the vertical shafts, which were built by the three engineers. In order not to be detected by a series of underground microphones that had been placed around the camp, the shafts were sunk some 30 feet, and had ladders 25 feet long. Another advantage of such a great depth was that it made the tunnels less vulnerable to the surface movement of vehicles such as carts.[10] At the base of each shaft, three chambers were built. The first was used for storing sand before it was dispersed elsewhere; the second served as a general storage chamber for equipment such as tools and lamps;

and the third, which was 5 feet long, 5½ feet high and 2½ feet wide, was used to house the most vital piece of equipment: the air pump. The designers and builders of the pumps were a Norwegian RAF Spitfire pilot, Jens Müller, and British officer Thomas 'Bob' Nelson. Two ordinary army kitbags were sewn together around a series of circular wooden frames to form an accordion-like tube, which was then mounted inside a long wooden box. Leather flaps were inserted halfway down the tube, and were reinforced with pieces of tin cut to size. These flaps, which acted as valves, would open and close, alternately causing one half of the tube to suck in the stale air, while the other half blew out fresh air. Attached to the tube was a handle, which was used to pull the whole assembly backwards and forwards, thereby creating the suction and delivery. The pipeline along which the air was delivered was made out of tins of the Canadian powdered milk Klim – 'milk' spelled in reverse – and this ran along the length of the tunnel. The pump also featured an exhaust, which led to the nearest chimney. 'The reason for this was that it was very moist air,' Nelson recalled, 'and if you had the outlet pipe in a visible position, you'd get a condensation trail . . . which would be visible.'[11] Nelson and Müller also devised a bypass system around the pumps, so that when the tunnel was not in use, the natural ventilation provided by the chimney kept the tunnel aerated.

By the end of May, the vertical shafts for all three tunnels had been completed. Out of caution, the working hours had been kept to a minimum – from 12.30 to 14.30 and from 22.00 to 23.50 – and no work was undertaken if there was more than one German in the compound.[12] It is hard to overestimate quite how much had been achieved in just two months, all of which had to be done under the watchfulness of Glemnitz and his ferrets. The stooges were doing their job well, and diversionary activities such as choir practices and open-air workshops for noisily making items such as baking dishes provided much-needed clamour to disguise the sounds of digging.[13] Although the escape committee was right to take such precautions, in the early days of the north compound the ferrets were by no means as effective as they might have been. Their biggest failing, it would appear, was their routine. 'It was extraordinary that, for several months, ferrets operated to such a timetable that it was nearly possible to set watches by their predictable entries and exits,' wrote Leonard Hall.[14]

As well as keeping the locations of the tunnels secret and providing them with air, there were other challenges that had to be overcome. The biggest problem, which had been the downfall of so many other tunnels, was the question of sand dispersal. Not only was quantity an issue, but so too was the colour, which was bright yellow – almost white – and therefore much lighter than that of the topsoil. The problem was solved by Lieutenant Commander Peter 'Hornblower' Fanshawe, who had navigated and been shot down in a Skua in the disastrous 1940 raid on the *Scharnhorst*.[15] Fanshawe's solution was to produce an invention that was as ingenious as the air pumps and the traps. He took two German handtowels, each measuring about 18 inches by 9 inches, and rolled them into two long tubes. These were then sewn down their length, but left unstitched at both ends. At the bottom, the tubes were closed with a big pin attached to a string, and then both tubes were attached to a pair of braces. The braces were worn, and the tubes ran down the wearer's trouser legs. A hole was then made in each trouser pocket, and the tubes were filled with sand. As each tube carried about 8 pounds of sand, the weight of the combined load resulted in the wearers having to adopt a somewhat comic gait, which earned them the nickname 'penguins'. 'We then waddled as inconspicuously as possible towards the sandy playing field,' recalled one Kriegie, 'indulged in some suitable activity such as throwing a medicine ball around, removed the pins, and shuffled sand through our trouser bottoms where it mingled into the ground and effectively disappeared. It was a Heath Robinson scheme, but it worked remarkably well.'[16]

Although this was the most celebrated method of dispersing sand, there were others. A team of South African Kriegies adopted a more simple system that involved wearing two pairs of trousers, the inner pair fitted with a release mechanism similar to that devised by Fanshawe. As around 30 pounds of sand could be held and dispersed, the walkers must have looked especially penguin-like. Even more straightforward was carrying sand in a blanket, which could hold some 24 pounds. During the warmer months, the Kriegies would roll up the blanket, and then unfold it on the ground before using it to sunbathe.[17] Even though all these methods of dispersal might have seemed sufficiently surreptitious, they were only carried out when Germans were not in the compound, which was usually for two hours around lunchtime, and in the summer, for two hours in the evening.[18] The quantities of sand that were dispersed were vast. Each shaft alone produced 12 tons of sand, which would have necessitated around 140 'penguin' outings. Each chamber produced 2 tons, and every 3½ feet of tunnel another single ton. It was later estimated that some 18,000 individual dispersal trips were made from the traps to the 23 dispersal areas. In total, approximately 200 'penguins' were employed.[19] One unexpected problem with sand was that it had a distinctive smell. In the rooms where it was loaded into the 'penguins', a tin of the most pungent tobacco was kept permanently burning in the corridor outside.[20] The smell of fresh pine so enjoyed by the new arrivals must have quickly been eradicated.

Sand was not only difficult to disperse, it also proved to be an extremely hazardous substance. The issue of sudden collapses was well known to the tunnellers, who constantly listened out for the crack that preceded any such downfall. The simple solution was to use the boards from the Kriegies' bunks to shore up the tunnels, and these proved immensely effective in providing support. Of course, this resulted in a concomitant lack of support in the beds, which caused some appreciable, but fruitless, expressions of ill feeling, as Walter Morison recalled: 'If someone came and said, "I want two of your bed boards," there was no good saying, "You can't have two of my bed boards." They had to go and your bed got progressively less and less smooth.'[21] As the bed boards were used up, the POWs had to decide upon which particular form of discomfort they would endure for the night. Some would choose to distribute the boards evenly; others would lay them together and curl up with their feet hitting the floor; and a few would simply let their bottoms hang down – presumably a technique that was not popular if one was on a top bunk.[22] The other hazard with sand was when it was hauled out by bucket and rope up the shaft: 'Occasionally somebody dropped the bucket,' said Ken Rees, 'and it was a bit nasty for the person underneath.'[23]

In fact, the whole process of tunnelling was more than a 'bit nasty'. Many of the Kriegies regarded the tunnellers as a 'breed apart', who were able to put up with the prospect of being buried alive, intense claustrophobia, heat, stuffy air and the smell from the fat lamps and their co-workers' bodies. The physical exertion required was enormous, and these were not men who were on diets that allowed for the rampant burning of calories. As one Kriegie put it simply: 'You could either do it or you couldn't.'[24] Even for those who could, the experience took some getting used to. Ken Rees recalled going down Harry for the first time, accompanied by Wellington pilot Flight Lieutenant Johnny Bull, who was a veteran tunneller. Bull was the father of a child who had been born since he'd been captured, which gave him not only a strong motive for escaping, but also a rather serious air.[25] Rees shared a room with Bull, and the two men had formed a strong friendship ever since Rees had fallen out of his bunk on his first night in the camp while having a nightmare about being shot down.

'What the hell do you think you are doing?' Bull had asked.

'I just baled out and my parachute wouldn't open.'

'Oh? Maybe next time you should just stay in the aircraft and crash with it.'[26]

Although Rees had already had a quick inspection of the tunnel a few days before, he was concerned that he would suffer from claustrophobia as he followed Bull.

> Luckily I didn't suffer from that at all. But it could be a bit worrying, because you were 30 feet down, nobody knew on the German side where you were, what you were doing, so if there had been any nasty fall you realised that you'd just about had it. There would be no means of rescuing you because they wouldn't even know where you were.[27]

As Bull crawled along, Rees crawled backwards behind him, so that he was in a position to collect the sand dug out by Bull and deposit it on the trolley. When the trolley was full, Rees would give it a tap, and it would be pulled back towards the shaft. As the men worked, the air quality in the tunnel would deteriorate, no matter how hard the pumps were being operated. Sometimes the flames from the fat lamps would flicker and die, leaving the men in darkness. Such moments would cause even the most hardened tunneller a moment of panic. On one such occasion, Rees remembered hearing an ominous rumble: 'We thought, "Oh God, the tunnel's caving in." It only lasted a matter of seconds but we realised afterwards it was a cart going down the road – all was over, but it was one of my most worrying moments down there.'[28] What made the air quality even poorer was the smell produced by the men. The sweat was bad enough, but what caused a real stench was urine and faeces. 'If you were caught short, you dug a little hole and did your best,' Rees wrote. 'It was no joke when someone had a dicky tum down there in the tunnel.'[29] At the end of a shift, the men would find themselves covered in sweat, sand and excrement, a combination that would cake their longjohns. After a while, as visually unappealing as it was, most tunnellers decided to work in the nude.[30]

As the excavations proceeded, the Germans began to get suspicious. Despite the depth of the tunnels, the underground listening devices, which were placed between each watchtower at a depth of 2 metres,[31] were picking up the sounds of subterranean activity. Manned by a Corporal Bening, microphones 53 and 54 started to detect loud noises in May around hut 104, the starting point of Harry. The hut was searched, but nothing was found. The sounds were ascribed to the activity at a nearby coal dump, but, incredibly, the Germans overlooked the fact that the noises were also being made at night.[32] Nothing less than wily, Hermann Glemnitz toured the compound, and stopped to ask dozens of Kriegies how many tunnels were being built. Although he knew he would never receive a straight answer, the escape committee was sufficiently worried that even by assembling a series of flippant answers, Glemnitz would have some clue as to the level of clandestine activity. All Kriegies were therefore ordered to ignore Glemnitz, no matter what he asked.[33]

As a result of their suspicions, it was during the summer months of 1943 that the Germans began to warn the POWs of the likely consequences of a mass escape. With the war going badly for Germany, and with an increase in British and American bombing raids on her cities, attitudes towards those Goebbels had

dubbed 'terror fliers' were becoming far less accommodating. What the prisoners could not know while
they tunnelled, but what was very clear to von
Lindeiner and his senior staff, was that the responsibility for POWs was being gradually wrestled away from
the Luftwaffe and placed into the clutches of less
civilised agencies of the Nazi state. In August, the
Kriminalpolizei – the Criminal Police, which was dove-
tailed with the Gestapo and was part of the
Reichssicherheitshauptamt (Reich Security Main Office
or RSHA) – took over responsibility for security
measures against escape, and the staff at Sagan saw this
as the thin end of a sinister wedge, as Heinrich Himmler
was now effectively in charge of all POW camps.
Prisoners captured by the police would no longer auto-
matically be returned to their camps, and could remain
in police custody.[34] In October, all POWs in Germany
were informed that any prisoner caught escaping while
wearing a German uniform or civilian clothes was liable
to be tried on the grounds of espionage, and would
inevitably be shot.[35] Bodies such as the Gestapo justified
such a measure on the basis of an unfounded fear that
the escapers were intending to join up with foreign
workers in order to carry out acts of sabotage and
foment resistance.[36] Furthermore, Lieutenant Günther
von Massow, the censor officer, suspected that a mass
escape would result in the SS taking over Stalag Luft III.
'I had no official information,' von Massow later stated,
'but I had watched this policy developing during the
years I had been connected with P.W. affairs.'[37] Von
Massow's concerns were shared by the Commandant,
who was worried about the interference by both the

Kripo and the Gestapo. 'He realised that he was not strong enough to fight them,' von Massow declared, 'and therefore decided to play one official off against the other.'[38]

Ultimately, von Lindeiner knew that no amount of politicking would save the POWs if they attempted a mass escape, and furthermore, he also knew that he would never be able to stop escape attempts from taking place. All that the Germans could therefore do was to impress upon the officers that attempts, if they were going to be made, should be done on a small scale, which would be less likely to attract the unwelcome attention of the Kripo and the Gestapo. Von Massow warned the Kriegies that 'an attempt at a mass escape might have dangerous consequences'.[39] In June, after one attempt at a large breakout via the delousing shed,[40] von Lindeiner warned the prisoners that another mass escape would see the Gestapo taking over the running of the camp.[41] By the middle of 1943, not one POW in Germany would have required any explanation as to what the Gestapo was capable of doing, and the knowledge that the Gestapo might treat mass escapers as potential saboteurs left the prisoners in little doubt as to what level of punishment would be meted out to those who embarked on mass escapes. In October, von Lindeiner wrote to the SBO, Group Captain Kellett, reiterating the order issued by the German High Command that 'any person found in the uniform of a German soldier or official or in civilian clothes must expect to be examined by a court martial on suspicion of espionage, sabotage, or banditry'.[42] Later that year, one Oberleutnant Schulz told Kellett that 'serious

consequences [were] likely to arise from a big break',
and that he thought 'there was a strong possibility of
murder'.[43]

Had the expression of such warnings, realistic though
they were, been revealed to the Kripo or the Gestapo,
charges of treason might well have been brought.
However, a few of the Germans dished out advice that
was even more helpful to the Kriegies. Corporal
Eberhard Hesse, who had worked as an interpreter at
Sagan since August 1942, warned Bushell himself that a
mass escape was less likely to succeed than a small one:

> The one disadvantage of these large-scale alarms was
> that they made all escape routes very difficult. For this
> reason, we later continually advised the RAF
> Intelligence Officer in Luft 3, S/L Roger Bushell, to limit
> the escapes to groups of 4 men because they would not
> cause a large scale alarm to be sounded and the chances
> of the escapees reaching home would be increased.[44]

Hermann Glemnitz held the same opinion. 'Maybe you
could get away with five men,' he commented after the
war, 'and then a month later another five men, but 78
men when all Germany was alerted at the same moment
– impossible to get away with it!'[45]

Both Hesse and Glemnitz were right. During the war,
the Gestapo and the Kripo had established a remarkably
effective system of nationwide searches that were
carried out in the event of emergencies. Known as the
Sonderfahndungsplan der Sipo und SD – the Special
Search Plan of the Security Police and Security Service –
the system was divided into three levels of severity:

Alpha, *Beta* and *Gross*. The *Grossfahndung* – Big Search Plan – was carried out rarely, and only when the emergency was felt to threaten national security. The first time a *Grossfahndung* was declared was in March 1943, when 43 Allied airmen, under the command of the indefatigable Wings Day, tunnelled out of Szubin. As soon as the escape was discovered, a *Grossfahndung* was raised, and the following agencies were alerted: the Gestapo, the Kripo, the regular Police (the Schutzpolizei), the Rural Police, the Motor Transport Service of the Schutzpolizei, the Ministry of Finance, the Frontier Patrol Service, the Ministry of Transport, the Hunting Office, the Chiefs of Mobilised Formations and Organisations, the Security Service (the Sicherheitsdienst or SD), the Waterways Protection Police, the Customs Frontier Guards, the Railway Police, the Railways Protection Service, the National Fire Protection Police, the Air Raid Precaution Police, the Volunteer Fire Brigades, the Technical Emergency Corps, the Auxiliary Rural Police, the State and Civil Forest and Hunting Protection Service, the National Labour Service, the General SS, the SA, the Nazi Motor Corps, the Nazi Aviation Corps, the Hitler Youth, the Hitler Youth Patrol Service, the Armed Forces, the Waffen-SS, the Army Patrol Service and, finally, the Auxiliary Mountain Police. It is worth listing all these organisations to emphasise quite how extensive the search was. In short, not one man in uniform within the borders of Greater Germany would have been unaware that there was a *Grossfahndung* and why it was in place. The Kripo and the Gestapo were also entitled to requisition men from at least ten of these organisations, but, most importantly, not from the armed forces. In addition, hotels, garages, railways and hospitals were notified. The result of this first *Grossfahndung* was absolutely spectacular. In total, 809 escaped POWs were captured, including all of those who had tunnelled out of Szubin. But the *Grossfahndung* claimed far more scalps that that; 8,281 foreign workers who had left their workplaces were also captured, as well as 4,825 other persons wanted by the police. In all, nearly 14,000 were caught.[46] The obvious question to pose is this: Who ultimately benefited from the mass breakout at Szubin?

Thanks to the repeated warnings issued by von Lindeiner and his men, Bushell and his team had a general awareness of the effectiveness of the *Grossfahndung*. They would also have heard about the ultimate failure of the breakout from Szubin by Wings Day himself, who was transferred back to Sagan after the escape. Although Bushell would not have been party to the figures detailed above, he would have heard enough from Germans such as Hesse and Pieber, and comrades such as Day, to indicate to him that a mass escape was unlikely to result in any more home runs *pro rata* than smaller attempts. If the object of the exercise was simply to 'keep the Germans busy', then that too was flawed, as the Germans being kept busy were not those fighting the Allies. The Germans did not pull troops off the front line to hunt POWs, but instead used a capacity that was already in place, and, crucially, these were not men who would have been used at the front line anyway. Could Bushell have known that? We cannot be sure, but it is reasonable to assume that he might have imagined what the British would have done in the event of a mass breakout of German POWs. He would have correctly reckoned that Allied front-line troops, or those immediately destined for the front line, would never have been redeployed away from theatre to hunt POWs in the Home Counties. Furthermore, Bushell might not have known the extent of the un-witting benefit to the Germans caused by the Szubin breakout, but he was surely intelligent enough to recog-nise that increased security caused by a mass escape would imperil other enemies of the Reich who were on the loose. In short, Bushell was engaging in an enter-prise that was extremely unlikely to succeed, would quite possibly end in some form of violent reprisal, and would queer the pitch for everybody else. It is therefore hard to disagree with Hermann Glemnitz when he described the Great Escape as 'a silly idea'. Smaller escapes – as Hesse had directly informed Bushell – would have resulted in more men getting home, no chance of a *Grossfahndung*, and no risk of the reprisals suggested by Schulz, von Massow and Pieber.[47]

Such an analysis should not be regarded as an expression of retrospective wisdom, because, as we shall see, Bushell and his fellow senior officers would be warned many more times. In addition, there were even some Kriegies who had their concerns about the whole plan – one of them being George Harsh. In his memoirs, Harsh claimed that at the time of the breakout, he had 'grave doubts' as to its wisdom and worth, and saw it as 'an act of typical military madness, a futile, empty gesture'. 'I do not believe that what we did affected the eventual outcome of that war by so much as one tittle,' he wrote.[48] Another doubter was Flight Lieutenant Paul Royle, who disputed that the escape would prove an irritant to the German forces. 'It's now said that a lot of German troops were employed or something, either to capture us or all the rest,' Royle said after the war, 'but I don't really see how that could have been the case, because seventy-three unarmed people couldn't have done very much harm. I think that's an exaggeration.'[49] Royle also doubted whether the motive for the escape was to deflect troops from the front: 'I think the motive for most was that they wanted to get out,' he said, 'and later on you can start deciding what the motives were. I don't think that I ever heard anybody ever talk about doing anything to the German army. They just wanted to get out.'[50] If those such as Harsh and Royle ever did express doubts like these at the time, it is doubtful whether they would have been brooked by Bushell. There was arrogance in his thinking, which was a product of both his personality and his desire to have a good war. There was also a refusal to acknowledge that the risks he was running with the lives of so many young men were as great as the camp staff repeatedly indicated. Perhaps blinded by an animosity towards all Germans, Bushell was not willing to trust decent men such as von Lindeiner, who were only his enemy *de jure*, and were his guardians *de facto*. Ironically, he, more than most other officers in Stalag Luft III, was aware of what the Nazis were capable of, and the words of men such as Hesse and Pieber must have rung true.

If the Great Escape is to be regarded as an act of reckless, counter-productive bravado, then the blame for it should not just be reserved for Bushell, but also for his fellow senior officers, Wings Day and the new SBO, Group Captain Herbert Massey, who had taken over from Kellett in April 1943. Although Massey, who had flown in the First World War, was of a similar generation to von Lindeiner, and may have shared the German's benevolent schoolmasterly attitude towards the young officers – 'a father to all of us' as one Kriegie remembered[51] – Massey was not the type of man to have urged Bushell to halt 'X activities'. Although the plan for the Great Escape was the sole vision of Bushell, Massey supported it completely. Similarly, Wings Day was not one to put a stop to Tom, Dick and Harry. As Alan Bryett said:

> Those three at the top had all agreed it. Group Captain Massey or Day could have vetoed the plan right from the start, but the enormity of it was known by the people at the top, and the risks of it were known by the people at the top as well.[52]

Bryett's words are only partially correct. The triumvirate of Bushell, Day and Massey claimed never to know exactly how serious the penalties were to be. In a statement he made when he was repatriated in 1944, Massey dismissed the significance of the 'threatened severe measures' which had been mentioned by another officer. He wrote:

> I do not attach much importance to the threat mentioned by Grocott, as threats of a like nature had been made in the past, both directly and indirectly, with a view to dissuading prisoners from attempting to

escape. I never got the impression that the High Command had decided on any sudden change of policy towards escaping.[53]

However, as we shall see, both Massey and his fellow senior officers would continue to be warned of the growing and significant danger that lay in wait for RAF officers outside the barbed wire, and it is unlikely that the likes of Massey were not able to sense that there had indeed been a change in policy.[54] The attitude of Massey, Bushell and Day to the risk was probably similar to that expressed by Richard Churchill.

> There was always going to be some risk if you were outside the wire and there were people with guns who could shoot at you. I suppose that for most of us . . . one had a certain comfort in the feeling that there was a Red Cross Convention in which it was laid down that it was an officer's duty to escape and one didn't expect too severe treatment if one was caught having done so.[55]

As we have seen, there was no Red Cross Convention enshrining a 'duty to escape', but Churchill's attitude towards the level of risk was widely shared. No Kriegie allowed himself to believe that what his fellow officers in the Luftwaffe were saying could really be true. 'Although . . . there were threats that they would kill us,' said Thomas Nelson, 'none of us had taken them seriously.'[56] Had Bushell done so, then this story would have been very different. What should also be stressed is that none of the Germans was telling the Kriegies not to try *any* form of escape; the warnings were exclusively reserved for mass escapes. It would have been perfectly feasible, and no less honourable, for Bushell to have adapted his plans and allowed his men to leak out of the camp, rather than flood out. By hitting the Nazis hard, he risked being hit back even harder, and hit back with a punch from which there could be no recovery. War is indeed a dangerous business, and risks must be taken, but not every risk has to be taken in order to achieve victory.

For their part, von Lindeiner and his men had no doubts that the situation for the POWs was becoming increasingly dangerous. There were rumours that German captives were being mistreated by the Allies, and there was an appetite for reprisal. One day, von Lindeiner summoned Simoleit into his office for a confidential discussion.

'Major Simoleit, you know our last information about bad treatment and even killing of German soldiers in England,' von Lindeiner began. 'We have to face a grave situation. What have we to do if Hitler wants more reprisals and sends us a strict order to shoot a number of our prisoners?'

Simoleit answered immediately.

'If I should receive such a dreadful order I would refuse to obey. I prefer in this case to be executed myself for military insubordination and would not try to save my miserable life by obeying.'

Von Lindeiner shook Simoleit's hand.

'We both know what we have to do.'[57]

The colonel and his major were honourable men, and clearly would have ended their own lives before executing any of their charges. But there were many in Nazi

Germany who thought differently. By digging their way out of Stalag Luft III, the POWs would shortly be placing themselves in the hands of such men.

Chapter Six

An Anglo-German Affair

THROUGHOUT THAT SUMMER, the work on the tunnels continued. Much of the digging was concentrated on Tom as it was the closest to the wire. Work on Harry was suspended, and Dick was used for storing sand from Tom, as well as equipment and contraband.[1] However, in late August, the escape committee received two pieces of bad news. The first was that the Americans would shortly be moved to the south compound, which meant that all the US officers who had helped with X activities would not be able to participate in the escape. The second was that the Germans were planning to build a west compound, which meant that the treeline into which Tom was to surface was about to be eradicated.[2] After much discussion, Bushell decided that work on Dick and Harry should be halted, and that the entire effort should be concentrated on Tom in order to give the 'cousins' a chance to get out. Within five days of the decision, Tom had advanced another 50 feet, and the woods were now just 40 feet away.[3]

However, the intensification of work resulted in shortcuts having to be made with security and sand dispersal. Glemnitz and his ferrets were beginning to notice an unusually high sand content in the Kriegies' gardens and, as a result of this, coupled with evidence from the microphone system, he ordered a search of hut 123, from which Tom started.[4] Although nothing was found, Bushell ruled, as a temporary solution, that the sand should now be stored in empty Red Cross boxes under the prisoners' beds. Unfortunately, the ferrets soon noticed a succession of POWs emerging from the hut carrying the boxes, and Glemnitz made another search, which was once again fruitless.[5] As a precaution, von Lindeiner banned any new boxes from entering the north compound, which meant that there was now no way of safely disposing of the sand. Bushell, reckoning that the tunnel was long enough, decided to stall, and mounted an operation to divert the ferrets' attention from hut 123. Soon, a succession of Kriegies was seen walking in and out of hut 119 carrying Red Cross boxes, which resulted in the hut being searched for four hours.[6] However, Glemnitz was no fool and, suspecting that he had been bluffed, he ordered a search of hut 123 after the morning *Appell*. From hut 122, Bushell and George Harsh could only watch. 'If we get away with it this time,' said Bushell, 'we'll make it. They're bound to concentrate on the other huts.'[7]

Just before eleven o'clock on 10 October, one of Glemnitz's men noticed a small crack in the corner of the cement floor of the small annexe.[8] He tapped around it with his metal probe, and was surprised to hear that the floor sounded hollow. Within a few minutes, Tom had been discovered. 'Glemnitz was beaming with a loathsome joy,' wrote Paul Brickhill. 'Even Rubberneck looked happy.'[9] According to Flight Lieutenant Flekser, Rubberneck said to the prisoners, 'You think I know bugger nothing; I know bugger all.'[10] Pictures were taken of a beaming Griese sticking his head out of the tunnel's trap, and the Germans even appeared to marvel at the quality of the construction. 'It had all the features of modern POW-technology,' noted von Lindeiner.[11] Less happy were the Kriegies, especially Bushell, who was 'in a vile mood all day'.[12] The only consolation lay in the Germans' ineptitude at destroying the tunnel. The normal method was simply to flood tunnels, which would cause them to collapse, but as Tom was 285 feet long, this was felt to be impracticable. Instead, charges were placed along its length and then detonated. This effectively transformed the tunnel into a long gun barrel, which resulted in the concrete floor around the trap being destroyed, and a large part of the hut's roof being blown off.[13]

A week later, Bushell and Wings Day summoned a meeting of the X Committee, in which the future of the two remaining tunnels was discussed. With the approaching tough Silesian winter, it was decided that no more escapes were to be made until the spring, and that Dick and Harry should be temporarily closed. Although Dick was now little more than a depot, Harry was 110 feet long, and therefore a third of the way to its intended exit in the woods immediately to the north of the compound.[14] As well as the imminent cold weather, Bushell was also keen to halt work in order to let the Germans think that the Kriegies were demoralised and had given up. At a subsequent meeting held in the camp theatre, Day reassured his fellow prisoners that their motivation to escape was just as strong. 'The Commandant wants to retire as a general,' he said. 'It's our job to see he's retired – but not as a general.'[15]

For all those present at that meeting, it would have been apparent that Day's return to the camp after the Szubin breakout represented a challenge to Bushell's position. Both men were formidable personalities and natural leaders, albeit of different varieties. 'Bushell was more of an intellectual leader,' said Richard Churchill. 'With his background and training as a barrister, he was obviously able to express himself readily and Day's leadership was more of the non-intellectual, "If I can do it, you certainly can" type.'[16] With two large egos in competition, it was inevitable that their relationship would be strained. 'I've been told that he [Day] and Bushell really clashed,' recalled Alex Cassie. 'They were two very different characters, and each figure was aware of their presence when they came into a room.'[17] The two men nevertheless did their best to conceal any friction. 'I think they were just very strong characters,' said Cassie, 'and both of them knew that, and each of them went to some effort not to make that apparent . . . The ordinary rank and file such as myself was quite unaware of it.'[18] However, some were adamant that there was in fact no tension between the two men. 'There was no issue at all,' said Sydney Dowse. 'They got on well. I think Day recognised Roger Bushell as the leader and Day just had the rank.'[19] Although both men deferred to the SBO, Group Captain Massey, there was no doubt in the eyes of the Kriegies that Day and Bushell were effectively the leaders of the POW population, with Bushell having the edge. Massey himself inspired mixed feelings. Alex Cassie said:

> He was a bit pompous. He wasn't a very tall man and his technique was to throw his head back so he would look down his nose, and he used this not as a device to show his superiority, but when he was dealing with the Germans. He looked down his nose at them. He was a man of great conscience. I liked him very much. I admired him. A lot of people didn't.[20]

In a community that was often as claustrophobic as the tunnels that lay under the huts, it is not surprising that such differences existed. In the main, the Kriegies got on with each other far better than might be expected, and it would be surprising if there had not been clashes between men with large egos stuck for years in the middle of a gloomy Polish forest.

Naturally, such a setting also formed the ideal stage for friendships that would last for lifetimes, but what was notable about Stalag Luft III was the number of strong relationships that were forged between the prisoners and their captors. In fact, the social cohesion between some of the Germans and the Kriegies was so strong that without it, the story of this book may well have never happened. It is quite possible to regard the Great Escape as the greatest-ever example of

Anglo-German cooperation, and it is deeply ironic that it happened during wartime. Of all the relationships that flourished, those between Corporal Eberhard 'Nikki' Hesse and officers such as Sydney Dowse and Tommy Calnan exemplify the extraordinary closeness that could exist across the barbed wire.

Born to a surgeon and his wife in Dresden in July 1918, Hesse was no run-of-the-mill NCO, and had been a prize-winning pupil at school before studying law at Freiburg University and in Vienna and Munich. While still a student he worked as an intern at Deutsche Bank and the Rhein-Main-Donau Canal Company, and by 1941, he had passed his government law examination at the Superior Provincial Court in Karlsruhe. Unlike many of his fellow students, Hesse had not joined any Nazi Party formations, and had even tried to leave Germany in 1939 to take up positions he had been offered in Switzerland, France and England, but the outbreak of war had stymied any such plans. In February 1941, Hesse was employed as a junior lawyer in the office of the Chief of the Kraków district in the German administration in Poland, which he found to be in a 'general state of confusion'. In July, he returned to Dresden, where he was called up for military service, and was sent to Russia as a lineman. However, in October, he fell sick with dysentery, and was hospitalised until March 1942, and then, after a period training recruits, he started working as an interpreter at Stalag Luft III in August.[21]

Hesse's dislike of the Nazis tempted him into helping the Kriegies, but he was understandably cautious. 'At first, I held back from cooperating with the P/Ws because I believed that although my help would be accepted, they would despise me for it,' he stated after the war. 'We German anti-Nazis could not see any sign that the Allies would differentiate between the Nazis and their German enemies.'[22] Hesse's sense of caution was also increased by what he claimed to be the 'un-cosmopolitan bearing' of some of the RAF officers, whom he found to be unworldly. Hesse's opinion may well have had some merit. While he had studied and worked in several countries, and spoke a few languages, many of the Kriegies would have travelled little, and their only tongue would have been English. To the average wartime RAF officer, a German such as Hesse would have been seen as merely 'just another Jerry', and the fact that he was an NCO would have also diminished him. Such barriers were soon dismantled after Hesse fell into long conversations with Sydney Dowse and Sergeant Deans, the senior NCO in the camp's NCO compound. 'They believed, just as I did, that the only normal thing for people with the same political ideas to do would be to cooperate,' said Hesse, 'and in this way, my fears were removed.'[23] Dowse quite reasonably suspected that Hesse was a plant, as the Germans regarded him as an incorrigible escaper. 'I was a much watched person,' Dowse recalled, 'marked, watched a lot, and he was put on to me, that was clear, and to find out all he could, and my job was to do the reverse.'[24] After several conversations, however, Dowse realised that Hesse's anti-Nazi convictions were sincere, and furthermore, that his desire to cooperate was genuine. 'I got very friendly,' said Dowse, 'and he got to be able to trust me and I got to be able to trust him, and we would talk about all sorts of things, his ambitions and after the war, and he began to realise that the Germans were losing.'[25]

Tommy Calnan, another officer who would later become friendly with Hesse, thought the German 'a nice honest kid, quite open in his views and absolutely terrified of being sent to the East front'. However, Calnan thought that Hesse's wish to help the Kriegies was born of a greater fear of his post-war fate: 'He was already convinced, in 1943, that Germany was going to lose the war and wanted desperately to have something in his favour on the records which he was certain we British maintained on our captors.'[26]

In January 1943, Hesse was appointed by Lieutenant von Massow to work with the POWs in the book depository of the camp's east compound. Shortly after-wards, Hesse learned that the SD had discovered that one of the Kriegies, Flight Lieutenant Peter Gardener, had been posting photographs and reports back to Britain concerning German anti-aircraft defences. Exactly how Gardener came by this information is unclear – it is likely that he was given it by a member of the camp staff – but the SD decided to allow Gardener to continue in order to gather enough evidence to bring him to a court martial. If convicted of espionage, there can be little doubt that Gardener would have been sent to a concentration camp, or perhaps worse. 'I was embittered by the way in which Gardener was to be led into a trap,' said Hesse, and he promptly tipped him off through another POW, Flight Lieutenant Watson. As a reward, Hesse was offered coffee and cigarettes, but he refused them, insisting to Watson that his actions had been motivated by his political hostility towards the Nazis rather than the need for nicotine and caffeine. Shortly afterwards, Sergeant Deans visited Hesse, and asked him, as a test of his anti-Nazism, if he would lend his pass so that it could be copied. 'I gave it to him on the same day because I trusted Sgt. Deans implicitly,' Hesse later stated, 'and knew that he would view my actions in the proper light.' Two days later, two sergeants, equipped with copies of Hesse's pass, escaped through the gate of their compound, but they were later recognised and recaptured.[27]

Hesse's willingness to help Sergeant Deans in such a flagrant fashion quickly came to the attention of the X Committee, and two days later, Hesse once again was allowing his pass to be copied for another escape attempt. On Saturday 12 June, Bob Vanderstok, the Dutch RAF Spitfire pilot, disguised himself as a German sergeant and led a party of POWs to the gate of the north compound. Claiming to be escorting the men to the delousing shed, Vanderstok waved his pink pass at the guard, who barely gave it a glance. 'We simply walked through,' Vanderstok wrote, '. . . and we marched out of the camp on the road along the edge of the forest of small pine trees.'[28] Unfortunately, just before the men were about to disappear into the woods, a sergeant saw them and, suspicious, fired his Luger repeatedly into the air. Within a few minutes, the party found itself interned in the guardhouse, en route to a fortnight in the 'cooler' – the solitary confinement unit. Vanderstok was repeatedly strip-searched, and he lost all his escape equipment – including the pass – although he did manage to hide a small roll of money in his hand as he undressed.[29]

Hesse's cooperation with the Kriegies was not just restricted to lending his pass. He brought in clothes, documents, radio parts, money, ration cards, maps and, most crucially for the war effort, intelligence.[30] In April, Hesse had passed on to Dowse information gathered from his brother, Dr Wolfgang Hesse, about the Peenemünde Army Research Centre that was developing missiles such as the V-1 and V-2.[31] This was an extremely sensitive piece of intelligence to supply, and although some Kriegies did not regard Hesse as being particularly brave,[32] he evidently had enough courage to betray his country, and would have certainly known the consequences of being caught. It is not clear whether the information supplied by Hesse to Dowse ultimately contributed to the Allied bombing of Peenemünde, but the very fact he was inclined to share such intelligence indicates the level of his willingness to help his notional enemy. Dowse and others had completely 'turned' Hesse, with the young corporal neither accepting payment for services rendered, nor requiring to be blackmailed. As we shall see, blackmailing was an effective, although distasteful, method of ensuring cooperation, but there was never a need to exert such pressure on Hesse. In fact, Hesse was so willing to express his sympathies that the POWs had to warn him 'not to grumble about the Third Reich' in case it was overheard by those Germans loyal to the regime.[33]

As a result of the 'delousing escape', Kriegies from the north compound were banned from working in the book depository, and were replaced by those from the east compound. Among them was Tommy Calnan, who was appointed as Hesse's 'liaison officer'. Along with Flight Lieutenant Robert Kee, Calnan was deter-mined to escape, and he asked for Hesse's assistance. One day, while Hesse was on duty at the camp gate, he saw a working party of Russian prisoners, and suggested to Calnan that the two men could infiltrate themselves amongst one such group.[34] Hesse did as much as he could to help, by supplying Russian identity armbands and turning a blind eye to Calnan's use of the typewriter in the book depository to produce a letter claiming that he and Kee were employees of a large chemical firm in Leipzig.[35] Hesse also gave the men two Dutch identity cards, which he himself had bought from a Dutch worker in Freiburg, whom he also asked to guide the escapees from Freiburg to the Swiss border. Hesse's final act of assistance was to hide Kee and Calnan in the attic of the book depository, from where the two officers escaped on 20 November. The follow-ing day, Hesse was arrested and all his possessions were searched, but since there was no evidence against him, he was released without charge. During his time at Stalag Luft III, Hesse would be searched eleven times and arrested twice, and each time he was freed.[36]

Although Calnan and Kee were captured a few days later, it is clear that without Hesse's help and imagin-ation, the escape attempt was unlikely to have been made. Curiously, Calnan's memoirs do not credit Hesse with this high level of assistance, and it is conceivable that Hesse was exaggerating his role in order to curry favour with his Allied interrogators after the war. Equally, Calnan may have minimised the importance of Hesse in order to make himself appear less reliant on the help of an enemy. On occasion, Calnan is

disparaging about Hesse, and displays a lack of appreciation towards someone who risked his freedom – and
possibly his life – in order to help the escape:

> I did not see why the fact that Nikki appeared to be a
> 'good' German on our side should make any difference.
> If he was for the high jump, it was his own fault. He had
> got himself into this situation with his eyes wide open.
> He knew my escape record.[37]

Whatever the truth, we can be sure that Hesse's
assistance was not insignificant – this was not an
isolated act, and there was a well-defined pattern of him
doing his utmost to help.

Hesse was by no means the only German who
assisted the Kriegies. In his post-war interrogation,
Hesse mentions those outside the camp who provided
not only escape equipment, but also intelligence. These
included a Fräulein Gisela Klute; Dr and Frau Peter
Felber; Fräulein Karin Sauren of Hauptstrasse 7 in
Aachen; and Hesse's brother, who told Hesse not only
about the V-weapons, but also about the Me-262 and
Me-163 jets, and no fewer than three Luftwaffe
research centres, including the institute at Rechlin.[38]
Thanks to the risks taken by such people, Stalag Luft III
began to acquire a reputation as a source of useful
intelligence, with Kriegies able to supply London with
information such as news of troop movements and
locations, details of anti-aircraft defences, German
morale, bomb damage and prices of foodstuffs. The
intelligence was not judged to be hugely important, but
it was certainly regarded as valuable, and had other

methods of intelligence-gathering been compromised, then the product emanating from camps such as Sagan would have been near priceless.[39]

Unfortunately, it is not known precisely how the individuals in Hesse's circle helped, but as well as supplying intelligence, it is conceivable that they forged passes and other documents. In the film *The Great Escape*, much is made of the ingenuity of the forgers, who were able to make near-exact replicas of just about any pass that was used in Nazi Germany. Although these calligraphic achievements are rightly celebrated, what is not mentioned is that the forgers received a great deal of assistance from Germans who lived many hundreds of miles away on the other side of the country. Alex Cassie, who was one of the most talented forgers, revealed one way in which documents such as gate passes were produced in collaboration with the enemy. First, a pass was pickpocketed from a guard, which was easily achieved in the winter months, as the guards kept their passes tucked into their cuffs rather than having to repeatedly extricate them from inside their tunics. The pass was immediately spirited away to someone such as Cassie or Tim Walenn, who noted its dimensions, what was written and printed on it, and what stamp was used. A thin slice of the card was removed in order to obtain a sample of its colour and thickness, and then the pass was 'depicked' back into the cuff of the guard, who never noticed it had been missing. A hand-drawn template was produced on paper, which was then given to one of the anti-Nazi guards, a Corporal Fischer, who stuffed it in his boot before going home on leave to the Ruhr, his pockets filled with the normal contraband items. At home, Fischer's wife reproduced the template with a typewriter, thereby providing a new and accurate template. This was then brought back to the camp, and reproduced by using a jelly press made from Red Cross jelly from which the colour had been removed.[40]

Hesse was also extremely candid about his fellow members of the camp staff who helped the prisoners. He lists Corporals Rickmers, Schmitzler and Schneider, all of whom worked as mail censors, and obtained both escape materials and intelligence – such as train times and when the guards were changed[41] – on the same scale as Hesse. Such material would be gathered when they were on leave or on duty trips to Holland, Belgium, France and Denmark, and then smuggled back into the camp. Rickmers even forwarded coded letters to England on behalf of Tommy Calnan, one of which contained a list of POWs who were being held by the Gestapo in Paris. The list may have been obtained by another member of the camp staff, who had gone to Paris on leave and had had his expenses paid for by the X Committee in order to bring back documents from the French Underground.[42] Unlike Hesse, some of these men appeared to be helping the Kriegies for material gain, and Rickmers regarded Hesse as being a 'silly idealist' for not availing himself of the proffered contents of Red Cross parcels.[43]

The liaison officer assigned to Rickmers was none other than Roger Bushell. It was Hesse who recommended Rickmers, as Rickmers was a friend of Lieutenant von Massow, and therefore privy to the goings-on in the camp administration. Hesse would also relay news of any German plans to Bushell, and Rickmers would in turn tell von Massow what Bushell required, and von Massow would then inform von Lindeiner. As he was at the heart of what we would today call the 'information loop', Bushell was in an extremely powerful position. 'At times S/L Bushell was practically in charge of the German, British and American camps,' Hesse stated, 'because nothing was done without his knowledge and approval.'[44] Nevertheless, not even the forceful Bushell could get everything he wanted. 'It is true, however, that Bushell demanded a great degree of subordination on the part of all concerned,' said Hesse, 'and it was sometimes difficult to comply with his demands.'[45]

Hesse's claims are significant, and there is no reason to be wary of them. He had shown himself to be utterly trustworthy – at least in the eyes of the Kriegies; as we shall see, after the war, he was fêted by the likes of Sydney Dowse.[46] The level of willing cooperation was extraordinary, and its significance has been neglected in previous accounts of the Great Escape. What Hesse and his fellow NCOs provided was extremely valuable, and without it, it is doubtful whether the X Committee could have mounted such an ambitious operation. It is understandable for reasons of national prestige that many accounts chose to make the undertaking an exclusively Allied affair, but in truth the Great Escape was as successful an Anglo-German venture as the marriage of Queen Victoria. Taken together, the five corporals and the five individuals outside the camp constitute a regrettably overlooked Resistance movement operating inside Nazi Germany. Although payments were made – just as they were to other Resistance operatives around Europe – the predominant motive of the group was not physical reward, but a desire to hit back at a hated regime. Hesse was later to claim that the group could have expanded, but Bushell was wary.

> [Bushell] warned me several times not to let the number of comrades working with me become too large, because he feared that politically unreliable men might find their way to us . . . In this way S/L Bushell clearly recognised what others who do not know Germany do not want to admit, namely that the larger a German resistance organisation is, the greater the danger of betrayal. Therefore: no large organisations![47]

Although the assertion that the Great Escape was an Anglo-German operation may appear surprising, it must be stressed that these ten were by no means the only Germans in cahoots with the Kriegies. The POWs also secured the assistance of numerous members of the camp staff through a mixture of bribery and blackmail. In fact, the assistance provided by this cadre of the corrupt was absolutely vital to the breakout, as even the official report compiled after the war made clear:

> Much of the most valuable work carried out by 'X' would have been totally impossible had it not been for the comparative ease with which it was possible to corrupt members of the German staff and Germans visiting the camp. The great majority of Germans seem to be quite willing to sell information of both military

and escape importance to Ps/W for a few cigarettes or some chocolate, coffee, etc. This traitorous streak is not confined only to other ranks but is found just as frequently among the officers. It is amazing what risks German personnel will take in order to obtain a few extra luxuries. The stupidity of the lower ranking Germans has to be seen to be believed. They literally throw themselves into the power of the prisoners, by such stupid actions as signing receipts for goods received from prisoners![48]

The *de haut en bas* tone of the report, written shortly after the war, is understandable, but underestimates quite how deprived the Germans were compared to their captives. Thanks to the Red Cross, the Kriegies were able to enjoy luxuries such as chocolate and cigarettes on a regular basis. While Germans received around twenty cigarettes per week, POWs were sometimes puffing through twice that number in a single day.[49] In addition, the POWs were far better nourished. For a long time in Sagan, the daily food ration of a German officer – which was lower than that for enlisted men – was 180 grams of bread, a small piece of butter, some cheese or sausage, and a bowl of thin vegetable soup for dinner. The rations for privates and NCOs were not considerably better. Meanwhile, in addition to their camp rations, the Kriegies received Red Cross parcels every ten days to a fortnight, which contained foods such as bacon, canned meat, milk, sugar, coffee, chocolate and butter – all items that were in extremely short supply in Germany. Gustav Simoleit recalled how the camp staff were not surprised to find that the

Kriegies often threw away their German rations, such as sauerkraut and potatoes.[50]

It was not just consumables such as tobacco that manifested the enormous disparity between the prisoners and their guards, but also items such as bedding and tableware. When a POW arrived at Sagan, he was issued, along with his bed and mattress, a knife, fork, spoon, dish, coffee cup, two blankets, three pieces of bed linen and a towel. Naturally, many of these items were used for nefarious purposes, and were often destroyed during such misapplication. From 15 January 1943 to 19 April 1944, 1,699 blankets, 192 bed covers, 161 pillow cases, 165 sheets, 3,424 towels, 655 mattresses, 1,212 bolsters, 34 chairs, 62 tables, 76 benches, 90 bunk beds, 246 watering cans, 1,219 knives, 582 forks, 408 spoons, 69 lamps and 30 shovels were all either lost or destroyed by the Kriegies. Although the cost of replacement was docked from the prisoners' pay, the German economy was taxed enough as it was, and having to resupply wilfully destroyed items was deeply resented, especially by those who had lost everything thanks to the bombs dropped by the same 'terror fliers' who were now being seen to lord it up in comparatively luxurious camps.[51] As the guards sat in their watchtowers, they would have looked down at the RAF and USAAF officers with a mixture of jealousy and contempt as the young foreigners played football, sunbathed, read books, went for a stroll, ate chocolate and, above all, smoked. Although the guard held the machine gun and was on the right side of the barbed wire, military service, economic strictures and the nature of the regime meant that he was as much a captive as the Kriegie. Despite what he read in the Nazi rags, the guard knew that the war was going the wrong way for Germany, from the simple fact that many of the rifles carried by the sentries were devoid of ammunition – an extraordinary piece of information that was apparently never shared with the Kriegies.[52] Furthermore, the average guard, as the RAF's official report asserts, was not the most dynamic of individuals. Major Hans Thiede, who was in charge of security in all of the Luftwaffe's POW camps, observed that the guards constituted a 'rabble of the halt, maimed, and blind with a sprinkling of mentally deranged whose only interest was the obtaining of cigarettes from the prisoners'.[53]

In any prison in which the prisoners are wealthier than their guards, corruption will always occur.[54] Nowhere was this immutable law more in evidence than in Stalag Luft III, as the charges made against the camp staff after the Great Escape make explicit: 'The most serious thing is that these German soldiers were ready to supply "Terror Airmen" with articles which served the purpose of escape and thus, through their own pleasure-seeking and yearning after tobacco, have become the betrayers of their own people and helpers of the enemy.'[55]

One of those who proved to be utterly corruptible was Corporal Erich Oest, who worked in the parcels office until Christmas 1943. Oest, who had lived in the United States, spoke perfect English, a qualification that on the surface appeared useful in a POW camp. However, during his time in North America, he had clearly acquired a sympathy for those who were now his enemy, and Oest became 'completely subservient to the prisoners'.[56] In return for cigarettes and other luxuries, Oest supplied the Kriegies with any item that they required. In the summer of 1943, he was arrested, and a search of his quarters uncovered a cache of English goods. Oest denied that he had been running an exchange, and claimed that the items were merely gifts. A somewhat forgiving von Lindeiner merely sentenced Oest to three days' close arrest, after which he was able to resume his job and his lucrative clandestine trading operation. In December, Oest was finally removed from his post. By his own admission, he had received some 4,000–6,000 cigarettes, many pounds of coffee, cocoa and raisins, and numerous bars of chocolate. He had also inveigled others into his scheme, including Corporal Lowerentz, who took over the 'business'; Corporals Gustav Wolter and Fischl; and Lance Corporal Bening. Corporal Wolter proved to be particularly useful for the X Committee, as he supplied maps of Eastern Europe, two lamps and one radio valve, as well as photo albums, tin openers, rakes, fruit and vegetables, and even whisky.[57] Another useful NCO was Sergeant Rohlmann, who was an electrical engineer and radio salesman in his civilian life. In return for 350–400 cigarettes, 6 or 7 bars of chocolate, 6 or 7 bars of soap and one tin of white pepper, Rohlmann supplied two British sergeants with enough equipment to build a radio transmitter and receiver.[58] Although not seemingly part of Oest's group, Lance Corporal Kasel also proved to be another source of vital escape material, supplying dyes, stamps and party badges.[59]

Of all these corrupt NCOs, potentially the most beneficial for the Great Escape was Lance Corporal

Bening, who was the technical chief of the underground listening system that had been laid to detect the sounds of tunnelling. As we have seen, the microphones had proved to be effective, but the interpretation of what they picked up had often been faulty, with the noises being put down to the activity of a nearby coal dump.[60] Despite it being a highly sophisticated system, there were members of the camp staff who were disappointed that it did not prove to be more effective. Ferrets such as Hermann Glemnitz suspected that the real problem therefore lay with the operators. 'I know that when we were in the North Camp [i.e. compound] we had too many who were bribed who were in that seismograph house,' Glemnitz claimed after the war.[61] The question is: was Glemnitz right? Lance Corporal Bening was certainly corrupt, and he had sold goods he had bought in Prague – such as pipes, wine, tin openers, photo albums, chessmen and candlesticks – to the British for the normal currencies of cigarettes, cocoa, tea and soap.[62] However, there is no direct evidence to show that Bening or any of those who worked in the microphone room were in fact bribed to turn a deaf ear, and we have already seen how microphones played a part in the discovery of Tom.[63]

Nevertheless, Glemnitz's suspicions remain understandable when considering that the entire listening system went offline for at least three critical months. On 19 December 1943, von Lindeiner ordered the system to be shut down so it could be extended to cover the new compounds that were being constructed. As a result, when work on Harry was resumed on 8 January 1944, there were no functioning microphones, and there would not be until a week after the Great Escape. Von Lindeiner would later defend his decision by stating his mistaken belief that tunnelling did not take place during the winter, and that therefore it did not matter if the system was not working.[64] In truth, the listening system did not need to be shut down for a matter of months, and it was perfectly feasible for the new extensions to be built separately from the existing network, and then simply connected together. This would have involved the entire system being offline for no more than a few days. One man who could have told von Lindeiner all this was none other than Lance Corporal Bening, but it appears that the NCO kept von Lindeiner in the dark. According to a later investigation, Bening was far too busy occupying his newly found free time by earning good money repairing radios – presumably those of civilians and soldiers – and therefore had no desire to quickly re-establish the listening system.[65] If Bening was bribed to keep the system offline, then that secret has gone to both his grave and that of the Kriegie who crossed his palm. What is reasonable to speculate is that had the system been switched on, then the Germans might well have detected Harry. Whether the information gleaned would have been precise enough to have led them to hut 104 is debatable, but it should be remembered that hut 123 was searched partly because of microphone evidence.

If bribery and appealing to political sympathy did not work in order to ensure Anglo-German cooperation, then there was a third method that usually worked: blackmail. One favoured method, as revealed above in the official report, was to ask Germans to sign receipts for goods they had received. Such documentation could then be used to blackmail the recipients, and it seems bizarre that any German would agree to fill in such forms, which can only be put down to a mixture of the aforementioned stupidity and the hackneyed German reputation for thoroughness. Bomber Command pilot Geoffrey Cornish was a member of the 'bribery department' and he recalled how a typical blackmail operation worked. On one occasion, a German was asked if he could bring in a magnetic needle for a 'physics experiment', although the man knew quite well that it would be used for a compass. A few days later, the German, 'trembling with fear', returned with the magnet, as well as various other useful items, and handed them over to Cornish. He waited expectantly to receive some luxuries in return, such as soap for his wife, chocolate for the children, and some Nescafé, which was, in the words of Cornish, 'liquid gold – better than gold'. Unfortunately for the German, Cornish told him that he had run out of such items, but that he might be able to recompense him if the German brought in a radio valve or 'something pretty hot'. The German refused, at which point Cornish set his trap:

'Well, if you don't, I'll tell them about the stuff you brought in previously, about the magnet.'

'You can't prove it,' the German replied.

'Yes I can.'

'You can't.'

In order to halt this exchange, one of Cornish's fellow Australians, Bush Parker, produced a receipt from the Sagan town hardware shop, which recorded the purchase of one magnet. 'The guy went absolutely ashen,' said Cornish. Parker, who was a magician in civilian life, then threw the receipt into the air, and it promptly disappeared.

'All right, I'll get it for you,' said the hapless German.

What the man could not have known was that the receipt had been provided by another guard who was already in the Kriegies' pay. If the German chose not to cooperate, then the POWs would simply report the corruption to one of the German officers, and the man would be punished with a lowering in rank. Unsurprisingly, many opted to assist. 'It was blackmail,' Cornish observed. 'It was lies, it was corruption – any weapon we had, we used for our German bribery department.'[66]

However, not all the Kriegies were comfortable with the idea of coercion, partly because it proved to be so pathetically easy to pull off. Even members of Glemnitz's ferret team were 'tame' enough to be bought with merely a cup of coffee, a few cigarettes and a bar of chocolate.[67] The uncontrolled expansion in 'turned Goons' resulted in a sensible concern for the security of escape projects, not least from Sydney Dowse:

> I was responsible for stopping too many people being involved in that. I said to Roger, 'Look, this is ridiculous, you've got to stop this. You can't have everybody trying to have all sorts of goons and people in, we don't know which will be informers and which won't and who will give us away.'

As a result of Dowse's plea, Bushell ordered that all blackmailing and bribery operations had to be cleared through the X Committee.[68]

As well as enlisted men, there was even an officer who cooperated with the POWs: Captain Hans Pieber. In December 1943, Pieber was asked by the Kriegies if they could borrow his Contax camera for a few hours in order to take photographs of a theatrical production. After consulting Captain Broili, the head of Department III, Pieber lent them the camera, which was promptly used to take photographs for false passes.[69] The charge sheet drawn up by the Germans after the Great Escape captures quite how reckless Pieber's actions were regarded as being:

> . . . the loan of the Contax to the prisoners is evidence of his lack of thought, his gullibility and his lack of responsibility . . . He should have realised, from his knowledge of the mentality of the prisoners, from the ban on allowing prisoners to have photos, and above all from the forged identity card photos that had been found, the danger that must follow from his irresponsible action.[70]

However, what the Germans did not know was that Pieber had done much more than simply lend his camera – he had also developed the film taken with it, and subsequently even supplied the Kriegies with a camera they could keep.[71] As Pieber was neither an unintelligent man nor, in the words of Major Thiede, 'mentally deranged', his reasons for his extraordinarily misguided assistance are hard to discern. The Germans thought he was overly pleased with the well-being of the prisoners, 'and thus clear-sighted and right-thinking soldiers and officers must accuse him of friendship with

England'.[72] Such a charge approximated that of treachery, but the Germans could not find proof that Pieber had gone quite that far. Besides, Pieber's political roots lay in Nazism, and he was unlikely to help the British out of political conviction, as Eberhard Hesse had done. With the knowledge that Pieber had been neither bribed nor blackmailed, the only motive that remains for his cooperation may lie in his sexuality. As we have seen, some Kriegies suspected Pieber of fancying an attractive young RAF officer called Peter Gates.[73] The two men struck up a friendship, partly because both men were interested in photography, and it was through this relationship that Pieber lent the Kriegies not only his camera, but also film and developing solutions.[74] If it is true that Pieber had what amounted to a schoolmaster's crush on one of his 'pupils', then that may explain why he came to abandon common sense and lend the Kriegies such vital equipment.

Through a combination of ideology, bribery, blackmail and, quite possibly, homosexual attraction, it is apparent that the apparatus running Stalag Luft III was hopelessly compromised. Von Lindeiner was presiding over a camp that was effectively being controlled by its economically dominant element: the POWs. The laws of the market were extremely effective, and cut through and burrowed under the barbed wire in a way that no human being ever could. Although the Germans were notionally in charge of the camp, they were no more so than the weak-willed parent who is dominated by an unruly child. The Germans gave the POWs just about everything they needed to escape. They provided passes, money, clothes, magnets, maps, intelligence, radio equipment, contacts, a camera and film, ration cards, dyes, badges, stamps, electric cabling and, quite possibly, turned a deaf ear to the microphones. The significance of this cannot be overstated, and before such an interpretation is dismissed as being cynical and overly revisionist, it is worth repeating the words of the official RAF report, which stated that 'much of the most valuable work carried out by "X" would have been totally impossible' without the assistance of corrupt Germans.[75] Such an interpretation does not diminish the ingenuity and boldness of the Kriegies, but instead supplements their achievements with those of their captors. Although few Germans could be proud of the corruptibility of their fellow countrymen, the actions of those such as Hesse should be venerated along with those who escaped. As we shall see, Sydney Dowse thought the very same.

Chapter Seven

Harry Reawakens

IN NOVEMBER 1943, the Kriegies set eyes on a man who would play an enormous part in their future: Oberregierungs- und Kriminalrat Max Wielen, the head of the Kripo in Breslau.[1] Wielen, who also held the rank of SS-Obersturmbannführer, visited the camp with Kriminalrat Brünner, the officer responsible for the prevention of escapes by POWs, and along with ten or twelve other men, conducted a search.[2] The men found little: some sketch maps, several compasses and a few other items. Wielen later noted how he thought that the camp was 'extremely difficult to supervise'. 'There was no means of properly controlling this barrack colony . . . ,' he stated. 'The loose dry sand made it easy to build tunnels. When subsequently 10,000 officers had to be accommodated, conditions became even more insecure.'[3] If the POWs were wary of Wielen and his

men, they would have been no more so than the camp
staff, who saw the visit by the Kripo as a demonstration
of Himmler's RSHA flexing its muscles over the
Luftwaffe's camps.[4] So far, von Lindeiner had been
spared such visits, and had only once been called upon
by the sister organisation of the Kripo – the Gestapo –
when an investigation was made into whether a POW
was permitted to send letters and parcels to his wife in
Vienna.

Von Lindeiner had also had the dubious pleasure of
holding a meeting with the Breslau Chief of Gestapo,
Oberregierungsrat Dr Wilhelm Scharpwinkel, during
the course of which Scharpwinkel took a telephone call
in which he ordered the liquidation of a prisoner. When
von Lindeiner asked Scharpwinkel whether it troubled
him to issue such an order, the Gestapo officer replied:

Three years ago, I was thinking just like you now. When
I was confronted with that type of situation for the first
time, I argued like you and did not sleep for several
nights. In the time that has passed since then, I have
come to the conclusion, however, that the life of a
single human being cannot play a role if the destiny of
the whole German race is at stake.[5]

As a result of the expression of such opinions, von
Lindeiner regarded Scharpwinkel as being unhinged, a
view that was shared by Max Wielen, who described
Scharpwinkel as 'intelligent, with a crazy streak in his
makeup, very temperamental, unscrupulous, brutal,
[an] extraordinarily keen worker, diligent, painstaking,
[a] rather unpleasant character, [with an] uneven

temper'.[6] Standing at 5 feet 9 inches, slim, with dark grey eyes and duelling scars on his face, it is tempting to see Scharpwinkel as the embodiment of the hackneyed image of the sinister Gestapo officer. Although von Lindeiner knew that he could call upon his services, and those of Wielen, he was reluctant to do so because he could not trust those who looked at him with 'their fanatically glowing eyes'.[7] Ultimately though, von Lindeiner wished to maintain his command, and he regarded the involvement of the two police forces as a necessary evil 'in order to save his own position'.[8] For the time being, however, both the Kriegies and the camp staff would remain free from the attentions of the Gestapo and Kripo.

Apart from this visit, the winter was quiet for both the Kriegies and their guards. Plays were produced, with Roger Bushell taking the perhaps appropriate part of Professor Higgins in *Pygmalion*. British and American movies were screened, and Christmas was a predictably hooch-fuelled celebration that left POW and German alike reeling in the snow. Fuelled by alcohol, at least twenty-two British and American officers were caught trying to scale the barbed-wire fence between their respective compounds, which resulted in the offenders spending New Year's Eve in the cooler.[9] Others found that the home brew had a somewhat more debilitating effect. Stephen Johnson recalled one fellow Kriegie who had indulged far too much and had thought it a good idea to go outside the hut for a stroll. Within seconds, he had lost both the use of his legs and his sense of direction, and had tried to support himself on the corner of the hut. 'Finally he decided to make for home on hands and knees,' Johnson wrote. 'After circling the hut twice, since the entrance seemed to have disappeared, he eventually found the door and made a dramatic entrance.'[10]

Nevertheless, the festive period also proved to be maudlin, with many missing their families. For some, such as Wings Day, this was their fifth Christmas behind the wire, and many wondered whether next Christmas would see them back in Surrey, or stuck in Sagan. The effect of such a lengthy captivity was starting to reveal itself in a severe decline in the mental health of some of the Kriegies. A visit by the Red Cross in February 1944 would reveal quite how bad the situation was becoming:

> The medical officers are very concerned about the growing number of psychosis cases; an increasing number of prisoners and particularly among those who have been in captivity for a long time, (3 or 4 years) are gradually losing their peace of mind, becoming more and more mentally unbalanced, some of them can hardly sleep any more and yet refuse to get up; they do not take part in any sort of entertainment and hardly talk to anybody; some of them develop a hatred for their comrades who share their room, rendering the common life extremely difficult.[11]

The British medical officers stressed that such POWs should be repatriated or interned in a neutral country, but the Germans were mindful that affecting lunacy was an age-old method of escape, and refused. Von Lindeiner acknowledged that there was a problem, and promised to allow more socialising between com-pounds, and to transfer Kriegies to other compounds in order to provide some social variety.[12]

The spirits of those keen on escaping were lifted by the outcome of a meeting of the X Committee on 4 January, in which it was determined to reopen Harry. Ken Rees recalled how his friend, master tunneller Johnny Bull, came rushing into his room with 'an excited grin on his usually sombre face' to announce that Bushell wanted to 'blitz' the tunnel, and finish it within two months, just in time for the start of spring.[13] A few days later, an inspection team was delighted to find that Harry had coped well over the winter. Some of the shoring was weak, the kitbags on the air pumps had rotted, and the airline of Klim tins was partially blocked with sand, but other than that, all 110 feet of the structure were fundamentally sound.[14] Three ten-strong teams of experienced diggers set to work, and soon the tunnel was advancing at a rate of 4 feet per day. By the end of that month, the first of the two 'halfway houses' was built, which acted as a hauling station and a resting point. As reminders of their ultimate destination, the Kriegies christened the first halfway house Piccadilly, the second Leicester Square.

Although the tunnelling proceeded smoothly, sand dispersal was rendered particularly difficult by the presence of snow and frozen soil. Hiding the sand under the barracks was impossible, as that was the first place Glemnitz and his ferrets always checked. Once again, it was Peter Fanshawe who came up with the solution, which was to dump the sand under the bank of raised seats in the theatre. A trap was made beneath one of the seats, and the space below was found to be sufficiently large to contain all of Harry's sand.[15] However, smuggling the sand to the theatre – a distance of some 200 yards – proved to be yet another technical challenge, as even the slightest leakage between hut 104 and the theatre would alert the ferrets. The trouser-leg tubes used by the 'penguins' were therefore ruled out, and replaced by sacks which could each contain 17½ pounds. Two of these were slung around the neck, and then carried under a greatcoat by teams of larger POWs in the hours of darkness before the nine o'clock lock-up. The sand was brought out of the tunnel in large kitbags that contained up to 100 pounds, and then transferred to a neighbouring hut and placed in a 'loading room'. From here, the spoil was loaded into the sacks, and the carriers made their way to the theatre along prepared routes. In the auditorium, the sand was dumped through the trapdoor into the cavity, in which especially short POWs worked to pack the sand tightly. If there were no ferrets patrolling the compound, the amount of sand dispersed could be impressive. On one day, while a ferret was kept distracted by one of the Kriegies, 4 tons were taken to the theatre in just two hours.[16]

As the tunnellers and the sand dispersers sweated with physical exertion, there were Kriegies who were involved in less strenuous but equally taxing escape activities. Among them were the forgers, who were ordered by Bushell to prepare around four hundred sets of documents for the escapees. As we have seen, Tim Walenn's department received much assistance from the Germans, but many passes and identity cards had to be produced by hand. Initially, the group only operated in the early afternoons from lunchtime to about three o'clock, when the Germans were asleep, but those hours would be lengthened. A library was the designated forgery room, which featured a map of Siam hanging from a blackboard. If a ferret approached, Alex Cassie would pretend to be giving a talk:

> I only had the first few words prepared. If a German was sighted anywhere near this area . . . we'd simply cover up our stuff or put them on our laps, and we'd just appear to be writing letters or listening to a lecture. My opening words were: 'And this is Bangkok. This is Siam. The main industries in Siam are bang and cock.' I didn't realise how prophetic that was.[17]

Perhaps regrettably, Cassie never had an opportunity to give his erudite exposition on South-East Asia.

In total, the forgers produced some 350 documents. The first fifty, high-priority, escapers would receive three documents each; the next fifty, two documents; and the remaining one hundred would each be issued with just a single travel permit, which was often somewhat crude. 'It might have passed a perfunctory examination,' said one Kriegie, 'but would not have deceived anybody of any authority.'[18] The more sophisticated documents were identity cards for foreign workers, leave passes and police residency permissions. Leave passes were stamped with 'Wehrkreis VIII, Bauabteilung BRESLAU' and 'Arbeiterlager SPROTTAU', which referred to two local labour camps. The identity cards were produced on brown paper, and were the size of a postcard. They each featured a photograph, a circular stamp, and sometimes remarks that indicated that the bearer was on special leave from a known armaments firm. The stamps read either 'Polizeiverwaltung SORAU' or 'Polizeipraesidium BERLIN, 132', but unfortunately, some of the stamps bore the words 'Polizeipraesident SORAU', which was a mistake, as there was no police president in Sorau, and the error proved to be useful to those searching for the escapees.[19]

The method by which the documents were produced by hand was no less impressive an achievement than the construction of the tunnels. Many of the materials used were stolen from the camp's small hospital by former medical students such as Bob Vanderstok, who helped himself to alcohol, glycerine, needles, tape, syringes and magnifying lenses used for eye tests. Soot, glycerine, ether and a pinch of mineral oil were combined to make black ink, which, unlike permitted watercolours, could not be smudged once it had dried.[20] Paper and cards would be commandeered by Tim Walenn from endpapers of books, and rubber stamps would be made from flying boots. New Kriegies would often find their footwear appropriated upon arrival, and returned within a couple of days with the rubber innards of the heels butchered. Walenn would then draw the stamp on the rubber with white ink, before handing it over to an Australian Wing Commander called Victor Wood, who would lie in a hollow in the playing field carving out the pattern and the lettering.[21] Without a typewriter, all the lettering on the documents – unless it was being typed by a collaborative German – had to be produced by hand. With some of the passes featuring fine whorled lines, a single document could take one man a month to produce, working five hours a day, every day.[22] To make them, brushes from painting sets supplied by the YMCA would be trimmed down to just five short hairs,[23] and if even one small mistake were made, the whole document would be discarded, although some errors could be rectified by burning a cigarette hole over them.[24] The need for such accuracy produced much eyestrain, but unlike in the film *The Great Escape*, there were no cases of blindness. Some, such as Frank Knight, gave up forging because of the strain, but he certainly did not suffer the same ocular fate as the character of Colin Blythe in the film.[25] Each member of the forgery department had his own speciality, with Alex Cassie specialising in German script. He said later:

> It sounds ridiculous, but it's very easy to imitate . . . Once you've learned the particular peculiarities of it, you can have a fair amount of latitude as far as accuracy is concerned. On the other hand, if it was sans serif, that was required to be absolutely spot on.[26]

Cassie also had a knack for forging signatures, which he did by writing them upside down, 'so your hand doesn't make the letters it's used to forming'.[27] One person for whom Cassie personally worked was Roger Bushell, who one day gave Cassie an original pass to modify. Bushell wanted a rubber stamp painted on to the document, which he wanted to be slightly smudged and set not quite straight. Cassie did as he was asked, and Bushell appeared to be delighted with the result. 'You know, Cass,' he said, 'we're going to put this in the Imperial War Museum and we'll visit it together.'[28]

As well as documentation, the other essential piece of escape equipment was clothing. The tailoring department was headed by Flight Lieutenant Tommy Guest, and its head tailor was the Czech Flight Lieutenant Bedrich Dvorak, whom Guest regarded as the 'cleverest tailor'.[29] The team was skilful enough to modify uniforms, blankets, sheets, quilts, towels and kitbags obtained from the Red Cross Clothing Store into all manner of civilian clothing. Collaborative Germans supplied dyes, insignia, badges, buckles and buttons, and confiscated civilian clothes sent by next-of-kin were simply pinched from the ferrets' store of such items.[30] Establishing what clothes were suitable for escapees was largely a matter of trial and error. Recaptured Kriegies would report back to Guest indicating whether their clothing was conspicuous, and whether it had even caused their arrest. One escapee told Guest that his overcoat, which had been made from a camel-hair blanket, had attracted rather too much attention because it was normally the type of coat worn by women. Others merely said that the clothes were too 'rough', but the biggest problem that Guest had to face was the matter of headwear. Soft cloth caps were relatively straightforward to produce, but escapees found that most men travelling on long-distance trains were more likely to affect smart felt Trilby-style hats. 'This presented us with a difficult problem,' Guest later wrote. 'We could not make felt hats, and it was very uncommon for people on the continent to travel without headgear.'[31] The only solution was to resort to bribery, but in this instance, collaboration did not yield its usual fruits, and Guest was to receive only two to three hats in eighteen months.

After the move to the north compound, the tailoring department was based in hut 121 and, like the forgers, the tailors only operated in the early afternoon, from 12.30 p.m. to 3.30 p.m.[32] Protected by a network of stooges under the command of Flight Lieutenant K. J. McMurdie, at least twelve Kriegies made a total of 6 pairs of workman's overalls, 12 German uniforms, 200 civilian jackets, 200 pairs of trousers, 40 overcoats, 100 suits, 250 caps, 40 ties and 10 haversacks.[33] Unlike the forged documents, the problem with the clothing was that it was difficult to hide. This was overcome by Major Jones of the USAAF, who, together with Lieutenants Williams and Bell, converted half the inner wall at the end of the hut into a panel that could swing out and expose a cavity some 5 to 7 inches deep.[34]

Throughout those first few months of 1944, other escape departments in Sagan were also working hard to fulfil their part of Bushell's plan. The mapmakers under Desmond Plunkett worked in the late afternoon and early evening to prepare at least two hundred maps of varying scales for the escapers. Many maps were acquired from the Germans and were reproduced with jelly presses. Ink was made from boiled-down pencil leads, and thin paper was either commandeered from the latrines or torn from hymn books. Another source of maps was MI9, the British secret service, which smuggled escape equipment such as money, maps and clothes to POW camps.[35] The organisation had tried to supply documents such as identity cards, but by the time it had received examples from which to work, the documentation had invariably changed.[36] MI9 also sent magnetised darning needles to use in compasses, as well as twelve completed compasses, but such numbers were insignificant compared to the five hundred compasses that Flight Lieutenants Hake and Russell produced in the camp.[37] No less vital was the work of the 'carpentry department' under John Williams, an Australian squadron leader, whose team produced the trolleys and rails that ran down Harry, dummy rifles and hiding places for escape equipment.[38] A two-strong 'metalwork department' produced the metal rims for the trolley wheels, as well as portable heating stoves, badges, buttons and buckles, while the 'leatherwork department', which consisted solely of one Flight Lieutenant L. Hockey, made uniform and cartridge belts, and holsters for holding dummy pistols.[39]

Meanwhile, work on Harry was going well, although the Germans were not without their suspicions. After *Appell* one morning, the Kriegies were startled to find a group of armed soldiers surrounding hut 104, and Griese and a team of ferrets searching inside. Paul Brickhill recalled how Bushell, Harsh, Ker-Ramsay and Floody walked around the compound, 'telling each other airily that Rubberneck didn't have a hope, and all of them feeling butterflies in their stomachs'.[40] For two to three hours, the Germans tore through the hut, and found nothing. An annoyed Griese emerged, and the onlooking POWs did well to mask any manifestations of relief. 'In the clear,' said one Kriegie, which earned him a sharp rebuke from Bushell: 'Not so! Now everyone has got to be even more careful.'[41] Bushell was right, as this was by no means the last of such searches to be carried out, and they were, it should be stressed, extremely thorough. One Kriegie, who kept his escape maps sewn into a waist belt, returned to his room and later noticed that the stitching on the belt looked a little different. He unpicked the stitches and found that the maps had been replaced with newspaper and a note which read, 'I hope these will do.'[42] Von Lindeiner ordered the searches at any time of day and night, as well as calling snap roll-calls, body searches and extensive inspections of the washrooms.[43]

Although it is unclear precisely why the Germans suspected hut 104, their reasons may lie in the fact that sounds of digging were heard underneath the cooler, which lay in a direct line between the fence and the hut. Glemnitz was among those who heard the noises, but he incorrectly blamed the microphone operators for not being able to ascertain the precise location.[44]

Chapter Eight

The Warnings

IF VON LINDEINER could not find the tunnel, then the best he could do was to advise the Kriegies of the folly of attempting a mass escape. In the middle of February 1944, he appealed directly to all the senior Allied officers, and essentially pleaded with them not to risk the lives of so many young men. Attended by, among others, Massey and Day, von Lindeiner stressed that the mood in Germany was most hostile to Allied airmen, owing to the effectiveness of the bombing campaign. He urged the officers to 'think of the mothers, women and children of your comrades, whose happiness will be in danger if some young hotheads try something foolish which will have no bearing on the outcome of the war'. The Commandant further hinted darkly at the likely fate of any who were captured while on the run:

Here, within the barbed wire of a POW camp, I am responsible with my life for the lives of the POWs entrusted to me. Here, I will protect you within my means, but outside of the barbed wire I am powerless. I beg you, take my words very seriously and act accordingly.[1]

This, then, marked von Lindeiner's last direct warning to the POWs. A loyalty to his Fatherland perhaps meant that he could not bring himself to make the dangers explicit; if he had told the senior Allied officers everything he knew perhaps they would have realised he was not bluffing. That month, von Lindeiner had received a word-of-mouth instruction from Colonel Ernst Wälde of Luftwaffe Inspektion 17 – the body that liaised between the German High Command and the POW camps run by the Luftwaffe – that any escaping POW who was picked up by the police would be held by them, handed over to the Kripo or Gestapo, and would no longer enjoy the protection of the Luftwaffe.[2] The fact that this order was not written down reveals that the Germans not only knew of its illegality, but also the dark consequences of the Gestapo and the Kripo taking responsibility for captured escapers. Von Lindeiner had seen at first hand what men like Dr Scharpwinkel in Breslau were capable of, and he had no wish to see his prisoners in the hands of those he regarded as 'beasts in their behaviour'.[3]

But despite his warning, the POWs thought von Lindeiner was bluffing, and the tunnellers kept digging. 'Obviously we weren't going to climb down on a warning from the German camp commandant,' recalled

Jimmy James. 'It may have been bluff as far as we knew.'[4] Besides, as James was later to reflect, 'Nobody thought seriously, if indeed they thought at all, of the possible, or probable, consequences of a mass escape on this scale.' James was perhaps well aware of the delusional aspect of this sort of thinking. 'How many of us had said, "I am not going to be shot down"? In war it is always the other fellow who is going to "buy it".'[5]

Nevertheless, the camp staff continued to warn the Kriegies against trying anything reckless. In February, Hans Pieber told at least five prisoners in one hut that it would be 'inadvisable to make any mass escapes in view of the previous threat by the Gestapo to take matters into their own hands in the camp'. Pieber even went so far as to suggest to the prisoners that if they were going to escape, then they should do so in groups of fewer than six men.[6] In March, less than a fortnight before the breakout, Unteroffizier von Schilling, the camp's welfare officer, visited his contact in the north compound, Flight Lieutenant Sedgwick Webster. Von Schilling told Webster that the Commandant had recently had meetings both at Oranienburg and with the Abwehr in Breslau. Von Lindeiner, von Schilling explained, was very worried that there was going to be a mass escape, and that if this took place, then 'he would be compelled to act in a manner that he would regret as an officer and a gentleman'. The consequences of any escape would not only be serious for those who escaped, but also for those who remained in the camp. Webster would have had no doubts as to von Schilling's subtext – the Commandant was indicating that any mass escape attempt might well result in executions.[7] In fact, von Schilling himself had issued a similar warning two months before, in which he had said, 'Don't have a mass break, something will happen.'[8] Even the hated figure of Corporal 'Rubberneck' Griese advised the prisoners against such an escape. 'If there is another escape,' he said ominously to Flight Lieutenant John Grocott, 'there will never be another.' After the escape, Grocott stated that he felt 'absolutely convinced' that Griese knew that a murderous reprisal would take place. 'They had tried every other method as a deterrent without any success,' said Grocott, 'and I always had a feeling that something of this nature would eventually arise if they found they could not keep us in.'[9]

Although Webster could not have known it, the warning was no bluff. On 4 March 1944, the head of the Gestapo, SS-Gruppenführer Heinrich Müller, at the order of the High Command of the Armed Forces, issued the now infamous 'Bullet Decree' in which re-captured Allied officers and NCOs – excepting British and Americans – were to be transported to Mauthausen concentration camp and shot. Crucially for British and American POWs, the decree also gave the army the latitude to hand over British and American escapees to the Gestapo.[10] The dissemination of this order through-out the Gestapo therefore prepared its personnel for the possibility that any POW might be executed.[11]

Unable to dissuade the Kriegies from continuing their game, or indeed to establish exactly what and where they were playing, von Lindeiner reluctantly called in the Kripo. That month he wrote to Kriminalrat Brünner in Breslau, and asked him not only for advice on camp security, but also for a special inspection. After a few days, Brünner did indeed visit the camp, spoke to Captain Broili, but then left without carrying out any inspection.[12] This curious episode raises two crucial questions. Why did von Lindeiner call in the Kripo, when he was so wary of them? And why did the Kripo not carry out a special inspection? The answers to both were touched upon by Jimmy James after the war, who reckoned that 'a rather nervous' von Lindeiner was attempting to abnegate responsibility for anything that might happen, and had even 'asked the Gestapo to come and take over'.[13] If that is the case, then von Lindeiner was clearly desperate enough to inflict those he hated upon those he respected: the Kriegies. However, such an analysis does not ring true with what we know of von Lindeiner's attitude, which appeared to be remarkably paternal towards the POWs, and it is unlikely – but not impossible – that he wanted the Gestapo to run the camp. Von Lindeiner's actions may be more reasonably explained by the simple need for him to cover his own posterior. If he could not find the tunnel, and the Kripo or Gestapo could not find the tunnel, then it would be impossible for those two police organisations to blame him if a mass breakout did occur. This bottom-covering exercise also explains the lack of will shown by the Kripo towards carrying out a special inspection. While one has sympathy for Jimmy James maintaining that the Gestapo 'wanted the tunnel to break so that they could make an example of us', there is no evidence for his assertion, and it is far more likely that neither the Gestapo nor the Kripo wanted to be seen to have been at fault in the event of an escape.[14] In short, von Lindeiner, Scharpwinkel and Wielen all knew that trouble was on its way, and not one of them wanted to be seen as having fathered it. The best that von Lindeiner could hope for was to share the paternity, but the Kripo and Gestapo were having none of it.

In his game of wits against the Kriegies, the Commandant was now left with one final move: to upset the board. Furthermore, he knew that he was running out of time, as he suspected that the breakout would occur simultaneously with the long-awaited Allied landings in France, which he anticipated to be at the end of March.[15] In January, the Germans had opened Belaria, a new compound built a few miles from Stalag Luft III, and some five hundred POWs from the east and centre compounds had already been transferred there. Von Lindeiner realised that Belaria would make the ideal new home for those he identified as the north compound's particularly escape-minded Kriegies, and on 1 March, he selected nineteen such men. Von Lindeiner chose wisely, as the men were all part of the X Organisation, and included luminaries such as Floody, Harsh, and Fanshawe. However, the group did not include the obvious leading light. 'Among them was originally Big X himself . . .' von Lindeiner later explained, 'but his transfer was halted at the last moment, at the instigation of several of my German colleagues.'[16] Bushell's absence from the list was a surprise, and it is often assumed that he was omitted because he had successfully given the impression that he no longer wished to run the risk of escaping.[17] However, this explanation contradicts the fact that it was well known throughout the German element of the camp that Bushell was a key personality amongst the Kriegies.

Eberhard Hesse, for example, reported after the war that the Germans knew that Bushell was 'in charge of the RAF Intelligence Section in Luft 3' and von Lindeiner would have certainly been party to this knowledge.[18] Those 'German colleagues' who persuaded von Lindeiner would also have known, and it is possible that they did not fancy the consequences of transferring Bushell. By moving him to Belaria, some Germans may have feared that his absence would have imperilled the profitable Anglo-German cooperation. Bushell was, after all, in the words of Eberhard Hesse, practically the leader of the whole of Stalag Luft III, and his friends on the other side of the barbed wire may have been just as loyal and dependent as those on his own side.

As we cannot be sure why Bushell was not sent to Belaria, further speculation would be fruitless, but the notion that he was no longer regarded as being a potential escaper is highly doubtful.

The first of March also represented another departure, albeit a temporary one. That day, the despised Corporal 'Rubberneck' Griese went on a fortnight's leave, which gave the Kriegies not only a much-needed boost in morale, but also the freedom to make far more rapid progress on Harry. Of all the members of the camp staff, it was Griese who suspected most strongly that 'tunnelling on a large scale was going on in North Compound', but, according to Eberhard Hesse, his superiors disagreed.[19] 'With Rubberneck away everything seemed to go smoothly,' Paul Brickhill observed, and in just nine days, the tunnel advanced by 100 feet. On the tenth day of Griese's leave, the whole of Leicester Square 'halfway house' was constructed, and after measuring the entire tunnel with a piece of string, Ker-Ramsay established that it was 344 feet long.[20] According to the surveyors, that meant that Harry was now some 7 feet behind the treeline. As the ground on the other side of the fence dropped down, it was estimated that the tunnellers only needed to construct a 22-foot shaft to reach the surface. 'Barring the unforeseen,' said Ker-Ramsay, 'I'll guarantee it before Rubberneck gets back.'[21] Building the shaft from bottom to top was far more difficult than digging down, as the sand kept falling into the tunnellers' faces. A solid box frame was constructed using bedposts and bed boards, and within four days, Johnny Bull and Ker-Ramsay had come to some pine roots, which made them think that they were inside the line of trees and no more than 2 feet from the surface.[22] After making a ceiling to support the ground and to stop a hapless German from falling in, on 14 March, Harry was effectively finished. Its construction had required 2,000 bed boards, 500 feet of wiring, 750 Klim tins, 370 feet of rope, 750 beading battens, and the dispersal of 130 tons of sand.[23] 'Looking back on it I am amazed at what we accomplished,' wrote Ken Rees. 'It was on a vast scale.'[24] For Roger Bushell, Harry represented much more than an immense logistical achievement. As the tunnel was being completed, Flight Lieutenant Flekser watched the expression of Big X as he waited in hut 104:

Roger stood with his arms folded across his chest, his face inscrutable, as he looked into the yawning hole at

his feet . . . I looked at Roger, and marvelled at the complete lack of visible emotion. Unfolding below him was
the culmination of his dream, tangible evidence of his
genius. Almost an extension of himself, the door to freedom was at that moment being unlocked by him.[25]

While Bushell started to deliberate when one of the
largest mass escapes of the war should take place, von
Lindeiner was, ironically enough, hosting a 2½-day
conference on the POW security situation, attended by
thirty-eight delegates, including heads of other camps,
senior staff from Sagan, Kriminalrat Brünner from
Breslau Kripo and Kriminalkommissar Läuffer
from Breslau Gestapo. The aims of the meeting were to
'exchange experiences' and to highlight 'new developments in security'. Von Lindeiner opened the meeting by
revealing that as some two thousand air force POWs
were being captured every month, there was a huge
demand for security officers. With no time to train such
men, the officers had to learn on the job, and von
Lindeiner suggested that visits should be encouraged to
see more experienced men at other camps. During the
discussions, Major Peschl from Stalag Luft VI in
Heydekrug spoke about how prisoners in air force
POW camps were very intelligent, and were issued with
'two commandments' – to escape, and not to fraternise
with the Germans. Peschl also discussed how the POWs
were immune from 'indoctrination along German lines',
because of 'severe internal control'. It is a measure,
perhaps, of Peschl's delusion that it did not occur to him
that the Kriegies may not have succumbed to indoctrination simply because they detested Nazism, and

therefore required no 'internal control', be it severe or mild. Von Lindeiner agreed with Peschl that the prisoners were 'on a high intellectual level', but thought that some indoctrination might be desirable, especially concerning the dangers of Bolshevism, as there were 'important differences among British personnel in their attitude towards Russia'. More ominously, von Lindeiner also mentioned 'instructing' the POWs on the Jews, but he noted that 'nothing can be done with regard to the Jewish question' in terms of propaganda.[26] As von Lindeiner wrote in his notes during the meeting, 'If I start to tell the British your Government is a crooked lot of Jewish Criminals, I immediately antagonise him. To start with I have to approach him in a different manner.'[27]

The following morning, the meeting was addressed by Brünner of the Kripo, who talked the attendees through the different search levels that could be instigated by the police.[28] Brünner noted how escapers from the Allied nations differed in their methods, with the British usually attempting to steal vehicles, including aircraft, while the Russians opted to march on foot for days, if not weeks. With the overstretched Kripo in Breslau arresting some one thousand individuals every month, Brünner underlined a previous remark made by von Lindeiner that 'prevention was better than cure', and asked for the military to assist the Kripo.[29] 'This is mainly applicable to Britishers who try their utmost to make the work of the Kripo difficult,' said Brünner. Had Roger Bushell been in attendance, he undoubtedly would have grinned at such a remark, as well as the subsequent observation by Brünner, in which he stated that the British and

American flying officers 'led the field' in the manufacture of escape equipment such as false passes. After the Kripo man had finished, von Lindeiner observed that the 'escape season' was approaching, although he could not have known quite how close it really was. One of the last to speak on the final day was Kriminalkommissar Läuffer of the Gestapo, who spoke about 'Prohibited Traffic with Prisoners of War', a topic that was also of significant, if unappreciated, relevance to the camp in which the meeting was being held. Läuffer reminded the attendees that 'careless talk in the presence of prisoners of war may have dangerous consequences'. As well as speaking about the demoralising effect on the armed forces of sexual relationships between German women and POWs who worked outside POW camps, Läuffer claimed that the Gestapo knew that 'illegal organisations' existed in all POW camps, and that one way of counteracting them was to introduce stool pigeons to 'detect traces of such forbidden activities'. At around noon on the third day of the conference, von Lindeiner concluded that 'to understand one another is everything', and underlined his homily by asking for 'friendly collaboration' between the agencies represented at the meeting.[30]

While von Lindeiner held his meeting, Corporal Griese returned from his fortnight's leave. His suspicions undimmed, Rubberneck ordered an immediate search of hut 104 on the first morning he was back. For four hours, he and his team of ferrets examined the building. 'It was the worst four hours we had known,' wrote Paul Brickhill.[31] But despite his renewed energy, Griese was unable to find the tunnel. 'He departed looking as miserable as ever, thank goodness,' recalled Ken Rees.[32] Although some Kriegies felt that another failed search had made Harry more secure, Roger Bushell thought the opposite, and decided that the breakout should be made as soon as possible. However, the biggest obstacle to acting quickly was the weather. According to Jimmy James, that winter was the coldest in thirty years, and about a foot of snow lay on the ground. For the majority of escapees, who would be travelling by foot, it would have been preferable to wait until the conditions had improved. But with the Germans so suspicious of the tunnel, Bushell knew that was not an option, and he decided that the best night to escape was 23/24 March, when there was no moon.[33] However, he was still worried that the weather would be too harsh, and that many would suffer from frostbite and exposure, and might even die. When he expressed his concerns to Wings Day, Day replied, 'Well, this is war, Roger. They can always give themselves up if the going gets too tough.'[34]

Judging by the above exchange, it appears that Bushell's resolve was also tempered with realism. While Day had a more 'hairy-scary' and gung-ho attitude towards escaping, Bushell's intellectualism led him to evaluate risk, at least on an operational, rather than strategic, level. That attitude was expressed in a conversation he had had with Flight Lieutenant Flekser, after Bushell had attended a lecture given by Flekser on Applied Mathematics and Probability.

'I am intrigued by the possible analogy between your poker game and our escape game,' Bushell said. 'Johnny [Bull] feels that your mathematical approach may add a new dimension to our planning.'

'Permutations and combinations of contingencies arise in both games,' Flekser replied. 'In poker, the odds can be calculated on each bet, and over time, if you are playing with people who rely on luck, you will win. Our game does not lend itself to precise calculation of the odds; nor do we have the luxury of time to smooth out and reverse a run of bad luck.'

'Are you saying that the laws of chance are of no practical value in our escape planning?'

At this point, Flekser recalled how Bushell's 'close eye-to-eye style of interrogation' had made him feel uncomfortable, and he stepped back a pace and started rubbing out the blackboard.

'On the contrary,' said Flekser. 'I am saying that if we are vigilantly abreast of the variables we can at least assign qualitative values in order to make the most promising choices. Also, as in poker, the element of bluffing – in our case misdirection – should play an important role.'

'Flex, it seems to me that the application of your approach to the escape game boils down to a disciplined employment of logic – which is precisely what I do. At least you have an analytical mind. As contingencies arise, I propose to discuss my planning with you. Let's see if my logic and your mathematics can meet.'[35]

Although Flekser never revealed quite how such an application was manifested, it is clear that the barrister in Bushell was keen to look at his own plan coldly and dispassionately. However, a vast part of him was the reckless downhill skier who rebelled against such analysis, and perhaps stopped him from looking at whether it was wise to engage in the activity at all.

Bushell may have weighed up the risks that lay along a particular course of action, but he never appeared to consider whether there were other courses he could try, courses that looked more modest but may have yielded better results. Bushell's flamboyance ultimately led him to take big risks, and no amount of 'disciplined employment of logic' was going to negate them. By the time Harry had been finished, there was to be no going back, snow or no snow.

With just nine days to go before the escape, there was much that the Kriegies had to do. With the documentation for all two hundred escapees requiring the addition of correct dates, the forgery department had to work overtime. Despite the poor lighting in the huts, those such as Alex Cassie and Tim Walenn had to break their own rules and work at night.[36] Desmond Plunkett and his mapmakers were similarly busy, as they had to finish producing two hundred bespoke maps. The pressure naturally caused mistakes to be made, and at one point, Plunkett's absent-mindedness nearly imperilled the entire breakout. A few days before the escape, the ferrets made a snap search of hut 101, in which Cassie and Plunkett were housed. While the Kriegies waited outside, Cassie recalled Plunkett suddenly turning white as he frantically frisked his pockets.

'I've left my book on my bed,' said Plunkett. 'If they find that, everything will be over.'

Plunkett's book, far from being some innocuous novel, contained the intended destination of every single escapee. If the Germans got hold of it, they would know exactly what was being planned for everybody.

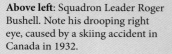

Above left: Squadron Leader Roger Bushell. Note his drooping right eye, caused by a skiing accident in Canada in 1932.

Above right: Bushell *sur la piste* in his characteristic devil-may-care style.

Right: Bushell in or after October 1936, displaying a nonchalance that would both attract and repel.

Bushell at the wedding of Viscount Curzon at St Paul's Cathedral in London in July 1935. Behind him walks Lady Georgiana 'Georgie' Curzon (*centre*).

Peggy Hamilton, to whom Bushell was engaged. A former dancer, she ended up marrying a lord.

Georgie and her son, Glen, photographed by Dorothy Wilding in 1937.

Left: Sydney Dowse, the Spitfire reconnaissance pilot who tried to persuade Bushell not to go on the Great Escape.

Below: A smirking Major Johnny Dodge after being captured, having escaped through the floor of a cattle truck.

Bottom left: Wing Commander Harry 'Wings' Day, a great friend and rival to Bushell, and a similarly diehard escaper.

Bottom right: Flight Lieutenant Desmond Plunkett's very English looks would make him hard to pass as 'Sergei Bulanov'.

Above: The much-respected chief 'ferret' Hermann Glemnitz pictured with his family.

Left: Lieutenant Günther von Massow, who would help Bushell throughout the war. The Commandant of Dulag Luft, Theo Rumpel, can be seen bottom left.

Below left: The Deputy Commandant of Stalag Luft III, Major Gustav Simoleit.

Below right: The aristocratic Colonel Friedrich-Wilhelm von Lindeiner, the Commandant of Stalag Luft III.

"PLEESE GENTLEMEN—
DONT SIT ON ZE
VARNING VIRE!"

Above: The loathed Corporal 'Rubberneck' Griese (*left*), with a fellow ferret.

Right: Captain Hans Pieber, caricatured by POW Ley Kenyon.

Below: Pieber (*left*) in conversation with Group Captain Herbert Massey, the camp's Senior British Officer from April 1943.

Left: Flight Sergeant Alfie 'Bill' Fripp as Launcelot Gobbo in *The Merchant of Venice*.

Right: Belgian pilot Bobby Laumans, who 'excited the hearts' of many POWs.

Below: 'To our women-starved lives, they looked absolutely great.' A production of *Girls, Girls, Girls* in March 1943.

Bottom: Interior of an officers' room by Flight Lieutenant Alex Cassie.

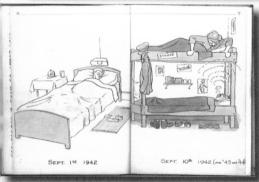

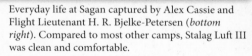

Everyday life at Sagan captured by Alex Cassie and Flight Lieutenant H. R. Bjelke-Petersen (*bottom right*). Compared to most other camps, Stalag Luft III was clean and comfortable.

P.O.W. No. 638

Above: A lean Roger Bushell (*right*) with Wing Commander Bob Stanford Tuck at Stalag Luft III.

Left: A self-portrait by Alex Cassie, who would oversee the forgery of hundreds of documents.

Below left: Suspected 'stool pigeon' Squadron Leader George Boyd Carpenter, who provided Wings Day with a contact address in Berlin.

Below right: The renegade officer. Railton Freeman, much detested by Bushell, who would besmirch the memory of Big X after the war.

'Plunkett was quite agitated,' said Cassie understatedly. 'He was a bit scatter-brained sometimes, but he kept his presence of mind most of the time.'

Fortunately for Plunkett, Tim Walenn was still inside the hut, feigning sickness in bed. As his bunk was near a window, Plunkett was able to whisper to him about the book, and asked him to wrap it up in a towel. Despite being nearly paralysed with panic, Plunkett then asked the ferrets whether they could pass his towel out to him, as he was due to have a wash in the shower block that morning. While the Germans were distracted, Walenn was able to hide not only Plunkett's book in the towel, but also a wash-bag full of rubber stamps. He then gave the whole package to a ferret, who obligingly passed it out to Plunkett.[37]

In the rush to get ready, mistakes were also made by the tailoring department. Airmen's greatcoats may have had their shoulder markings removed, but in some cases, telltale 'AM' – Air Ministry – labels remained on the lining. The 'AM' label would also remain on some pairs of trousers, and naval greatcoats would retain their service buttons. One escaper's greatcoat even bore the label of the famous Savile Row tailor Gieves & Hawkes, whose clothes were unlikely to be worn by many Germans in 1944.[38] As Jimmy James was later to observe, much of the clothing worn by the escapees was only 'vaguely civilian', consisting as it did of modified – yet still discernible – pieces of uniform and battledress.[39] RAF tunics were a popular choice, and merely had their service buttons replaced, although in several instances, not only the buttons remained, but also the rank markings and even the RAF wings.[40] According to one escaper, very few of those heading down the tunnel were dressed in 'anything resembling civilian clothes', with most in 'more or less military dress'.[41] Today, it is unclear quite why the escape clothing was not better disguised. Clearly, no matter how talented the likes of Dvorak and Guest, it was impossible to produce two hundred entirely convincing outfits, and very few of the escapers were issued with what could genuinely have been described as civilian clothes. Unlike with the forging of documents, tailoring offers more latitude with the accuracy of reproduction, and there was perhaps a sense of having to 'make do'. As most of the escapers were not expected to be successful, and were merely to provide fodder for Bushell's 'massive flap', there was no point in issuing clothing that could have passed the closest inspection, especially to those whose linguistic inability meant that they could not pass as a German or a foreign worker. Besides, many Kriegies felt that the wearing of adapted uniforms, or clothes that still bore Air Ministry labels, made it harder for the Germans to accuse them of spying. As we shall see, in the post-war investigations and trials, determining what the escapers were wearing was vital in order to establish that they had not been tasked with the capital offence of espionage.

As well as finalising and assembling escape equipment, the X Committee had to decide who was going to escape. Some six hundred Kriegies had been engaged on work connected with the breakout, and from these, two hundred had to be selected. The first thirty places were awarded to those who were felt to have the best chance of making a 'home run', either because they spoke

German fluently or had plenty of escape experience. Among them were Bushell himself, Sydney Dowse, Bob Vanderstok, Tim Walenn, Johnny Bull, Johnny Marshall, Desmond Plunkett, Bedrich Dvorak, Johnny Dodge, Jens Müller and his fellow Norwegian, Per Bergsland. These names were all placed into a hat, and then drawn in the order in which they were to exit the tunnel. Bushell drew number four. Then the names of forty prominent workers were selected, and then twenty were drawn. After that, thirty important workers were added, and another twenty drawn. Finally, the rest of the names were added, and the running order of the remaining 130 was decided.[42] Of the four hundred POWs who were left, there were some who had deliberately chosen not to go. One of the primary reasons was claustrophobia, an anxiety disorder suffered by, among others, Alex Cassie. A few weeks before Harry was completed, he was shown the tunnel to see whether he could cope going down it. 'I didn't like it . . . ,' he recalled. 'I just looked along it and thought, "God no." Always when I go into tunnels of any kind, I'm happier when I come out.'[43] The X Committee did its best to ensure that none of the escapees shared Cassie's phobia, and in the main, claustrophobics chose not to go not just out of fear, but also because a panic attack in the middle of the tunnel could have had disastrous consequences. However, as we shall see, this vetting process was not entirely watertight.

After the draw had been made, the next few days before the 23rd were taken up with briefing the escapees, and establishing whether everybody had the correct kit and documentation. The first thirty, who would be travelling by train, were provided with brief-cases, identity cards, ration cards, money, letters from German firms and authorisations to allow them to travel by train. However, they carried little food and only small maps of the frontiers where they intended to cross, as it was felt that the presence of detailed maps and large amounts of food would not tally with their disguises as professional men. Another forty were to travel by workmen's trains, with the remainder going by foot.[44] This largest group was known as the 'hard-arsers', for the obvious reason that they would be tramping through a freezing and unforgiving landscape of thick forest and inhospitable villages. Despite carry-ing escape rations made from chocolate and oatmeal, food would be scarce, and shelter would be hard to find. It was only during the preparations that the scale of the challenge became truly apparent to those who had made the draw. Ken Rees recalled how he and his friend and escaping partner, Red Noble, simultaneously looked out of the window at the conditions and shared the same thought: 'Would we be able to do it, to make it the 60-odd miles to the Czech border, walking mostly by night, sheltering by day wherever we could find a hole?'[45] Although Rees still felt confident, there were other hard-arsers, such as Jack Lyon, who felt anything but. 'The chances would have been minimal in good conditions,' he observed, 'but absolutely impossible in those sorts. No one really expected this category to make it, but that wasn't the objective, was it?'[46]

On 20 March, Ker-Ramsay and Marshall inspected all the escapers and their outfits, as well as briefing them on how to go down the tunnel, by lying flat on the trolley and holding out their belongings while they were pulled along. Each of the briefcases carried by the train travellers had to be inspected to make sure that it would fit through and not dislodge the bed boards. Despite the cold weather, blanket rolls were forbidden, as they might have got caught on the boards or under the wheels of the trolleys.[47] While members of the X Committee taught first-timers about German customs, Bushell personally briefed all of the escapers, and checked their cover stories.[48]

It was at this stage that Roger Bushell was to receive a final warning not to go on the escape. The man who issued it to him was not a German, but Sydney Dowse.

'Whatever you do, you must not go out,' Dowse pleaded, 'because I've got it on very firm grounds from Hesse that should you ever go out, there'll be no more of you. You're likely to be shot.'

Dowse repeated the warning, begging Bushell not to go, insisting that Bushell was more valuable as Big X, 'organising things and getting things done, [rather than] getting out, getting captured again, getting shot, or getting put away in a very special concentration camp'.

'Dynamo,' Bushell replied, 'that's fine, but I'm going.'

Dowse later reflected that Bushell's attitude was 'quite arrogant'. 'He was very confident,' Dowse recalled. 'I begged him not to go, I really did.'[49]

As well as Bushell, there was another element of the escape that could not be told what to do: the weather. When the prisoners woke up on the morning of the 23rd, the first thing they saw through their windows was a fresh covering of snow. Bushell immediately consulted Flying Officer Leonard Hall, an RAF meteorologist who had fallen into captivity when his boat had been torpedoed. Hall's reckoning was that the weather would not deteriorate, and a heavy cloud cover would obscure any starlight or what little moonlight there might have been. Bushell discussed his options with the X Committee, and it was decided to delay the escape by twenty-four hours in order to take advantage of any thaw.[50] The next morning, temperatures had indeed improved. 'There was a hint of mildness in the air,' recalled Paul Brickhill, 'and the white carpet was wet on top and a little squashy underfoot.'[51] Once again, Hall was asked for a forecast. 'I asked for, and was allowed, fifteen minutes or so to walk round the circuit and glean what I could from the sky and the wind conditions,' he later wrote. 'Needless to say, no weather maps were available and I could only draw on my knowledge of weather patterns, cloud formations, wind speeds and directions.'[52] At around eleven thirty, Hall went to Bushell's room and gave him his opinion: the cloud would stay in place, and there would be no deterioration. As Hall described it, his forecast was akin to the 'making of bricks without straw', but it was to prove immensely accurate. Although he could not have known it, the pressure was rising, and the cold front with its snow was moving east.[53]

'Right,' said Bushell, jumping to his feet. 'We go tonight.'[54]

Chapter Nine

The Great Escape

FOR THE GERMANS, Friday 24 March was just another day, although they strongly suspected an imminent escape. The Kriegies, however, managed to keep any displays of excitement well under control, especially at afternoon *Appell* at five o'clock. 'I remember as this German went down the row counting *eins, zwei, drei, vier, fünf*...,' recalled Frank Waddington. 'I thought the next time you count us, mate, you're going to have a shock, because I knew they were going out that night.'[1] After the roll-call, the escapers went back to their huts for a last supper. 'The tension in the room was stomach-churning,' wrote Ken Rees, 'almost worse than before any operation I could remember.'[2] In Alex Cassie's room, Cassie was the only one of seven not to be escaping, and he cooked his companions a nourishing meal. The Kriegies ate as much as they could, not knowing how long they would have to rely on their escape rations. The atmosphere was tense, as it was in so many other rooms throughout the compound, but, as Cassie recalled, 'we tried to keep it under control' with banter. Those leaving him behind were Tim Walenn, Ley Kenyon, Gordon Brettell, Henri Picard, Desmond Plunkett and Anthony Hayter. As Cassie said goodbye to each of the men in turn, the banter was replaced by something more serious. Brettell, who had just celebrated his twenty-ninth birthday, said, 'Cass, if I don't get back, will you explain it all to my parents?' Tim Walenn left a gold watch he had been given by his parents for his twenty-first birthday. After the farewells, the men slipped out into the dusk and headed for hut 104. Cassie looked round the empty room, feeling deflated. 'I was left surveying the vast amount of washing-up that needed to be done,' he said. 'It drove it home to me then that I was the only one left in that room.'[3] Of the six men who departed, Cassie was only ever to see two again.

Throughout the early evening, hut 104 filled up with the two hundred escapers; it is a measure of the effectiveness of the X Organisation's security that for many, this was the first time they learned of the tunnel's location.[4] The officers nervously waited for the start of the breakout, which was scheduled for 8.45 p.m.[5] 'There was little talk, no joking, and practically no walking around,' said Bob Vanderstok.[6] Some affected nonchalance and pretended to sleep or solved crosswords, while others checked and rechecked their clothing, rations and papers.[7] After the Germans had shut down the hut and closed the windows at 9 p.m., the air quality began to deteriorate as the Kriegies sweated and smoked. 'It got so hot in there with all the bods that before long you could actually see steam . . .' recalled one POW. 'We couldn't make out what was going on.'[8] Dressed in many different outfits, the escapers were truly a motley crew. 'The variety of their disguises was unbelievable,' recalled Alan Bryett. 'There were chaps dressed as German soldiers, German civilians, there was [even] a chap dressed as a German sailor.'[9] Perhaps the smartest disguise was worn by Bushell himself, who was wearing a pin-stripe grey suit, a light-blue shirt, a red-and-blue striped tie, a narrow-brimmed hat, and was carrying a polished leather briefcase. 'Roger looked every inch the French businessman he purported to be,' observed Flight Lieutenant Flekser.[10] Accompanying Bushell was Pilot Officer Bernard Scheidhauer, who had served in the Free French Air Force and 131 Squadron of the RAF. Fluent in English, German and French, the 22-year-old was the ideal escaping partner for Bushell, who intended to make contact with the French Resistance and head over the Pyrenees to Spain.[11] Unlike many of the Kriegies, Bushell appeared to be relaxed, and he walked around the hut, checking that all were ready. Jens Müller recalled how Bushell walked into a room shared by him and Bernard 'Pop' Green, who was working on a crossword:

[Pop] was the keenest and most passionate crossword puzzler I'd ever met, and he was dead to the outside world. But suddenly he looked up. The commander of the whole operation had walked into the room. There was silence, as all of us looked towards the man who had organised and planned the whole thing. We expected him to say a few words. He just said, 'Good luck, boys', and then he walked out.[12]

Bushell's calm demeanour was the inverse of the mood down in the tunnel itself, which had been soured by the first of many mishaps that would afflict the breakout that night. The first two men sent down were Johnny Bull and Johnny Marshall, who had been tasked with opening the exit. However, when Bull climbed up the shaft a little after 8 p.m., he found that the protective ceiling had swollen with damp and was immovable.[13] For over two hours, Bull and Marshall worked as quickly and calmly as possible to move the woodwork, and finally, at around 10.15 p.m., Bull was able to tentatively stick his head out into the cold air. What he saw appalled him. The exit was not in the woods, but some 15 feet short, and right in the middle of the open ground between the line of trees and the barbed wire. Worse still, a guard tower loomed just 15 yards away.[14] Bull ducked back inside the tunnel, and passed on the bad news to not only Marshall, but also Bushell and Sydney Dowse, who were now waiting at the end of the tunnel. 'We were pretty horrified,' Dowse said later. 'We thought it bloody bad management, whoever had made the arrangement, or done the measurement. I've forgotten who did it. He was an idiot in my view, because he had got it wrong.'[15]

Dowse's 'forgetfulness' was likely to have been born out of a desire to protect the identity of the 'idiot', whose name has never been revealed. However, despite

Dowse's understandable frustration, the blame for the tunnel falling short cannot be rested on any single pair of shoulders. The responsibility for determining the length of the tunnel was that of Desmond Plunkett's mapmaking team, which was tasked with surveying the north compound, and measuring the distance between the huts, as well as between the huts and the barbed wire. According to the official RAF report, 'the results of their work were put on paper and handed to the tunnel engineers'.[16] It has recently emerged that the individual responsible for establishing the length of the tunnel was Jens Müller, who, according to Canadian Spitfire pilot John Weir, 'did the triangulation and figured how far to get to the trees'.[17] However, it would be unfair to blame Müller, as, unknown to him, the tunnel was built sloping downwards until Piccadilly Circus, after which it sloped up. This fundamental feature of the tunnel appeared to be forgotten when Ker-Ramsay took the final measurement, and because of its inclines, the tunnel therefore covered less distance than was required.[18] As a result, if blame is to be apportioned – and to do so seems churlish – then it should be shared by both Ker-Ramsay and his tunnelling team, and Plunkett's team of surveyors.

However, it is also possible that Harry did indeed end up in the woods as planned. Thanks to the mythologising influence of the movie, the fact that the exit fell short is considered a definitive component of the story of the Great Escape. Nevertheless, there are a few pieces of evidence that suggest that Harry did in fact reach the woods, or was so close to the treeline as to make little difference. The first can be found in a detailed drawing

of the tunnel made by Ley Kenyon in his wartime logbook. The picture, which appears to have been drawn
and annotated after the escape – and it would have been
an appalling security risk to have done so before –
clearly shows the tunnel emerging into the trees.
Furthermore, a caption to the picture states that the exit
was '20 feet inside' the woods.[19] Another piece of
evidence is contained in the testimony Unteroffizier
Petzold gave to the Allies some six months after the
escape. Petzold, who had served at the camp from May
1943 to August 1944 and was captured fighting at
Schijndel in the Netherlands in September, was on guard
duty at the outer gate of the north compound on the
night of the escape, and recalled how a search party
found the tunnel's exit 'in the woods at a distance of
10m from the road on the outside of the north
compound'.[20] Finally, there are two photographs taken
by the Germans of the exit of the tunnel, which both
suggest that it lay inside the treeline. The first is taken
from above, and shows Corporal Griese climbing up the
shaft, around the opening of which can clearly be seen
tree roots. The second shows a reconstructed scene of a
prisoner emerging from the hole, and in the background
can be seen what looks like the base of a tree. These
photographs are contained in an album called 'Tunnel
to Freedom' that can be found at the Royal Air Force
Museum in Hendon, north London, and both are
captioned 'Harry – break through in the woods'.[21]
Is it therefore possible that Harry did emerge
amongst the trees, and that the whole story of the
tunnel falling short is in fact a myth engendered by the
movie and populist accounts such as that by Paul

Brickhill? Despite the evidence above, it seems unlikely. The majority of testimonies and memoirs made by the surviving escapers refer to Harry not reaching the tree-line, and although it is tempting to subscribe to the old Russian maxim that nobody lies like an eyewitness, in this instance, too many of the accounts coincide rather than conflict.[22] The best evidence to support the tunnel falling short is by taking measurements from an aerial photograph of the camp taken in the latter stages of the war.[23] We know from Ker-Ramsay's string that the tunnel was exactly 344 feet long, and we should be confident that that measurement was accurate.[24] As we also know that Harry started under a stove at the north end of hut 104, and as the chimney of that stove is just discernible on the photograph, we can also be certain of the tunnel's starting point. Although there is no scale on the photograph, it is possible to establish distance by overlaying reference points on contemporary satellite images. A line representing 344 feet drawn from the northernmost chimney finishes just north of the perimeter road, and about 50 feet from a guard tower. This projected exit also comes up some 15–20 feet before a hedge-like screen erected by the ferrets, behind which they would hide to spy on the Kriegies in the compound. All of these distances tally with most of the testimonies, although the treeline in the photograph is approximately 80 feet from the exit, which is con-siderably further than the usually quoted figure of around 10–20 feet.[25] This discrepancy may be indicative of the Germans having moved back the treeline after the breakout – and that the aerial photograph was taken subsequent to this deforestation – rather than any gross and deliberate inaccuracy concocted by the Kriegies to hide their blushes. In addition, the edge of the forest was not clearly defined, and the ground between it and the road was an amalgam of scrub and the hedges erected by the ferrets. Although this lack of definition may account for the mistake, there are other, more likely reasons. The only instruments for making a trigonometrical survey available to Plunkett and his team were 'very crude' and 'home-made', and an error of some 10 per cent in establishing the correct length was perhaps inevitable.[26] In addition, it was hardly possible for the Kriegies to stand at the fence for several minutes at a time looking into the wood and holding up their instruments without attracting suspicion. Other possible reasons for the error, such as taking the measurement from the wall of the hut, or worse still, from the compound's fence, may be discounted, as they would suggest gross incompetence rather than an understandable mistake.

What then of the evidence that suggests that the tunnel did in fact reach the woods? As regards Kenyon's drawing and Petzold's testimony, we can only conclude that the two men were mistaken. The roots visible in the photograph of the shaft are almost certainly remnants of the trees that were felled during the ground clearance when the camp was established. Furthermore, the tree shown in the picture of the emerging 'escaper' may just be a stump, and there were plenty of those throughout the compound, much to the irritation of the Kriegies.

However, even though it is clear that the tunnel did not emerge into woods, how much of a problem was it? In the post-war RAF report, no mention is made of the shortfall, and although this could be put down to an application of gloss, the report is reasonably candid about other errors.[27] Very few, if any, of the testimonies made by the surviving escapers after the war specifically mention the location of the exit as being a handicap, and instead merely refer in general terms to the many 'hitches' that afflicted the breakout. It would appear that the location of the exit only assumed a dramatic significance when Paul Brickhill's 1951 account, *The Great Escape*, was published, upon which the movie was based. Perhaps tellingly, recollections made by Kriegies after 1951 will invariably mention the shortfall, but those made before do not. This lack of emphasis would suggest that the location of the exit, although not ideal, was not quite the disaster that someone like Sydney Dowse would later portray it. The watchtower was, after all, 50 feet away, and its occupant surveyed the inside of the camp rather than the woods behind him. The ferrets' hedges were close, and they afforded ample cover. There was also no moon, and with plenty of snow lying on the ground, the escapers could crawl into the woods in darkness and in near silence. Furthermore, the Kriegies quickly developed a solution that ensured they would not be spotted by any guard patrolling the perimeter road. A rope was tied to the top rung of the exit ladder, which was then led by Johnny Bull to a position behind one of the hedges from where he could keep watch. Instructions were swiftly relayed down the tunnel that Bull would give the rope two tugs to indicate that all was clear, and that it was safe to emerge.[28]

As soon as Bull was in position, the next man to leave

Harry was his fellow tunnel engineer Johnny Marshall, who emerged into the night at just after ten thirty. Carrying maps, a compass, 200 Reichsmarks, food, and papers that claimed he was in fact one Petr Kovalkov, a glass worker living in Burgos, Marshall wore a civilian outfit consisting of Royal Australian Air Force blue serge trousers, an RAF tunic made to look like a civilian jacket, a skiing cap, and an airman's overcoat dyed dark grey and fitted with civilian buttons. His escaping partner was the next man out, Flight Lieutenant Ernst Valenta, a Wellington navigator with the Czechoslovakian-manned 311 Squadron. Together, the two men planned to take the train from Sagan to Breslau, where they would change to catch a train at 3 a.m. to head 80 miles south to Mittelwalde,[29] which was just 2½ miles from the Czech border. Once they had crossed into Valenta's homeland, the pair hoped to contact an underground organisation, and if that failed, they intended to make for Yugoslavia, where they would join Tito's partisans.[30]

Marshall and Valenta hurried about 100 yards into the woods, where they waited, as arranged, for more escapers. Within a few minutes they were joined by Bushell; Scheidhauer; Flight Lieutenants Rupert Stevens, Johannes Gouws, Nils Fugelsang, Hallada Espelid and Romas Marcinkus; Tim Walenn; Bedrich Dvorak and Desmond Plunkett.[31] It is worth noting that fewer than half of this twelve-strong batch of escapers was British – two were Czech, two Norwegian, one South African, one French, and even, in the form of Marcinkus, one Lithuanian. Today, the Great Escape is often regarded as a very British tale, but some four in every ten men who left the tunnel were not in fact from the United Kingdom. Although the breakout was led and inspired by a Briton – albeit one born and partially raised in South Africa – the level of international co-operation means that the Great Escape should not be coveted by any one nation.

It was at this point that Bushell issued his last orders to members of the X Organisation. With the escape running nearly two hours late, three trains had already been missed, and Bushell told the group to split into twos and threes and to catch a train leaving Sagan station at 11 p.m.[32] The timing would be tight, as the station was just under half a mile away, and the escapers would have to navigate through the dark woods to find it. Marshall and Valenta headed off, and within a few minutes they got lost. While they were searching, at around 11 p.m. the sound of an air-raid siren filled the air, and when they eventually found the entrance to the subway that ran under the tracks to the station, its doors had been locked. A ticket collector emerged from the darkness of the entrance and told the two men to go to the air-raid shelter, but Valenta insisted that they should be allowed through as they had a train to catch. However, the ticket collector was adamant, and told the escapers that nobody was allowed into the station during an air raid. Frustrated by officialdom, Marshall and Valenta retreated to the woods, where they discussed their options. They could either wait for the air raid to end and hopefully catch the 1 a.m. train, or they could walk the 90 miles to the Czech border. Although the snow and the temperature made the second option unappealing, neither man wished to risk staying in the vicinity of the tunnel, and so, instead of catching a train, they became hard-arsers.[33]

While Marshall and Valenta were getting lost, a few members of the early batch of escapers were having more luck. Dvorak and Plunkett arrived at the station just as the air-raid siren sounded, and were accosted by a German warrant officer who insisted that they should go to the shelter. As they were entering the shelter, they heard the announcement of the train from Berlin to Breslau arriving at platform 3, and they gave the man the slip.[34] Within a few minutes, they had managed to get on a third-class carriage on the train without buying a ticket.[35] While they stood in the corridor, they saw Bushell, who said nothing to them, but simply squeezed Plunkett's hand.[36]

Bob Vanderstok was also enjoying some good fortune. The nineteenth escaper to exit the tunnel, the Dutchman was travelling by himself and making for Holland. Posing as a Dutch worker, Vanderstok was wearing a naval jacket and trousers, an Australian greatcoat, RAF boots with their tops cut off and a beret that had been made in the camp.[37] According to his memoirs, his departure from the tunnel had certainly been dramatic. As he was emerging, he had spotted the silhouette of a guard standing between the exit and the fence, looking straight towards him. 'He just stood there and never said a word,' Vanderstok recalled. 'Then I noticed the thin stream of urine and I realised that he was standing with his back toward me ... pissing.'[38] After the guard had finished, Vanderstok scrambled from the tunnel and disappeared into the woods, where he found a path. As he made for the station, the air-raid siren sounded, and knowing that the station would be shut he decided to wait it out in the woods rather than attempt to find an air-raid shelter. Suddenly, he heard a voice coming from 15 feet behind him.

'Stop! Who are you? Where are you going?'

The words were in German. Vanderstok turned to see a soldier aiming a rifle at him.

'Ah, good evening,' Vanderstok replied. 'I am a foreign worker and I am on my way to the railway station.' He then told the soldier that he had been caught outside on his way to the station, and that he hadn't managed to find a shelter.

'Oh nonsense!' the soldier replied. 'As long as you are with me, no trouble. This path will take you to the station. Go to the shelter there.'

Vanderstok thanked the soldier and then swiftly followed the path.[39]

Although both these incidents seem very dramatic, it is unlikely that they took place. In his interview given to MI9 on 11–12 July 1944, Vanderstok states that he 'got out of the tunnel without incident'. The Dutchman may have deemed the story of the urinating guard not worth recounting to MI9, but its veracity seems particularly fragile when it is considered in relation to the fact that he told MI9 that his sylvan challenger was in fact a civilian, who even kindly escorted him to the station.[40] It is a pity that Vanderstok should have invented such incidents, as the true story of his escape is dramatic enough. Age might be considered an excuse for inaccurate recall, but not for outright embellishment.

When Vanderstok arrived at the station, he saw one of his fellow escapees, Squadron Leader Thomas Kirby-Green, the seventeenth man to leave the tunnel, talking in Spanish to another Kriegie. With his long dark hair and swarthy looks, Kirby-Green certainly looked the Hispanic he was pretending to be, but a sharp-eyed female employee of Department VI of the camp – the censor's office – was suspicious of him. She asked a military policeman to check his papers, and while he did so, she approached Vanderstok and asked him a number of questions about his identity and his destination. Vanderstok informed her that he worked as a draughtsman for the Siemens Bau Union, and was able to satisfy her with his cover story. After the questioning had finished, the policeman approached the woman and told her that the papers of the 'Spanish worker' were all in order.[41] The temptation for Kirby-Green and Vanderstok to have exchanged relieved glances must have been immense, but both men acted as if they were strangers to each other. At three thirty, the train to Breslau arrived, and Vanderstok found himself crushed into a second-class carriage. 'I could hardly believe it,' he later wrote. 'I had gotten out of the goddam camp and here I was, standing in the corridor of a train car, on my way to Breslau.'[42]

If the air raid was creating difficulties for those who had already left the tunnel, it was far more problematic for those still inside it. When the siren sounded, the camp's power was shut down in order to remove any illumination that might prove useful to the Allied aircraft. As the tunnel's lights ran off the hut's electricity supply, this meant that the entire length of Harry was cast into complete darkness. For many of the Kriegies, the temptation to yield to an incipient sense of panic must have been huge. 'The confinement, the stuffiness, the fear of moving in case of a fall, combining with the blackness, gave rise to claustrophobia, and nerves were at a snapping point,' observed Paul Brickhill.[43] Alan Bryett put it somewhat more laconically. The lack of light, he recalled, was 'a very depressing morale loss'.[44] Ironically, this latest delay was caused by the actions of their RAF comrades in Bomber Command, who were carrying out their last major raid on Berlin of the war. A force of 811 aircraft, consisting of 577 Lancasters, 216 Halifaxes and 18 Mosquitos, was making for the German capital, although the night's strong northerly wind saw many of the planes scattered away from the target.[45] Ken Rees, who was waiting in the hut, thought he could hear 'a distant familiar roar, which pleased us a lot'.[46] After some confusion, light was eventually restored with a series of fat lamps, although the solution was hardly ideal. Not only was the quality of light poor and the fumes choking, there was also a strong risk that they could set light to an escaper's clothing, and thereby set the whole tunnel ablaze.[47]

As the breakout slowly continued, it would be beset by other problems, many of which were caused by human error and resulted in a systemic near-breakdown. One of the most vital tasks that was neglected was the hauling through of the escapers along the tunnel, which was the responsibility of every twentieth escapee. Wings Day would later recall how the escape was delayed partly by 'some of the officers who should have remained to haul the others . . . leaving without being relieved'.[48] Sydney Dowse, who was supposed to be the third to leave the tunnel, found himself demoted to the twenty-first because an unidentified Kriegie had forgotten to relieve him of haulage duties at the end of the tunnel, and had mistakenly relieved a hauler in one of the two halfway houses.

> They made a muck of things down below. The chap who was supposed to relieve me, instead of relieving me, he relieved the people below. In the tunnel there were two other areas, and then the out. Some idiot made a mess of relief, and I was there much longer than I should have been.[49]

After a while, Wings Day came up the tunnel, and was surprised to find Dowse still *in situ*.

'Bloody hell!' he exclaimed. 'What the hell are you doing here, Dynamo?'

'I haven't been relieved, that's why,' Dowse replied. 'So-and-so is supposed to relieve me.'

'Well, he's down at the other place.'

'Bloody idiot!'

'For Christ's sake,' said Day. 'Go out, and I'll relieve you.'[50]

Another avoidable problem was the propensity of escapees to go down the tunnel carrying or wearing too much. Although they had been ordered to divest themselves of blankets, too many Kriegies tried to get through with all manner of encumbrances, including cases and too many layers of clothes. As a result, according to Day, some of the officers got stuck.[51] On perhaps two or more occasions, this resulted in the tunnel collapsing. One of these collapses was caused by James 'Cookie' Long, whose broad shoulders dislodged some of the shoring. Long was able to dig himself out, and his hauler, Thomas Nelson, managed to pull him along to the next halfway house. Nelson then crawled back through the tunnel, and for the next half an hour attempted to repair the damage. 'I had in darkness more or less to work replacing frames and packing in the sand behind the frame . . . ,' he said, 'and then trying to spread the surplus sand along the tunnel in order to open up this business again.'[52] Such work was of course dangerous and time-consuming, and it was fortunate that none of the collapses resulted in the termination of the breakout.

Another problem was the onset of claustrophobia in those with less experience of tunnels. Alan Bryett recalled one delay that was caused by a Kriegie suffering from an anxiety attack. 'I don't know who it was,' he said, 'but one of the fellows had got halfway along and had got claustrophobia. Very difficult to move him out. In the end he was moved and people started going.'[53] Ken Rees thought that at least two escapers panicked, which resulted in two separate falls, one of which was repaired by his friend Red Noble and Robert Ker-Ramsay. Rees also remarked that many of the escapers were 'very nervous', and needed quite some encouragement to go down the tunnel.[54] According to Ivo Tonder, one of those who suffered was Johnny Dodge. 'He had already escaped several times, but never underground, probably because of his stocky frame,' Tonder recalled. 'It was his first time deep in the tunnel, and he was suffering from claustrophobia. He had almost kicked me to death by the time he got past me and onto the trolley.'[55] In his memoirs, George Harsh claims that three escapers were victims of claustrophobia, one of whom was no less a figure than a squadron leader with a DFC and bar, who had to be tied up and passed back to the surface. 'As soon as he was brought into the room his panic melted, and he slunk shamefacedly off into the barracks,' Harsh wrote.[56] Another victim, according to Harsh, was a 'large, powerful Australian' who had been a champion swimmer, and who had to be knocked cold with the handle of a tool so that he could be dragged back to the entrance of the tunnel.[57] Once again, it would appear that a former Kriegie has sought to embellish the story of the Great Escape. Although there can be no doubt that some did have anxiety attacks, the idea that panicking escapers were tied up or knocked unconscious is ludicrous, as to have done so would have risked a fight that could have caused a bad collapse. Harsh's account is also dubious, as he claims to have been in the north compound during the time of the escape, whereas he had in fact been dispatched to Belaria some three weeks before.[58]

Despite the late start, the tunnel's shortfall, the air raid, the lack of regular haulage, and the collapses caused by bulk and panic, the Great Escape somehow managed to limp on. At 1.20 a.m., the forty-seventh man – in the form of Flight Lieutenant Albert Armstrong – left the tunnel.[59] The rate of escape soon fell to one man every fourteen minutes, which was a far cry from the intended rate of one every two to three

minutes.[60] During the small hours, it became apparent
to those in hut 104 that nothing like two hundred were
going to get out. 'There was a great air of depression,'
said Alan Bryett, 'because a lot of us saw our one
chance of freedom being snatched from us. And what's
worse, we're going to be caught red-handed with lots
and lots of things we shouldn't have.'[61] At 4.30 a.m.,
with dawn less than an hour away, Flight Lieutenant
William Cameron exited Harry as the sixty-ninth
escapee.[62]

As with many of the escapers lower down the order,
Cameron was a hard-arser, and along with Flight
Lieutenant A. B. Thompson, he simply started walking
through the freezing pine forest, where they hid when it
got light.[63] Most of those who had hoped to catch trains
had been successful, and as daybreak approached, they
were well on their way to various destinations around
the Reich, including Berlin, Frankfurt (Oder), Lissa and
Breslau. Jens Müller, who was travelling with his fellow
Norwegian Per Bergsland, was initially nervous while
he waited for the train at Sagan station, and felt that his
fellow passengers were staring at him. However, he
soon discovered that this was not the case, and that the
platform was thronging with people from all over
Europe. Just after 2 a.m., their train came into the
station – somewhat surprisingly on time – and Müller
and Bergsland squeezed into a third-class compartment.
There was no illumination in the carriage, but from the
dim blue light cast by the platform lamps Müller could
just discern their fellow passengers, who were, judging
by their conversation, mainly Polish and Czech
workers. Most were slumped on the uncomfortable

benches and were trying to sleep, while others sat on suitcases or packages in the corridors. As the train rattled slowly towards Frankfurt (Oder), the only incident was the arrival of a woman with a buggy containing two children. 'She was clearly conscious of wanting to be a true German mother,' Müller recalled, 'and in an authoritative voice, she ordered those in the cabin to make room for her and her children.'[64]

Back at the camp, at 4.50 a.m. it was decided by Ker-Ramsay that the eighty-seventh man – Ken Rees – would be the last to escape.[65] Behind the ferrets' hedge, Flight Lieutenant Roy Langlois was manning the signalling rope, and had done so for at least an hour. According to Paul Brickhill, at around 4 a.m., Langlois had been horrified to witness the approach of a guard near the exit of the tunnel, who then proceeded to defecate within just 4 feet of the opening.[66] The story is now part of the legend of the Great Escape, and a less scatological version of this close shave features in many retellings. However, it is highly likely that the story is untrue, as it does not appear in the testimony of Langlois contained in the report made to the RAF, and neither does it appear in any other primary source. Its supposed verisimilitude stems from its presence in an endless validation loop of stories about the escape, stories that get a little taller upon each retelling.

What we can be sure of is that just after 5 a.m., Langlois watched as Squadron Leader Laurence Reavell-Carter heaved himself out as the seventy-sixth escapee. Reavell-Carter, who had thrown the discus at the Berlin Olympics eight years before, was disguised as a Hungarian worker and carrying a Li-lo that was intended to help him get across rivers. After receiving the 'all clear' tugs on the rope, Reavell-Carter crawled into the woods, where he awaited the arrival of the other eight members of his escaping party.[67] The next to emerge was Flight Lieutenant Alfred Ogilvie, who was wearing army battle-dress and a greatcoat, and he managed to join Reavell-Carter in the woods without any mishap, where the two men waited for Flight Lieutenant Michael Shand.[68] Shand, who was disguised as a Romanian worker, received the all clear and crawled along the ground, until he suddenly felt some more tugs on the rope.[69] Shand lay still, unable to see what was going on behind him. Further down the rope, just 5 yards from the exit, was Squadron Leader Len Trent, who was also crawling towards the woods. He too lay still when he felt the tugs.[70] The cause of Langlois's warning was the approach of a guard, who had noticed some movement in the trees and was walking towards them.[71] With the area nearly cast in daylight, Langlois could tell that the guard was looking at the track carved by the crawling escapers, and after a few more seconds, the German noticed the vapour issuing from the hole in the ground.[72] From their respective positions, Langlois, Reavell-Carter and Ogilvie watched as the guard raised his rifle and pointed it towards the ground. Reavell-Carter was the first to react. Fearing that the guard was about to shoot, he ran out of the wood shouting, 'Don't shoot! Don't shoot!' The guard let off a round, but into the air, whereupon Trent jumped up and implored him in German not to fire.[73] According to Great Escape myth, Trent's linguistic skills were less than perfect, and instead of shouting *'nicht schiessen'*, he was in fact saying *'nicht scheissen'*, and was therefore imploring the guard not to empty his bowels.[74] Two of the Kriegies decided to exploit the ensuing confusion. Michael Shand, who was nearer to cover than Trent, leaped to his feet and dashed into the woods. There, he met Alfred Ogilvie, and the two men ran in a westerly direction. Ogilvie soon tripped, and instead of waiting, Shand continued to run, and they were separated.[75]

Coming up the tunnel's exit shaft at the moment of discovery was Bob McBride, who was to be the eightieth man to leave the tunnel, albeit straight into the custody of the guard, who was now blowing his whistle and attempting to ensure that the four men – Langlois, Trent, Reavell-Carter, and McBride – did not run away. Not far behind McBride were at least half a dozen officers, who included Ken Rees, who was travelling between Leicester Square and the exit shaft when he heard the shot.[76] Without pausing, he backed up his trolley to the halfway house, whereupon two other Kriegies – Joe Moul and Clive Saxelby – shot past him on their hands and knees. 'I called to Sax, telling him to take it easy or he'd bring the damned thing down,' Rees recalled.[77] Saxelby ignored Rees, and continued to go down the tunnel in a kind of kangaroo hopping motion. Rees followed him, all the time fearing that a German would come down the tunnel and fire a shot down it. 'All I would need was to be stuck in a cave-in with a bullet up my backside,' Rees wrote.[78] In order to lessen the chances of that happening, Rees frantically tried to kick in the shoring to deliberately cause a collapse behind him, but in the true spirit of

Sod's Law, the wood wouldn't budge.[79] Eventually, Rees reached the entrance chamber, climbed up the ladder, and the tunnel was swiftly closed down, with the stove replaced over the entrance.[80]

The scene in the hut was chaotic. Not wishing to be captured with any incriminating escape equipment, the 120 remaining officers set light to their forged passes and identity documents. With eight or ten bonfires smouldering away, the building soon filled with acrid grey smoke.[81] Compasses were crushed under foot, and money was hidden in mattresses. Civilian buttons were ripped off clothes, and were either hidden or burned.[82] Some Kriegies, such as Arthur Cole, decided to try to get back to their own huts. Cole jumped through a window, and ran the 100 yards over to his block. 'I rushed across it,' he recalled, 'tripped over a tree root and fell down onto my hands, came up straight away, carried on and dived through a window into my own block and went back to my own bed.' Cole was lucky to have tripped. According to a friend who was watching Cole's private great escape, it was thanks to the offending root that Cole was not shot by a guard who was training a rifle on him from the other side of the wire.[83] After a few minutes, a guard appeared in the hut, accompanied by a dog. Uncertain of what to do, he simply ordered everyone to their rooms inside the hut, while the Kriegies found that by feeding it escape rations, the dog was just as corruptible as its human comrades.[84]

At the exit, the guard's whistled entreaties and gunshot were soon answered. A senior NCO rushed up to Unteroffizier Petzold, who was on duty at the outer gate of the north compound, and asked him where the shot had come from. Petzold directed him towards the woods. Soon afterwards, Petzold watched the NCO escort the four men to the guardroom, where they were searched by a duty officer, who found money, maps and passes stamped with 'Arbeitsamt BRESLAU' and 'Polizei BRESLAU' which stated that the men were French workers.[85] However, in his testimony, Reavell-Carter claimed that he at least was able to burn his papers and maps in the stove.[86] It mattered little, for with papers or without, nothing was going to ameliorate the ire of von Lindeiner, who had been informed by Broili of the escape at around 5.20.[87] About ten minutes later, he appeared in the guardroom with Pieber and Broili, and began to question the men. Broili demanded to know how many had escaped, a question that was met with no response. 'That will be so much the worse for you,' Broili ominously replied. At this point, von Lindeiner lost his temper, and went into a terrific rage. 'He was virtually incoherent in his speech,' said Reavell-Carter, 'and he did mention that the Gestapo would have a hand in the affair.'[88] While the four Kriegies were being shouted at, a search party was heading into the woods. It soon found numerous tracks through the snow, whose routes were later reported to be 'devious'.[89] This was a generous inter-pretation, for the snaking nature of the tracks was more a product of the escapers getting lost than deliberately leaving a trail that was hard to follow. What quickly became apparent was that a great number had escaped, and that most had headed to the station.

Surprisingly, it took the Germans almost an hour to

establish that hut 104 was the source of the tunnel. Corporal 'Charlie' Pilz had gone down the exit shaft, but so far, he had not emerged. At around 6.30, four machine guns were mounted around the block and trained on it.[90] Von Lindeiner walked in, 'wearing a face like thunder', and ordered the POWs to file out into the snow.[91] There, in addition to the machine gunners, the Kriegies were faced by eight more guards with tommy guns, and another twenty with drawn revolvers. 'They were livid,' said Alan Bryett. 'I have never seen men so annoyed. They were *furious*.'[92] Perhaps the most irate was Corporal 'Rubberneck' Griese, whose face, according to Ken Rees, had turned 'deep purple with frustrated rage'. Griese had a particular animus towards Rees, and when he saw him and Red Noble emerge from the hut, he turned a deeper shade of purple. He ordered the two men to strip off, an order which Rees and Noble followed slowly, owing to both the cold and a desire to manifest some truculence. This was too much for Griese, who barked at two guards to tear off the men's coats. 'By this time, though, I was feeling pretty fed up with being pushed around myself,' Rees recalled. 'I wrenched myself free of the guard and gave him a defiant shove.'[93] Griese went almost apoplectic, and pointed his revolver at Rees's face. Fortunately, von Lindeiner emerged from hut 104 at that moment, and ordered Griese to lower his weapon. Rees and Noble then stripped down to their underpants and vests, and were marched to the cooler.[94] 'We were bitterly disappointed after all our hard work,' said Rees. 'The hope of getting home was almost nil. It was just the thought that you were escaping, freedom as it were.

But at the time there was always the hope you'd get home.'[95]

The strip searches were endured by all those who had been found in hut 104. Von Lindeiner watched over the proceedings, still unable to contain his anger. The sounds of laughter and mockery issuing from two of the officers instantly earned them a place in the cooler along with Rees and Noble.[96] 'So you want to be out?' he said to the shivering officers. 'Wait till the Gestapo gets hold of you.'[97] Although most understandably took this as a threat, it was more likely that the Commandant was publicly anticipating that the Gestapo would take over the camp. As well as fearing for his own future, von Lindeiner felt personally let down by the Kriegies, and especially by Group Captain Massey, with whom he thought he had a rapport: 'I believed that he, being responsible for the well-being and future of so many young men, would stop them from going through with this senseless if not childish adventure. How bitterly I was deceived.'[98] During the searches, there was one moment of levity, when Major Simoleit ran out of the hut over to hut 101, in order to speak to the compound's adjutant, Squadron Leader Bill Jennens. Simoleit had to admit sheepishly that his men were still unable to find the entrance to the tunnel, and that they were worried that Corporal Pilz might be suffocating. Would it be possible, Simoleit enquired, for Jennens to open up the trap? Simoleit escorted Jennens to the hut, but when they arrived, they found that a Kriegie had taken pity on Pilz – who they had heard desperately scratching away for quite some time – and had let him out.[99]

While von Lindeiner was supervising the search, his staff were busy telephoning some forty-two agencies and offices that needed to be informed of the breakout. These included both the Kripo and the Abwehr in Breslau, Luftwaffe Inspektion 17, as well as all nearby air bases, railway stations and police stations.[100] At that time, the Germans had no precise idea of how many had escaped, but the tracks in the woods would have allowed them to estimate that the figure could be counted in tens, if not scores. As well as not knowing the number, the Germans could only assume that the officers were dressed similarly to the four who had already been captured. A cable sent a little later that day from the Sipo (Security Police) in Warsaw, and intercepted by the British, reveals quite how little the Germans knew. '. . . Apparently they had on over their uniforms overcoats smeared with sand and are pretending to be French civilian workers. Probably direction of flight BERLIN and/or BRESLAU but it is also quite possible that they are making for the General Gouvernement [occupied Poland].'[101]

Max Wielen of the Kripo received the call from the camp at around six o'clock that morning, which he immediately shared with Kriminalrat Brünner.[102] Unsure of how many officers were on the loose, Wielen's first action was to give the order for a *Kriegsfahndung*, which was a lower level of search than the all-out *Grossfahndung*. However, after discussing the matter with his colleague Kriminalkommissar Dr Günther Absalon, Wielen decided to raise the search to the full *Grossfahndung*.[103] Absalon, although junior in rank to Wielen, was undoubtedly the more intelligent. Well educated, hard-working, a successful detective, and described by his superior as 'very slick, very diligent and keen in big cases', Absalon looked as if he might go far through the ranks of the Kripo.[104] In his early thirties, tall, slim and fair, he certainly looked the part, especially when dressed in the uniform of a captain in the SS, a rank he held by virtue of his role in the Kripo. Most fittingly, von Lindeiner would later describe Absalon as a 'good German type with polished manners – the perfect drawing-room criminal'.[105] However, as none of the officers at the Breslau Kripo station could give the final authority for a nationwide search, Wielen had to contact the Kripo's head office in Berlin, which constituted Department V of Himmler's RSHA. The officer in charge of Wartime Searches was Oberregierungsrat and SS-Obersturmbannführer Dr Richard Schultze, who in turn reported to the head of the Kripo, SS-Gruppenführer and Police General Arthur Nebe.[106]

One of the Third Reich's more enigmatic and contradictory figures, Nebe had been a career detective in the Kripo since 1920, and had joined the Nazi Party in 1931. However, he claimed to renounce his Nazism when in 1934 he was ordered – and had refused – to kill Hitler's rival, Gregor Strasser. Despite his supposed animus towards the regime, Nebe nevertheless radiated enough apparent loyalty to command one of the murderous *Einsatzgruppen* in Russia. However, in private, Nebe's doubts saw him forge contacts with resisters such as Hans Bernd Gisevius and Hans Oster, who were part of a conspiracy to overthrow Hitler that would famously come to fruition four months after the

Great Escape.[107] It was Nebe, then, who gave the authorisation for a *Grossfahndung*, but as we shall see, Nebe was to play a far more critical role in determining the fates of those on the run.

In the camp, the strip searches were completed by about eight thirty, after which the officers were sent for a photographic check. Finally, at eleven o'clock, nearly six hours after the discovery of the tunnel, a roll-call was held.[108] Despite the cold, this was one *Appell* that the Kriegies were happy to let drag on, and they took their time lining up, much to the frustration of the Germans, who grew increasingly annoyed. After taking a count, it was established that some seventy-six men had escaped, but the trickier challenge facing von Lindeiner and his men was establishing their identities. In order to make matters more difficult, many officers had deliberately altered their appearance – beards had been shaved off or grown, and moustaches had turned into beards or had simply been dispensed with. 'All this sounds remarkably stupid and petty,' said Alan Bryett, 'but it was vital because it delayed for hours the actual assessing of which people had got out.'[109] In order not to alert the Germans before the escape, the X Committee had made sure that not every Kriegie had practised such radical facial topiary. But for those who did get rid of their beards, the process was not entirely pleasant. The only barber-shop implements available were scissors and blunt razors, and many were sporting sore faces as they waited in the cold.[110] But such pain was as nothing compared to that felt by one man on that parade ground: Colonel von Lindeiner. He knew that his career was in ruins, and by nine o'clock that morning he had already personally telephoned Luftwaffe Inspektion 17 asking for the normal legal proceedings to be instigated against him in the event of a mass escape.[111] More than anything else, von Lindeiner felt let down. 'The result was shocking,' he later wrote. 'Seventy-six men were missing. For me, what was personally distressing was the revelation that for the last six weeks, the warnings that I had expressed with such deep seriousness to those responsible for the POWs were just like grass in the wind.'[112]

Chapter Ten

Early Fallers

ALTHOUGH MOST OF the escapers preferred to travel either in pairs or singly, some officers thought that it would be safer to form larger groups. Between around 1.15 a.m. and 1.45 a.m., a party of some twelve assembled in the woods, all of whom were disguised as foreign workers from a local mill going on leave.[1] The group included: Johnny Bull; Johnny Dodge; Jimmy James; Flight Lieutenants James Wernham, Bernard Green, Reginald Kierath and Antoni Kiewnarski; Lieutenant Douglas Poynter; Flying Officers Kazimierz Pawluk and Jerzy Mondschein; Pilot Officer Sotiris Skanziklas; and Squadron Leader John Williams.[2] Once again, this collection reveals quite how cosmopolitan the Great Escape really was. Of these men, just half were British, and the rest were Australian, Polish and Greek. Rather than catching a train at Sagan station, this group walked nearly 5 miles southeast to the small station at the hamlet of Tschiebsdorf.[3] As they walked, it quickly became apparent just how bleak the conditions were. 'Once we came to a clearing across which the north wind cut like a knife,' Jimmy James recalled. 'Several voices were raised in anguish.'[4] At Tschiebsdorf, Mondschein bought the entire party third-class rail tickets to the small village of Boberrohrsdorf, some 45 miles southeast of Tschiebsdorf, and 4 miles west of the large town and major railway junction of Hirschberg.[5] Alighting at Boberrohrsdorf meant that the escapers would not be subject to any security checks at a larger station and, by all accounts, the party left the train without any incident at some point between nine o'clock and eleven o'clock. It was here that the group split up.[6]

Douglas Poynter decided to travel alone, and after walking through the picturesque Boberrohrsdorf and crossing the river, he spent the day hiding in a wood on the village's southern outskirts. At four o'clock, Poynter made his move, and headed southwest across country. Unfortunately, it began to snow, and even for a healthy 24-year-old, the going was exceptionally tough. Protected only by his adapted naval uniform and a camp-made cloth cap, Poynter certainly felt the extreme cold, and after walking some 7½ miles and reaching the railway line between Hirschberg and the Czech village of Polaun,[7] he felt completely exhausted. Eschewing his role as a hard-arser, Poynter opted to travel by train, and he bought a third-class ticket for Polaun from a nearby station, possibly that at Petersdorf.[8] The train arrived at six o'clock, just after he had bought his ticket, which meant that a policeman on duty at the station was only able to give his papers a cursory glance.

As the train snaked its way over the Reisengebirge mountain range that marked the boundary between Germany and the Protectorate of Bohemia and Moravia, Poynter might have felt that he was making some significant progress. However, at around nine o'clock, two policemen and a member of the Hitler Youth boarded the train, and proceeded to examine everybody's papers. The policemen looked at his documents closely, and returned them, declaring that they were in order. The Hitler Youth then studied them and, showing a keener eye than those of his elders, spotted a defect. Poynter was arrested, but he continued to protest his innocence and maintained that he was a French worker on leave. At the next stop, Poynter was removed from the train and taken to the police station at Hammersdorf, where he was searched, interrogated and accused of having escaped from Stalag Luft III.[9] Poynter denied the accusation, whereupon the police decided to send him to the Kripo headquarters at Hirschberg. Two soldiers soon arrived to collect him, but just before he left Hammersdorf, Poynter finally admitted to the chief of police that he had indeed escaped from Sagan. Late that night, or possibly in the small hours of the following day, Poynter found himself incarcerated in Hirschberg, his only bitter-sweet consolation being that he was in good company: seven other members of the group were also being held there.[10]

Among them were Johnny Dodge and James Wernham, who had chosen to travel together after leaving the train at Boberrohrsdorf. The two men had walked down the river from the village to a small station on the outskirts of Hirschberg, where at around two o'clock Wernham had unsuccessfully tried to buy tickets to a town on the Czech frontier. Rather than risk heading into Hirschberg proper, Dodge and Wernham walked northwest along a main road, but, as so many of the escapers, they found they were ill equipped for tramping through snow, and they decided to chance their luck at the main station. Once again, Wernham was unable to buy tickets, but Dodge had better luck, and managed to get tickets to a town near the frontier, which was likely to have been Schreiberhau.[11] At four o'clock, the men boarded their carriage, but before the train had even departed, they found themselves being questioned by a plain-clothed policeman, who asked them where they were going, what they were doing, and who they were going to meet. Dodge and Wernham did their best, but the policeman was unimpressed, and they were arrested and taken to the railway station's police office. After being interrogated for around fifteen minutes, the two men admitted their real identities, and were transferred to the Kripo headquarters.[12]

Also present were Jimmy James, Green, Pawluk, Skanziklas and Kiewnarski. Like Dodge, Wernham and Poynter, James and Skanziklas had found that hard-arsing was physically dangerous, if not impossible. After they had left Boberrohrsdorf station, they tried to make their way south across country to the border, but they were defeated by the cold and the snow, which was sometimes at waist height.[13] As with all the other hard-arsers, James and Skanziklas were hardly dressed for

traversing snow-covered mountain ranges, with James
merely sporting a modified RAF officer's tunic and – of
all things – a pair of Middle East tropical trousers.[14] 'I
had been used to Canadian winters of 30°F and more
below zero,' James recalled, 'but I began to see that survival might be in question for both of us, with our
limited rations and thin clothing, if we went on over the
mountains in these conditions.'[15] After a few hours, the
two men decided to head down to Hirschberg, from
where they hoped to catch a train to take them across
the border. When they arrived at the ticket office at
around five thirty that afternoon, their dishevelled
appearance attracted the attention of a policeman, who
demanded to see their papers. Within less than
a minute, the two men had been arrested and they were
taken to the Kripo headquarters.[16]

The experience of the 56-year-old Bernard Green
illustrates with even more clarity quite how badly prepared and purposeless so many of the escapers were. At
Boberrohrsdorf station, Green watched most of the
party turn left out of the station and head towards
the village, whereas he noticed that Bull and
Mondschein turned right to take a road that bore west.
Green followed them for around 200–300 yards, but he
lost them at a bend, and chose – for no apparent reason
– to walk north on his own. 'It was heavy going as the
roads were thick with snow,' he said, 'but I gradually
worked my way round south again so that I approached
the village . . . from the north.' Like Poynter, Green then
hid in a wood, and watched the village for about two
hours, during which time he weighed up his options.
Realising that the snow made it impossible to skirt

round Boberrohrsdorf, Green decided to simply walk through the village. He managed to cross the bridge over the river with no difficulty, but just as he was on the verge of leaving, he was stopped by a German soldier on police duty, who asked him for his papers. When Green informed him that he was heading for Czechoslovakia, the soldier enquired as to why Green had left his train at Boberrohrsdorf. Green replied that he had lost all his money gambling, and could only afford to travel so far, an explanation that did little to convince the soldier, who escorted him to the post office, from where several calls were made. One of these was to the police station at Hirschberg, a place where Green soon found himself being interrogated before being locked up at the Kripo HQ with his seven fellow escapers.[17]

At the headquarters, the first to be questioned was Jimmy James, who was led through the door of an anteroom marked 'Kriminal Polizei' and then into a larger room in which a slight, bald-headed, bespectacled man wearing a suit was sitting behind a desk. Although James later suspected that the man was from the Gestapo, he has yet to be identified, and it is more likely that the official was indeed a member of the Kripo.[18] Also in the room were, as James later described, 'various other people', including a typist.[19] The small man fired out a number of questions, requesting details about the tunnel, the number of escapers, and what time James had left the tunnel. James refused to supply any details, and told the man that escaping was a military occupation, which earned him a 'disparaging interjection' from the official, in which he accused the

Kriegies of acting like 'boy scouts'. Eventually, the small man's patience expired, and he ordered James to be thrown into a cell, whereupon he fell asleep. After two hours, James was awoken, and re-interrogated by the small man, although on this occasion his presence was supplemented by some figures wearing SS uniforms. James was tired and dazed, and the small man took advantage of his state by screaming and shouting at him. Nevertheless, James remained tight-lipped, and he was sent back to the cells.[20]

The other seven prisoners received similar treatment, although it appears that only James was interrogated twice. Some recalled a second interrogator who was a tall, thin, grey-haired man, with an aquiline face and long fingers, who spoke English with a drawling voice from a curved mouth which bore a cynical expression.[21] In a mixture of German and poor English, Douglas Poynter was asked where he had been heading; why he was going south; whether he had been ordered to escape; whether he was heading to the same location as the other escapers; and the source of his civilian clothes and his identity papers. He was warned that being in possession of such papers was dangerous, as the Germans had no way of establishing whether Poynter really was an escaped British officer.[22] The prisoners found this element of their interrogation menacing, as it seemed to suggest that the Germans were trying to establish whether the men were acting as spies or saboteurs rather than as mere escapers.[23] Apart from that of James, none of the interrogations seemed to last particularly long – that of Green was just twenty minutes[24] – and the Kriegies suffered neither acts nor threats of violence. In this instance, it would appear that the Kripo – and possibly the Gestapo – broke no international conventions regarding the treatment of POWs. Darkly hinting that the men might be suspected of attempted espionage or sabotage should be seen – at this stage of events – as nothing more than a form of aggressive questioning that intimated the prospect of capital punishment in order to loosen a prisoner's tongue. After all, the British did the same at Camp 020, the interrogation centre in south London for captured Axis agents.[25]

After the interrogations, the eight men were then handcuffed and marched to Hirschberg gaol and placed in a single cell. Six of the men slept on mattresses on the floor, with the other two sharing a wooden bench. The only thing that brought any form of respite from the harsh conditions was the presence of an attractive young Polish woman who brought them their food. 'Even the forbidding presence of the Meister [chief warder] could not detract from the pleasure of my first contact with the opposite sex for four years,' recalled Jimmy James.[26]

In total, none of those held at Hirschberg had travelled much further than 50 miles, and they had spent, on average, around fifteen hours on the run. It was evident that the most redoubtable enemy faced by the escapers was the weather, although the effects of the *Grossfahndung* were all too apparent. Had the weather been better, then it is feasible that the eight men might have avoided capture for longer by skirting around trains and major towns, but walking through rural communities – which are famously wary of strangers –

had its own risks. To be blunt, their chances were absurdly poor, and even if the object had simply been in some way to hamper the German war effort, there seems to be little evidence that the actions of these eight men struck even the lightest of blows against the German Reich. Such an assertion may seem unduly harsh, but the notion of 'keeping the Germans busy' was, after all, one of the reasons why Bushell had chosen to organise a mass breakout, and it is upon those reasons that the escape should be judged.

Captured POWs were not the only ones the Germans were interrogating. From around midday on the 25th, the camp started to receive many visitors who were focusing their attention not upon the Kriegies, but upon those who were guarding them. The first to arrive was Colonel Ernst Wälde of Luftwaffe Inspektion 17, who was tasked with producing a report for Hermann Göring himself. An hour later saw the arrival of four members of the Breslau Kripo and Gestapo: Brünner, Absalon, Kriminalsekretär Scholz and Kriminalinspektor Hänsel.[27] One of the POWs, George Atkinson, witnessed their arrival. 'They certainly fitted the bill,' he recalled. 'There was a little chap with a cloak and all the equipment one associates with the Gestapo on the official illustrations of them. They were in charge, and were very heated under the collar.'[28] Unsurprisingly, Absalon and Brünner strongly suspected that there had been a significant degree of complicity between the guards and their prisoners and, as we have already seen, their suspicions were correct. After making some initial enquiries, it soon became apparent to the Kripo team that their investigations would take some time, and Absalon swiftly established an office in the Sagan police station just off the market square, and staffed it with Scholz, two other assistants and a female typist.[29] For the next few weeks, Absalon and his team would question scores of members of the camp staff, but he would find progress frustratingly slow. He soon discovered that not only were those he questioned unwilling to betray each other, but also that his best witnesses could only be found among the POWs, none of whom was likely to cooperate with a Kripo investigation.[30] That afternoon saw one more arrival of note: that of Colonel Müller, the chief of staff of the Inspector General of the Prisoner-of-War Organisation, and Adolf Hitler's special envoy, General Otto Röttig.[31]

The next day, Sunday 26 March, von Lindeiner received two staff officers from the Luftgau-Kommando III as well as the Deputy Judge Advocate General, Dr Garbe. The three men issued the Commandant with a writ that relieved von Lindeiner of his command, and also ordered him to remain in the camp until the court-martial proceedings had started.[32] The writ also stipulated that his duties should be taken over by the next senior officer, which resulted in Lieutenant Colonel Erich Cordes stepping into von Lindeiner's boots. This was an unfortunate appointment, as Cordes had only been posted to the camp for training purposes, and knew little about how to manage Kriegies.[33] For von Lindeiner, the strain was unbearable, and he found himself incapable of resting or eating properly for many days after the escape. On 29 March, he collapsed with severe heart palpitations, and he was only saved by the actions of a doctor who was living a few rooms away. He was dispatched to his home, Jeschkendorf Manor, where he was told to recuperate, and to prepare himself for his court martial.[34]

That Sunday morning also marked the departure from the camp of Colonels Wälde and Müller.[35] Both men filed their reports to their immediate superiors, and by that afternoon, their words were being discussed by Hitler, Himmler, Göring and Field Marshal Wilhelm Keitel, the Supreme Commander of the German armed forces, at the Berghof, Hitler's home in the Bavarian Alps above Berchtesgaden. The breakout had come at a particularly bad time for the German leader. On the Eastern Front, the 1st Panzer Army was in danger of being encircled by the Soviets, and just a few days before, Hitler had summoned his field marshals to the Berghof to sign a document declaring their loyalty.[36] The Allied bombing raids had hardly improved his temper, and furthermore, Hitler's health was suffering, and he had been too ill to address the nation on Heroes' Memorial Day on 12 March.[37] Furthermore, Hitler was in a mood for reprisal. Just three days before, on the evening of 23 March, he had given the order for thirty Italians to be shot for each of the thirty-three German policemen who had been killed by a partisan bomb in Rome that morning. The German revenge, he said, 'would make the world tremble' and a quarter of Rome should be destroyed.[38]

As no minutes were ever made of the meeting between these four men, it is hard to establish precisely what course the discussion took. After the war at the International Military Tribunal at Nuremberg, Göring would mendaciously claim that he had not been present, and Keitel's account of the meeting was enormously at odds with how he had reported it to a fellow officer immediately afterwards.[39] What is clear is that Himmler, Göring and Keitel each abnegated responsibility for the escape and passed the buck. Both Göring and Himmler reprimanded Keitel for allowing so many prisoners to escape, a charge refuted by the Field Marshal, who declared that his command had nothing to do with the camp. Keitel indicated that responsibility lay at the feet of Göring, as the camp was run by the Luftwaffe.[40] According to many accounts, an infuriated Hitler stopped the bickering by issuing a very straightforward order: all those recaptured should be shot.[41] The brutality of Hitler's order was true to his customary form, and it seems not one of those gathered openly disagreed, and they only raised questions of practicality rather than principle. Göring merely argued that shooting all those recaptured would look suspicious. Hitler agreed, and ordered that the number should be reduced to 'more than half', which the men in the room found more palatable.[42] The story of Göring's cynical suggestion is perhaps apocryphal, as there is no record of it in any primary source, and it first appears in Paul Brickhill's book *The Great Escape*, after which the story was recycled *ad nauseam*. Keitel's response to Hitler's order is also unclear, although it is commonly assumed that he manifested his usual obsequiousness in front of his Führer, and readily agreed to the shootings.[43] Again, there is no evidence for this response, and in his testimony at Nuremberg, Keitel was adamant that he had objected to Hitler's order. 'I said that this procedure was impossible,' Keitel would later testify. 'The general excitement led Hitler to declare again and with considerable emphasis, "I am ordering you to retain them, Himmler; you are not to give them up."'[44] The Field Marshal then went on to claim that he in fact wanted to save some of the prisoners, and that it was thanks to him that the numbers to be killed were reduced: 'I put up a fight for the men who had already come back and who should, according to the original order, be brought out again and handed over to the police. I succeeded in doing it; but I could not do anything more.'[45] The notion that Keitel, who would later be hanged as a major war criminal, was acting out of a humanitarian concern for RAF 'terror fliers' seems questionable, but, according to one of his officers, Keitel did indeed seek to save some of the recaptured escapers by insisting that any prisoners who had been detained by members of the armed forces were to be sent back to the camp rather than handed over to the Kripo or the Gestapo.[46] Those who seek to exculpate Keitel look to his testimony at Nuremberg as evidence that the Field Marshal was extremely reluctant to have anything to do with the shootings, but this goes against what we know of Keitel's pliable nature and willingness to sign orders of similar murderousness.[47] Whatever the nature of the conversation that took place that day in the Berghof, the end result was the same: more than half of any of those recaptured were to be shot.

After the meeting, Keitel summoned two senior officers, General von Grävenitz, the head of the prisoner inspectorate of the OKW (the Supreme Command of the Armed Forces), and von Grävenitz's deputy, Major

General Adolf Westhoff. When the two men entered the room, they found their superior agitated and nervous.

'Gentlemen, this is a bad business!' Keitel announced. 'This morning, Göring reproached me in the presence of Himmler for having let some more POWs escape. It was unheard of.'

The Field Marshal described how Himmler had also complained, and then declared, 'Gentlemen, these escapes must stop. We must set an example. We shall take very severe measures. I can only tell you that the men who have escaped will be shot; probably the majority of them are dead already.'

Von Grävenitz was appalled, and he said as much.

'But, sir, that's out of the question. Escape isn't a dishonourable offence. That is specifically laid down in the [Geneva] Convention.'

'I don't care a damn,' Keitel snapped back. 'We discussed it in the Führer's presence and it cannot be altered.'[48]

Privately, von Grävenitz promised that if any escapers were captured by the Wehrmacht, they would be handed back to the camp rather than to the Kripo and the Gestapo. 'In this particular case only those caught by our people were brought back to the camp,' Major General Westhoff recalled, 'that is, those caught by soldiers.'[49]

No matter how decently Keitel's underlings would claim to behave, the matter was largely out of their hands. The following morning, that of Monday 27 March, Himmler personally addressed a top-secret order to the head of the RSHA, SS-Obergruppenführer and General der Polizei Ernst Kaltenbrunner, which was only to be distributed to heads of departments.

The increase of escapes by officer POWs is a menace to internal security. I am disappointed and indignant about the inefficient security measures. As a deterrent, the Führer has ordered that more than half of the escaped officers are to be shot. Therefore I order that Department V [the Kripo] hand over for interrogation to Department IV [the Gestapo] more than half of the recaptured officers. After interrogation the officers are to be returned to their original camp and to be shot en route. The shootings will be explained by the fact that the recaptured officers were shot whilst trying to escape, or because they offered resistance, so that nothing can be proved later. Department IV will report the shootings to Department V, giving this reason. In the event of future escapes, my decision will be awaited as to whether the same procedure is to be adopted. Prominent personalities will be exempted, their names will be reported to me and my decision awaited.[50]

This text would become known as the notorious 'Sagan Order', and it exemplifies like few other documents the brutality and deceitfulness at the heart of the Third Reich. One of its more noteworthy and repellent features is the insistence on faux-legality, in which departments were ordered to produce reports that both the sender and the recipient knew to be false.

Throughout that day, several meetings were held in the headquarters of the RSHA on Prinz-Albrechtstrasse in Berlin. One was called by von Grävenitz, although he did not personally attend; he was represented by Colonel von Reurmont. Colonel Wälde was also present, as were Arthur Nebe and the chief of the

Gestapo, Heinrich Müller, both of whom, as heads of departments, had seen the Sagan Order. The meeting was told of the conference that had taken place at the Berghof the previous day, although according to Wälde, the precise nature of the measures decided upon was not disclosed. It was only towards the end of the meeting that Müller announced that some ten to fifteen escapers had already been shot. This remark caused, claimed Wälde, a 'shattering effect', as it became clear what had been decided upon, and that the decision had been made by the 'highest authority'.[51] Müller's assertion that some of the officers had been shot by the time of the meeting was incorrect, but his words would prove prophetic. Wälde was so appalled by what he heard that he informed his superior, Lieutenant General Walter Grosch, who in turn complained to his superior, General Helmuth Förster, that the order contravened the Geneva Convention. Förster reported the matter to Field Marshal Erhard Milch, whose next line of action, in the words of a later investigation, 'would be to approach Göring and so complete the circle of complete stagnation'. In fact, there is no record that either Milch or Förster took the matter any further.[52]

Another meeting held that day was between Arthur Nebe, Oberregierungsrat Richard Schultze and Max Wielen, who had been telegraphed at noon to report to Berlin. Wielen arrived at Nebe's bomb-damaged office on Werderscher Markt after a long train journey at around eight thirty that evening, whereupon the head of the Kripo offered him a seat on a red leather sofa and restorative coffee and sandwiches.[53] Nebe told Wielen about the meeting at the Berghof, and then showed him the Sagan Order. Wielen later stated that Nebe 'appeared shocked at this order; he was very distressed'.[54] He subsequently heard that Nebe had had trouble sleeping, and had camped out on the sofa in his office for 'nights on end', although Nebe's unsettled condition may have been more a product of overwork and having to fight a turf war with Heinrich Müller, who was trying to absorb the Kripo into the Gestapo.[55] Wielen himself claimed to be very much against the idea of executing recaptured officers. 'I was too appalled at the horrible step to be taken and opposed its execution,' he stated. 'I said that it was against the laws of war and that it was bound to lead to reprisals against our own officers, who were prisoners-of-war in English camps, and that I absolutely refused to take any responsibility.'[56] Dr Schultze nodded at Wielen's objection, but said little or nothing. Nebe told Wielen that it was not possible to ascertain whether the order was actually against the Geneva Convention, which Wielen must have known to be a lie.[57] 'We have no possibility to check the legality of this action at all,' Nebe declared, 'maybe we are dealing here with the question of reprisals. We cannot refer the matter to any other authority. Ways, measures and means of high policy cannot be checked or controlled by us.'[58] So spoke the former leader of an *Einsatzgruppe*. Nebe then further attempted to reassure Wielen by telling him that he would in fact be taking no responsibility, as the Gestapo would be acting 'completely independently' and besides, there was no way of disobeying an order that had come straight from Hitler, otherwise Wielen would 'have to bear the consequences', which, according to Wielen, meant facing an SS court martial and being shot.[59] All Wielen had to do was to 'preserve absolute secrecy' and not to make 'difficulties vis-à-vis the Staatspolizei [the Gestapo]'.[60] If those were indeed Nebe's words, then what he was effectively asking Wielen was to hand over men caught by the Breslau Kripo to the Gestapo, and therefore to send them to their deaths. It is hard to see how such an order absolved Wielen of any responsibility for the intended murders.

At the end of the meeting Wielen was dismissed and took the night train back to Breslau. When he returned home, he spoke to his wife, and told her that he thanked God he had not been asked to carry out the executions himself, as he would not have been able to do so.[61] 'My husband was mortified,' said Eva Wielen later, 'he was terrified and deeply shocked about this order.'[62] After catching up on some sleep the following morning, he telephoned Dr Wilhelm Scharpwinkel, his opposite number at the Breslau Gestapo, and asked him whether he had received any orders from Heinrich Müller. Scharpwinkel denied any knowledge, and asked Wielen to see him, which merely involved Wielen crossing the road. 'I told him what I had heard in Berlin,' said Wielen. 'I declare explicitly that I had no instructions to do so, but the case in question was of such an extremely singular nature that I felt I had to tell him about the Führer order.'

'I'll do this personally,' said Scharpwinkel, who then repeated his words. 'I'll do this personally.'[63]

While the Germans were haggling over the bureaucratic niceties of mass murder, many of their intended victims were being caught easily. By the evening of Monday 27th, just under seventy-two hours since the tunnel broke, sixty-one of the seventy-six Kriegies on the run had been recaptured.[64] They included Flight Lieutenants Edgar Humphreys and Paul Royle, who were among the hard-arsers, and, like so many other Kriegies, neither man had a well-developed escape plan. 'We walked south, and not north, and that's about as good as it was,' said Royle.[65] Both men found the temperatures so low and energy-sapping that they ate their rations within two hours, and when daylight broke, they rested up in a pine forest. After trying to sleep, the two men continued at nightfall, but at around two thirty in the morning of 26 March, they were stopped near Tiefenfurt, some 16 miles south of Sagan, by a member of the Landwacht, the German Home Guard.[66] 'Somebody just came up and captured us,' Royle recalled. 'Some old chap, he just got us, and that was that.'[67] A policeman and a soldier then took the two men to the small police station in the village, where they were given a perfunctory search, and then placed in a cell. Within thirty minutes, they were joined by another escaper, Flight Lieutenant Albert Armstrong.[68] Like Humphreys and Royle, Armstrong had done little more than head south, although he had mostly travelled alone. Stymied by too many snowdrifts, he decided to walk along a road, with the perhaps predictable result that he was stopped by members of the Landwacht at 2 a.m. on 26 March.[69] A few hours later, the cell was augmented by Ernst Valenta and Johnny Marshall, who, after failing to catch their train at Sagan station, had walked south until lying up in a pine forest at

9 a.m. 'We hid in a fir plantation all that day,' Marshall recalled, 'during which time it snowed heavily and we suffered badly from exposure and cold.' They set off again in the evening, but at 4 a.m., they were stopped by two members of the Landwacht and escorted to the cell at Tiefenfurt.[70] Because of the ineffectiveness of the Landwacht searches, the officers were able to burn and destroy their papers and escape equipment, although they kept their money, and Armstrong managed to reconvert his tunic so that he once more looked like an airman.[71]

Later that morning, the five escapers were taken by five uniformed policemen in a van to Sagan, where they were put in a police cell, and then completely stripped and searched. At the police station they were joined by ten other officers, and at eleven o'clock that night, a group of nineteen escapees were taken in a lorry 40 miles south to Görlitz. Before they left, a worried Colonel von Lindeiner telephoned Kriminalkommissar Absalon and asked for the prisoners to be returned to the camp, but Absalon refused, saying that since von Lindeiner was suspended, he was under no obligation to listen to his instructions.[72] The van was escorted by cars containing uniformed police armed with machine guns, and at 2.30 a.m. on the morning of 27 March, the men were placed three or four to a cell in Görlitz's civilian prison.

Royle shared his cell with Alfred Ogilvie and Flight Lieutenant Charles Hall.[73] The story of Ogilvie's escape attempt was sadly similar to that of so many others. After becoming separated from Michael Shand in the woods, Ogilvie walked south, spent the day hiding in the woods, and was captured at dawn on 26 March by a member of the Landwacht outside the small town of Halbau, 10 miles south of Sagan. Ogilvie was taken to an inn, where he was interrogated, and after two hours he was joined by Hall, Flight Lieutenant A. B. Thompson and Flight Lieutenant Brian Evans.[74] Thompson had also been caught on the 26th near Halbau by a member of the Landwacht, who were proving to be extremely capable at spotting the escapees.[75] All these escapers were transferred to Görlitz. Michael Shand had fared somewhat better, and by eight o'clock on the morning of 29 March, he had reached Kohlfurt, some 28 miles south of Sagan.[76] However, while he was hiding near the railway station waiting for a goods train, he was discovered by a railway worker, and by that evening he too found himself in Görlitz.[77]

The area around Halbau also marked the nemesis of the escape of Richard Churchill and Thomas 'Bob' Nelson, who, like nearly all the other hard-arsers, had headed south. Not wishing to leave tracks in the firebreaks in the forests, Churchill and Nelson battled their way through undergrowth, which naturally resulted in their making slow progress. After resting during the day, they decided the following night to walk down the firebreaks and occasionally head off into the undergrowth in order to confuse any pursuers.[78] As well as the snow and the undergrowth, other natural obstacles came in the form of rivers and streams, which, owing to the melting snow, were extremely full. With bridges likely to be guarded, Churchill and Nelson realised that fording was their only option, and consequently their trousers and boots quickly became wet as they struggled through water and bog that came up to their knees. At one point that night they came to a large river or a canal. Churchill told Nelson to stay behind while he went to examine it. 'I then crept forward on hands and knees to this river,' said Churchill, 'and putting out my hand I found that it was very hard, which was a surprise. It turned out to be the main autobahn running into Poland.'[79] Confirmation that the supposed body of water was a road came in the form of an approaching car, which caused Churchill to retreat back to Nelson's hiding place, where the two men discussed their options. After deciding to cross the road, they carried on plodding through the woods, but their progress was excruciatingly slow. The men faced a dilemma: either stick to the woods and make a small amount of distance from the camp; or risk walking along a road, where there were bound to be checkpoints. They opted for the latter, and although they were not stopped, what slowed them down was the cold and a lack of water. 'We were in a very bad condition in relation to exposure,' said Nelson, 'so we decided that we'd have to seek some shelter even if it meant an increased risk.'[80]

In the early hours of the morning of Sunday 26 March, an exhausted Churchill and Nelson burrowed their way into a barn stuffed full of hay, where they intended to stay until the hue and cry had died down. They stripped off their wet clothes and managed to warm themselves up, but their bigger problem was still thirst. After it had grown dark, they crept into a nearby village, where they found a water pump. Despite dogs barking, the two men worked the pump, which, in the words of

Churchill, 'creaked and squeaked most alarmingly'.[81]
Surprisingly, no villager appeared to wake, and the
escapees returned to their lodging. '[It was] a very risky
thing to do,' Nelson recalled, 'because we knew we
were increasing the risk of capture. But we were really
in a bad shape at this stage.'[82] At around noon on the
27th, the officers heard the sound of locals searching
through the hay with pitchforks. Churchill and Nelson
remained still, hoping not to be impaled and that the
search would not be thorough. Unfortunately, it was,
and the pair were ignominiously hauled out of the hay,
and walked down to an inn in a village near Halbau,
where the men managed to hide their false papers
behind a piano. At one o'clock, the Burgomaster of
Halbau collected them and drove them to Sagan
police station, from where they were transferred to
Görlitz.[83]

Also held in Görlitz were Flight Lieutenants Anthony
Bethell and James 'Cookie' Long, who had been
captured on 28 March. After leaving the tunnel at
around 4 a.m. as the sixty-fifth man out, Bethell's job
was to assemble a team of ten men and to lead them
towards open country to the south and west of the
camp. The plan was to avoid both the railway station
and a guarded electrical transformer by walking north
for 200–300 yards, then heading west, and then walking south through a stretch of open country between the
Russian compound and a railway line running southwest. 'What was proposed and what happened were at
variance,' Bethell later drily declared. As the group
walked north, they heard a shot ringing out behind
them – presumably that let off by the guard when he

discovered the tunnel – and the men scattered. Bethell found himself with Long running through some kind of rubbish dump near the Russian camp, and through sheer luck they eventually managed to find themselves in open country. Bethell later ruefully reflected that his leadership of the team 'was hardly a model of navigation or of execution'.[84]

The two men walked north for 1¼ miles, before deciding to rest up for the day. They hid themselves in a fir-tree plantation, and made themselves as comfortable as possible by using branches as bedding. 'With good boots on and warm clothing we were in reasonable shape for a daylight wait,' Bethell recalled. However, there was one discomforting element: answering the call of nature. After clearing some snow, and dropping his trousers, Bethell realised that he had put his underpants on beneath a woolly one-piece combination. As a result, he had to strip almost completely in order to be able to defecate. 'It was a long and cold exercise!' he observed. That night, Long and Bethell headed northwest along the Frankfurt (Oder) railway line. After walking for some 10 miles, they arrived at a barn on the southern outskirts of Benau at about 6 a.m. on 26 March.[85] They climbed up into the hayloft, ate some raisins, dry porridge and chocolate, covered themselves in hay and fell asleep. At one point, somebody entered the barn, but if they were searching for escapers, they were not looking very hard, and Bethell and Long remained undisturbed.

That night, the two men headed towards Benau, which they hoped to circumnavigate as they journeyed north. However, the going was immensely difficult, as the thaw had turned the ploughed fields into near quagmires. 'Each step required effort and we were getting nowhere fast,' wrote Bethell. 'We were also getting very, very wet and dirty.'[86] Realising that they were wasting their time, the two men returned to the barn at 4 a.m. on 27 March and spent the day drying out. With the conditions so terrible, the pair decided to try to stow away on a slow-moving freight train. Although they had originally intended to go to Czechoslovakia, they now hoped to reach Stettin, from where they could find a boat to take them to Sweden. That night they walked to a nearby marshalling yard, but the only trains they saw were travelling too quickly, and all Bethell and Long could do was to crouch down in wet bushes as the locomotives steamed past.[87] Once again, frustrated, damp and miserable, Bethell and Long returned to 'their' barn. They discussed their options, and decided that their only course was to travel by daylight, and so, at around 11 a.m. on 28 March, they tried for a second time to skirt around Benau.

The two men headed for some woods to the west of the village, and for a couple of hours, their luck held. However, at around 2 p.m., just as they were walking down a cart track that led to the railway line, they suddenly heard a voice behind them shouting, 'Halt!' They turned to see two members of the German Home Guard pointing their rifles and advancing towards them. Bethell and Long put their hands up, and as they were frogmarched down into Benau, a slow-moving freight train trundled past them. 'It was not our day!' Bethell rued. After being shut in the village's small jail, the two Kriegies were transferred to Sorau, before being

sent back down to Sagan. There, the two men expected
to end up in the cooler at the camp, but instead, on the
evening of 29 March, they were taken to Görlitz.[88]

Among their fellow prisoners at Görlitz were Flying
Officers Henry Birkland and Denys Street, and Flight
Lieutenant Leslie Brodrick, whose escape attempt was
perhaps the most pitiful of all. After splitting up from a
larger group, the officers walked south in an attempt to
reach the Czech border. Like their fellow hard-arsers,
the men rested during the day, and at around 5 p.m.
they once more set off. 'That was a bad night,' said
Brodrick, 'because we couldn't get out of this forested
land and the trees seemed closer and the snow seemed
deeper and pretty soon we were just struggling along,
stopping every fifty yards.'[89] The only water they had to
drink came from ditches, and the men found that they
were not as fit and as strong as they had thought. On
the morning of the 26th, the trio hid inside some
bushes, and spent the day doing their best to keep
warm. 'It was so miserable and cold,' Brodrick recalled,
'everything was wet through, the blanket roll was as
heavy as lead.'[90] Because of the cold, the men started
walking again before nightfall, but their progress was
agonisingly slow. In the middle of the night, Birkland
grew delirious and began talking to himself, and whenever the party stopped, it grew increasingly difficult to
make him continue. Street and Brodrick eventually
realised that the situation was hopeless. 'We decided to
give ourselves up,' Brodrick recalled, 'as we were wet
and suffering from the effects of the cold.'[91] They
approached a cottage, in which they soon discovered
that four soldiers were billeted. The escapees were

promptly arrested and taken to the local police station, where they managed to destroy their false papers in a fire. 'In two and a half days we'd covered only two or three kilometres,' said Brodrick. 'I don't think we really thought we'd make it. I mean it's a bit stupid, isn't it, to walk down to Czechoslovakia?'[92]

Although Brodrick's estimate of the distance the three men covered is excessively low, the experience of the three men shows just how unlikely it was for the hard-arsers to make any significant progress, let alone to 'keep the Germans busy'. The fact that the three men gave themselves up is indicative of – to use Brodrick's words – quite how 'stupid' the plan really was. Even with better weather, the men's chances would have still been poor, as they lacked suitable supplies and clothing. Had the escape taken place later in the year, when the weather was warmer, the hard-arsers would have been exposed to more daylight hours, and having to pass incognito through rural areas in which the population would have been working outside. Come snow or shine, the hard-arsers' task was both almost impossible and entirely pointless. Any sense of freedom was entirely illusory. As Brodrick was to observe, 'By the time we did get caught it was a relief in some ways that it was over.'[93]

Not all those who were captured so early had covered quite such insignificant distances. Like so many, Flight Lieutenant Ivo Tonder and Flying Officer John Stower had walked south from the camp, but for them Halbau and its environs did not mark the end of their escapade. By the early morning of the 26th, they had reached Kohlfurt, where they rested for the day. That evening, they walked south, heading for the Czech border, but at seven o'clock in the morning they were spotted near Stolzenberg by a girl, and Tonder and Stower soon found themselves being chased by three civilians and a dog. They headed back north, and by the time they had arrived at Rothwasser, some 3 miles south of Kohlfurt, they had evaded their pursuers.[94] Deciding that train travel was more secure, Tonder and Stower boarded a train at Kohlfurt that took them to Görlitz, where they arrived at two o'clock that afternoon. From there, they took a train south to Reichenberg, but at some point after the train passed Zittau, two German 'civilian officials' and several military policemen entered their compartment and asked for their papers. Although these appeared to be in order, one of the officials noted that their clothes – converted RAF NCOs' uniforms – were similar to those worn by some captured escapers who were being held in Reichenberg, and the two men were searched. The discovery of their POW identity discs resulted in their swift arrests and conveyance to Reichenberg's civilian prison.[95] When they arrived, the two men found some familiar faces. Among them were those of Johnny Bull, Jerzy Mondschein, Reginald Kierath and John Williams. All four of these men had been part of the group that had taken the train from Tschiebsdorf to the small village of Boberrohrsdorf, and after splitting into pairs, they had reunited in order to climb over the Reisengebirge mountain range, where they had been caught by a mountain patrol.[96]

At the time of their capture, Tonder and Stower had made it some 80 miles from the camp. However, in his memoirs, Tonder falsely claimed to have travelled a far greater distance, and stated that he and Stower managed to reach the Baltic port of Stettin after boarding the train at Kohlfurt, which is a distance of some 175 miles. 'Unfortunately there we had no luck with the foreign sailors,' Tonder wrote. 'We were terribly disappointed, but there was nothing to be done. Uncomplainingly we set off down south again.'[97] Tonder then claimed – absurdly – that the two men returned to the Kohlfurt area, and were only then arrested near Zittau. Once again, it is a pity that one of the Great Escapers should have resorted to fabrication in order to amplify a story that requires no such treatment. Tonder's motive for claiming to have travelled such a large distance was possibly born from a sense of frustration that he did not get much further, but such a tall tale surely skews the historical record of a subject that has attracted more than enough exaggeration.

However, there were some Kriegies who really were heading for Stettin.[98] These included Wings Day and Flying Officer Pawel Tobolski, who were making for the port via Berlin, a journey of some 220 miles. Because of the delays in the tunnel, Day and Tobolski had missed the 11 p.m. train from Sagan to Berlin, but after eventually arriving at the station at 12.45 a.m., they were lucky to catch a train leaving just fifteen minutes later.[99] Both had adopted unconventional disguises, with Day posing as a renegade Irish colonel who had been held prisoner since 1940 and had been converted to Nazism, while Tobolski was dressed in the uniform of a Luftwaffe corporal and acting as the escort of 'Colonel Brown'.[100] After arriving in Berlin in the early morning, the two men made their way 4½ miles across the city from the Silesian station to a fourth-floor flat at Winterfeldstrasse 22, about a mile south of the Tiergarten.[101] Living there were a German-Jewish couple called Kunis, as well as their lodger, a young Dane called Erik Engel, who was reputed to have contacts with the Danish Resistance.[102]

The address had been provided to Day by a Squadron Leader George Boyd Carpenter, who had arrived in Stalag Luft III in February 1944.[103] For the Kriegies – and even for historians – Boyd Carpenter was and is an enigmatic figure. A night-fighter pilot, he had been moved from Dulag Luft on or around 1 October 1943, and had spent a few months in Berlin ostensibly helping a group of British renegades make pro-Axis broadcasts to the Allies, although he claimed his real purpose was to gather intelligence. Adopting the pseudonym 'Herr Carter', Boyd Carpenter was housed at the Auto-Hotel at Saldernstrasse 5–7 in Charlottenburg, and according to one of the British collaborators, the squadron leader did 'practically nothing' apart from sabotaging some 432 telephone boxes, and write letters to his cousin in England in code.[104] In January, Boyd Carpenter was arrested by the Gestapo for shoplifting a coat, and having realised that he was more a menace than an asset, the Germans sent him to Stalag Luft III.[105] Unsurprisingly, his fellow officers were suspicious, and after Bushell had interrogated him, Boyd Carpenter was placed under barrack arrest and was watched day and night. Wings Day was apparently less suspicious, and he spent many hours questioning Boyd Carpenter about Berlin, and how to behave on the streets of the German capital in a way that would not attract attention.[106]

Unfortunately for Day and Tobolski, neither the Kunis couple nor their lodger proved to be particularly helpful contacts. Although Engel had once claimed that he could help 'Herr Carter' escape to Sweden via Denmark, it soon emerged that his promise was hollow; he had probably just been trying to impress Boyd Carpenter.[107] However, the Kunis couple did provide the two escapers with not only a divan for the night, but also two hearty meals. On the afternoon of the following day, Sunday 26th, Day and Tobolski separated in order to work out their next steps, and they agreed to meet up on Monday at Winterfeldtplatz. Day occupied his time drinking in bars and reconnoitring timetables to Stettin – from where the two men hoped to catch a boat to Sweden – and he spent an uncomfortable night in an air-raid shelter, narrowly avoiding the police checking his identity papers. Tobolski, meanwhile, had a refreshing night at a transit centre for servicemen, and when the two men reunited, the Pole was fresh-faced and well fed.[108] That day, they took the train to Stettin, where, once again, the contacts they had been supplied did not bear fruit. Tobolski therefore approached his sister, who lived on the outskirts of town, and she allowed them to use her husband's toolshed on his allotment in order to stay the night.[109]

It was not until the afternoon of Tuesday 28th that their luck seemingly began to improve. After a tentative approach by Day, some members of a French POW working party agreed to put them up in their barracks until Day and Tobolski could work out how to stow away to Sweden. After a good night's sleep, the two men decided to lie low in the barracks, but at some point between 10 and 11 a.m., two plain-clothed Gestapo men entered the room, brandishing revolvers, and demanding to know the whereabouts of the two 'Tommies'. There was no doubt in Day's mind that they had been betrayed, and the two men were arrested and marched through the streets of Stettin to the Gestapo headquarters with their hands on their heads. During his interrogation, by an officer Day described as being 'quite civil', it was revealed that they had indeed been betrayed by an informer, but that as it was normal Gestapo practice eventually to reveal the identity of informers to their fellow countrymen, Day could at least draw some solace from the fact that the man would one day receive his just deserts.[110]

Day and Tobolski had managed to travel some 225 miles, but that distance was easily surpassed by two pairs of Kriegies – Squadron Leader James Catanach and Flight Lieutenant Arnold Christensen; and Lieutenants Hallada Espelid and Nils Fugelsang – who had reached Flensburg on the Danish border on Sunday 26 March after a train journey of some 400 miles. However, all four men were arrested that night during random police checks, and were brought to the police prison in the town.[111] The next morning, they were interrogated by Obermeister Paul Linke and Kriminalsekretär Günther of the Kripo, who found that their four detainees were most unforthcoming about the details of their escape, or how they had obtained their identity papers and money. All that the captured officers told the Germans was that they had bought train tickets in either Sagan or Breslau, and had travelled via Berlin, and had not been subject to any controls.[112]

Some of the most impressive distances were achieved by those travelling alone. Like Day and Tobolski, Lieutenant Alexander Neely also reached Stettin, where he hoped – but failed – to meet his fellow escapees on the 28th. Unable to make any contact with anybody who could help him get to Sweden, Neely decided to head to France by slow trains, on which he felt searches would be less likely. He arrived in Berlin at ten thirty that evening, spent the night in a hotel, and the next morning risked the express train to Munich, on which he was arrested in the evening.[113]

Second Lieutenant Raymond van Wymeersch of the Free French Air Force had been the nineteenth or twentieth man to leave the tunnel, and at Sagan station he had accidentally caught a train to Lissa instead of Breslau.[114] After doubling back, he eventually arrived at Breslau at nine o'clock the next morning, from where he bought a ticket direct to Paris. After leaving Breslau at 11.10 a.m., the Frenchman remained on the train as it passed though Dresden, Leipzig, Frankfurt and Saarbrücken. His papers stated that he was a French worker on leave from Siemens in Breslau, and they held good until he reached Metz on 26 March, where he was arrested by the Gestapo after travelling over 500 miles.[115]

At 8.30 the following morning, on the road between Mulhouse and Altkirch, some 60 miles south of Strasbourg, three members of the Landwacht arrested Flight Lieutenant Anthony Hayter as he walked south. Although his papers – which showed that he was a Danish national – appeared to pass muster, the Landwacht men had received orders to take every foreigner to the Gendarmerie, and Hayter soon found himself at the headquarters at Zillisheim. There, Hayter was interrogated by the Meister of the Gendarmerie, an NCO called Welter, who noticed several errors with his documentation. 'When I checked his papers more closely I noticed that the pass he had was false,' Welter stated, 'that it had several office stamps of different colours and that it purported to be made out at the Police Headquarters at Leipzig. The photograph was unsatisfactory and Leipzig was spelt with a "ch" at the end.'[116] Hayter was forced to admit that he had indeed escaped from Sagan, at which point he was promptly arrested.

Another Kriegie who had travelled solo and managed an equally impressive distance was Flying Officer Dennis Cochran, who was arrested just south of Lörrach, about 500 miles from Sagan, and an agonising 1½ miles from the Swiss border near Basel.[117]

Among those who had covered the greatest distance were Roger Bushell and Bernard Scheidhauer, who by around noon on Sunday 26 March were boarding a train that would take them some 80 miles west from Ludwigshafen am Rhein to Saarbrücken on the French border. Since they had left the tunnel, the two men had travelled some 500 miles, and hoped to be in France by the middle of that afternoon and shortly to contact the Resistance. However, on the train to Saarbrücken, their luck began to dwindle. A policeman checked their papers, and declared that he was not satisfied. Although Bushell and Scheidhauer might have felt concerned, their worries were perhaps alleviated by the fact that the papers of four other passengers were seemingly not in order either. After arriving at Saarbrücken at around 2.30 p.m., the policeman removed the men from the train, and took them to see Fritz Bender, a Kripo man employed at the railway station to check passes and identity papers. Bender examined the papers of all six men, and found that two sets were not in order: those of Bushell and Scheidhauer. Although the officers claimed to be French workers from Breslau on their way to France on holiday, Bender noticed that their papers did not bear a Labour Exchange stamp. Bender therefore arrested them, and took them to the local Kripo headquarters at Schlossplatz 1 and 2.[118]

According to a Gestapo employee called Gustav Pitz, another reason why Bender arrested the two men was because one of them said 'yes' in English in response to one of Bender's questions, rather than saying '*oui*'.[119] As Scheidhauer was French, and Bushell's first language was English, it seems likely that if this slip did take place, then it was made by Big X himself. Of course, this account of the arrest of Bushell and Scheidhauer is markedly different from the fictionalised version portrayed in the film *The Great Escape*, in which it is the escaping partner of 'Bartlett', 'Sandy MacDonald', who makes the error in response to a Gestapo officer wishing him 'good luck'. The film's version of events is now so strongly imprinted that it even appears in histories of the escape, and it is Scheidhauer who makes the error.[120] However, this simply has no basis in truth, and should be regarded as yet another piece of Great Escape mythology, and, furthermore, a slur upon the Frenchman.

At the Kripo headquarters, Bushell and Scheidhauer were interrogated in the office of Kriminalobersekretär Jakob Hartz. Scheidhauer was questioned first, and Hartz noticed that the fingerprint on his civil pass did not appear to be correct. Scheidhauer laughed, and invited Hartz to take his fingerprints in order to check. The Kripo officer did not take up the offer, and instead continued with his interrogation, and after a little while, Scheidhauer admitted that his papers were false, and that he had escaped from Sagan. Hartz then quizzed Scheidhauer about his travelling companion, and the Frenchman denied knowing him.[121] Hartz turned his attention to Bushell, who realised that it was pointless to maintain his cover story, and he too revealed his true identity.

The two men were then separated, and Bushell was subsequently interrogated by Kriminalkommissar Ludwig Kehl, whose regular duties involved investigating suicides and sudden deaths. Kehl offered Bushell food and cigarettes, which he accepted, and during the questioning, Bushell revealed that he had been educated at Cambridge, when he had joined the RAF, and his civilian occupation as a barrister.[122] The following day, on Monday 27th, Bushell was questioned by a Kriminalinspektor Bahr, to whom Bushell expressed his gratitude for the 'excellent and gentle treatment' that he was receiving from the Kripo, which was not what he had been expecting. Bushell then asked for something to smoke, and Bahr handed him five cigarettes.

'How can I make up for it?' asked a delighted Bushell.

'I do it with pleasure,' Bahr replied, 'in order that a

charitable hand may extend to my son who is a prisoner in Russia.'

During the interrogation, Bushell told the Kripo more about his legal career, and how he had travelled all over Germany during peacetime. In addition, he said that he was wealthy, which somehow increased his 'thirst after liberty' that had been 'irresistible behind the barbed wire'.[123]

At first glance, it seems puzzling that Bushell, with his supposed animus towards the Germans, should have readily offered so much information to his captors. According to the testimonies of all those who saw Bushell while he was being held by the Kripo, his demeanour seemed to be anything but truculent, and he even appeared to radiate a superficial bonhomie. Of course, it is possible that all the Kripo members who were interviewed after the war were lying about Bushell's behaviour and treatment, but there is no compelling reason to doubt their statements. The Kripo was not, after all, the Gestapo, and there was no point in torturing or terrorising their captives. As the Sagan Order had not worked its way through the system at the time of the arrest and the interrogations, for the Kripo this was still a straightforward matter of handling escaped POWs. With Bushell and Scheidhauer ignorant of what was being planned in offices in Berlin, there was no need on their part for them to be anything but polite and cooperative. None of those involved would gain anything by superfluous posturing or displays of bolshiness and muscle-flexing. What is also worth noting is that Bushell's name did not appear to register any alarm with the Kripo. If his name was indeed – as is often claimed – on a Gestapo blacklist, then it appears that those in Department IV of the RSHA had not shared it with their colleagues in Department V.

That afternoon, Bushell and Scheidhauer were taken some 2 miles by car up to the Lerchesflur Court Prison on Hohewacht. While they waited to be returned to Sagan, a telegram arrived at the Kripo headquarters in Saarbrücken from Department V in Berlin that ordered any recaptured officers from Sagan to be handed over to the Gestapo for 'political interrogation'. Furthermore, the telegram stated that the prisoners would be taken to Berlin for a 'final interrogation', and that copies of the initial Kripo interrogation should be forwarded to the RSHA.

It would appear that the Kripo in Saarbrücken did nothing until the arrival of two Gestapo men at their headquarters in the early hours of Wednesday 29 March.[124] The two men were Emil Schulz and Walter Breithaupt, who maintained the vehicles run by the Saarbrücken Gestapo. Aged thirty-six, Schulz had been brought up on his parents' farm in the Saarland, and after leaving school he became a miner for six years. In 1928, he spent a year at the police school in Bonn, after which he served in the regular police in Essen, Munich and Saarbrücken. In 1938, he joined the Gestapo as well as the Nazi Party, and he progressed surely through the ranks to become a Kriminalsekretär, or First Class Detective Sergeant. In 1934, he had married one Angela Lambert, and the couple had had two daughters, Ingeborg and Helga.[125] According to Ingeborg, Schulz's wife was very uneasy about her husband's membership of the Gestapo. 'For a long time, my father wore a uniform,' Ingeborg recalled, 'and then one day he came home with no uniform, and my mother said, "That's not good, I do not like it, Emil." The Gestapo usually wore no uniforms – they were undercover.'[126]

Schulz knew precisely why he had been sent to collect Bushell and Scheidhauer that morning, and he was deeply uneasy about it. Some time between 11 p.m. and midnight, he had been summoned to the office of the chief of the Saarbrücken Gestapo, Dr Leopold Spann, who had a telegram lying in front of him on his desk. Spann started by asking Schulz whether he had been in action, which Schulz denied.

'What I am telling you now remains between us,' continued Spann. 'There are two English RAF officers [sic] in the Lerchesflur prison at Saarbrücken, who had escaped. These are to be shot on orders of the RSHA.'

Schulz expressed some reservations, which Spann did not brook.

'You are acting on my orders,' he said, 'and you will follow my instructions.'

Spann then asked Schulz if he knew of a suitable place to carry out the killings, and told him to bear in mind that the location should not be too distant in order to save petrol.[127] Spann's greater concern for fuel economy than for committing murder speaks volumes about his mindset. At some stage during the conversation, Spann spoke over the telephone to the head of the Kripo in Saarbrücken, Kriminaldirektor Dingermann, who reportedly objected to having to hand over Bushell and Scheidhauer. Spann told him that as it was a direct order from the RSHA, there was nothing either man could do about it, and at around

4.30 a.m., Schulz and Breithaupt arrived at the Lerchesflur prison.[128]

When the Gestapo men turned up, Bushell and Scheidhauer were standing ready, their luggage by their sides. Schulz was surprised that the men were in fact officers. 'They both looked very down at heel,' he said later, 'so that I had the impression that these people had not an opportunity to tidy themselves up for a period of weeks at least.'[129] 'It all went very quickly,' recalled Walter Breithaupt, who watched Schulz dealing with his Kripo counterpart and filling in the required paperwork. The four men then drove to the Gestapo headquarters, where Schulz told Breithaupt to stay with the two officers in the ground-floor lobby while he went up to see Spann. While they waited, Bushell and Scheidhauer exchanged some words in English, which Breithaupt could not understand.[130] A few minutes later, Schulz returned, and gesticulated to the prisoners that they should follow him with their luggage to the car, which was parked immediately outside the building. Breithaupt placed the cases in the boot, and Schulz then proceeded to handcuff the two men. Bushell protested, telling Schulz in German that applying manacles was not 'compatible with the honour of an officer', but Schulz said that he had been ordered to do so.[131] Shortly afterwards, Spann emerged, and informed Bushell and Scheidhauer that they were being taken to a POW camp. The officers were then placed in the back with Schulz sitting between them, while Spann sat in the front next to Breithaupt.[132]

At this stage, Bushell and Scheidhauer would have been extremely anxious. Not only would they

have detected Schulz's undoubted nervousness, but the
officers would have also wondered why it required
the Gestapo to transfer them to a POW camp – a task
that could easily have been undertaken by the Kripo.
The early hour was also an ominous sign. Although it is
impossible to substantiate, both Bushell and Scheidhauer
– and especially Bushell – must have strongly suspected
that they were being driven to their deaths.

Chapter Eleven

'This dirty work'

WHILE THE PRISONERS were being recaptured, at the RSHA in Berlin a list was being assembled. At around 10 a.m. on Tuesday 28 March, Kriminalrat Dr Hans Merten of the Kripo was ordered to see the head of the department for Wartime Searches, Oberregierungsrat and SS-Obersturmbannführer Dr Richard Schultze. On the day of the breakout, the 39-year-old Merten had been posted to the department to act as an extra pair of hands, and he had been occupied preparing notices for the *German Police Gazette*, sending and receiving telegrams, making and recording telephone calls, and reporting captures to Nebe. Schultze informed Merten that owing to a shortage of staff, Merten's presence was required immediately over at Nebe's office on Werderscher Markt, where two telegrams urgently needed drafting. 'Get there quickly!' Schultze urged.[1] Merten took the tram, and he eventually arrived at eleven o'clock. As ordered, he drafted the two telegrams, which seemed perfectly unexceptional, and he showed them to Nebe, who signed them. The head of the Kripo then issued Merten with another order:

'Take the teleprints which contain the individual captures, write down the names and places in which the recaptured men are now, and find their personal file cards for me. You have heard about the Führer Order?'

Merten replied that he had.

'Then you know what to do,' Nebe continued. 'I will bring Müller a further list at lunchtime. Without a heading, without anything, just the names of the recaptured men and their present whereabouts, then a new line. The rest is done by Department IV [the Gestapo]. Give me the personal file cards as soon as possible so that I can tell you who is to be on this list, and who not.'[2]

Because Merten was privy to the Sagan Order, he was in no doubt as to what inclusion on the list meant. Although a list had already been drawn up the previous day, it did not include the names of those since captured, and it took Merten more time than he anticipated locating these Kriegies' personal file cards. Working in the office of Nebe's adjutant, Merten was not even permitted to pause during a forty-five-minute air-raid warning, and he observed that Nebe was highly agitated. 'I attribute Nebe's excited and uncontrolled behaviour to the fact that he was aware of the monstrosity of the deed which he was about to carry out,' he later recalled.[3] Merten presented Nebe with eight to ten cards, which Nebe examined while asking which of the men had wives and children. The Kripo chief started allocating each of the cards to one of two piles he had in front of him. One pile meant death, the other, life. 'He is for it,' said Nebe, looking at one card, and then placing it down on one pile. At another card, he exclaimed, 'He is so young. No!' and placed the card on the other pile. With a further card, Nebe enquired as to whether the man had children. Merten said that he did not, and Nebe placed the card on the first pile. Soon, there were several cards in both piles. Nebe studied the pile, and then swapped a single card from one to the other. He then handed one of the piles over, and snapped at Merten: 'Now quickly, the list!' Merten took the four or five cards through to Nebe's shorthand typist and dictated the supplementary list, which was then passed through to the Gestapo. Merten would later claim that his emotions were mixed as he read the names. 'I wanted at least to delay the evil deed,' he said, 'and at the same time ensure that I got clear of this dirty work.'[4]

Such was the method by which the extinction of fifty young lives was decided. If Merten's recollection is to be trusted, then Nebe was at least displaying some humanity in his selection process, a humanity that he had apparently not shown when his *Einsatzgruppe* B liquidated some 46,000 men, women and children in and around Minsk and Smolensk from June to November 1941.[5] It is possible that Nebe did indeed find the selection process emotionally difficult. In Russia, he was not looking at faces or names, and was simply ordering the deaths of swathes of anonymous humans – or people he presumably regarded as being subhuman – from behind a desk. Here, Nebe was looking directly at men young enough to be his sons, men who were neither Jews nor Communists, men who he must have known were guilty of nothing more than wanting to taste freedom rather than committing sabotage or acts of terrorism. Furthermore, it was hardly as if Nebe was an enthusiastic supporter of the regime – his semi-detached involvement in what would become known as the July Bomb Plot was evidence of that.[6] Nebe may indeed have felt revulsion at what he had to do, but he, like so many other Nazis, was simply acting in a way that kept the regime in power – he was following orders.

The murders began the following morning. Perhaps the first two escapers to die were Squadron Leader Thomas Kirby-Green and Flying Officer Gordon Kidder, who had been arrested on the morning of the 28th by some local gendarmerie in a small cottage in a wood near the Czech village of Vsetín, some 230 miles southeast of Sagan.[7] The pair had made good progress, and had reached the town of Kunčice, a few miles south of Moravská Ostrava, on the evening of the 25th, where they had stayed at 262 Senovska Street in the house of one Anna Lisova.[8] Today, it is unclear who Lisova was and, indeed, what stood at Senovska Street, but it is possible that Lisova was a member of the Czech Underground, and that number 262 may have been some form of hotel. Certainly, the two men were confident enough to supply her with their contact addresses – Gordon Kidder declared that he was from St Catharines, Ontario, and Kirby-Green gave the address of his bank, Lloyds at 6 Pall Mall, London – so it seems likely that Lisova was active in the Resistance. The following morning, Lisova supplied them with a map and directions to Uherské Hradiště, some 80 miles southwest, and even saw them on to a train at a nearby station.[9] As the men were captured two days later in a small cottage in a wood just 25 miles south of Kunčice, it is possible that they may have got off the train quickly and decided instead to hard-arse, as, after their arrest, their clothes were found to be very shabby and torn.[10] The two men were taken to the headquarters of the Grenzpolizei – the Frontier Police – in Zlin, where they were questioned by Kriminalassistent Kurt Kruger, and Kriminalassistent Erich Zacharias of the Gestapo, who was attached to the Grenzpolizei.[11]

Of all those responsible for the ensuing atrocities, the character of the 32-year-old Zacharias is perhaps the most disquieting. Described after the war as being a plausible liar, cowardly, very dangerous, and with 'no sense of honour whatsoever', Zacharias possessed all the attributes of a criminal while wearing the uniform of a policeman.[12] In fact, Zacharias had killed before, and in the most horrific fashion. One day, after he had conducted a particularly violent interrogation, he was annoyed to find that a young Czech woman had been sitting outside the room, and had heard the proceedings. Worried that the woman might reveal the extent of his brutality to his Gestapo colleagues, Zacharias decided to take the woman to lunch. Some 6 miles outside Zlin, Zacharias stopped his car, raped the woman, shot her dead, and then buried her beside the road. Afterwards, he returned to Zlin to enjoy his lunch. 'He showed neither remorse for the act nor compunction about describing it,' recalled one of his post-war interrogators.[13]

At some point on the afternoon of the 28th, Zacharias had a meeting with the head of the Gestapo in Zlin, Kriminalrat Hans Ziegler, a corpulent 45-year-old former brewer from Odelzhausen near Dachau.[14] According to Zacharias, Ziegler informed him that the two prisoners were 'very important', as they were in touch with the Underground, and that a Gestapo officer would shortly be arriving from Brno, some 50 miles west.[15] That officer was Kriminalsekretär Adolf Knippelberg, a 36-year-old Viennese, who was driven to the Gestapo headquarters in Zlin by Fritz Schwarzer.[16] After Knippelberg arrived, Ziegler explained to him and Zacharias that he had received orders that Kidder and Kirby-Green were to be shot. 'I imagine that you should drive up almost to Moravská Ostrava,' he suggested, 'where you have a break for urination, and at this opportunity the shooting can take place.' Mindful of practicalities, Ziegler added: 'In this way it will not be very far to Moravská Ostrava and the corpses will not have to lie on the road too long.' Neither Zacharias nor Knippelberg appeared to make any significant protest, and merely concerned them-selves with logistical matters. Knippelberg said that he would 'attend to the formalities' in Moravská Ostrava, and have the bodies taken to a crematorium. As they would be travelling in two cars, Knippelberg asked whether Zacharias could lead the way, as he knew the area better, and would be able to find a suitable spot. Zacharias claimed to have expressed some reluctance at some point during the meeting, although Ziegler apparently reassured him by stating that 'everything would be carried out and handled in such a way that no difficulties whatsoever could arise'. Zacharias would recall:

> I carried out the task first because it was an order, and also because I was assured that nothing could happen to me later, and also because I justified myself in that there was a war on and that the airmen might have killed already many hundreds of civilians by bombing.[17]

Towards the end of the meeting, at around 8–9 p.m., Ziegler telephoned Friedrich Kiowsky, a Gestapo driver who was working for the Grenzpolizei. Ziegler ordered Kiowsky to ready his car in order to take the two POWs from the police prison to Breslau, and furthermore, he was not to discuss the matter with anybody else in the station. Kiowsky went down to the garage, but before he could fetch the prisoners, he was joined by Zacharias, who informed him that he first needed to pick up Kurt Kruger and an interpreter called Hager from their homes in order to carry out a further interrogation.[18] Kiowsky did as he was ordered, and Kirby-Green and Kidder were eventually collected from the prison and delivered to the headquarters of the Grenzpolizei at around 11 p.m.[19] The two officers were taken down to the cells by Kiowsky and Zacharias, where they were interrogated by Kruger and Hager, and, a little later, by Hans Ziegler. During the questioning, one of the prisoners complained to Ziegler about being forced to wear handcuffs, to which Ziegler responded that 'when vagabonds were encountered in the streets, they would be treated like vagabonds'.[20] Even if the two men were scruffy after a few days on the run, it appeared they tried to maintain an aura of dignity. According to one Gestapo employee, the officers – both of whom were comparatively tall – 'seemed quite self-possessed and entirely confident'.[21] Had Kirby-Green and Kidder known the nature of the conversation that took place between Zacharias and Knippelberg immediately after their interrogation, it is likely they would not have displayed such composure. The two Gestapo men discussed the precise details of the forthcoming murders, with Zacharias and Knippelberg agreeing that the prisoners should remain handcuffed, and that they should take a position 1 metre behind the victims while they were urinating. When Knippelberg raised his arm, Zacharias would take that as the signal to shoot, and both men would be killed simultaneously. After this discussion, Zacharias continued with his regular night-time duties for another couple of hours.[22]

Just before 2 a.m., Ziegler informed Kiowsky and Fritz Schwarzer that they should get ready to depart and to prepare their two cars. However, Kiowsky was concerned that his car did not have enough petrol to get to Breslau, which was some 200 miles north by road, and told Ziegler of his worry. 'You will not have to drive to Breslau,' Ziegler replied, which made Kiowsky suspect that the two prisoners were shortly destined to die. This suspicion was bolstered when he saw Zacharias loading a gun and putting it in his coat pocket.[23] Kirby-Green and Kidder were then brought from the cells, and placed in the two cars. Kidder was placed in Zacharias's car, which was driven by Kiowsky, and Kirby-Green in Knippelberg's, which was driven by Schwarzer.

Zacharias sat in the front of the car, and the journey was largely conducted in silence. At one point, after they had passed the town of Friedeck, some 15 miles south of Moravská Ostrava, Kiowsky quietly asked Zacharias what was going to happen to the two men. Knowing that Kidder spoke some German, Zacharias surreptitiously turned down the thumb of his right hand. 'Then I knew for the first time that the two men were going to be shot,' Kiowsky recalled.[24] It is inconceivable that at this stage – unless he was asleep – Gordon Kidder had no inkling of his fate, not least because Zacharias ordered Kiowsky to slow down while he scanned the countryside in the dim early morning light for a suitable place to stop, which was hardly the order given by a man merely seeking a place to urinate.[25]

At around 4.30 a.m., Zacharias found a suitable location some 5 to 7 miles south of Moravská Ostrava, and the two cars drew to a halt. The landscape was flat and desolate, with snow-covered fields on both sides of the road. Just up ahead to the left was a small barn, which Zacharias would have assumed to be uninhabited. In the middle distance, about a mile away, the outskirts of a small town – perhaps Vratimov – might have just been visible at that hour.[26] Zacharias told Kidder that they were stopping to relieve themselves, and both prisoners – still in their handcuffs – were soon standing at the edge of the road, urinating into a 2-foot-deep drainage ditch. Knippelberg and Zacharias took their positions about a yard behind each man, and Knippelberg raised his right hand and pointed his pistol towards the rear of Kirby-Green's head. 'This was for me the time for action,' Zacharias recalled, 'so that I could fire simultaneously with Knippelberg.'[27] Zacharias pulled his pistol out of his coat pocket and aimed it at the left side of Kidder's back in order to shoot him through his heart. Zacharias fired, and Kidder twisted and collapsed, his cuffed hands still held in front of him while he urinated. As he did so, Zacharias fired again, this time above the Canadian's right ear and into his temple.[28] The Gestapo man stood so close to his victim that the area around the second round's entry hole was scorched from the pistol's discharge.[29] Zacharias then shouted over to Knippelberg, 'What's happening?' Knippelberg replied that Kirby-Green was dead, and Zacharias bent down to see whether Kidder was in the same condition. He checked for a pulse, looked at his eyes, and confirmed that his prisoner had also been killed. Zacharias ran over to Knippelberg and looked down at Kirby-Green, and could see a wound on the back of his head.[30] Meanwhile, Kiowsky and Schwarzer, who had been sharing a cigarette, watched as Knippelberg told Zacharias to remove the prisoners' handcuffs, and to remain by the bodies while he and Schwarzer drove into Moravská Ostrava to fetch an ambulance to remove the bodies.[31] Before he left, Knippelberg told the three Gestapo men that the two prisoners had been shot while escaping, and that all were 'to give evidence unanimously to this effect' and, other than at the official inquiry, they were to remain absolutely silent.[32]

Zacharias and Kiowsky anxiously waited for Knippelberg's return. 'I wanted the corpses to disappear as quickly as possible from the road,' Zacharias later claimed, 'so as not to give an exhibition [*sic*] to the many workers going to work.'[33] Knippelberg arrived at the Gestapo station in Moravská Ostrava at around 5 a.m., where he requested a driver and a van. A Czech policeman by the name of Emil Schreier was summoned, and he was ordered to drive towards Friedeck with Knippelberg and Schwarzer following. At the murder site, the body of Kirby-Green was placed in the van first, and Kidder was placed on top of him. 'I noticed no wounds on the body of the second man,' Schreier recalled. 'I saw only blood flowing from the nose, mouth and one ear.'[34] As soon as the bodies were loaded, Zacharias and Kiowsky turned round and drove back to Zlin, while Knippelberg and Schwarzer headed to Moravská Ostrava with the bodies. Shortly before 6 a.m., they arrived at the crematorium, where they were assisted by an employee called Frantisek Krupa, who was ordered to open the door to the mortuary. The bodies were then placed on the floor, and Knippelberg and Schwarzer searched through their clothes and removed any personal effects. The door of the mortuary was then sealed, and Knippelberg declared that nobody was to enter.[35]

Later that morning, at around 9.30 a.m., Zacharias and Kiowsky arrived back at Zlin, where they reported to Ziegler. 'Herr Kriminalrat,' said Zacharias, 'everything is all right and Knippelberg is having the corpses examined by a doctor, and having them sent to the crematorium.' Ziegler appeared satisfied, and then told Zacharias that he should go home and get some sleep, because he looked 'terrible'.[36] While Zacharias and Kiowsky headed to their beds, back in Moravská

SO **YOU** DESIGNED THE LONDON UNDERGROUND?

A prophetic cartoon painted by American officer
Tom Young in the logbook of Ley Kenyon.

"GOOD LUCK"
Tom Young
USA

Above: Tins of KLIM powdered milk were joined together to make air lines for the tunnels.

Right: Instructions given to the 'stooges' who looked out for Glemnitz and his ferrets when they patrolled the north compound.

Below left: The trolley and railway line used to transport spoil along the length of the escape tunnel Harry.

Below right: The stove in Room 23 of Hut 104, which concealed the entrance to Harry.

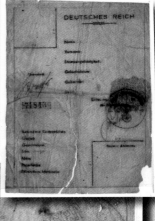

Above left: Rubberneck working Harry's air pump, designed by Jens Müller and Bob Nelson.

Above right: A ferret modelling the sacks worn under a pair of POW's trousers which would be used secretly to dispose of sand.

Right and below: Templates of passes produced by Alex Cassie's forgery department. These would be passed to a friendly German and reproduced on a typewriter outside the camp and then copied using a homemade jelly press.

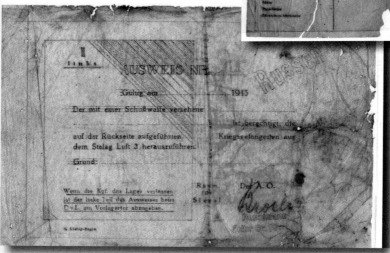

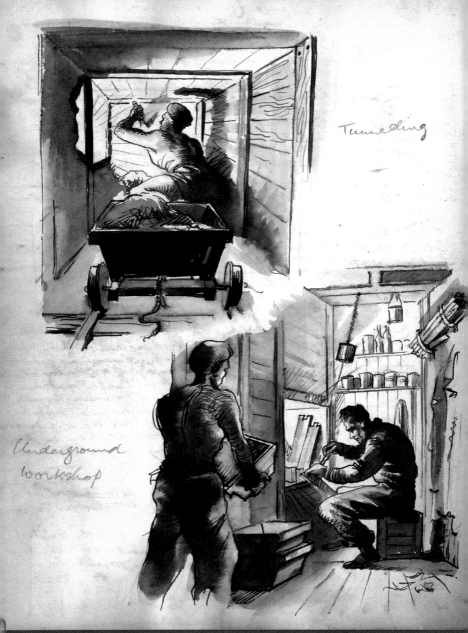

Tunnelling

Underground
workshop

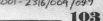

Air pump
and pumper.

Roger Bushell
Big "X"

Squadron Leader
Roger Bushell

Paintings by Ley Kenyon
of the construction of
Harry. To the right is a
portrait of Bushell – 'a
big criminal' – which
successfully captures the
increasing coldness and
haughtiness of 'Big X'.

"EIN GROSSE
VERBRECHEN"

Above: The entrance to Harry with the stove removed.

Right: A beaming Rubberneck emerges from the entrance to Tom.

Below left: Looking down Harry's 30-foot entrance shaft.

Below right: The first few yards of Harry. The tunnel would run for some 344 feet.

Top: A trolley complete with rope inside Harry.

Above left: A ferret climbs out of Harry's exit shaft.

Above right: The ladder in Harry's exit shaft.

Right: A German reconstruction of a POW emerging from Harry.

An ashamed Alex Cassie, who suffered from claustrophobia, was the only man in his room who did not go down Harry. Those marked with crosses were subsequently shot dead by the Gestapo.

GOING DOWN! — THE EXODUS OF ROOM 4.
BY THE ONE WHO STAYED.

A. CASSIE
1/4/44

Four of the Great Escapers photographed in their escape kit. From left: Squadron Leader James Catanach (Australia), Flying Officer Arnold Christensen (New Zealand), Lieutenant Nils Fugelsang (Norway) and Lieutenant Hallada Espelid (Norway).

Ostrava Knippelberg's work was still not done. At 10 a.m., he returned to the mortuary with another Gestapo man and a doctor, who examined the bodies and then resealed the mortuary.[37]

While the corpses of Kirby-Green and Kidder lay in the crematorium, the Gestapo men busied themselves with their fabrications. After a few hours' sleep, Zacharias was back in his office by 2 p.m., where he spoke to a senior colleague, Kriminalobersekretär Karl Raska, who had been a member of the Zlin Gestapo since March 1939. Raska had seen a telex arrive from the Gestapo station at Moravská Ostrava at eight thirty that morning, in which it was reported that the two POWs had been shot 'while trying to escape'. Raska asked exactly what had happened, and Zacharias told him that he and Knippelberg had been standing behind the men while they urinated, until 'they both began to run, as if on a word of command, straight across the field'. According to Zacharias's official version, he and Knippelberg drew their firearms and shot at the men, who continued to run a short distance before falling to the ground, dead. Raska enquired as to whether the men were handcuffed, which Zacharias denied, stating that POWs were not permitted to be restrained in such a way.[38] Raska later claimed that he totally disbelieved Zacharias's story, and he had much cause to do so, not least because transporting POWs was not normally carried out by Zacharias and high-ranking members of other Gestapo stations, and at Zlin, it was usually entrusted to a Kriminalassistent called Karel Locher. In addition, the use of two cars stoked Raska's suspicions, as fuel was strictly rationed. Finally, the nocturnal transfer also looked extremely suspect. 'All these circumstances drew me to the conclusion that both Zacharias and the official from Brno [Knippelberg] had shot the two officer-prisoners dead in accordance with orders given them,' said Raska, 'without their action being justified by any attempt to escape on the part of the hand-cuffed prisoners of war.'[39] If Raska did indeed hold such misgivings, and was not expressing them simply to curry favour with his post-war interrogators, then he un-doubtedly kept them to himself. As a Gestapo officer, he knew better than to cross his own organisation.

At 9.30 a.m. the following day, Knippelberg returned to the crematorium for the second time, accompanied by two other men. There, Frantisek Krupa was ordered to cremate the bodies immediately, and not to provide coffins. Kirby-Green and Kidder were therefore burned merely in what Krupa described as their civilian suits. Kirby-Green was cremated first, and his ashes were put into urn number 6385. Kidder's were placed into urn 6386. Two days later, on 1 April, a Gestapo official collected the remains.[40]

Kirby-Green and Kidder were aged just twenty-six and twenty-nine respectively when they were shot by men they never knew for the 'crime' of wishing to taste freedom. There would be another forty-eight such homicides, many of which took place in similar locations, and carried out by men such as Zacharias who thought that obeying orders was a defence for committing murder. As we shall see, quite a few of these killers acted on an assumption that a refusal to shoot would have resulted in their own deaths, a belief that was almost entirely groundless, but – crucially – an assumption that was seldom tested, owing to moral weakness and a culture of obedience. Furthermore, many of the Gestapo men who shot the Great Escapers sought justification for their actions in the fact that they were shooting men who had bombed their fellow citizens, therefore they were carrying out a legitimate, quasi-biblical form of justice, albeit one that was not sanctioned by a court. We have already seen how the German populace had a strong animosity towards Allied airmen, an attitude fostered by Goebbels' propaganda ministry, which conveniently forgot that the Luftwaffe had carried out equally punitive raids on civilian populations earlier in the war.[41] Nevertheless, this hatred was undeniably – and understandably – genuine, and it was felt particularly strongly for the RAF. One USAAF airman, First Lieutenant William E. Koch of the 301st Bombardment Group of the Fifteenth Air Force, witnessed it after landing by parachute near Linz when his B-17 had been shot down. Koch was surrounded by thirty to forty angry civilians, one of whom was pointing a shotgun at his face. 'Are you English or American?' a voice asked. Koch said that he was American, whereupon the gun was lowered. 'It's good you are an American,' said the voice, 'because had you said you were English, my friend would have blown your head off.' Koch reckoned that, after years of nocturnal raids by the British, 'the Germans decided that if they killed every English airman, the word would get back to England and they would stop night-time bombing'.[42] Many downed British airmen were indeed shot by angry civilians, killings to which those in authority turned a blind eye. It is quite likely that men like Zacharias did share this enmity, hatched both from viscera and vengeance, and even though they were aware that shooting men such as Thomas Kirby-Green in the back of the head was illegal – hence the cover-up and fabrication – it was perhaps not considered unacceptable by the communities they policed.

Such people had been sold the idea that they constituted a blessed 'community of fate', yet, night after night, they had endured deathly rain from the skies. To them, the notion that a downed member of a Lancaster that had just been dropping high explosives on their town could simply walk into the safe environment of a POW camp must have seemed anathema.[43] Such an attitude was crystallised in a broadcast made the following May on Goebbels' General European Service by William Joyce – more commonly known as 'Lord Haw-Haw'.

> After all, if an enemy airman comes down almost to the housetop level and opens a withering fire upon helpless civilians; if he kills a child and is subsequently brought down himself, can I reasonably be expected to strike a blow at the father of that child if he wants to come to grips with the murderer? I do not know of any moral law which could justify you in making such a request of me.[44]

If the Luftwaffe could no longer bomb Britain, then the German civilians could at least get their own back – so the logic went – by killing those who were killing them. This does not in any way excuse the murderers of the Great Escapers, but it does contextualise their actions. Although there can be no grounds for such killings, revenge is perhaps a more honourable defence than merely following orders.

As well as acting out of obedience – and possibly from vengeance – the motives of some of the murderers appear to have been rooted in a form of uneasy corporate loyalty. At around the same time as the killing of Kirby-Green and Kidder on the morning of 29 March, Flight Lieutenants Rupert Stevens and Johannes Gouws were shot some 30 miles north of Munich on the side of the autobahn heading towards Ingolstadt.[45] Today, it remains unclear exactly where and how the two men were captured, but by the evening of 28 March, they had been incarcerated in the Munich police headquarters on Ettstrasse. Just after midnight, the two men were collected by two Gestapo officers – Kriminalkommissar Martin Schermer and Kriminalsekretär Eduard Geith – and were driven by a Gestapo driver called Johann Schneider the few hundred yards to the Gestapo headquarters in the Wittelsbach Palace.[46] Dressed in civilian clothes, and wearing a blue overcoat and a trench coat, Gouws and Stevens were locked in the cells while their fate was discussed in Schermer's office by Geith, Schneider, Schermer and Kriminalsekretär Emil Weil, a 34-year-old former member of the Bavarian political police who had joined the Gestapo in 1938.[47] It was Schermer who briefed the men, acting on the direct orders of the head of the Munich Gestapo, Oberregierungsrat and Obersturmbannführer Dr Oswald Schäfer. Schermer explained that the four of them had been entrusted with a 'Top Secret matter', and that the prisoners were to be shot on the way back to their POW camp. In order to secure their silence and complicity, Schermer made the four men clasp hands, a gesture not uncommonly associated with men about to go into battle.[48]

As was typical with all those who murdered the escaping officers, very few – if any – objections were raised when the orders were received. Weil later recalled that after the handclasp, Schermer said that the order had come from an authority higher than the RSHA, from which Weil inferred that it had been issued by either Himmler or Hitler. Nevertheless, he was not entirely certain whether the order had any legitimacy. 'I was not quite clear whether it was legal or not legal to kill in this case,' Weil later stated, 'but the manner prescribed made it quite clear to me that it must have emanated from a higher authority.'[49] If he did still have any doubts, then Weil kept them to himself, as he later claimed that it was impossible for him to have even asked for an explanation of the reasoning behind the order – let alone its legality – because this would have been regarded as being in-subordinate.[50] Besides, Weil had other reasons to keep quiet, not least because he was a quarter Jewish, a racial inconvenience that meant he, unlike so many of his colleagues, could never be a member of the SS. Resentful of this exclusion, Weil would complain to a colleague that he wanted to leave the Gestapo, but an application to transfer to the Wehrmacht in 1941 had been denied. Although he would later mendaciously insist that his superiors did not know of his Jewish ancestry, Weil was undoubtedly trapped in his role as a secret policeman.[51] As a result, neither he nor any of his colleagues expressed any misgivings about shooting Gouws and Stevens. Indeed, the only objections seemed to be grimly practical rather than moral. Geith recalled:

Everyone present discussed the execution of the order, and we did not come to any fixed conclusion. I think, I may say that Weil had the same inhibitions as myself, to carry out the actions as such with our duty pistols . . . because with them a mistake was most to be feared.[52]

Schneider, who had served on the Russian front, then proposed that he would shoot the men with a machine pistol, as he was 'certain of himself' and 'there would be no mistake'.[53] Schermer agreed with Schneider's suggestion, and Geith observed that he and Weil 'were also content with this solution'. With the gunman selected, all that remained to be discussed was the location of the killings, and from where Schneider would fire. After an hour, at about 3 a.m., the meeting ended, and, according to Geith, the men passed the time until departure with 'unimportant conversation', with some even managing to doze a little.[54] It is clearly disturbing that these four men were able to indulge in chitchat and sleep on such an occasion. Although Geith, Schermer and Weil were doubtless secretly pleased that they were not pulling the trigger, each man must have known that their culpability was equivalent.

At around 4 a.m., Gouws and Stevens were interrogated. As none of the three Gestapo officers spoke good English, and with only one of the POWs speaking patchy German, the interrogation lasted at least an hour, much to the annoyance of Schermer. After the prisoners supplied brief résumés of their military careers and details of how they had escaped and which towns they had travelled through, the two men were stripped and searched. According to Eduard Geith, the Gestapo officers were keen to carry out this specific task as decently as possible. 'The search room was always kept at a good room temperature and no bodily harm could be contracted by the prisoners in this respect,' Geith stated. 'In the execution of our duty . . . Weil as well as I maintained complete decency.'[55] The irony of those about to commit murder being concerned with maintaining their intended victims' dignity is all too apparent.

After the interrogation and the search, Gouws and Stevens were manacled together and then placed in the back of a car. Weil and Geith sat on two folding seats opposite them, and Schermer sat in the front next to Schneider, who was driving. Dawn started to break as they left Munich's northern limits, and after heading up the autobahn for around 25 miles, at approximately 6 a.m. Schermer ordered Schneider to stop. The car pulled up next to a small meadow in front of a wood some 20 yards away. Schermer then turned to the RAF officers and issued a single-word command: 'Urinate.'[56] The two men, accompanied by Weil and Geith, walked 5 yards into the meadow. Schermer pointed at the machine pistol hidden under Schneider's seat, and then ordered the driver to get out. Schneider took the gun, inserted a magazine, and took up his position, leaning against the luggage box at the rear of the car. Schermer stood 3 feet to his right and started gesticulating towards Schneider. 'He was very excited,' recalled Schneider, 'and he pointed with his hands in the direction of the prisoners and said to me in an excited and hushed voice, "Shoot, shoot."' Schneider fired a short burst at each prisoner, and Gouws and Stevens both immediately collapsed.[57] The four Gestapo men ran up to inspect their victims, and Geith noticed that one of them was still twitching and told Schneider. 'Edi, go away,' said Schneider, 'I'll see to that.' Schneider aimed at the man's head, shot twice, and the movement stopped.[58]

As soon as death was confirmed, the Gestapo men engaged in a cover-up that would typify those carried out after the murders of the Great Escapers. Geith immediately removed the handcuffs that connected the dead men. As he did so, Schermer noticed that one of the officers wore a wristwatch, which he removed and pocketed. Branches from the nearby fir trees were placed over the bodies, and Weil and Geith fired several shots from their Walther PPKs into the woods in order to leave evidence of 'pursuit shots'. The car was then pushed forward some 5 yards, and Schneider's spent cartridge cases were gathered up and scattered around the new position of the vehicle. After Schermer was satisfied that the scene now looked like the aftermath of a thwarted escape rather than a murder, he and Schneider drove to Pfaffenhofen to find the coroner and a doctor.[59] While Geith and Weil waited with the bodies, two patrolling members of the local gendarmerie happened to approach on bicycles and asked Geith and Weil what was going on. After showing the policemen their passes, the Gestapo officers refused to offer an explanation, as their superior officer – Schermer – had the matter in hand. That answer seemed to partially satisfy the senior of the two policemen, who cycled away and left his colleague to stay at the scene.[60] Eventually, after around an hour, Schermer returned, accompanied by a Dr Max Reber and the coroner, who lifted up the fir branches covering the bodies, and declared, 'Yes, there is certainly no more to be done here.' Although Geith could not subsequently be certain, it appeared that neither the coroner nor the doctor studied the bodies too closely, or, if they did, neither man was willing to start asking awkward questions.[61]

After the coroner and the doctor departed, the corpses were moved into a slight dip so that they could not be spotted from the road, and the Gestapo men drove back to Munich, leaving their victims to be guarded by the junior policeman. Back at the Gestapo headquarters, Schermer instructed Geith to hand over the dead men's effects – including the watch – to Dr Schäfer. The Munich Gestapo chief studied them, and picked out an open packet of cigarettes, which he handed to Geith, telling him that he might as well smoke them. After performing a handclasp with Schäfer, a grateful Geith shared out the tobacco with Weil and Schneider.[62] Such were the spoils of murder. Two days later, at 9 a.m. on 31 March, the bodies of Gouws and Stevens were cremated by the State Funeral Office. Each cremation cost 36 Reichsmarks and 90 pfennigs, with the invoices being sent to Schermer of the Gestapo.[63] When the bill arrived, the Gestapo paid for the costs from the money it had confiscated from its two victims.[64]

Another fourteen Great Escapers were shot on the

same day as Kirby-Green, Kidder, Gouws and Stevens. Wednesday 29 March also saw the murders of Johnny Bull, Squadron Leader John Williams, Jerzy Mondschein and Reginald Kierath, who had been held in the same cell at the Kripo headquarters in Reichenberg with Ivo Tonder and John Stower.[65] At some point early that morning, the four men were taken away and shot on the orders of the Reichenberg Gestapo chief, Bernhard Baatz. It remains unclear who actually killed the four men, but it is likely to have been a combination of two Gestapo men called Robert Weyland and Robert Weissmann, although it is quite possible that more were involved.[66] What remains particularly unsettling about these murders is that Baatz wrote his letter to the crematorium in Brüx the night *before* the men were killed. After listing the names of the four men, Baatz had written that 'those named were killed during an escape attempt' and had added that no third parties were to blame.[67] Also murdered that morning were Romas Marcinkus, Tim Walenn, Gordon Brettell and Henri Picard, three of whom had been roommates with Alex Cassie.[68] Captured near Danzig, the four men were driven about 15 miles south to a wood near the village of Gross Trampken, where they were shot in the back by several members of the Danzig Gestapo, which was headed by Dr Günther Venediger.[69] Among those who carried out the shooting were Kriminalsekretär Reinhold Bruchardt, and possibly Oberassistent Julius Hug, as well as three other Gestapo men called Asal, Fels and Rörer. At about seven o'clock that morning, Gestapo driver Willi Reimer was ordered to drive a 2½-ton lorry to the wood, into which the bodies were loaded and transported back to the Gestapo headquarters in Danzig and quickly cremated.[70]

If some Gestapo officers found it distressing to shoot unarmed and manacled men in the back, there were others for whom such a task was little more than an inconvenience. Among them was the 35-year-old SS-Sturmbannführer and Kriminalkommissar Johannes Post, who worked for the Gestapo in Kiel. A committed Nazi, Post had joined the Party in December 1930, and had become a full-time officer in the SA. In October 1935, he joined the Gestapo in Elbing in what was then West Prussia.[71] After passing through the Sipo Officers' School in Berlin in February 1939, Post became a Kriminalkommissar, and had served in towns and cities occupied by the Nazis, such as Troppau, Radom and Stettin, before being posted to Kiel.[72] Tall, corpulent, with blue eyes and swept-back fair hair, he was feared even by his fellow Gestapo officers, who regarded him as a sadist because of his 'well-known brutal behaviour'.[73] Post, therefore, was the ideal man to be entrusted by the head of the Kiel Gestapo, Fritz Schmidt, to carry out the murders of James Catanach, Arnold Christensen, Hallada Espelid and Nils Fugelsang, all of whom were being held by the Kripo in Flensburg.

Post was given his initial orders at around eight o'clock on the morning of 29 March by Schmidt, who told him to prepare himself to escort some prisoners that day. About an hour later, Schmidt summoned Post and his colleague, Oskar Schmidt, and he explained exactly what the duty entailed – the two officers were to find a discreet location on the road between Kiel and

Neumünster where the four prisoners could be shot. Post and Schmidt did as they were ordered, and after driving some 7 miles south out of Kiel, they found a ploughed field surrounded by a thick hedgerow to the southwest of the village of Voorde.[74] After they had returned, Fritz Schmidt called another meeting, which was attended by both Post and Oskar Schmidt, as well as by officers Hans Kähler, Walter Jacobs and Franz Schmidt, and two drivers, Artur Denkmann and Wilhelm Struve. According to Oskar Schmidt, Fritz Schmidt read out a telegram from SS-Obergruppen-führer Kaltenbrunner, head of the RSHA, saying that the four RAF officers were to be shot while escaping, and that anybody not complying with this order 'will have to reckon with immediate sentence of death and punitive measures against his family'. As with many such meetings held at other Gestapo headquarters that day, the discussion was finalised with a handclasp.[75]

For Johannes Post, the fact that the prisoners were in Flensburg must have proved irksome. Flensburg was a drive of over 50 miles, and by the time the party had driven there, interrogated the prisoners, completed the paperwork, driven to the murder site, shot the prisoners, and then returned to Kiel to brief Schmidt, Post ran the risk of missing a night at the theatre he had planned with his girlfriend, one Marianne Heidt. The team left almost immediately, and drove up to Flensburg in two cars: a six-seater Adler and a four-seater Mercedes 231.[76] They arrived at around one o'clock, although presumably to Post's frustration, the chief of the local Gestapo insisted on standing his Kiel colleagues lunch at the Harmonie restaurant.[77] While the officers dined, the two drivers discussed a problem with Struve's Adler, which had developed a mechanical fault, and Struve asked Denkmann to watch out for him as they made their return journey.[78] After half an hour, the officers emerged from the restaurant, and by just after two o'clock, the four prisoners were being subjected to cursory interrogations, which did little more than confirm names and ranks.[79]

At around three o'clock, the two cars left Flensburg. In the Mercedes 231 driven by Denkmann sat Post, Kähler and Catanach, with the remaining three prisoners being escorted by Jacobs, Franz Schmidt and Oskar Schmidt in the Adler driven by Struve. As they headed south, Post – who spoke sufficient English – engaged Catanach in small talk. He offered his intended victim a cigarette, which the Australian refused because he was a non-smoker. At one point, the car drove over a viaduct over the Kiel Canal, which Catanach observed had often been targeted by the RAF.[80] Unfortunately for Post, progress was not as swift as he may have wished, as the Adler's engine trouble slowed it down, and Denkmann repeatedly had to stop in order to allow Struve to catch up.[81] Because of the delay, Post was now concerned that he would not get to the theatre on time, so he ordered Denkmann to drive via the centre of Kiel, in order to drop off one of the tickets with Heidt on the Hansastrasse.[82] Denkmann told Post that such a detour would add some 20 miles to the journey, but Post was insistent. 'You take the way which I tell you,' he snapped.[83] As a result of the diversion, the two cars were separated, but nevertheless, Post's car arrived at the scene of the imminent murders before the faltering Adler.

It was now around 4 p.m., and the impatient Post was in no mind to wait for the other car. He ordered Kähler to remove the handcuffs from Catanach and then told both men to get out. With his hand clutching his pistol in the right pocket of his coat, Post walked Catanach across the cobbled carriageway to the gate that led into the field. Kähler followed, holding a carbine. After passing through the gate, Catanach would have seen a view of gently rolling fields dotted with occasional copses. It would be the last thing he saw, as a few seconds later, Post shot him between the shoulder blades, straight through his heart. Catanach let out a short cry, and then fell dead to the ground. A few minutes later, the car containing the other prisoners arrived, and Christensen, Espelid and Fugelsang were marched into the field with their hands tied behind their backs. Escorting them were Oskar Schmidt, Franz Schmidt and Walter Jacobs.[84] As they turned into the field, the RAF officers saw the body of Catanach, and they started to scream in terror and tried to run away.[85] It is worth noting that Post could easily have hidden the body, but it is a measure of his callousness that he left it there for the prisoners to see. '*Los!*' he shouted at the three Gestapo men. 'Why don't you shoot?' Shortly afterwards, three shots rang out – fired by the two Schmidts and Jacobs – and the men fell to the ground. Although two were killed instantly, one prisoner, perhaps Espelid, was still moving. Post shouted at Kähler to finish the man off with the carbine, but Kähler hesitated, whereupon Post grabbed the weapon from him and shot Espelid through the head.[86] Post repeated the gruesome procedure with Fugelsang and

Christensen, and then removed the handcuffs from all three.[87]

What happened next was the familiar pattern of fabrication, involving bodies being moved, the crematorium being contacted and false statements drawn up. Post drove back to Kiel with Denkmann and Kähler, and instructed Kähler to sort out the tiresome details such as transporting the bodies. Despite all the delays, Post managed to make it to the theatre on time with his girlfriend.[88]

Two more of the Great Escapers who lost their lives that day were Bernard Scheidhauer and Roger Bushell. After leaving the Gestapo headquarters at Schlossplatz 15 in Saarbrücken,[89] Walter Breithaupt drove the two officers, along with Emil Schulz and Leopold Spann, east out of the town in the direction of Homburg.[90] After heading down the autobahn for just over half a mile, Spann ordered Breithaupt to stop, and the three Gestapo men got out of the car and looked around. Spann asked his colleagues whether they thought the location was suitable, and a consensus seemed to emerge that it was not. 'Later,' said Spann, who ignored a request from the prisoners to have their handcuffs removed.[91] Breithaupt drove past Homburg, and then headed towards Mannheim-Ludwigshafen via Kaiserslautern. After they had driven some 3 miles from Kaiserslautern, Spann once more stopped the car and he and Schulz got out.[92] Smoking cigarettes, the two men had a brief discussion, and then beckoned Breithaupt over and told him what was about to happen. 'Remember what happens to our wives and children during the air raids on our cities,' said one of the Gestapo officers.[93]

Schulz and Spann told Bushell and Scheidhauer that they could leave the car in order to relieve themselves. Bushell gestured towards his handcuffs, and Schulz removed them from both prisoners, who shook the cramp free from their arms. Spann warned them that if they tried to escape, they would be shot, the threat of which was reinforced by the fact that both he and Schulz had drawn their pistols. Bushell and Scheidhauer walked 5 yards back from the car, and about 2 yards away from the road, and began to urinate. Schulz and Spann then took up their positions, and almost simultaneously shot the two men in their backs.[94] Scheidhauer was killed immediately and fell forward on to his face. Bushell, however, had fallen on to his right side, and as he lay, he turned on to his back and started to convulse. 'I lay on the ground and shot him through the left temple,' Schulz recalled, 'whereupon death took place immediately.'[95]

After examining the bodies, Spann told Schulz to remain with them while he and Breithaupt returned to Saarbrücken to fetch a lorry. On the drive back to Gestapo headquarters, Spann told Breithaupt that he was not to talk to anybody about what had happened, and if he were ever asked, he was to say that the men had been shot while trying to escape. When they arrived at Schlossplatz, Spann ordered a driver called Peter Schmidt to help Breithaupt collect the bodies, and to place them in a large wooden coffin-like box filled with sawdust that was taken from the cellar of the headquarters.[96] It is telling that the Gestapo kept such equipment to hand. In all, it took Breithaupt two hours to travel to and from the site of the murder, and when he returned, he, Schulz and Schmidt loaded the bodies into the box and then on to the back of a covered Opel Blitz lorry. By around nine o'clock that morning, Schulz and his cargo drew into the courtyard at Schlossplatz, and Schulz reported to Spann, who told him that the disposal of the bodies would be handled by Kriminalkommissar Preuss and that Schulz could carry on with his normal duties.[97]

In the meantime, it appears either that Spann was not entirely certain how to get rid of the bodies, or that Preuss was not available, and so once again, Spann called upon Schulz to help. Spann told Schulz to take the bodies to Neue Bremm, a small Gestapo-run concentration camp situated 3 miles south of Gestapo headquarters.[98] There, Schulz delivered the bodies to the camp's commandant, SS-Untersturmführer Fritz Schmoll, who ran Neue Bremm with extreme brutality and used to hold executions of prisoners in the camp's courtyard. Schmoll was emphatically not the type to ask awkward questions, and he deposited the bodies in a hut in the women's section of the camp, and ordered nobody to enter. Schmoll then asked Olga Braun, a shorthand typist, to type up two death certificates, which stated that both men had been 'shot whilst trying to escape'. Braun was curious, and asked Schmoll about the killings. 'That does not concern you,' Schmoll replied, 'you have no questions to ask – type, and the matter will be settled.'[99] (It is worth observing that Schmoll's words unwittingly encapsulated how bureaucracy in Nazi Germany was used to mask criminality.)

The following day, Spann arrived to inspect the

bodies, accompanied by Dr Zeitzler, the head of the Saarbrücken Health Department.[100] Perhaps unsurprisingly, Zeitzler did little more than sign the two death certificates – here was another man who knew better than to ask questions such as how an escaping prisoner had been shot in the temple at close range. Later that day, the bodies were collected by Josef Allgeier, a driver for a local firm of undertakers called Hubert Laubach, based at Nauwieserstrasse 27.[101] Allgeier noticed that the two coffins bore cards that stipulated that they were not to be opened, a requirement that was emphasised in person by Schmoll. The driver then took his cargo to Saarbrücken's south cemetery, where it remained for two days.[102] On 1 April at 9 a.m., Roger Bushell's body was cremated by the 48-year-old Rudolf Schriever, who had been working at the crematorium since 1930. Schriever placed the ashes into urn number 127/1872, and made an entry in the death register. At nine thirty, Scheidhauer was cremated, and his ashes were put into urn 127/1871.[103] At some point – it is unclear when – the urns were delivered by a member of the Gestapo to the Kripo headquarters on Schlossplatz. They were deposited in the office of Kriminalkommissar Ludwig Kehl, who just a few days before had interrogated Bushell and had given him food and cigarettes. The urns were spotted by his colleague Wilma Klee, who asked Kehl whether they contained the remains of the two men. Kehl confirmed that they did, and, as Klee later reported, 'he himself regretted their deaths'.[104]

So ended the life of Roger Bushell, his death – for a Kripo officer in a small town in Germany – nothing more than a source of regret. Bushell's murder was of course no more tragic and horrific than the forty-nine other deaths that took place, but it is hard to think of a more unsuitable demise for such a dynamic and brave figure. Had Bushell considered the manner of his passing – and everybody who fought did reflect on how he or she might die – then he would have wanted to have died the Spitfire pilot's death, blasted into fiery smithereens during a dogfight against a chivalrous opponent. There are few, if any, good deaths in war, but the barbaric indignity of being crudely shot in the back while urinating by a man who was simply following orders was a particularly bad death, and was commensurate neither with the supposed offence nor with the nature of the man. Bushell and his fellow victims were not rapists or looters who might have expected such a form of execution, but were simply young men who wanted to regain the freedom they had enjoyed behind their control columns. As we have seen, the escapers had most certainly been warned that terrible consequences would occur in the event of a mass breakout, but Bushell could not have anticipated quite how terrible they were to be. Nevertheless, Bushell's insistence on a *grand coup* despite much cautioning against it was indeed reckless, and indirectly led to the deaths of himself and forty-nine other young men.

Such an analysis may not be attractive to many, who might argue that this was war, and risks have to be taken. After all, it is part of an officer's job to send men to their deaths. On the surface this position seems reasonable, but it ignores the fact that not all risks have to be taken to win wars, and certainly not those risks whose taking gains little or no benefit. The Great Escape did not alter the course of the war in any way whatsoever, and not one fewer Allied serviceman was killed as a result of the breakout. There had been other mass breakouts from other camps, but nobody then – or today – supposed that anything was gained when, for example, Wings Day led forty-three Allied airmen out of Szubin in March 1943.[105] As we have seen, thanks to the efficacy of the *Grossfahndungen* in rounding up not only escaping POWs but also thousands of other wanted persons, such mass escapes actually helped the Germans.[106] The difference between other great escapes and the Great Escape was the simple and horrific fact that most of those who escaped through Harry were murdered. As a result of an understandable desire to memorialise – and for those deaths to 'mean something' – the Great Escape has been elevated into a component of national mythology. Had the murders not taken place, then it is likely that the tale of Bushell and Tom, Dick and Harry would be as obscure as that of any of the other mass breakouts. How many today remember the escape in June 1943 of sixty-five Allied POWs through a tunnel at Oflag VIIB at Eichstätt?[107] Or the construction of three tunnels – also called Tom, Dick and Harry – built during the winter of 1943 to 1944 at the same camp?[108]

It is therefore possible to argue that the lives of the Great Escapers were wasted. All their deaths served to prove was that Nazism was brutal and murderous – a fact well known to many. It is hard to draw any significant meaning from, for example, the murder of

Flying Officer Dennis Cochran, who was just twenty-two years old on 31 March when he was shot in the back of the head by Kriminalsekretär Otto Preiss on a track off the road leading up to Natzweiler concentration camp.[109] And what was the point of the murder of the 27-year-old John Stower, who was taken from the cell he shared with Ivo Tonder at Reichenberg that same day, and shot in an unknown location by an unknown Gestapo officer? Both of these young men were alone when they were killed, and each might have asked the simple question 'Why?' – if they had ever had the chance.

There is no satisfactory response to that; or at least, no response that can bring satisfaction. For the parents of the Great Escapers, there could be no comfort that they had lost their sons while they were in the midst of battle, doing their bit for freedom. Their sons were killed simply because they had annoyed someone. That was the obvious cause of the deaths, but it does not reveal why the men were put in such a dangerous position, for which there were many reasons. First, the escapers desired freedom – but that freedom was illusory, as very few could ever hope to gain it through escape. Secondly, there was the notion that escaping was some sort of sport – but the enjoyment quickly wore off after a few hours in freezing conditions dressed in hopelessly inadequate clothing. Thirdly, there was the need to be seen to be doing *something* against the enemy – but the mass searches engendered by mass breakouts inadvertently helped the Germans, so that motive too was flawed. And, even if a POW did make a 'home run', the impact of such an achievement on the war effort was negligible.

The final reason comes in the form of Roger Bushell, who had an enormous influence on his younger officers through his charisma and forceful personality. It was Bushell who ultimately decided to mount a mass escape, despite the repeated warnings made against doing so. It would of course be wrong to lay the blame for the murders on his shoulders, but Bushell was in a position to judge whether the risks – both explicit and implicit – in adopting such a strategy were worth taking. After all, what did Bushell hope to gain by launching the Great Escape? Did he really think that he would be hitting the Germans hard, or were his reasons rooted in something more egotistical? Until he was shot down in May 1940, Bushell had never tasted significant failure, and for the last four years of his life, his actions can be seen as an understandable attempt to make up for that failure. What is less creditable, however, is Bushell's desire to involve others in a project that was unsound, doomed, dangerous and superfluous to the war effort. This is not to argue that nothing should have been done, but it is clear that a more realistic approach to escaping might have offered greater reward. Why was it not enough for Bushell to mount a series of smaller escapes, which would have had more opportunities for success, and less chance of reprisal? In an awful sense, it was only through the murders that the legend of Bushell was created. Had the reprisals not taken place, Bushell would be remembered no more than the now forgotten officer who led the June 1943 mass breakout from Eichstätt.

Chapter Twelve

An 'atmosphere of sudden death'

AFTER THEY HAD been captured, almost half of the Great Escapers found themselves incarcerated in the civilian prison at Görlitz. Among them were Richard Churchill and Thomas Nelson, who had been sent there after their arrest on 26 March near Halbau.[1] The conditions in the prison were tough, with four POWs crammed into cells designed for single prisoners and only measuring 8 feet by 5. A bucket in the corner served as a lavatory, and a wooden bench that could be folded into the wall acted as a bed. The only light came from a single barred window set high up, but as it could not be opened, it provided no ventilation. With almost no food, it is hardly surprising that Nelson later described the situation as a 'very uncomfortable set-up'.[2]

Coupled with such deprivations was an overarching

sense of fear engendered by interrogation and disappearance. From time to time, the POWs were taken either singly or in pairs to the Gestapo headquarters, a Baroque-inspired townhouse on Augustastrasse 31. There, the POWs were sat on a stool in front of a table in a dimly lit room and questioned by Dr Wilhelm Scharpwinkel[3] and two or three other Gestapo officers, who wished to interpret the escape as something more sinister. 'They were very keen to produce a scenario where it wasn't just a breakout of officers from an RAF prison camp,' Richard Churchill recalled, 'but was in some way a spy operation or the equivalent of a Commando raid.' According to Churchill, the Gestapo's line of questioning focused on the notion that the escapers were intending to foment an uprising in the former Czechoslovakia, or even in Germany itself, all of which Churchill later dismissed as being 'fairy tale stuff'.[4] Despite the absurd accusations, the interrogations were very frightening. 'It was very unpleasant questioning of the third degree type,' said Thomas Nelson. 'There was no physical violence used as far as I was concerned, but considerable mental violence or pressures and threats that we would be killed, and so on, which none of us I think took very seriously.'[5] Others, however, did appear to take the threats seriously. 'I wasn't beaten up,' said Richard Churchill, 'but the atmosphere of sudden death being quite possible was all around one all the time.'[6] Many of the officers were told they were going to be shot, and at least two – Flight Lieutenants Alastair Gunn and Michael Casey – were told they were going to 'lose their heads'.[7] One officer was told that he was in the hands of 'what you would call in English, the secret service' and that 'anything might happen to you without protection'. When the POW replied that he was protected by the Geneva Convention, there was no response, but merely 'a half laugh'.[8] Even one of the Gestapo interrogators found Scharpwinkel's manner alarming, with one noticing that he became 'very excited' when the POWs refused to answer questions about the escape.[9]

However, it was the disappearances that the POWs found most disquieting. Lifted up by his cellmates, Churchill was once able to look out of the window into the courtyard below, where he saw six of his fellow officers. '[They were] being taken out by men dressed in black leather coats and trilby hats who were clearly Gestapo and put into motor cars,' he recalled. Unfortunately for Churchill, he was spotted, and a few moments later, the cell door was unlocked and in came the largest man he had ever seen. 'He must have been seven feet tall and weighed seventeen stone or more,' said Churchill. 'He came into the narrow cell, plucked me from the shoulders of the other inmate, and threw me from one end of the cell to the other as if I'd been a small sack of rice.' The man, who was wearing the trademark Gestapo coat and hat, informed Churchill that it was forbidden to look out of the window. 'I thought my last moment had come,' said Churchill. However, to Churchill's surprise, the man left the room as quickly as he had entered it. 'This certainly woke me up to the condition we were now in,' Churchill recalled, 'and the rest of us in the cell with me, that this wasn't prisoner-of-war officers' camp treatment.'[10]

Every few days, groups of POWs were taken from the prison and were never to return. Their names were called out, and Nelson and Churchill noted them down, believing that the men were going back to Sagan. 'We thought we were rather badly done by,' said Nelson, 'because the other people had finished their interrogation and gone back to a relatively comfortable camp.'[11] On 30 March, the Gestapo took six officers away. A second party left the following day, comprising ten POWs, and on 1 April, four were driven off. On 6 April, a fourth party of officers was taken, which left just nine Great Escapers in the prison. Later that day, eight further names were called out, including those of Nelson and Churchill, and the men were put in a lorry and taken back to Stalag Luft III, where they were locked in the cooler. Just one POW – James 'Cookie' Long – remained in the prison.[12] 'We assumed at that time that we were the . . . last people to leave Görlitz,' said Nelson, 'and all the people earlier arrived back in the camp.'[13] But of course Nelson was wrong, because as he and his fellow officers were shortly to discover, all those who had left Görlitz in the other parties had been shot.

Their murders were masterminded by Scharpwinkel, and were carried out by numerous members of the Breslau and Görlitz Gestapo.[14] Among those who were party to the killings was the 56-year-old Kriminalinspektor Richard Hänsel, who had assisted with the interrogations at Görlitz. Although it is not entirely clear which killings Hänsel witnessed, it is likely to be those of Flight Lieutenants Albert Hake, Michael Casey, George Wiley and Thomas Leigh, Flying Officer

John Pohé, and Squadron Leader Ian Cross, who left Görlitz at 1 p.m. on 30 March.[15] The convoy of four vehicles, which comprised three cars and one lorry, headed in the direction of Sagan, and drove via Penzig, Rauscha and Halbau.[16] At 3.30 p.m., about 5 miles north of Halbau, and just 3 miles south of Stalag Luft III, Scharpwinkel ordered the convoy to halt on a wooded stretch of the road. The prisoners were told to form a column, and were guarded by at least six Gestapo men, two of whom were carrying submachine guns. For the next five minutes, nothing appeared to happen, and the prisoners stretched their legs. Hänsel even fetched himself some bread and butter from his briefcase in his car as he had missed his lunch. When he returned, he saw Scharpwinkel gesticulating to the POWs that they should move into the woods.[17] The officers did so, and were followed by Scharpwinkel; Kriminalkommissar Läuffer, who had attended von Lindeiner's conference a fortnight before;[18] Kriminalrat Dankert; Kriminalinspektor Hampel; Kriminalrat Erwin Wieczorek; and Kriminalobersekretär Walter Lux, who was carrying a submachine gun.[19] While Hänsel was waiting by the side of the road eating his slice of bread, he heard two bursts of automatic fire. Abandoning his lunch, he ran into the woods. There, sprawled amongst the trees, were the bodies of the prisoners. All of the men, Hänsel noticed, appeared to have been shot in the back, in the region of the heart. When Hänsel asked what had happened, Kriminalinspektor Hampel told him that the men had tried to escape.[20] Hänsel didn't believe his colleague for a moment, but he kept quiet. 'They would have been crazy to try to escape with men armed with machine pistols standing so close behind them,' he recalled. 'Their chance of getting away was so slight.'[21]

Scharpwinkel then ordered Hänsel and a driver, Kriminalrat Kühnel, to go to Halbau immediately and to telephone an undertaker in Görlitz to collect the bodies and to cremate them. Hänsel went to the home of Halbau's *Amtsvorsteher* – superintendent – where it took him an hour and half to get through to Görlitz. Hänsel eventually returned to the scene of the murders at around 6 p.m., by which time only four of his colleagues – including Lux and Hampel – remained. While the six men waited for the undertaker, Hänsel overheard Lux saying to one of the Gestapo men, 'Tomorrow, or the day after, we'll be going to Hirschberg.'[22] At 8.30 p.m., the undertaker arrived, and Hänsel and Kühnel escorted the bodies back to Görlitz, where they were formally handed over to the crematorium at 11.30 p.m.

Although Hänsel did not know what Lux was planning to do at Hirschberg, he might well have been able to guess. Imprisoned there were four men whose names had ended up on the wrong pile in Nebe's office – Flight Lieutenants James Wernham and Antoni Kiewnarski, Pilot Officer Sotiris Skanziklas and Flying Officer Kazimierz Pawluk. At around midday on 31 March, Scharpwinkel sent for the 38-year-old Kriminalrat Erwin Wieczorek, who had joined the Breslau Gestapo in 1933, and had served in Koblenz, Kassel, and Wilhelmshaven.[23] Scharpwinkel ordered Wieczorek to select two men, and to drive to Hirschberg to 'escort' four of the recaptured Sagan escapers.

Wieczorek knew exactly what his chief meant, as a few days before, Scharpwinkel had told him and a handful of other senior Breslau Gestapo officers about Hitler's order. Wieczorek chose Kriminalsekretär Schampera and Kriminalangestellter Tögel to accompany him, and shortly afterwards, the three men departed as part of a convoy of three cars and drove the 70 miles west to Hirschberg. Also included in the convoy were Scharpwinkel himself, and Kriminalsekretär Walter Pattke. After arriving in Hirschberg, Scharpwinkel interrogated the four men at the Gestapo headquarters, and then announced that he would be taking them back to Sagan, and that if they attempted to escape, they would be shot.[24]

The convoy of four cars departed at 6 p.m., and headed north towards Sagan. After driving for just half an hour, Scharpwinkel ordered the convoy to stop. On this occasion, the Gestapo chief had decided on a different form of subterfuge, and declared that his car had broken down. All four cars were to draw close together, and the prisoners were permitted to relieve themselves on the side of the road between the second and third cars. As two Gestapo men ostensibly tinkered under the bonnet of Scharpwinkel's car, the remaining members of the escort stood near the prisoners. However, Wieczorek later claimed that he and his driver had gone to help with the breakdown, 'in order intentionally to avoid participation in the action which had been ordered'. According to Wieczorek, he heard an order being shouted out and then shots being fired. 'The reports of the tommy guns at so short a distance were actually very loud,' Wieczorek said, an admission that makes it unlikely, despite the darkness, that he did not actually see the murders taking place. Nevertheless, he did admit to seeing the dead bodies, which were lying six to seven paces from the edge of the road.[25] Once again, the now customary arrangements for dealing with the corpses were made, and after a few hours, the Gestapo men drove back to Breslau. 'During the journey hardly anyone spoke,' said Wieczorek. 'On the one hand we were all tired, and on the other hand, I suppose, more or less depressed by the incident.'[26] Such was the level of sympathy shown.

In total, Wilhelm Scharpwinkel coordinated the murder of around thirty of the Great Escapers. The circumstances of the deaths of most of his victims remain opaque, and no accounts of the killings on or around 6 April of Flight Lieutenants William Grisman, Alastair Gunn, Harold Milford, James 'Cookie' Long and John F. Williams; Flying Officers Denys Street, Stanislaw Krol and Pawel Tobolski; and Lieutenant Clement McGarr are known to exist.[27] What is clear is that the majority of the victims were killed by pistol shots taken by Gestapo officers, and the depiction in the film of the escapers being mown down by a heavy machine gun is inaccurate. However, at least ten of the escapers were killed in a manner redolent of the celluloid depiction, and this slaughter was witnessed by a driver with the Breslau Gestapo called Oberscharführer Robert Schröder. The victims were the members of the second party of POWs which had left Görlitz, and comprised Flying Officers Włodzimierz Kolanowski, Robert Stewart and Henry Birkland, and Flight Lieutenants Ernst Valenta, Edgar Humphreys,

George McGill, Cyril Swain, Charles Hall, Patrick Langford and Brian Evans. The men had been taken to Breslau for interrogation, and at about 7 p.m. one evening, they were placed in a lorry and taken on the road to Sagan, with a car driven by Schröder in the lead. The night was freezing, and about halfway to Sagan, the vehicles stopped in order to let the guards and the prisoners urinate. 'The lorry was about 40 metres behind me,' Schröder recalled. 'I was sitting alone in the car when I suddenly heard shouts, followed immediately by a mad firing of machine-pistols.' Schröder jumped out of the car and ran back to see the POWs lying on the ground, some of whom were on the road, and the others on the slope nearby. When Schröder asked what had happened, the response he was given was sadly predictable: that some of the prisoners wanted to escape, 'and that they all had caught it'.[28]

Although most of the Gestapo officers carried out the murders either willingly or with few qualms, there were some who felt deeply unsettled by their orders. Of these, the case of Alfred Schimmel is perhaps the most pertinent. As the senior Gestapo officer in the Alsace, it was Schimmel who was responsible for the killing of 23-year-old Flight Lieutenant Anthony Hayter, who had been arrested on 27 March, 60 miles south of Strasbourg.[29] Unlike many of the murderers, the 38-year-old Schimmel had been a practising solicitor before joining the Gestapo, and had studied law at the universities of Heidelberg, Munich and Würzburg. After nearly three years working in the Bavarian and Reich civil service and the Bavarian political police,

Schimmel was transferred to the Munich Gestapo in May 1938 to head up the Internal Political Department with the rank of Regierungsrat.[30] Schimmel would later state that his appointment to the Gestapo had merely been a 'question of reorganisation' and that he had had no say in the move, a claim that was not entirely without foundation, as the Bavarian political police was merged by Himmler into the Gestapo.[31] In April 1942, Schimmel was transferred to Strasbourg to head up the Gestapo unit in the Alsace, which was subordinate to the office of the Befehlshaber der Sicherheitspolizei und des SD (the Commander of the Security Police and SD, or BdS) which by January 1944 was headed by Dr Erich Isselhorst.[32] Despite being relatively senior, it appears that the bespectacled and bookish Schimmel was not admired by the head of the Gestapo, Heinrich Müller, who, according to Schimmel, regarded him as being 'too soft' to serve in the organisation. In the spring of 1944, Schimmel had been ordered to visit the office of the RSHA in Strasbourg, where he was informed that he would never be promoted because Müller had always blocked it, on the grounds that Schimmel was 'not sufficiently hard for service for the Gestapo'.[33]

At the time of the Great Escape, Schimmel found himself in Berlin, where he was temporarily attached to Department III of the RSHA, where he was learning administrative and legal procedures in Office A5, and to where he was shortly going to be transferred. By 5 April – his birthday – Schimmel had returned to Strasbourg, and he started work proper at his office at Sängerhofstrasse 14 the following day.[34] At eleven o'clock that morning, two Kripo officials arrived, bringing with them Flight

Lieutenant Hayter, who, they told Schimmel, was being transferred into his custody. Schimmel was perplexed, as he claimed not to have heard of the *Grossfahndung* while he was in Berlin, and neither was he aware of the Sagan Order.[35] He telephoned the head of the local Kripo, who simply informed him that he was under orders to hand Hayter over to the Gestapo. Schimmel then called Isselhorst, but he was out to lunch. Schimmel then told Hayter to sit down, offered him a cigarette, and had a brief conversation with him before going out for lunch himself.[36]

Upon his return at around 1 p.m., Schimmel was handed a cable that had been sent by Heinrich Müller. The cable ordered Schimmel to drive Hayter in the direction of Breslau, and to have him shot en route whilst he was attempting to escape. The body was to be disposed of by an undertaker, and the ashes were to be handed to the Kripo in Strasbourg before being forwarded to Berlin. A few years later Schimmel would say:

> I could not understand this order, because first that an office of the Gestapo should be burdened with such a task; secondly . . . because although it was such a serious matter, no reason was given for it and I asked myself how I was going to justify the execution of such an order in front of myself and in front of my officials.[37]

Claiming to be in shock, Schimmel put through an urgent call to Müller himself, who was exasperated when Schimmel expressed his qualms.

'The order is absolutely clear and intelligible,' Müller

replied sharply. 'The order is to be carried out in the way it is laid down in the teleprint. You cannot doubt its legality because it comes from Hitler.'

Schimmel continued to raise objections, which only served to further irritate the Gestapo head.

'Schimmel, I know your soft attitude, there is no doubt in this matter. Either you carry out the order, or you must expect to be arrested and shot because of refusal to obey an order and because of betraying a state secret.'[38]

Schimmel claimed to have been shaken by Müller's reply, and even though he had been told that the order had come from Hitler – whose word really was law – Schimmel decided to consult Isselhorst. Unfortunately for Schimmel, his immediate superior had served in a series of *Einsatzgruppen* from September 1942 to October 1943, and was phlegmatic about the killing of a solitary British RAF officer.[39] Instead of offering Schimmel some consolatory advice, he helpfully suggested that Schimmel could arrange for the execution to take place on the road to Natzweiler concentration camp, where the body could then be easily disposed of.[40] Isselhorst then enquired as to who Schimmel had in mind to carry out the order, and Schimmel said that he was not certain, but possibly Kriminalkommissar Max Diessner and Kriminalsekretär Heinrich Hilker.[41]

When he returned to his office, Schimmel assessed his options. 'I once again considered whether it would not after all be possible to avoid carrying out this order,' he later stated.[42] He would claim that had he refused to obey, he would have been sent to a concentration camp to receive 'special treatment' – which meant being shot on the spot. Under the principle of *Sippenhaft* – literally, 'kin detention' – Schimmel also expected his wife and young daughter to be arrested, as well as his elderly parents.[43] Another course Schimmel considered was to escape to Switzerland with Hayter. 'My thought was to take the prisoner with me into my flat for the night,' he recalled, 'and drive him in the direction of the Swiss border the next morning.' However, Schimmel dismissed the idea, as the border was completely closed to traffic, and the frontier zone itself was some 2 miles wide, and anybody who entered it was regarded as suspicious and could be checked. 'I abandoned the plan in the end,' Schimmel said, 'because I would have had to leave my family behind. I had to reckon with my wife and child being arrested at once on my escape.'[44] Schimmel also considered simply walking Hayter out of the building and letting him run away, but he suspected that the POW would have stood no chance, and such an act would have resulted in Schimmel's arrest and have simply delayed Hayter's death. 'I saw no practical possibility of saving him,' Schimmel claimed, 'although it was horrible for me to occupy myself with the execution of this order.'[45]

Although the question of whether Schimmel and his fellow Gestapo officers would have been shot had they refused to obey the Sagan Order will be examined later, it is worthwhile to reflect on whether Schimmel was being truthful when he claimed to have agonised over the killing of Hayter. After all, when Schimmel was relating the motives behind his actions, he was fighting for his own life in a courtroom, and most people in similar circumstances would not hesitate to dissemble. By that stage, Schimmel had already lied frequently about the murder, and he had variously claimed to have been in Oslo at the time, or in Berlin, or in Strasbourg but to have never seen any order.[46] Schimmel's words cannot be trusted, but his later statements, made after more thorough interrogations (and that is emphatically not a euphemism for violence), do have an air of verisimilitude. They are also markedly different from those made by his fellow Gestapo officers, who, in the main, do not reveal any deliberation about the killings. It is possible that the well-educated and clever Schimmel was trying to adopt the same skin-saving, inculpatory attitude as Albert Speer had done at Nuremberg. However, his character and background make it equally plausible that Schimmel had indeed been anxious about an order that, although technically legal in Hitler's Germany, was barbaric in the eyes of any decent human being, let alone – or, to be cynical, even – a lawyer. It is very tempting to simply dismiss every word ever uttered by every Gestapo officer, but that would be to accept the caricature of that organisation as a realistic portrait. As a body, it is right to consider the Gestapo a force for evil, but it cannot be said that all its members were in themselves evil, or were psychopathic or similarly mentally disturbed. It would be more absurd to suppose that a middle-class 38-year-old husband and father, who had studied law and had worked as a civil servant, was more likely to kill willingly than reluctantly. This does not deny that such men can make eager homicides, but even in the Third Reich, there were men – who may have included Schimmel himself – who still possessed compasses with needles of sufficient moral magnetism.

Despite his deliberations, Schimmel did decide to organise the killing of Anthony Hayter. A better man, when faced with such a task, would have chosen to do it himself, but Schimmel passed on the duty to two of his subordinates, thereby creating three murderers rather than just one. Schimmel briefed Diessner and Hilker to kill Hayter near Natzweiler, and then to take his body to be cremated there. The Gestapo chief added that the order was a 'rotten business', but that he could not do anything about it, and that he was sorry to have to pass the matter on to them.[47] Schimmel also had another concern. As a church-going Protestant, he was reluctant to have Hayter shot the following day, as it was Good Friday. 'I could not go to church knowing that that was happening,' he said later.[48]

At around 3 p.m. that afternoon, Diessner and Hilker left the Gestapo office with Hayter, and were driven to Natzweiler by a driver called Hässle.[49] After a drive of some 35 miles, the car was stopped about half a mile from the camp at a turning into a wood. Hayter was ordered to get out and to relieve himself, and while he did so, Diessner chatted to him. The conversation was cut short when Hilker suddenly came up on the side of Hayter and shot him in the temple. Death was apparently instantaneous. The Gestapo then man-handled Hayter's body into the car, and they deposited it at the concentration camp, giving orders for the urn containing his ashes to be sent down to Schimmel in Strasbourg when it was ready.[50] It is likely that Hayter's body was cremated by Franz Berg, a Kapo whose job was to stoke the fires in the crematorium. For Berg, burning the body of the young airman would have been of no consequence. During his time at Natzweiler, he had cremated between 5,000 and 7,000 bodies, at an average rate of some 500 per month.[51] A few days later, the urn arrived at the Gestapo headquarters, and Schimmel forwarded it to the Kripo. He then dispatched a cable to Müller in Berlin, telling him his orders had been carried out. 'Ever since it happened,' Schimmel recalled just over two years later, 'this case has never left me in inner peace. I felt that one day it would be my doom.'[52]

Chapter Thirteen

'No *one* wounded?'

BACK AT STALAG LUFT III, the mood among the POWs was one of a mixture of cautious celebration and nervous anticipation. Many supposed that the Germans were bound to take some form of reprisal. 'The escape had broken a world's record for the length of a kriegy [*sic*] tunnel and another world's record for the number of officers escaped,' Paul Brickhill wrote. 'That was bound to be interpreted by the Master Race as a direct insult to The System.'[1] 'There was a sense of triumph,' said Leonard Hall, 'and almost of unreality.'[2] 'An uneasy feeling permeated the camp,' recalled Flight Lieutenant Flekser. 'Day followed day, without any news of the escapees.'[3] For some, such as Alan Bryett, the lack of information boded well. 'The initial news was very optimistic,' he said. 'There was a very large number – some fifty or sixty – who had obviously got away and were not coming back.'[4] However, not all were so hopeful, and many found it ominously unlikely that not a single POW had seemingly been captured, and it was a cause of relief when some of the escapees eventually did return. Those who came back told of being held in Görlitz and interrogations by the Gestapo, which was unsettling enough, but what worried the returning Kriegies were the fates of those they knew had been recaptured. Jack Rae said:

> They were sort of saying, 'Hasn't Johnny come back? And Jim, where is he?' A little bit of unease set in, but we thought, 'Oh, they've probably been moved to another prison camp or sent them to Colditz or something.' We weren't terribly worried to start with at all.[5]

What the POWs did not know was the piece of news given to the temporary Commandant, Lieutenant Colonel Erich Cordes, on the evening of Tuesday 4 April. In a telephone call made from Berlin, Cordes was told that forty-one of the POWs had been shot, and that he was to pass this information on to the senior British officers. Cordes replied that he wanted to have a statement in writing issued by Berlin that would contain the exact words he was to use, and this arrived the following day.[6] On the morning of Thursday 6th, Group Captain Massey was informed by an upset Hans Pieber that he and his interpreter, Squadron Leader Philip Murray, were to report to the Commandant's office at 11 a.m.[7] Pieber had made little effort to hide his distress throughout that morning's *Appell*, as he said to some of the Kriegies, 'It is not a very nice day.' When they asked him what the matter was, he could only say, 'You will find out later.'[8] When Massey and Murray arrived at the office, Cordes stood up and delivered Berlin's words in German.

> I have been instructed by my higher authority to communicate to you this report. The Senior British Officer is to be informed that as a result of a tunnel from which 76 officers escaped from Stalag Luft III, North Compound, 41 of these officers have been shot whilst resisting arrest or attempting further escape after arrest.

Murray translated these words for Massey, who then asked Cordes how many of the men had been wounded. The Commandant was clearly ill at ease, and stiffly responded, 'My higher authority only permits me to read this report and not to answer questions, or to give any further information.' Massey persisted, and repeated the question. Cordes said that he understood that none had been wounded.[9] Massey's voice then rose.

'*No one* wounded?' he asked. 'Do you mean to tell me forty-one can be shot in those circumstances and that all were killed and no one was wounded?'

'I am to read you this report,' Cordes replied, 'and that is all I can do.'[10]

Massey then asked for the names of the dead, information that the Commandant said he would supply as soon as possible. Massey also requested Cordes to inform the senior officers in all the other compounds, including those at Belaria, which Cordes agreed to do.

After that, the meeting broke up and Massey and Murray were escorted back by Pieber, who was clearly upset by the news.

'Please do not think that the Luftwaffe had anything to do with this dreadful thing,' he said. 'We do not wish to be associated with it. It is terrible . . . terrible.'[11]

After arriving back at the compound, Massey asked for the senior officer of every room in each barrack to report to him in the theatre. Already, rumours were spreading around the camp that 'something dreadful' had taken place, but such rumours were commonplace, with some supposing that Massey was to announce a German reprisal on the level of stopping Red Cross parcels.[12] When he broke the news to the three hundred officers who had gathered, the theatre fell silent. 'A lot of people suddenly felt sick,' Paul Brickhill later wrote. 'Still in a stunned silence we filed out of the theatre and within two minutes the news had spread to everyone in the compound.'[13] At that evening's *Appell*, the atmosphere was unsurprisingly tense. 'It was conducted with a silence that you could cut with a knife,' said Arthur Cole. 'It was the only weapon we had against them, but it was quite a powerful one.'[14] The mood among the POWs was, according to RAF Marine Craft Officer Edward Chapman, one of a mixture of 'anger, revulsion and vile hatred'. 'We stood there,' he recalled, 'and I've never known such silence . . . The Germans were cringing. They could feel it. There wasn't a sound. They were sort of cowed, and they went off with their tails between their legs.'[15] Despite their justified anger, the Kriegies realised that their captors were not to blame. 'They were as dumbfounded as we,' said John Acquier, a British wireless officer with the Royal Canadian Air Force. 'As far as the Germans were concerned, it was an embarrassment.'[16] Hans Pieber, observed Cole, was in tears. 'Everybody was stricken to hear the official announcement and to find out that the rumour was true,' Pieber later said. 'We knew instantly that this must have been done by the Gestapo.'[17]

Later that day, Massey wrote to Cordes, expressing his 'very gravest misgivings' at the news, and requested that he have a meeting with none other than the head of the Luftwaffe, Hermann Göring, 'in order that I may be given full details of the whole occurrence, and hear his views as brother, though enemy, soldier'.[18] Massey's appeal did not bear fruit, and on the following day, he wrote two further letters, in which he asked for a meeting with the senior officers of the other compounds, and also that the remains of the deceased POWs should be brought to Sagan for burial in the British and American cemetery. Massey also advised Cordes that the compound would go into mourning throughout the whole of Easter, and no games or entertainments would take place. Furthermore, after the *Appell* on the evening of 7 April – Good Friday – a service would be held to commemorate the dead.[19] The service was a particularly tense affair. As a further mark of remembrance, every Kriegie had cut the bottom off his black uniform tie, and had sewn it on to his sleeve as a black diamond. While the prisoners sang 'O Valiant Hearts', the Germans were sufficiently wary of an uprising that they had positioned machine guns all around.[20] When the Kriegies solemnly and slowly walked back to their huts, a sentry fired a volley of warning shots over their heads.[21]

For the next week, the compound was in shock. The air of unreality was not helped by the Germans' bewildering decision on 11 April to remove the clothes of all those who had escaped and to store them in the *Vorlager*.[22] This gave rise to much speculation, abetted by Pieber, that the escapees were in fact still alive, and that the clothing was required by the Gestapo in order to improve the captives' appearance.[23] Other rumours were to follow. On 12 April, an American officer, who had been receiving treatment at the German hospital in Bunzlau, reported that he had met a Belgian POW on a train who had told him that twenty-four British men had been brought to his camp, Stalag VIIIA at Siegersdorf, on the 4th of that month.[24] Corporal Rickmers, who had passed on coded messages to Britain on behalf of Tommy Calnan,[25] reported that Roger Bushell had been caught in the Flensburg area disguised as a nun, and had been shot.[26]

Despite all these rumours, none possessed enough credibility to stop a memorial service being held on Thursday 13 April. 'I cannot recall any parade, in captivity or out, which was executed with more solemnity and precision,' wrote Flight Lieutenant Cy Grant from British Guiana.[27] However, there was a strange coda to the service, which revealed a startling insensitivity on behalf of the Germans. During the pro-ceedings, some of the Kriegies noticed, in the words of Flight Lieutenant David Codd, 'some strange activities going on the other side of the parade ground'. 'With admirable British aplomb, the Memorial Service con-tinued,' wrote Codd, but as soon as it was over, a crowd of POWs rushed over to see what was happening.[28] The

Kriegies were startled to see a group of British soldiers holding some of the camp staff captive. One of the soldiers cuffed a German around the head, while another prodded a wounded German with the butt of his rifle. 'The uniforms were so perfect!' recalled Cy Grant. 'Our hopes so tangible.' But then the Kriegies noticed a movie camera in the background, recording the whole scene as 'evidence' of British atrocities. The Kriegies soon twigged and started to protest, but the Germans carried on filming their propaganda. However, the interruptions grew too loud and frequent, and a sergeant toting a pistol eventually ordered the Kriegies back to their huts. Grant found the episode a 'heartless riposte' to the memorial service, which was both 'inconceivable and callous'.[29] Others saw a lighter side, and had sarcastically clapped each of the 'takes'. 'At least this diversion gave us something other than the massacre to think about,' David Codd recalled.[30]

Two days later, on Saturday 15 April, Hans Pieber presented a list that contained forty-seven names.[31] It was pinned to the camp noticeboard, and a crowd swiftly gathered around it, gasping and cursing as the names of friends were spotted or read out.[32] Naturally, some of the Kriegies who had not made it down the tunnel reflected on what they now regarded as their good fortune. 'I realised that if I'd got out, I was fairly certain I would have been one of the fifty because my record wasn't too good,' said Ken Rees. 'I felt it was a very lucky escape.' But relief soon gave way to grief. When Rees discovered that his friend and roommate Johnny Bull had been shot, he was devastated:

When I was back in my bunk, I would look across to his bunk and think 'God'. He had been shot down and his baby had been born afterwards and he had never seen it. I just couldn't get over the fact that he was not going to go home and would never see his wife and child.[33]

Three days later, a further three names appeared: those of Stanislaw Krol, Pawel Tobolski and James 'Cookie' Long.[34] Of these, Long was probably the last of the Great Escapers to have been shot, and he was murdered on or around 12 April on the orders of Wilhelm Scharpwinkel. Although the grieving would continue, the Kriegies reacted in a more sanguine way than civilians might have done. According to Paul Royle, morale did not significantly diminish. 'I don't recall any particular effect,' he said. 'People were probably pretty cross about it. But remember every single person had been very nearly killed a week or a month or a year ago or so, so you took a very different attitude towards life.'[35]

Chapter Fourteen

Later Fallers and Finishers

BY MIDNIGHT OF 27 March, fewer than forty-eight hours after the breakout, sixty-one of the seventy-six Great Escapers had been recaptured.[1] As we have seen, the Kriegies faced numerous impediments, the most significant of which were the harsh weather conditions and the effectiveness of the *Grossfahndung*. Of these, the *Grossfahndung* represented the greater danger, as nearly every man in uniform in the Reich was looking for the escapees. The Kripo's War Search Head Office in Berlin issued regular special updates in the *Deutsches Kriminalpolizeiblatt* (*German Kripo Newsletter*), which was circulated to various agencies all over Greater Germany. As well as detailing the escapers' clothing and papers, the updates insisted that 'especially energetic searches are to be made in connection with the special search measures already ordered'.[2] The efforts clearly paid off, because by 29 March, just four days after the breakout, only seven were still on the run. As a result, the *Grossfahndung* was reduced to a *Kriegsfahndung*, although checks on railways and borders were to be continued in full force, and the Wehrmacht were to maintain 'adequate forces' in their search.[3]

Among the seven were Sydney Dowse and Polish Flying Officer Stanislaw 'Danny' Krol, who were the twenty-first and twenty-second men to leave the tunnel. Dowse was wearing a civilian suit and a greatcoat that had been dyed plum red, and with his blond hair, he was attempting to pass himself off as a Danish worker. Krol was wearing an RAF officer's greatcoat, under which he had several pullovers, and was posing as a Slav worker. Unlike many of the other escapers, Dowse possessed a three weeks' supply of food coupons, which meant that he and Krol would not have to subsist on escape rations.[4] Initially, Dowse had wanted to travel by train on his own to Berlin, where he was to stay with a contact for two weeks, before moving on to the port of Danzig.[5] However, when he went to Sagan station, he decided to change his plan. 'I saw all these bloody Kriegies around,' he recalled, 'and I thought, "Somebody's going to give the game away, they're going to be noticed."'[6] Dowse also feared that the tunnel, because of the shortfall of the exit, would soon be discovered, and after discussing the matter with Krol, who claimed to have contacts in the Polish Underground, the two men decided to team up and walk southeast along the railway line in the direction of Liegnitz, which was some 44 miles away.[7]

What also distinguished Krol and Dowse from the

other hard-arsers was the fact that they travelled during the day. 'We didn't walk at night,' said Dowse, 'because there were always curfews and things like that.'[8] The pair also opted not to trudge through muddy, thawing fields, and instead brazenly walked on pavements and through towns. As well as making the going easier, Dowse correctly surmised that going across country was simply more conspicuous.[9] This also overcame another problem encountered by many of the escapers: the inevitability of looking like tramps. In addition, Dowse had somehow managed to wangle an electric razor, which did much to negate the effects of living rough. The two men also tried to keep their clothes as clean as possible, although, as Dowse observed, many people in wartime occupied Poland were hardly models of personal hygiene.[10] The pair had another advantage: both seemed physically very fit. Whereas some other escapers, perhaps weakened by a relatively sedentary lifestyle and poor nutrition behind barbed wire, became exhausted after just two days, Dowse and Krol managed to maintain a good pace and survived on very little sustenance. 'We'd go as long as you could without eating,' said Dowse. 'And when you'd get really peckish you'd have a little to eat and go on. You had to ration it.'[11] Within two or three days, the pair had made it past Liegnitz, and turned to walk east towards Breslau – a distance of over 40 miles.

Despite their good progress, the hard-arsing was by no means straightforward. The days were, in Dowse's words, 'pretty damn cold', and there was the odd close shave. At one point, they were stopped by some civilians who resembled members of the Home Guard, and were asked where they were going. When it swiftly became clear that the answers they were giving were not satisfactory, Dowse and Krol adopted a tactic used by criminals and errant schoolboys the world over: they legged it. 'Once we started crossing the field they didn't want to follow,' Dowse recalled. 'It was very funny because we ran right across this field and we stopped right under this big tree. We thought they'd come and follow us, but they didn't!'[12]

Within a few days, the pair had passed through Breslau, and they pushed on eastwards, passing through Oels and then towards Kempen.[13] On the afternoon of 5 April, after covering 140 miles in twelve days and with the weather worsening, the two men decided to rest in the hayloft of a barn 2½ miles west of Kempen. 'We went in against my wishes,' said Dowse, 'but Danny wanted to go into the barn and sleep. He was getting cold and tired.'[14] At some point the following day, the farmer came to thresh his grain, and despite their keeping still, the two escapees were soon spotted. Krol explained to the man – who was a *Volksdeutscher* – that they were Polish workers escaping from Germany, and the farmer appeared to show some sympathy. He told them they could stay until the evening, and he even supplied them with bread and coffee. However, half an hour later, at around 4 p.m., a member of the Hitler Youth happened to enter the barn and after seeing its unkempt inhabitants, he rushed off to fetch some members of the Home Guard.[15] 'We didn't have time to get out,' said Dowse. 'They treated us very well. No brutality, none at all.'[16]

The two men were arrested and taken to the Kripo at

Oels, where they were interrogated. For the time being, while Dowse acted dumb, Krol maintained that they were Polish workers, and their reason for sleeping in the barn was that they had been out walking and had not made it back home in time. This unlikely story was further undermined when Krol supplied a manifestly invented address. 'Of course they realised it was total rubbish,' said Dowse, 'and the game was up then.' The two then revealed who they really were. 'They realised I was English, and there was no point trying to hide it. I couldn't speak Polish, and I couldn't pretend to be dumb for too long!'[17] After discovering they were escapees from Sagan, the Kripo telephoned the Gestapo in Breslau, who stipulated that Dowse and Krol should be handcuffed and incarcerated in the civilian prison in Oels. Both men were also stripped of their belongings and searched, during which Dowse's false papers were discovered.[18] The prisoners were then locked in separate cells, and held for six days. Both were individually interrogated by a Luftwaffe officer and the prison governor, who told them that they would shortly be returning to Sagan. However, on 12 April, Dowse was informed by the governor that only Krol was being sent back to Sagan, whereas he was to be taken by the Gestapo to Berlin.[19]

Dowse's escort arrived that same day. 'I knew that they belonged to the Gestapo because they had small green passes about which I made a joke,' Dowse recalled. He also noticed that both men were carrying revolvers under their left armpits. Dowse asked the men what was going to happen to Krol, and even enquired as to whether the Pole was going to be shot.

'Good gracious me,' came the reply, 'he is being sent back to Sagan – we can promise that.' Dowse asked if he could say goodbye, but he was refused.[20] Nevertheless, as he was walked through the main hall, Dowse quickly ran off to Krol's cell, and shouted through the door that he was being sent to Berlin. Krol was deeply alarmed.

'Don't leave me!' he implored. 'I've had it if you leave me! I'm finished!'

Dowse tried to reassure him.

'You're all right, Danny,' he said. 'They're taking you back to Sagan. They've told me you are. But I've got to go with them.'

Krol was unconvinced.

'Don't leave me,' he begged. 'Don't leave me! I've had it if you leave me.'

At the time, Dowse felt that Krol was overreacting. 'I didn't believe they would do a cold shooting,' he recalled. 'There hadn't been any at that time.'[21]

Of course, by 6 April, dozens had already been murdered in such shootings, but Dowse could not have known that. It would be the last time the two men saw each other. Dowse was put on a train and locked in a private compartment with his escort for the trip to Berlin.[22] From there, he was taken to Sachsenhausen concentration camp, where he was reunited with three of his fellow Great Escapers – Jimmy James, Johnny Dodge and Wings Day – all of whom were regarded by the Germans as being particularly persistent escapers and therefore deserving of especially punitive incarceration.[23] Krol, meanwhile, was taken from his cell and told that he was going back to Sagan. His suspicions that he was 'finished' proved to be grimly accurate. In an unknown location, somewhere between Oels and Sagan, an unknown Gestapo officer shot him dead.

With the arrest of Dowse and Krol, just five of the Great Escapers remained on the run. These were the two Norwegians Jens Müller and Per Bergsland, the Dutchman Bob Vanderstok, and the Czech Bedrich 'Freddie' Dvorak, who was accompanied by the last remaining Briton, Desmond Plunkett. On the morning of 6 April, Plunkett and Dvorak were waking up in a hotel in Pardubitz in occupied Czechoslovakia after an eventful and circuitous journey of some 400 miles.[24] Since Plunkett had had his hand squeezed by Roger Bushell on the train from Sagan to Breslau on the morning of the breakout,[25] the two men had had many narrow escapes, some of which were the products of the *Grossfahndung* and others of Plunkett's comical bumbling.

Like many of their fellow escapees, Dvorak and Plunkett were disguised as foreign workers, and were in possession of two forged brown official passes. Dvorak was posing as one 'Bohumil Dostal' and Plunkett as 'Sergei Bulanov', both of whom supposedly worked at the Siemens factory in Breslau and were taking some leave.[26] Their only plan, in as much as one existed, was to get into occupied Czechoslovakia and to take it from there.[27] As the train headed southeast towards Breslau, Dvorak and Plunkett overheard a conversation that made them realise quite how much the Germans detested men such as them. In the next compartment, a woman from Berlin was violently bemoaning the damage caused to her city, and left her fellow passengers in no doubt as to what she would do if she ever came face to face with an Allied airman.[28] Plunkett and Dvorak were doubtless glad when they alighted at Breslau at around 12.45 a.m.[29] However, they did face the problem of getting past the ticket barriers without tickets. Fortunately, they found that the ticket collector was having an argument with a fellow passenger, and so the two Kriegies were able to blend themselves into the large crowd passing unchecked through the gate.[30]

From Breslau, Dvorak and Plunkett had hoped to catch the 1 a.m. train that would take them 50 miles south to Glatz, but the service had been cancelled.[31] As a result, the pair had to wait in the busy booking hall for a nervous and sleepless five hours. Also waiting for a train were Roger Bushell and Bernard Scheidhauer, but according to Plunkett, the Frenchman was taking advantage of his newly found freedom by 'spending every spare moment catching up with pleasures he had missed in camp'. If the implication of this is true, and Scheidhauer was indeed seeking to exercise his libido, then he was running an enormous risk. Bushell spoke to Plunkett and Dvorak briefly in French about the escape, and mentioned that he and Scheidhauer needed to head back to Sagan if they wanted to get to France.[32] At five thirty, just as dawn was breaking, the escapers were alarmed to hear a loudspeaker calling for two Gestapo officers to report to the station office. 'We were then sure that the escape had been discovered,' Plunkett recalled.[33] Luckily for the escapers, the train to Glatz was on time, and by 6 a.m., the pair were on the slow train south.

The compartment was packed, and Plunkett and Dvorak did their best to get some sleep. However, Plunkett had the misfortune of sitting next to a particularly loquacious German who wished to have a conversation. As Plunkett's command of the language was minimal, the best he could manage was to mutter about how the weather was particularly cold, which was not, as Plunkett would later observe, 'very profound for that time of year'.[34] The German soon gave up, and the escapers managed to rest, and by 11 a.m., they had alighted at Glatz, from where they intended to walk some 13 miles to the border with occupied Czechoslovakia. Finding the snow too deep, Dvorak and Plunkett instead took the next train 14 miles up the track to the busy resort town of Bad Reinerz, which was less than 3 miles from the frontier.[35] Once again, the escapers managed to outwit any checks at the station by blending in as best they could with the throng of holiday-makers clutching suitcases and skiing equipment.[36] After passing through the barrier, Plunkett urgently needed to urinate, and after he had finished, he let out a long sigh and said – in English – 'That's better!' A German standing at the next cubicle looked over in disbelief, and Plunkett fled the lavatory. Dvorak was none too happy, and swore copiously at his escaping partner in Czech as they stumbled up the snow-covered slopes.[37]

Both Dvorak and Plunkett found it hard work to climb up to the border. Not only was the snow deep and their clothes hopelessly ill suited, but also the physical effort drained them. As they trudged, a German on skis swept past them and enquired as to why they weren't similarly equipped. The best excuse the escapers could formulate was that they had not expected such poor weather. It was doubtful that the skier believed them, but it appeared that he valued his holiday more than the security of the border, and so he skied on.[38] Later that afternoon they arrived at a small village on the border called Güsshübel, where they visited a barber, to whom Dvorak revealed that they were escaped POWs.[39] 'He nearly had a fit and wanted to run away,' Plunkett recalled, but Dvorak managed to persuade the man to help them. He led them to the border, and brought them along a woodland path that avoided the customs house and dropped down to the Czech town of Novi Hradek.[40] Although crossing the border had involved little more than jumping across a small stream, by then the two men were exhausted and extremely cold. Their clothes and shoes were soaking, and as night approached, they knew they had to find shelter. Fortunately, their impromptu guide knew the owner of a hotel in Novi Hradek, and after telling him they were escaped POWs, the guide asked if they could stay the night. The hotelier, a man called Kožovsky,[41] agreed, and within half an hour, the escapers were drying out in front of a stove and being given food and drink. Their fellow hotel guests seemed too absorbed by gambling and alcohol to notice the two bedraggled strangers in their midst.[42]

Kožovsky allowed his two guests to stay for three nights while he and the barber made arrangements for the escapers to stay elsewhere. On the morning of Tuesday 28 March, Dvorak and Plunkett were taken to a barn near Neustadt, where the men slept badly after the comparative luxury of the hotel.[43] The barn also felt insecure, a feeling borne out when a farmer discovered them while he was loading hay into his cart. Dvorak told him they were escaping POWs, and that he must help them, but the man refused and said he would report them. Dvorak grabbed him before he could run away, and told him: 'If that is your attitude, we will kill you here and now.'[44] The threat worked, and the farmer agreed to let them stay. Dvorak and Plunkett endured four uncomfortable nights in the straw, and on the evening of Saturday 1 April, the farmer told them they had to leave. He led them part of the way to the hamlet of Spy, and then abandoned them en route. With no contact in the hamlet, Dvorak and Plunkett knocked on every door, but that seemed to do little more than rouse the canine population. Eventually, they met a farmer milking his cows, who said they could stay in his barn until 4 a.m. When he came to wake them, Dvorak and Plunkett were so tired they were unable to move, and so the farmer let them stay the day.[45]

On the evening of Sunday 2 April, the pair walked 8 miles south to Opočno, where they hoped to catch a train. As they approached the railway junction at four o'clock the following morning, they were stopped by a Czech policeman, who apologetically explained that there had been a mass breakout of POWs, and that he was required to search them. As he frisked and questioned Plunkett and Dvorak, the policeman grew suspicious, and was perturbed by the fact that 'Sergei Bulanov' no longer had the moustache he was sporting in his identity document. Plunkett explained that he had recently shaved it off. The policeman then asked about their line of work, and if indeed they were workmen, why weren't they carrying their tools? Dvorak said they were looking for spares. The policeman was less than impressed, and said that their story 'stank'. Both men now feared the worst. However, for some reason – either through secret sympathy or laziness – the policeman waved them on.[46]

After a tortuous journey via Kolin and Pardubitz, Plunkett and Dvorak arrived in Prague on the evening of Monday 3rd. There, they hoped to get in touch with another contact, but failed, and instead found themselves trudging the city's back streets until they got a train back out to Kolin. As they stepped on to the platform, a policeman noticed Plunkett's dishevelled appearance and demanded to see his identity card. Luckily for 'Sergei Bulanov' the accuracy of the forgery passed the inspection, but Dvorak gave Plunkett a dressing down for his scruffiness.[47] After a visit to a barber, there then followed two days of shuttling between hotels in Kolin, Prague and Pardubitz. In Kolin, they stayed at the Jellinek Hotel, where the manager supplied them with not only food and money, but also the disquieting information that the Germans had shot nine Czech civilians for helping prisoners of war at Jungbunzlau in central Bohemia.[48] With the realisation that their peregrinations were unnecessarily risking lives, the two men eventually decided to head towards Bregenz, from where they hoped to enter Switzerland. On the morning of Thursday 6 April, they left Pardubitz and travelled once more to Prague, where they stayed the night at the home of the manager of a roadhouse.[49] At 9 p.m. on Good Friday, they arrived at the picturesque cathedral town of Taus, which was just

6½ miles from the German border, but some 230 miles from Bregenz.[50] When they checked into their hotel, Plunkett and Dvorak were disturbed to find that the manager's son examined their documents rather too closely, and the men were set on edge. Dvorak said that they should leave the town immediately, whereas Plunkett insisted that they stay. Dvorak's temper was not helped when Plunkett once more drew attention to himself as he was going to the lavatory. On this occasion, as he was feeling his way down a dark corridor, he collided with a fellow guest, and fell on top of him. The man was a German, and even though both men apologised for the mishap, Dvorak was angry with his partner's clumsiness.[51]

The next morning was Easter Saturday, and the two men slipped out early from the hotel and took a train 20 miles east to Klattau.[52] As it was a holiday season, the train was crowded, and extra policemen had been drafted at the checkpoints. Dvorak went first, and he was nodded through. When it came to Plunkett's turn, a policeman asked to see his documents. Once more, his identity card appeared to satisfy its umpteenth scrutiny, but on this occasion, Plunkett was asked for his leave papers – papers he did not possess.[53] Realising that his partner was in trouble, Dvorak now had two options – he could keep walking, or he could come back to help Plunkett. Bravely, he chose the latter, and told the policeman that they were visiting the town to see friends. The policeman did not buy it, and within an hour, the two men found themselves in a cell in Klattau's police headquarters.[54]

Plunkett and Dvorak were held by the police until 10

April, when they were transferred into the hands of the Klattau Gestapo.[55] There, they were repeatedly interrogated by a large and violently angry Gestapo man, who was convinced that the two men were not escaped POWs, but were in fact spies who had been dropped by parachute in order to commit sabotage. At one point, their interrogator grew so angry that Plunkett thought the man was about to have a heart attack.[56] Aware that the Gestapo man's lack of composure revealed a weakness, Dvorak and Plunkett kept quiet, and on 4 May, they were transferred to the Gestapo headquarters at Pankratz Prison in Prague.[57] In total, Plunkett and Dvorak were held by the Gestapo for some seven months, during which time both men were interrogated but never tortured.[58] Nevertheless, the men's health suffered, not only from excessive weight loss, but also from the extreme mental anxiety of living under the threat of execution for so long. Gestapo officers would remove prisoners from their cells and shoot them on a whim, and at times, Plunkett wished that his turn would come, rather than having to endure the wait for what felt like the inevitable.[59] Also held in Pankratz was Ivo Tonder, who was transferred from Reichenberg to the prison on 17 April and held in solitary confinement.[60] Tonder's cell consisted of nothing more than a hard iron bed and a small table and chair. After establishing communication with neighbouring cells by banging on the wall, Tonder soon discovered that the only way to get any drinking water was to drink from the lavatory. 'But I had my self-respect,' he recalled. 'Then I said to myself that if I flushed the water, clean water would flow in. But I used it just for washing because I never had

enough resolve to swallow it. I just sat there, and
nothing happened.'[61]

Eventually, on 30 November, Tonder and Dvorak
were transferred to Stalag Luft I at Barth.[62] Plunkett was
sent to Barth at the end of January 1945, after enduring
a particularly unpleasant two months in solitary confinement at the Wehrmacht's Hradin Prison in Prague.[63]
The experience of incarceration left him as little more
than a shell, and when he learned of the murders of his
fellow escapers, he convinced himself that he was
responsible for their deaths by letting something slip
during interrogation. To make matters worse, the
American POWs at Barth also accused him of being a
stool pigeon, and after just four days at the camp he
suffered a complete mental breakdown and was
hospitalised.[64] It would take him months to recover.

Of the three Great Escapers who remained away from
the clutches of their pursuers, it is of significance that
not one of them was British. Two – Müller and
Bergsland – were Norwegian, and Bob Vanderstok was
Dutch. One of the lesser problems faced by the escapers
was that many of them looked unmistakably British.
This certainly applied to Desmond Plunkett, whose
ruddy complexion and red hair smacked more of his
native Haywards Heath than, say, Heidelberg.[65]
Plunkett's untidy appearance cannot have helped, but
even if his grooming had been more refined, it is still
likely that his face would have continued to attract the
eyes of those manning checkpoints. When one looks at
a wartime picture of Plunkett with his moustache – presumably similar to that on his identity documents – it is

hard to make it correspond with a Mitteleuropean worker called 'Sergei Bulanov'. Indeed it is hard to picture a more English face. In short, Desmond Plunkett looked very much like a man called Desmond Plunkett.[66]

Being Scandinavian, both Jens Müller and Per Bergsland blended in well as they made their way from Sagan on the 2.04 a.m. train north to Frankfurt (Oder) on the morning of the breakout.[67] The two men had the further advantage of not needing to adopt different nationalities, and so Norwegian Spitfire pilot Per Bergsland was now simply Norwegian worker Olaf Andersen, complete with papers that showed that he was employed by Siemens in Frankfurt and that he had been working on an electrical transformer in a village near Sagan.[68] Müller was also posing as a Norwegian worker and had similar papers that explained why he was travelling from Sagan to Frankfurt. In addition, both men carried another set of documents that purportedly gave them permission to travel from Frankfurt up to Stettin, from where they hoped to catch a boat to Sweden. Each bore two letters supposedly issued by Siemens, addressed 'to whom it may concern', and stating that the men were required to do some important work in the port, and that they were to receive as much assistance as possible to help them on their way.[69] Müller and Bergsland also carried around 160 Reichsmarks each, sandwiches, bread and margarine, Danish sausages, changes of underwear and socks, toothpaste and soap, and were wearing civilian suits modified from RAF and Royal Marines uniforms.[70] 'We felt that we were very well prepared,' Müller recalled, and he was right.[71] Compared to the hard-arsers, Müller and Bergsland were carrying practically a whole delicatessen and unimaginable wealth. It is a measure of how much confidence the X Organisation had placed in them that they had been issued with so many resources.

At around 6 a.m. on 25 March, their train pulled into Frankfurt and they alighted without any mishap. As they stood in the booking hall, Müller and Bergsland faced their first dilemma: they had a choice of two trains. The first, which went directly to Stettin, was a slow train and, as such, would be subject to few, if any, security checks. However, this train did not leave until the afternoon. The second option was to take a faster train and change at Küstrin, but this would be subject to checks, although it had the advantage of leaving in an hour. Confident in their documentation, and mindful of getting as far away as possible, they opted for the latter. They bought their tickets and then went for a stroll around the town. 'This did not feel comfortable,' Müller later wrote, 'because the streets were so empty at that early hour in the morning. We were happy when we got back into the station.'[72]

The train was on time, and, as it happened, Müller and Bergsland were not asked to show their papers as they headed a mere 20 miles north. They arrived at Küstrin at 8 a.m., and decided to get some breakfast before their connection to Stettin left at 10 a.m. The station café was almost full, and the two men managed to find a table that had just been vacated by some German soldiers. After ordering some beer, they ate some of their own sandwiches, and as they did so, two of their fellow escapers came and sat next to them.

Neither pair of men acknowledged each other's presence, and after draining their beers, the two escapees left the table. 'They gave us a weak smile as they left,' Müller recalled, 'and we nodded slightly. Good luck!'[73] Müller and Bergsland finished off their somewhat alcoholic breakfast. Bergsland lit a cigarette, and the two men idly watched the people around them while they chatted.[74]

Suddenly, Bergsland leaned in towards Müller.

'Don't look up,' he whispered, 'but there's an inspector coming right towards us.'

Bergsland stubbed out his cigarette as a young, sharp-faced corporal in the military police approached the table and requested their papers. Müller noticed that the man had 'hard eyes'. Bergsland took out his wallet, and Müller did the same, doing his best not to let his hand shake.

'Soldiers?' the corporal asked.

'No,' they replied. 'Norwegian workers.'

The German studied their papers closely. Bergsland and Müller exchanged a nervous glance as the corporal looked through a selection of passes, which even included identity cards supposedly issued by a Wehrmacht unit in Berlin, showing that the bearers were trusted foreign workers.[75]

'Good!' said the corporal finally. He handed back their papers and saluted. The two escapers did their best not to exhale too sharply. 'The atmosphere in the waiting-room felt very oppressive,' Müller observed. 'Out on the platform was much better.'[76] The train to Stettin couldn't come quickly enough, and thankfully for the two Norwegians, it arrived on time. Just before 10 a.m., they boarded their third-class compartment and did their best to relax as the train started its 70-mile, three-hour journey.

'I felt somewhat uneasy when we got off the train at Stettin,' Müller recalled. 'But nothing happened. We walked past the ticket-collector without fuss, and soon we were on the street outside the station.'[77] The two men now had at least four hours to kill until dusk, when they were due to visit a brothel on Klein Oder Strasse.[78] Their reason for the visit was not to procure entertainment, but to receive help from a contact supplied by the X Organisation.[79] Müller and Bergsland walked along the waterfront, trying to remember the layout of the city from maps they had seen back at Sagan. At one point, they entered the business district, which lay largely in ruins. 'The Royal Air Force had apparently not liked the business district in Stettin,' Müller wryly commented.[80] Eventually, the pair found themselves walking down a wide, bustling street called Grüne Schanze, which featured several hotels, shops, restaurants, and bars – into one of which they entered. Unable to buy any food because they lacked ration coupons, they instead ordered two pale lagers, which they drank slowly. They then ordered two more, while Müller enviously eyed a fat woman who was tucking into a giant bowl of vegetable soup.[81] Fearing that they would attract attention by staying too long, the two escapers soon left the bar and tramped the streets. Fortunately, they passed a cinema, which perfectly suited their purposes; they spent two hours watching a film, which was, in the words of Müller, 'even worse than we had expected'.[82]

At around five o'clock, they left the cinema and made

their way to Klein Oder Strasse 16. The road lay in the old town; the surrounding streets were dark, filthy, narrow and insalubrious.[83] Klein Oder Strasse was particularly seedy, and groups of men stood threateningly in the shadows while the pair walked slowly past the address.[84] Müller knocked on the door and waited. No sound came from within. Growing impatient, Müller knocked again, and still there was no reply. A figure broke away from one of the huddles of men and asked them in broken German what they wanted. Before Müller could answer, the man, who was Polish, then asked whether they had anything to sell on the black market. 'No,' Müller replied, 'I was looking for a place where I could get a girl.' The man appeared unwilling to help, and Bergsland realised that they would have to play along with him. He showed the man some tobacco, and said that he would trade it for some bread coupons. The Pole quickly disappeared, and returned with 2 kilograms' worth of coupons, for which Bergsland also had to surrender his pullover.[85] After the transaction had taken place, Müller asked the man if he knew where they could find some Swedish sailors. 'Sure!' he said. 'Come with me.' The man then knocked on the door of number 17 and went inside, leaving the two Norwegians on the pavement. He returned a few minutes later, accompanied by a Swedish sailor who said that he would be more than willing to help them. His boat was leaving for Gothenburg early the following morning, so could they come back at ten o'clock that evening?[86]

Müller and Bergsland agreed, and once more found themselves at the bar on Grüne Schanze drinking lager and eating up what remained of their food. They tried to stay as long as possible, but with people staring at them, they thought it time to leave. They next visited a wine bar, where there seemed to be very little wine on offer, and so they ordered yet more beer. For an hour, they chatted to the German landlord, and at one point, Müller accidentally said something in English, but the man did not appear to hear. Instead, he seemed more preoccupied with kicking a map of Britain he kept behind the bar, which Müller noticed had countless boot marks on it.[87]

After finishing their beers, the two Norwegians walked back to Klein Oder Strasse, and found themselves outside the door to number 17 at 9.30 p.m. Bergsland decided to go into the house anyway, and after a short while he came back out with the revelation that the house was in fact the brothel – the X Organisation had mistaken number 17 for 16. The two young men entered the building, which bore the inscription: 'Only for Foreigners – Germans Forbidden'.[88] The scene that greeted them must have been a significant culture shock for two young Norwegian students-cum-pilots who had spent the best part of two years in the all-male environment of Stalag Luft III. Dozens of young men were packed into a 'waiting-room', ready to be attended to by the exclusively French and Czech prostitutes. A slim young Czech woman sashayed from one punter to another, regaling them with dirty stories. 'It seemed that she knew every single person,' Müller observed.[89] The Swedish sailor soon appeared, but the two Kriegies were still transfixed. 'For a while we stood and watched this strange scene,' wrote Müller, 'until he told us to come along.'[90]

Müller and Bergsland followed the sailor out of the brothel and southwest down Klein Oder Strasse towards the station. The man then led them over a bridge across the Oder river, and they found themselves in an area of dark streets. After a couple of minutes, the sailor insisted that they stop for a drink at a small bar. Just as they had received their orders, the air-raid siren sounded, and they rushed into the streets seemingly to find a shelter.[91] However, the sailor instead took them to the pier where his ship was berthed, and told Müller and Bergsland to wait by some railway freight. He said that he would go on board and whistle when they should follow him. 'Per and I hid in the darkness under one of the goods-wagons and strained both eyes and ears . . . ,' Müller recalled. 'Several times we thought we heard the agreed signal, but we found that our imagination was playing tricks with us.'[92] While they waited, they heard the sound of jackboots clacking against the ground, and the two escapers froze when three police-men drew near to the wagons. One of them lit his torch, but it was only in order to look at his watch, and the policemen continued walking.

After fifteen minutes of waiting, one of the steamers left the harbour, but Müller and Bergsland, still trusting their contact, continued to wait. However, within a few cold hours, it dawned on them that the ship had prob-ably left and they had been let down. Refusing to give up hope, they waited a while longer, but their luck was out. The two men climbed inside a covered wagon and tried to get some sleep, despite the cold temperature and the flimsiness of their clothes.[93] At 3 a.m., they left the wagon, and went back into town, desperate to find

a bed. They even tried number 17 and various neighbouring houses, but they had no luck. As a result,
Müller and Bergsland had to roam the streets for the
rest of the night. 'It's pretty tiring trudging up and down
the street at a pace that does not seem suspiciously
slow,' Müller wrote. 'We had to constantly pretend that
we should be somewhere, and we had to be fast.'[94] As
dawn came up and the streets started to fill, the
escapers could relax their pace. They found a railway
café and ate some breakfast, but the coffee – or what
passed for it – could not revive them. An hour later, they
found a hotel, and after having a remarkably early beer
in its restaurant, they asked the manager if they could
have a room for the day. The manager eyed them
suspiciously, scrutinised their papers, and agreed. 'I fell
asleep as soon as my head lay against the pillow,' Müller
recalled.[95]

Exhausted after a lack of sleep – and perhaps beer at
breakfast – the two men slept until five o'clock that
afternoon, 26 March. They got up quickly, paid their
bill, and hurried back to Klein Oder Strasse 17 in order
to find some more Swedish sailors. Just as they arrived,
they saw two sailors emerging from the brothel, and
Müller told them that they needed to escape. Without
any equivocation, the Swedes immediately agreed, and
within minutes, the four men were on a tram heading
out of the city towards the dock at Parnitz, where they
arrived at around 6.30 p.m.[96] Unfortunately, the party
had travelled one stop too far, and as they doubled back
on themselves, they had to cross a small bridge, which
was guarded. The policeman asked to see their papers,
and the two Swedes produced theirs first. After

examining them, he nodded them through. Bergsland and Müller started to produce their documents, but the policeman, assuming they were part of the same crew, nodded them through.[97]

The two Norwegians enjoyed similar treatment at the gangway to the ship, where a policeman was having an animated chat with his friend, and simply waved the four men aboard. The Swedes took Müller and Bergsland to their cabin, and plied them with bread and butter, smoked sausage, and – best of all – Swedish export beer, which tasted 'indescribably good' after the seemingly intravenous consumption of light German lagers.[98] However, such luxurious hospitality soon had to end, as the sailors trusted neither their captain nor some of their fellow crew members, which meant that the two escapers would have to hide somewhere other than the cabin. Furthermore, as the ship was not going to be sailing until the morning of the 28th, Müller and Bergsland would need to be hidden for the best part of thirty-six hours. Out in the corridor, one of the sailors opened a hatch that led down to the anchor chain compartment, and told the Norwegians to follow him down the ladder. The compartment was damp and cold, and consisted of bulkheads, and various water and bilge tanks. Behind one of the water tanks, the sailor said there was a small space where they could hide and be able to stretch their legs under the tank. The two men crawled through a narrow gap above the tank, and as they did so, scraped some of the skin off their legs. When they sat down in the corner, they found there was less space than there had appeared to be and, worse still, Müller's long legs could be seen sticking out from beneath the tank. The sailor's solution was to cover them in assorted chandlery such as tarpaulin and chicken wire, upon which wooden beams were placed. 'It would have to be an extremely conscientious and dutiful watchman who would come to examine our hiding-place,' Müller observed.[99]

For the next twenty-four hours, the two men stayed under the pile of marine detritus, occasionally leaving the hiding place to stretch their legs. The following evening, they were brought upstairs for some food, and found themselves being laughed at because of the blackness of their faces, which were covered in oil and dirt. After being fed and given – inevitably – more beer, Müller and Bergsland had to return to their hiding place and wait for the ship to be inspected before it set sail. The sailor said he would knock on the hatch five times when the inspection was taking place. 'And so we began to wait again,' Müller later wrote. 'One hour. Two hours. My limbs started to ache, and we got up to stretch our legs. We were pretty nervous, so we got back down again after a few minutes.'[100] Suddenly, they heard five knocks, and before the echo of the last knock had died away, they heard footsteps above them. Fifteen minutes passed, during which Müller and Bergsland tried to remain motionless. Then the hatch opened, and they could hear someone coming down the ladder. They heard shouts in German:

'What's down there?'

'Nothing,' came the reply.

'No, I'll have a look!'

The man entered the room and shone his torch around. The escapers could hear him breathing as he clambered over bulkheads and anchor chains. He approached the hiding place and pressed down on a roll of wire mesh that was covering Müller. 'I felt his hand on my shoulder,' Müller recalled. 'I held my breath. I tried not to tremble, but I was absolutely sure he could hear my heart beating.'

The man then let out another shout:

'No! All good!'

As he climbed back out, Müller and Bergsland remained motionless. Eventually, they started whispering to each other, and they decided they should keep still, as they had been told ships were often subjected to random searches at the mouth of the harbour.[101] They waited for another six hours, until they were relieved by their friendly sailor. Over sandwiches and beer, the Swede told the stowaways that he would have hit the German over the head with a wrench had he discovered them. As they talked, Müller and Bergsland looked through the porthole, and saw lights: it was the coast of Sweden. However, as Gothenburg was still many hours away, the sailor advised them to go back to the compartment, and he supplied them with yet more beer.[102]

At 11 p.m on the evening of Wednesday 29 March, just 118 hours after they had gone down Harry, Müller and Bergsland landed at Gothenburg.[103] As the two men stepped on to Swedish soil, Müller could have shouted for joy, but he did not want to attract the attention of the frontier police. However, like their German counterparts in Stettin, the guards did not bother to check the papers of all the crew, and the Norwegians managed to avoid any scrutiny. As soon as they had left the port area, they summoned a taxi, which took them to the

British Consulate. After they had explained who they were, the diplomat who received them offered them a drink – which in this instance was not a beer but a cup of tea. 'It was not until we were well inside the consulate and sat down with our cup of tea in front of us, that Per and I felt completely secure,' Müller claimed.[104] The following day, the escapers were sent to Stockholm, where they spent a few days writing reports at the British Legation. On the evening of Thursday 6 April, the two men were driven out to Bromma Airport, where they were immediately put on to two waiting Mosquitoes. In a little over three hours, and after a flight of around 800 miles, they landed at RAF Leuchars in Scotland in the early hours of the following day. 'I did not know where I was until I heard a couple of Scots talking to each other in the dark,' Müller recalled. 'The tone was not to be mistaken.'[105]

In the parlance of the escaping fraternity, Müller and Bergsland had made 'home runs', and they were the first of the Great Escapers to have done so. Their achievement was considerable, and both men proved they had the resourcefulness that merited the X Organisation supplying them with so much money and documentation. As has been established, the two Norwegians had a distinct advantage in that they did not have to adopt a different nationality, but that was not the only key to their success. Their journey to Stettin was comparatively short – just over 150 miles – and instead of being made on foot through half-frozen, muddy fields, it was made on crowded, anonymous trains. Notwithstanding the wrong house number, they had also benefited from reliable intelligence from the

X Organisation concerning the brothel. Both men also had good judgement and that other essential ingredient luck, without which no escape can ever be successful. Despite the odd mishap, their flight from Sagan was a textbook example of how to get away. It is therefore unfortunate that the other escapers who headed to Stettin were not able to make similar contacts to those forged by Müller and Bergsland. Wings Day and Pawel Tobolski arrived in the port on Monday 27th, and Alexander Neely on the following day, and none of them were able to locate the brothel. It would appear that the men had found Klein Oder Strasse 16 'unlocked and empty' and therefore assumed that the brothel had been shut down as part of 'some swift police purge'.[106] Had they knocked on the door of number 17, or made discreet enquiries at a nearby bar, then they too may well have ended up stowing away to Sweden.

If the journey made by Bergsland and Müller was relatively short and swift, then that made by Bob Vanderstok was anything but. On the morning of the escape, the Dutch Spitfire pilot took the 3.30 a.m. train from Sagan that arrived at Breslau at 5 a.m.[107] Vanderstok found the station to be extremely dimly lit, and after purchasing a 43-Reichsmark third-class ticket from Breslau to Alkmaar in Holland, a journey of some 700 miles, he bought himself a 'stale glass of beer'.[108] While he waited for the train to Dresden, Vanderstok noticed some of his fellow escapers, including Bushell and Scheidhauer, Gouws and Stevens, and John Stower, but he avoided making contact.[109] Like his fellow escapers, Vanderstok found that every train was packed, and he was lucky to get a seat for the 170-mile ride to the Saxony capital. 'Passengers were tired,' he observed. 'They sat on the floor and some of them must have eaten salami. The smell of garlic and dirty bodies was awful. But when somebody tried to open a window, a stream of protests forced the man to shut it again.'[110]

Vanderstok arrived in Dresden at 10 a.m. With his connection to Bentheim on the Dutch border not leaving until 8 p.m., he spent the day lying low in cinemas, drinking beer and eating bread and sausage. When he boarded the train that evening, he once again found it packed, and he shared his compartment with six civilians and two soldiers. During the 13-hour journey, Vanderstok had his papers checked on four occasions, and once by a Gestapo agent wearing a trademark black leather coat.[111] At Bentheim, all the passengers had to leave the train to pass through the border control, which was manned by another leather-coated Gestapo man, to whom Vanderstok showed his train ticket and forged travel permit. The permit was made out for one 'Hendrik Beeldman', an employee of Siemens in Breslau who had permission to travel to Holland between 24 March and 9 April.[112] The Gestapo officer examined it closely, and then asked where 'Herr Beeldman' was travelling. Vanderstok told him, and the man simply scribbled his initials on the permit and waved him through. Vanderstok now travelled on to Oldenzaal, from where he bought a ticket to Utrecht, fearing that the station at Alkmaar would be monitored. 'It was entirely possible that a smart ferret or Gestapo agent had figured out which tickets to Holland were bought on 24 March at Sagan or some place near Sagan,' Vanderstok reasoned.[113]

Utrecht had the added advantage of being Vanderstok's university town, and as a result, he knew a few people in whom he could trust. Among them were two academics: a biologist called Professor Koningsberg; and a physiologist called Professor Jacob Jongbloed. Vanderstok called on the house of Koningsberg first, which was situated near the university's Botanic Gardens. The professor and his wife and daughter were immediately accommodating, and offered Vanderstok an Indonesian-style meal that even featured fried bananas taken from the gardens. 'I smiled and was a little overcome by so much warmth and trust at this reception,' Vanderstok recalled, 'which all of us knew to be a life-threatening situation.'[114] About an hour later, the gathering was joined by Professor Jongbloed, a former member of the Royal Dutch Air Force who had held his chair since April 1942, and specialised in aviation physiology.[115] The group discussed the situation in occupied Holland, and how people were starting to burn their furniture to provide heating. Nevertheless, it seemed as though the Koningsberg household was still able to afford some creature comforts, and that afternoon, Vanderstok was able to soak in a warm bath.

Vanderstok stayed with the Koningsbergs for the next three nights, and on the morning of Wednesday 29 March, he walked round to the home of Professor Jongbloed.[116] The door was answered by Jongbloed's wife, who urged Vanderstok to come in quickly, as her husband was apparently well known for being anti-German. The professor emerged from a room, and led Vanderstok out into the back garden. 'I must apologise for this strange procedure,' he said. 'But believe me, we are not safe at all.' Jongbloed climbed over the fence at the rear of the garden, and Vanderstok followed. They then walked through the neighbour's garden and house and came out on to a street with a tramway. Jongbloed told Vanderstok to take the tram to its last stop, which was 12 miles away to the east in the small town of Amersfoort. There, Vanderstok would find a policeman who worked for the Dutch Underground, and who would help to send him down an escape line that led back to Britain, via the Pyrenees and Gibraltar. 'I began to realise that every move I made was planned,' Vanderstok recalled, 'and that I was in a situation which I didn't like.'[117]

Vanderstok's misgivings were understandable, and they were not entirely groundless. For the next sixteen nights, he hid in the attic bedroom of the policeman, a man called 'Officer Ottens', whose wife and seven children referred to their new houseguest as 'Uncle Bob'. On one occasion, Vanderstok had to share his bed with a French spy, who saw the arrangement as being opportune for homosexuality. 'My response was rapid and clear,' Vanderstok recalled, 'and he retreated to the side of the bed with a bloody nose and a punch in the ribs.'[118] As well as having to endure the risks of molestation, Vanderstok was not entirely trusted by those who were charged with protecting him. Many members of the Underground thought he might be a stool pigeon, not least because they could not believe his almost picaresque odyssey of escaping to Britain, becoming a Spitfire pilot, being shot down, and then managing to escape once again. When Vanderstok was eventually issued with a new false identity document, he found it to be an out-dated version, and, what was worse, he was given an address in Brussels that he knew from fellow Stalag Luft III POWs to be a Gestapo trap.[119]

Frustrated by the seeming ineffectiveness of the Underground, Vanderstok decided to go it alone. Just before he left, however, the Underground did manage to supply him with some money, and the address of a farm near Maastricht, some 120 miles south and on the Belgian border. As he sat on the train, Vanderstok was relieved to find that security was lighter than it was in Germany, and the only document that was checked was his legitimate train ticket. At some point on the afternoon of 16 April, Vanderstok arrived at the farmhouse, which was on the banks of the River Maas.[120] He stayed there for two days, before cycling some 20 miles north to Echt, where he was accommodated in a large white house inhabited by a couple who were called the 'Count and Countess of Harreveldt' – a name which Vanderstok doubted. In the early hours of 19 April, a woman led him by bicycle down to Geule aan de Maas, where they were met by two Belgian men with German Shepherds next to a farmhouse.[121] The men, one of whom was called Arnold Bollen,[122] escorted him down to the bank of the Maas, where Vanderstok was ushered on to a black rowing boat hiding among some reeds. On the other side of the river, some 300 feet away, was Belgium and the village of Uikhoven. After being joined in the boat by the two men and one of the dogs, Vanderstok was rowed across in silence. 'It took almost half an hour to cross the water,' he recalled. 'At the Belgian side, there again were reeds which engulfed us, until I felt a slight bump as the boat came to a stop.'[123]

The men equipped Vanderstok with another bicycle and a Belgian identity card, and he was told to make for Hasselt, where he could stay with a contact. The journey was only 20 miles, and Vanderstok would have arrived in the town in the early morning. At this point, it is now unclear with whom Vanderstok stayed and what help he received, but what is known is that at two o'clock on the afternoon of Friday 21 April, he had arrived in Brussels at the Gare du Nord.[124] He was to stay in the city for over a month, at the imposing villa owned by a wealthy family called Haenecour at 14 Avenue Kamerdelle in the southern suburb of Uccle. Once again, Vanderstok was consigned to an attic bedroom and referred to as 'Uncle Bob' by the family, which consisted of five children. For the next few weeks, Vanderstok settled into family life, eating with the family in the dining room, and even playing tennis with friends and visitors on the house's private court.[125] There is no doubt that the Haenecours were taking an enormous risk by sheltering 'Uncle Bob', and as each day passed, Vanderstok was aware that the jeopardy increased. Finally, on 24 May, exactly two months after he had crawled out of Harry, Vanderstok was given a third-class ticket to Paris, as well as the necessary travel permits and some French and Belgian currency.[126] He was also supplied with the address of a contact in Toulouse where he would be able to stay until the final stage of his escape – the crossing of the Pyrenees – was set in place.

Vanderstok arrived in Paris at eleven o'clock the

following evening, after a 200-mile journey that took more than twenty-four hours, owing to bomb-damaged railway lines. Once again, thanks to the chaos and the crowds, the last of the Great Escapers had neither his papers nor his tickets checked, and his greater concern was hunger. At Gare du Nord, Vanderstok visited a 'filthy restaurant and bought a surprisingly good meal', and then fell asleep in the waiting room.[127] On the morning of the 26th, he headed down to the Gare Saint-Lazare, where he surrendered his travel permit and bought a second-class ticket for the 440-mile journey south to Toulouse. Compared to his experiences travelling between Brussels and Paris, this train ride was luxurious, and Vanderstok was able to eat well at the station restaurants in Lyons and Rodez, and could even wash down his meals with glasses of wine.[128] Vanderstok stayed in Toulouse until 9 June, when he took a train 50 miles southwest to Boulogne-sur-Gesse, accompanied by two fellow countrymen and escorted by a guide.[129] The two Dutchmen were both spies, one of whom was called Rudy, and had worked for Philips in Eindhoven, and the other a Roman Catholic priest who claimed to be part of the Underground in Limburg.[130]

By 11 June, the group had been taken to a farmhouse near Vignaut, which, as the condor flew, was just 10½ miles from the Spanish border. It was here that Vanderstok met the men and women with whom he was to attempt to cross the Pyrenees. They included two lieutenants from the United States Army Air Corps called McPherson and Stonebarger, and two RAF pilots called Flight Officer Thomas and Flight Sergeant

Shaughnessy. Also with them were a French officer, a Russian, and a French woman who had escorted Stonebarger, Thomas and Shaughnessy down from Paris.[131] For the next few days, the party remained at the farmhouse, and then, on 14 June, they were struck with terrible luck. Their designated guide – a stocky Frenchman by the name of Pierre – was shot dead by the Germans while he was returning to the farmhouse after collecting some food.[132] However, within two days, a new guide was found, a man called Felix.[133]

Finally, on or around 16 June, the party set off south towards the border, walking principally through the Forêt de Cagire, and keeping to the east of the villages of Saint-Pé-d'Ardet and Melles. The going was immensely tough, especially for Stonebarger, who appeared to be suffering from a fever. At one point, he insisted that the group should go on without him, but McPherson and Vanderstok geed him along. The walk lasted for two nights, and as the group climbed, the temperatures dropped and the inclines grew steeper. 'We walked all night, hours and hours of walking in the dark,' Vanderstok later wrote. 'None of us had any idea of direction anymore.'[134] Food was minimal, consisting of just a little bread and the occasional cup of milk scavenged from farms. On the morning of 18 June, the group huddled together in a freezing cave, with Stonebarger's condition worsening. Nevertheless, the guide was determined that they should make their final push for the border sooner rather than later. '*Allons, mes amis,*' he said, '*marchez [sic] encore une fois.*'[135]

After hours spent tramping through ice and snow, the group eventually reached the top of the mountain range.

The altitude and the wind made the temperature unbearable, but their guide reassured them by saying that the going would be easier from there on. After another hour, he suddenly stopped and pointed towards a grassy mountain pass.

'On the other side is Spain,' the guide told them. 'It is easy going from now on. You're on your own now. So good luck, and *bon jour* [sic].'[136]

The guide then turned round and walked away. Vanderstok estimated the distance to the border – and therefore freedom – to be just 2 miles. After a journey of some 1,800 miles that had lasted more than twelve weeks, he was determined that nothing would now go wrong. Vanderstok grew increasingly nervous as they approached the frontier. 'I constantly scanned the land – left, right, and behind us,' he recalled.[137] Stonebarger continued to struggle, but the others urged him onwards. A stretch of pine trees afforded the group some welcome cover, although progress was delayed by the fact that the path snaked steadily uphill. However, after another exhausting hour or so, the five men finally reached the frontier. Vanderstok delightedly stamped on the wet grass and announced, 'Hey, fellows! We're in Spain!'[138]

Although Vanderstok had technically escaped, he cajoled his fellow escapers to keep going, for fear that a passing German might be tempted to take a shot at them from across the border. After about half a mile, they were stopped by a Spanish policeman, and the group soon found themselves in the nearby village of Canejan. Over the next few days, the group was taken south through a succession of increasingly large towns, and subjected to numerous interrogations to ascertain the identity of its members and to check none of them were Communist spies. On 22 June, they arrived in Lleida, where they made contact with the British Consul the following day. For the next six nights, they stayed at a hotel, before being transferred to the British Embassy in Madrid, which they reached on 5 July.[139] When he arrived at the embassy, Vanderstok could not help but notice that something was wrong. 'It was time for a celebration, time for a party,' he observed, 'but the atmosphere was subdued.'[140] He soon discovered the reason, as by that time news of the murders had reached Britain. Vanderstok was left speechless, and as he walked around Madrid over the following days, he wanted to machine-gun every German he saw and heard.[141]

By 8 July, Vanderstok had reached Gibraltar, which was British territory. There, he bought two postcards, and sent one to his family in Holland, and the other to 'Heye Schaper' at Stalag Luft III. After stating that the 'ice cream cones were terrific', he signed the postcard from 'Roberto del Baston' – a literal translation of his own name.[142] When the card arrived, his former fellow Kriegies would finally know that a third member of the Great Escapers had made a 'home run'. On the night of Monday 10 July, Vanderstok was flown from Gibraltar and landed the following morning at Whitchurch Airport, 3 miles south of Bristol.[143] There, he presented himself to a Wing Commander, who congratulated him, and told him to report to the RAF in London, and to the Directorate of Netherlands Airpower on Fleet Street. 'Well, so long, Van,' said the officer. 'And again, well done, old chap.'[144]

Chapter Fifteen

Helpless Outrage and Cover-up

THE URNS STARTED arriving at Stalag Luft III on 15 May.[1] They were brought to the camp in batches over the course of two months, deposited at night by Gestapo men who drove a private car. 'I did not know who the Gestapo people were,' Hans Pieber recalled. 'They did not know where to place them and they eventually put them in a room near the sick quarters.' By 27 May, some twenty-nine had arrived, and Cordes and Pieber escorted a group of senior British officers to see them. Each urn bore the name and rank of the officer, as well as the place where they had been cremated. Pieber noticed that many featured the towns of Breslau and Görlitz.[2] Some time later, the urns were shown to the rest of the camp. 'The compound was in shock at the sight of the fifty urns,' wrote Flight Lieutenant Flekser, 'neatly aligned on a trestle table placed by the Germans alongside the theatre. A mood of helpless outrage and dejection permeated the camp.'[3] In their diaries, many of the Kriegies wrote out the list of their fifty murdered comrades in acts of private remembrance.[4] More poignantly still, on 14 June, the clothing of the dead men, which had been removed by the Germans two months before, was returned to the camp.[5] These clothes were then auctioned off. 'Clothing was extremely short and things would sell at the most ridiculous prices,' one Kriegie remembered. 'Nobody had any money, they used to make a cheque out to be cashed at the end of the war. So a thing like a silk scarf might sell for £25 or something quite ridiculous.'[6] Representatives from each of the dead men's rooms were entrusted with cataloguing the men's personal property. 'In some cases, there was pathetically little,' said Alex Cassie, who had lost four of his roommates.[7]

The news of the murders would not stay inside the camp for long. On 17 April, the Swiss camp inspector, Gabriel Naville, visited Sagan on a routine inspection. Upon arrival, Cordes told him about the escape and the killings, which at that point numbered forty-seven. Naville was informed that some of the deaths were brought about by the POWs offering resistance on recapture, and others by launching new escapes.[8] The inspector then asked von Lindeiner about the killings, and he stated that he was entirely ignorant of the fate of the escapers.[9] Although von Lindeiner appeared reluctant to speculate, the British officers were more than willing, and they told Naville that it was 'absolutely impossible' that so many should have been shot in such a way. Not only did every Kriegie know that to resist capture was dangerous folly, but those who had returned from Görlitz, such as Richard Churchill and Thomas Nelson, had been able to communicate from their present home in the cooler how they had seen the prisoners being taken away in manacles. The officers could only conclude that the men had been 'summarily executed by the Gestapo'.[10]

An unsatisfied Naville left the camp the following day and filed his report a few days later to the Head of the Special Division of the Swiss Legation in Berlin, who in turn personally approached the Legal Division of the German Foreign Ministry. The Swiss told the Germans that an inquiry into the deaths was a 'necessity', and that they were also surprised that no announcement had been made, especially as the killings appeared to have taken place almost a month earlier.[11] For the time being, the Germans remained silent. On 12 May, Naville's report finally arrived at the British Embassy in Berne, which transmitted a summary of its findings to the British Foreign Office that afternoon. The embassy urged the Foreign Office to ask the Swiss to 'take up the matter at the highest possible level in Berlin and press strongly for an immediate official statement on behalf of the German Government'.[12] It would not be until the following week, on Friday 19 May, that the British Government would finally issue its own statement, which was delivered by the Foreign Secretary, Anthony Eden, on the floor of the House of Commons. Eden announced that forty-seven officers had been shot, and that their next-of-kin had been informed. After being questioned by Edgar Granville, the MP for Eye, Eden said that the Government would 'certainly consider' the publication of the names, but would not do so for the time being.[13]

Although the British Government did its best to handle the matter delicately for the sake of the relatives, such conscientiousness was not manifested by some elements of the press. On Tuesday 23 May, the *Daily Express* splashed with the headline 'Prison Camp Shootings Were Mass Murder', and reported that the killings were 'carried out by a group of guards who lost their heads and shot prisoners haphazard in barracks, courtyards and workshops'. Under the byline of 'E. D. Masterman' in Stockholm, the story also 'revealed' that the massacre took place on 22 March – some two days before the escape – and that it was witnessed by those who had managed to flee the slaughter.[14] This shocking piece of fabrication caused near apoplexy in many Whitehall departments, including the Air Ministry, the War Office, and the Foreign Office, which contacted the British Embassy in the Swedish capital for elucidation as to the origins of the article.

A reply came swiftly from the Military Attaché, Colonel R. Sutton Pratt, who reported that on the 22nd he had had a meeting with Masterman, who was in fact a Hungarian called 'Demaitre' and held a French passport. In the opinion of the Stockholm press corps, Demaitre was 'an unscrupulous journalist', who had often written about events before they had occurred in the hope that the march of time would 'put him right'. During the meeting, Sutton Pratt gave Demaitre the same minimal amount of information about the escape that he had given to four other journalists that day, but this did not appear to satisfy Demaitre.[15] The journalist

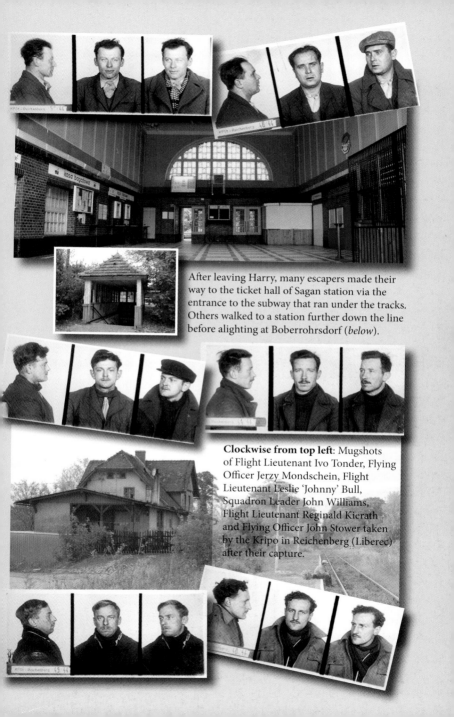

After leaving Harry, many escapers made their way to the ticket hall of Sagan station via the entrance to the subway that ran under the tracks. Others walked to a station further down the line before alighting at Boberrohrsdorf (*below*).

Clockwise from top left: Mugshots of Flight Lieutenant Ivo Tonder, Flying Officer Jerzy Mondschein, Flight Lieutenant Leslie 'Johnny' Bull, Squadron Leader John Williams, Flight Lieutenant Reginald Kierath and Flying Officer John Stower taken by the Kripo in Reichenberg (Liberec) after their capture.

The station at Kohlfurt (Gmina Węgliniec) from where Ivo Tonder and John Stower boarded a train for Görlitz, and where, in the goods yard, Michael Shand was arrested.

Background: The picturesque village of Boberrohrsdorf (Siedlęcin) through which twelve of the Great Escapers would pass before splitting into smaller parties. At the time of the escape it was covered by several feet of snow.

A barn near Tiefenfurt (Parowa), some 16 miles south of Sagan, near where Flight Lieutenants Edgar Humphreys and Paul Royle were captured.

Above: The Kripo headquarters at Schlossplatz 1 and 2 in Saarbrücken, where Bushell and Scheidhauer were taken after being detained at the railway station.

Left: The Görlitz Gestapo headquarters at Augustastrasse 31, where many of the Great Escapers were interrogated.

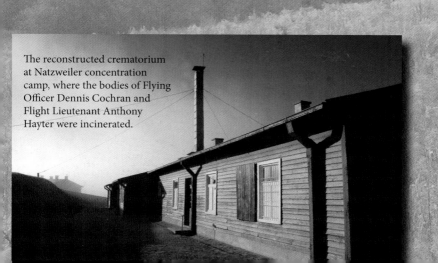

The reconstructed crematorium at Natzweiler concentration camp, where the bodies of Flying Officer Dennis Cochran and Flight Lieutenant Anthony Hayter were incinerated.

Left: Fritz Schmidt, the head of the Kiel Gestapo, ordered the deaths of Catanach, Christensen, Fugelsang and Espelid, whose murders near the village of Voorde were recreated by the RAF's Special Investigation Branch (*below*).

Bottom left: Kriminalkommissar Günther Absalon of the Kripo in Breslau (Wrocław) in his SS uniform.

Bottom right: Absalon with his son. Lindeiner described him as 'the perfect drawing-room criminal'.

The psychopathic Kriminalassistent Erich Zacharias of the Gestapo (*right*) shot Flying Officer Gordon Kidder on the orders of Kriminalrat Hans Ziegler, the head of the Zlin Gestapo (*below right*) and Kriminalsekretär Adolf Knippelberg (*below left*) of the Gestapo at Brno. The murders of Kidder and Squadron Leader Thomas Kirby-Green a few miles south of Moravská Ostrava were reconstructed by the RAF after the war (*bottom*).

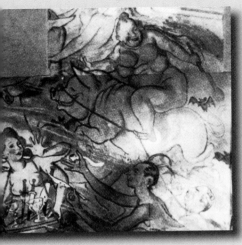

Above left: The mural in the central Brno hotel whose caricature of Franz Schauschütz was invaluable for the RAF Special Investigation Branch.

Above right: The photograph of Kriminal-kommissar Johannes Post and his mistress skiing in the Harz mountains that led Flight Lieutenant Frank McKenna to identify Post in the Minden Holding Centre.

Right: Post (*left*) and Alsace Gestapo chief Alfred Schimmel on trial.

Below: Post in the dock at the No. 1 Courtroom of the Curiohaus in Hamburg in July 1947.

Above: Kriminalsekretär Emil Schulz of the Saarbrücken Gestapo on trial for the murder of Roger Bushell.

Right: Saarbrücken Gestapo chief Dr Leopold Spann, who shot Bushell's escape partner, Pilot Officer Bernard Scheidhauer.

Below: A drawing by Gestapo driver Walter Breithaupt of the shooting of Bushell and Scheidhauer.

Above: The memorial to the Great Escapers near the site of the camp in Sagan (Zagan) in Poland.

Right: The site of Harry today. Little of the camp still stands.

Below left: Bushell's gravestone at the Old Garrison Cemetery in Poznan in Poland.

Below right: Georgie's gravestone at the Holy Trinity Church in Penn Street village in Buckinghamshire.

appeared to be convinced – presumably through ill-educated guesswork – that the killings had taken place in some sort of random fashion within the camp, and Sutton Pratt denied Demaitre's implication that the men had been gunned down after a rush for the gate.[16] Demaitre then asked whether any other journalists were better informed than he, to which Sutton Pratt replied – perhaps naively – that one reporter did indeed know some 'minor details' about the escape itself. For Demaitre, this seemed to suggest that he was being treated as a poor relation, and he told Sutton Pratt – in a similarly naive vein – that no journalist should receive preferential treatment over any other when it came to the breaking of news.[17] In a fit of pique, and concerned that he might be scooped, Demaitre decided to file his story anyway. After it had appeared, an angry Sutton Pratt called another meeting, and quizzed the journalist as to his source. Although Demaitre did not acknowledge that he had no source – and it was impossible for him to have had one – he told the attaché 'that it has done no harm, and the odds are that it was probably basically correct anyway'.[18]

Demaitre was wrong on two counts. Not only was his story untrue, he was also recklessly misguided when he supposed it to be harmless. For those such as C. Challen of MI9, the article was a 'piece of shocking invention' that would cause 'utter consternation, alarm and despondency . . . not only amongst the relatives of Prisoners of War, but men in the fighting services who may become prisoners themselves, and all people, throughout the civilised world, who are interested in their welfare'. For Challen, the story was so blatantly wrong that he supposed it could have been planted by the Germans themselves, in order to shift the blame from the Gestapo and on to the armed forces. Challen also wondered whether the story might act as a 'red flag in front of the Germans' that would only serve as an inducement to commit further similar atrocities.[19] The head of MI9, Major Norman Crockatt, was equally disturbed, and declared that the 'damaging effect on morale of P/W and aircrews (British and American) cannot be assessed'.[20] Captain V. A. R. Isham, who had also worked at MI9 until he was invalided out in 1942,[21] summed up the irony of a British newspaper unwittingly playing into the Germans' hands when he wondered, 'What can we do in otherwise total war being fought for freedom?!'[22]

In all likelihood, the story was not a German plant, and there is no evidence to suggest that it was. It appears that the Germans ignored the report – after all, they could hardly deny it by reporting what had actually taken place. Instead, the German Foreign Office, in cahoots with Section C – the search section – of the Reichs Kripo Office in Berlin, attempted to formulate a version of events that it hoped would be palatable. Several meetings took place between Dr Erich Albrecht of the Foreign Office and Kriminaldirektor Amend of Section C, during which a frustrated Albrecht, in the words of one Kripo official, 'expressed his extreme consternation at the diplomatic effect of this order [the Sagan Order] of Himmler, and compared it with the losing of a great battle'. Furthermore, Albrecht thought that 'in the diplomatic field, it meant a set-back for years'.[23] It is hard to imagine what sort of diplomatic traction Dr Albrecht supposed the German Foreign Office enjoyed with its British counterpart after nearly five years of war, and it is fair to assume that the diplomat was as deluded as his master, Joachim von Ribbentrop. As a result of the meetings, two sets of lies were drafted. The first was a supposedly 'exact' version, which was drawn from the Gestapo reports that claimed the men were shot while trying to escape. This version was dismissed, mainly because of the 'great frequency with which the same reasons were given'. The second version was a modification of the first, and attempted to add verisimilitude by inventing new ways in which the officers had died. These included drownings and traffic accidents, but in the main, the most common cause was that given by the Gestapo.[24]

During the same period, other agencies within the Nazi state apparatus were also desperately trying to establish another version of the truth. After a conference held at the Gestapo headquarters on Prinz-Albrechtstrasse, Walter Schellenberg, the head of the Ausland-SD – the SS Foreign Intelligence Service – witnessed a conversation between Kaltenbrunner, Nebe and Müller, during which the head of the Kripo and the head of the Gestapo revealed how they had been liaising with the Foreign Office on how to deal with a protest against the killings made by the Red Cross. Kaltenbrunner discussed, in the words of Schellenberg, 'what form one could best cover up the actually effected shootings in each individual case', and he suggested that the deaths could perhaps be explained by a variety of causes, including air raids, and, those hardy favourites, 'shooting while attempting to escape and while offering resistance'.[25]

Kaltenbrunner's inability to think of anything more imaginative reveals quite how stymied the Gestapo found itself in trying to explain how fifty escaping prisoners were not only shot, but shot and killed. Immediately after the murders had taken place, every participating Gestapo station had sent to Berlin a short report that was more or less identical, just as the Sagan Order had stipulated: 'The shootings will be explained by the fact that the recaptured officers were shot whilst trying to escape, or because they offered resistance.' Kriminalkommissar Peter Mohr, who worked in the Kripo's Section C, recalled how the first set of reports 'were very brief' and 'contained only Rank and Name of the shot officer in question, with the reason for shooting as already described'.[26] It quickly became apparent to Müller that more detail was required if the reports were to have any chance of being believed by an investigating authority such as the Red Cross. The Gestapo head clearly did not relish having to make up for the flaws in Himmler's order, and, like many a bad boss, he vented his frustration on his subordinates.

On the Tuesday after Eden's statement, Müller held a conference that was attended by, among others, Nebe, Scharpwinkel, Wielen, and Mohr.[27] During the course of the meeting, Müller had the gall openly to berate Scharpwinkel for the murders.

'A fine business of yours, this Breslau affair,' Müller raged. 'Shooting prisoners! It has brought diplomatic difficulties. You will be up in front of an international court!'

According to Peter Mohr, Scharpwinkel was 'very embarrassed' to be the subject of such ludicrously unjust treatment. Müller eventually calmed down, and then told the men that there was the possibility of an inquiry by the Red Cross, and that von Ribbentrop had also asked Himmler for an exact report of what had happened. Müller therefore ordered that each of the Gestapo stations had to submit much longer reports, which were to be dated the same as the original reports, but were not to be marked '*Geheime Reichssache*' – Top State Secret – as the new versions of the killings would appear legitimate and not require any such discretion. Of course, what Müller was ordering was an exercise in futility, as the implausible causes of death had already been reported, and all that could essentially be changed were the details. 'I had a very unsavoury impression of this conference,' Mohr later stated. 'Not a word was said about the existence of the Reichsführer's Sagan Order. I was surprised and upset at the way these gentlemen made a stage act of the whole thing.'[28]

What followed was a pathetic and transparent attempt to create a series of documents that stood no chance of fooling anyone. A typical example was the case of the Gestapo in Karlsruhe, which had been tasked with the killing of Dennis Cochran.[29] One of those party to that murder was Kriminalkommissar Walter Herberg, who was called away from the cinema at six o'clock one Sunday afternoon to go to the flat of Josef Gmeiner, the head of the Karlsruhe Gestapo. Gmeiner told Herberg that he had to travel immediately to Berlin, as the report their station had filed was deemed to be inadequate. Herberg had to take with him some blank sheets of Karlsruhe Gestapo letter paper, all of which had been signed by Gmeiner. After a tortuous journey, Herberg arrived in Berlin late the following afternoon, and reported to Müller on Tuesday morning. The head of the Gestapo appeared to be in a foul mood. 'Müller was very indignant about the report from Karlsruhe,' Herberg recalled. 'He declared we had no imagination, every report sounded alike.' This was rich, as the Karlsruhe Gestapo had only supplied what they had been ordered to supply. Müller then told Herberg to describe the location in which Cochran had been shot, after which Müller dictated a new report on the death to a secretary, who typed it upon the blank sheets supplied by Herberg. Müller's version of Cochran's death now featured the Gestapo's car suffering a puncture, with Cochran taking advantage of the breakdown by trying to flee, and then being shot twice in the process. Once it was complete, Herberg was dismissed, and went back to Karlsruhe that day.[30]

In Strasbourg, Alfred Schimmel found himself also having to concoct a new version of events, which 'revealed' that Anthony Hayter had in fact tried to escape whilst urinating 'at a spot somewhat out of view', and was therefore shot. The new report was taken to Müller in person by Kriminalsekretär Heinrich Hilker.[31] In Kiel, Gestapo driver Artur Denkmann was summoned to Room 33 in the headquarters, where he and the other participants in the murders of Catanach, Christensen, Espelid and Fugelsang were told by Johannes Post that Berlin had not accepted his report. Post then addressed Denkmann directly, and presented him with a possible new version of the killings.

'Two of the prisoners wanted to escape towards the

road,' Post said, 'and wanted to seize the two cars; during this, you and Struve shot one each.'

Denkmann, who had not actually pulled a trigger, was unsurprisingly outraged by the suggestion.

'But why this?' he asked. 'Do tell the truth how it happened, if it is all in order. I refuse most decidedly and indignantly to support such lies.'

Denkmann then added that he did not even possess a firearm, as it had been lost during an air raid in Hamburg in July the year before. Post tried to mollify Denkmann by telling him that it was just a formality, but Denkmann was adamant that he would have nothing to do with it. Post dismissed him, but an hour later, Denkmann was given a dressing down by the head of the Kiel Gestapo, Fritz Schmidt, who told him that if he created any difficulties, then 'something unpleasant' would happen to him. Denkmann still refused to take the blame.

'I would never consent to anything such as Post demanded of Struve and me,' he said, 'because this would be a great lie and even to our detriment.'

Schmidt repeated Post's assertion that the whole process was 'a pure formality', but Denkmann replied that he could not 'support even a formality if it is untrue'. After seeming to display remarkable patience in front of a truculent junior employee, Schmidt finally snapped, and shouted at Denkmann to get out of his office, and ended the exchange with the ominous words, 'I shall see to it that you keep your mouth shut.'[32] Although it is now unclear whether Post's new report ascribed two of the killings to Struve and Denkmann, it is possible that it did, as it would appear that

Denkmann did indeed keep his mouth shut. Although his superiors appeared not to know it, the driver's stepfather had been sent to Mauthausen concentration camp in 1938, where he had supposedly died from an illness in 1942. Under the principle of *Sippenhaft*, Denkmann later claimed that he risked meeting a similar fate, especially if his refusal to play along with the new report of the murders caused an inquiry into his background.[33]

By the end of May, Müller had received all his new reports, although it would appear that if they were seen by the German Foreign Office, they were not considered sufficiently plausible. Eventually, on 12 June, the Foreign Office did issue a Diplomatic Note that tried to explain away the murders with yet another concocted version of events. It claimed that in March there were several mass escapes all over Germany, involving some thousands of prisoners. These breakouts were 'systematically prepared' and 'had political and military objectives' which 'represented an attempt on public security in Germany and were intended to paralyse administrative and police authorities'. Therefore, the regime had no other option but to issue 'severe orders' to search units to 'pursue at all costs all who failed to halt when challenged or offered resistance or made renewed attempts to escape after capture, and to make use of weapons until fugitives had been deprived of all possibility of resistance or further flight'. The statement then mendaciously asserted that the fifty officers from Stalag Luft III were merely a 'residual number of prisoners' against whom weapons had to be used.[34] Unsurprisingly, neither the Swiss nor the British believed a word of the Note, and, significantly, nor did the Luftwaffe, whose Air Attaché in Geneva issued the following statement:

> A serious view is taken by the OKW [the German High Command], especially the GAF [German Air Force], of the death of the RAF officers trying to escape. Realised by them this will have repercussions on British attitude towards German Army and Air Force at end of war. They are anxious to convey to British Government that victims were handed over to SS on instructions from 'Highest Quarters'.[35]

The attaché also acknowledged that the official German statement was very 'thin'.[36]

Apart from its obvious absurdity, one of the reasons why the British did not believe the statement was because they were able to speak directly to some of the Kriegies who had been in Stalag Luft III, including Group Captain Massey, the former Senior British Officer. In an astonishing piece of oversight, the Germans had repatriated Massey and several other officers on medical grounds, and they had arrived in Britain on 22 May after leaving the camp on 11 April.[37] As a result, the Air Ministry had assembled a Court of Inquiry at RAF Weeton in Lancashire on 29 May, in which Massey and eleven other officers gave a full account of all they knew about both the escape and the killings. Massey had told the court that he had heard that none of those who had been taken by the Gestapo from Görlitz had been returned to the camp, and, specifically, that he had learned that Ernst Valenta and Denys Street had been shot.[38]

On Tuesday 20 June, a memorial service was held at the Church of St Martin-in-the-Fields in London. The service was attended by some one thousand people, including not only the next-of-kin and the great and good from the RAF and the Air Ministry, but also many London workers, who had queued up to join the service.[39] The names of all fifty murdered officers were printed in the order of service, with Roger Bushell's name appearing at the top. The service featured three hymns – 'For All The Saints Who From Their Labours Rest', 'Let Saints On Earth In Concert Sing', 'I Vow To Thee, My Country' – and one of the lessons included the following passage from the Wisdom of Solomon:

> In the sight of the unwise they seemed to die; and their departure is taken for misery, and their going from us to be utter destruction: but they are in peace. For though they be punished in the sight of men, yet is their hope full of immortality.[40]

'Music and prayer best suited the mood of private grief and public tragedy that underlay the service,' wrote one observer.[41] That sense of private grief was also noted in *The Times*. 'In the ceremony there was nothing for tears, but pride in service faithfully rendered.' At the end of the service, the 'Last Post' was played, with 'the pedal notes of the organ suggesting in such a vivid fashion the passing of aircraft that one could imagine that a squadron was flying past in tribute'.[42]

Three days later, on Friday 23 June, Anthony Eden made another statement on the murders. After giving the House of Commons more details about the escape and the murders, and rejecting the contents of the German Note, Eden concluded that the Government was 'firmly resolved that these foul criminals shall be tracked down to the last man wherever they may take refuge,' and that 'when the war is over they will be brought to exemplary justice'.[43] The House was unanimous in its support, and on 3 July, Eden was to receive a telegram from James Catanach's father in Melbourne, Australia, who stated that he wished to show his appreciation 'of the serious consideration by the British Government to this odious crime'.[44]

The Germans reacted sourly, and the following month, had the gall to rebuke Eden for making his statement before the findings of the German 'investigations' had been published. Furthermore, the Foreign Secretary, because of the punitive Allied bombing campaign, lacked the 'moral right to say anything at all in this question or to raise a complaint against anyone else'. As a result, the German Government stated that it would decline to make any further announcements about the shooting.[45] Shortly afterwards, Müller, in a last attempt to divest himself of the whole affair, handed over all his files on the Sagan case to his counterpart in the Kripo, Artur Nebe, who in turn passed them to Peter Mohr. When Mohr asked Nebe what he was to do with the files, Nebe simply said, 'Put them in the fire. You'll find out soon enough what to do with them.' Mohr gained the impression that his Kripo head was 'visibly relieved to be rid of them'.[46]

As well as ineptly arranging the cover-up, the Germans were indeed carrying out extensive investigations, but not of the kind they had implied in their

statement. The only genuine inquiries they were con-
ducting were those by Kriminalkommissar Günther
Absalon and his team.[47] Since his arrival on the day of
the escape, Absalon had led the investigation into corruption at Stalag Luft III with a mixture of oily charm
and intelligence. His approach may not have endeared
him to his fellow Germans, but it was to prove fairly
effective. Dressed immaculately in his SS field uniform,
clutching a voluminous blue notebook, and arriving at
the camp on a regular basis in a grey Mercedes, Absalon
was to become a familiar figure to Kriegie and German
alike.[48] The British even nicknamed him 'My son, my
son', because of the Old Testament resonance of his
surname.[49] Working on the entirely correct hypothesis
that the escapers must have been helped by those who
were guarding them, Absalon ordered extensive
searches of the German section of the camp in order to
find items such as chocolate and cigarettes from Red
Cross parcels.[50] Unfortunately for Absalon, the contraband he did find would provide him with his best
evidence of corruption. As a charge sheet – perhaps
written by Absalon – later noted, those who were suspected of corruption were unlikely to betray each other,
and the only witnesses were the Kriegies themselves,
who both remained silent and were considered
'excluded as a means of conviction'.[51]

As a result, Absalon relied more on interrogation,
threat and even espionage to wheedle out the truth.
Among those interrogated was Joachim Ziegenhorn,
who worked as a mail censor at the camp. After the
'delousing shed escape' in June 1943,[52] Ziegenhorn was
twice interrogated by the Gestapo for several hours, and

accused of being pro-British and a believer in 'English propaganda'. Although the Gestapo could find no proof of wrongdoing, his passport was confiscated, and his parents were also interrogated and their home was searched. At the time of the Great Escape, Ziegenhorn was in hospital, although this did not stop Absalon from having him sent to Breslau jail, where he was held for two days and subjected to several interrogations.[53]

Being a relatively junior member of the camp staff, Ziegenhorn was unlikely to have answered back to his interrogators, but there were those who did. When Gustav Simoleit defended the actions of von Lindeiner, he was told 'it would be better for me "to take care of my own head"'. During his interrogation, Simoleit was accused of being responsible not only for the breakout, but also for the 'unbearable situation' in the camp. Simoleit wrote:

> I tried to defend myself with the clear fact that my department was not responsible for custody and guarding of the prisoners. I pointed out that all my actions and activities were in strict accord with the Geneva Convention and even with former orders of the German High Command of the armed forces.

Such a defence carried little weight, and Simoleit was threatened with being sent to a frontline fighting unit – a posting that was colloquially known as being sent to a *Himmelfahrtskommando*, a 'heaven-bound squad'. Fortunately for Simoleit, he was saved by the appointment of the camp's new permanent Commandant, Colonel Braune, who refused to take up his position if he were deprived of his most experienced officers.[54]

It is not clear who questioned Simoleit, but judging by the tenor of the interrogation, it was likely to have been Kriminalsekretär Scholz, who played the 'bad cop' to the 'good cop' played by Absalon. Lieutenant Günther von Massow, the censor officer, found that Absalon always behaved politely, and even with courtesy. When von Massow's wife was arrested, von Massow asked Absalon to ensure that she was brought home by car, to which Absalon agreed. As with the questioning of Simoleit, von Massow himself was told that he had been too 'favourable' with the Kriegies – an accusation not without substance – although Absalon was unable to find any compelling evidence of corruption. As a result, according to von Massow's suspicions, Absalon placed a spy in the lieutenant's office, and ordered a search of his flat, where foodstuffs such as cheese and butter were found. Von Massow was arrested on 3 May and charged with 'contravening rationing regulations', although the accused was adamant that he was innocent, maintaining that the supposed contraband was not of the kind supplied to the Kriegies.[55] Absalon reserved his greatest unctuousness for von Lindeiner, who was recovering from his coronary episode at his home, Jeschkendorf Manor. The former Commandant recalled how Absalon tried to gain von Lindeiner's trust while sitting next to his sick bed. The elderly colonel was, however, too wily for the policeman's assurances that he was simply there to help, and remained mostly tight-lipped. 'My caution was soon proved to be justified,' von Lindeiner recalled, 'as it was reported to me that those I had mentioned only in passing had been immediately called in for questioning, regardless of whether they were members of the camp staff or not.' When Absalon realised that von Lindeiner would not confide in him, he tried to earn the trust of the Commandant's secretary and his adjutant (Gustav Simoleit), although both approaches were similarly fruitless.[56]

By the middle of September, Absalon and his team had drawn up their charge sheet. The list featured three officers – von Lindeiner; Captain Broili, the head of the camp's counter-intelligence department; and Captain Pieber – and eight NCOs, including Erich Oest, Gustav Wolter and Fritz Bening. Unsurprisingly, von Lindeiner attracted the greatest number of charges, and he was accused of intentional dereliction of duty, constant disobeying of orders, endangering the preparedness of the German army, neglecting his duty of oversight over his subordinates, and constantly ignoring the rules concerning contact with the prisoners. Broili's charges were similar, as were those of Pieber, although the latter was also accused of 'careless actions that had furthered the enterprise of the enemy', which referred to the loan of his Contax camera. The NCOs were accused of constant disobedience of orders 'resulting in detriment and danger to life, or to foreign property, or to the security of the Reich', as well as a litany of other charges concerning corruption and the nature of their contact with the prisoners.[57]

The court martial started on 4 October.[58] Von Lindeiner had no complaint with the conduct of the proceedings, which he felt to be 'factual and honourable', although he was taken aback by the severity of the punishment called for by the prosecution: eighteen months in jail and demotion.[59] After five days, von Lindeiner was found guilty of neglect of duty for not keeping the underground microphones in operation; continual disobedience for allowing the prisoners to keep tin cans; neglect of 'supervisional duties' for continuing to employ Erich Oest, who was known to be corrupt; and, last, 'forbidden intercourse' with the prisoners, such as shaking hands and accepting cups of tea. However, most significantly, and perhaps most disappointingly for Absalon, the court declared that 'no guilt attaches to L. in the successful mass escape'. Nevertheless, von Lindeiner was sentenced to a year's imprisonment in a fortress.[60] Mindful that twelve months in the hands of the Gestapo would do no wonders for his health, von Lindeiner decided to pull a time-honoured trick used by soldiers immemorial to avoid an unpleasant duty: he pretended to be mentally ill. Towards the end of October, a psychiatrist declared that he suffered from 'an advanced stage of mental disturbance' and instead of being incarcerated, he was admitted to an army hospital in Görlitz.[61] His fellow defendants were not quite so fortunate, and received custodial sentences that ranged from a few months to two years.

Back at Stalag Luft III, the Kriegies were of course largely unaware of such events, and were instead trying to adjust to the new regime under Colonel Braune. A visit by Gabriel Naville in June found that the Kriegies still felt 'insecure', and that relations between the British and the Germans were 'very strained'. However, the

British appeared to respect Braune, who was considered firm but fair, and, to paraphrase Naville, the British knew where they stood.[62] What Naville would not have been privy to were the activities of the X Organisation, which may have lost its Svengali and, in the words of Lieutenant Charles Woehrle, 'the brains of the camp',[63] but it did try to continue in the same spirit. Any efforts made were largely the product of keeping face, and a new tunnel – 'George' – was started from underneath the theatre.[64] Work on the tunnel took place over the summer, despite the lack of what Paul Brickhill called a 'definite policy just yet on mass escapes'.[65] By the time winter arrived, George had reached just beyond the wire, after which it was sealed. The likely purpose of the tunnel, which was never used, was to act as a contingency in the event that the Nazis ordered the POW population to be massacred.[66] After the killing of the fifty, the Kriegies thought their captors were capable of anything, and courses were held in unarmed warfare and self-defence in order to prepare for the type of event that had been imagined by 'E. D. Masterman'.[67] Ironically enough, during that summer, MI9 finally managed to smuggle some really useful equipment into the camp. Two complete civilian suits and hats arrived, as well as a typewriter, a camera with films and developing materials, forged documents and stamps.[68] Unfortunately, none of this material was to be used.

In addition to the tunnel, very few other escapes were attempted. The new Senior British Officer, Group Captain Wilson, stipulated that the danger was just too great, and in September, a coded message was received from MI9 stating that 'escape was no longer considered a duty'.[69] As we have seen, there was in fact no formal duty to escape, but it was quite clear that the murders – if their purpose was to act as both retribution and warning – had served the Germans well. Furthermore, if such a violent admonition were not enough, during the summer, posters had appeared in camps throughout the Reich advising British POWs that 'the escape from prison camps is no longer a sport'. After outrageously claiming that Germany had 'only punished recaptured prisoners of war with minor disciplinary punishment', the poster warned that escapers ran the risk of entering 'death zones', where all trespassers could be 'immediately shot on sight'. Of course, as these zones were not delineated, this effectively gave the Germans an unwarranted carte blanche to shoot any escaper at any time, and could act as a convenient *post hoc* justification for murder that Müller would have relished when he was having to explain away the killings of the Great Escapers. In short, the poster warned, 'the chances of preserving your life are almost nil!' and it exhorted prisoners 'to stay in the camp where you will be safe!'[70] Had the poster appeared before the Great Escape, it is debatable whether the Kriegies in Stalag Luft III would have taken it seriously, but in the wake of the killings, it could not simply be dismissed as a piece of empty propaganda. Prisoners in other camps also heeded its words, not just because they would have heard of the Sagan murders, but also because other escaping POWs had been shot in similar circumstances. In April, two British officers, Major Wadeson and Captain McKenzie, had escaped from Oflag 8F near Liegnitz, some 60 miles southeast of Sagan. In June, urns containing the ashes of the two men were returned to the camp, along with the predictable statement that they had been 'shot whilst attempting to re-escape'.[71]

If the appetite for escaping was not what it was, there was certainly a desire to commemorate those who had died. Towards the end of the summer, the Commandant gave permission for the British to erect a mausoleum for the urns outside the camp, and thirty officers were selected to carry out the work, operating in shifts of a maximum of twelve men, each of whom had promised not to try to escape.[72] The materials and the stone were donated by von Lindeiner himself, and a brass plate carrying an inscription was paid for by the War Prisoners' Aid section of the World's Alliance of Young Men's Christian Associations.[73] Constructed in the shape of an altar, the memorial bore three scrolls representing each of the three tunnels, and upon which the names of the fifty were carved. On 4 December, a brief funeral service was held, which was attended by twenty-three officers, Gabriel Naville, and Colonel Braune's adjutant. After wreaths were laid, a company of German guards fired a salute in honour of the fallen.[74] The monument still stands today.

Chapter Sixteen

Exemplary Justice?

IN EARLY APRIL 1945, just a fortnight before the Americans entered a partially ruined Munich, Kriminalsekretär Emil Weil was ordered by his chief, Dr Oswald Schäfer, to visit the city's funeral office. As the city had suffered some seventy Allied air raids, the registers in the office featured thousands of names, but Weil was told to look for just two: those of two men he had helped to kill. After explaining his orders to the office's deputy director, Weil was shown the appropriate register, where he quickly found the names of Johannes Gouws and Rupert Stevens. Then, with a typewriter rubber and a penknife, Weil erased the two names. He reported back to Schäfer, who ordered him to perform a similar task two days later at the Munich police headquarters on Ettstrasse, where the two men had been held. After consulting an Inspector Wörlein, who in turn discussed it with the Chief of Police, Weil was told that the police would be happy to oblige, and that the Gestapo officer could leave it to them. Weil then visited the Kripo, where he spoke to a Kriminalrat Haselsberger, who was 'in charge of secret matters'. 'I told him my instructions,' Weil recalled. 'He had a black note book fetched and I crossed out these two names with Indian ink.'[1] At first, it seems extraordinary that after terrorising an entire city for over a decade, the Munich Gestapo was concerned with covering the evidence of just two murders. However, the efforts made by Schäfer reveal quite how unusual it was for the Gestapo to have killed Allied POWs. Both he and his colleagues would have been aware that their membership of the Gestapo would shortly make them wanted men, but to be associated with such high-profile killings might make them especially sought-after by the approaching Allies.

The erasing of such records would not be the only barrier for those tasked with bringing men like Schäfer and Weil to what Eden had promised to be 'exemplary justice'. As the war ended, tens of thousands of Nazi criminals went into hiding, adopting false identities and blending in with the millions of refugees and soldiers who were either on the road or crammed into over-crowded internment camps. With Germany's physical and bureaucratic infrastructures in chaos, the priority of the Allies was to prevent anarchy and starvation, not to mount thousands of time-consuming and costly man-hunts. The investigation teams that were established were hopelessly under-staffed and under-resourced, which was partly the product of a lack of political will to act on a larger scale. Although many fine words were said during the war, not least in Moscow in October 1943, when the Allies promised to pursue the criminals 'to the uttermost ends of the earth and . . . deliver them to the accusers in order that justice may be done', in truth such declarations did little more than reaffirm the moral high ground rather than offer up anything practical. Bodies that were formed to create legal frameworks and to assemble evidence, such as the United Nations War Crimes Commission and the Central Registry of War Criminals and Security Suspects, ended up as little more than talking shops or beset by administrative and technical problems that rendered them woefully ineffective. Had the fleeing Nazis known quite how incapable were the efforts being made to find them, many might have stayed at home rather than undergone arduous journeys to far-flung destinations such as Buenos Aires or Damascus.[2]

This, then, was the environment in which the unit tasked with hunting the killers of the Great Escapers had to operate. The officers and men were drawn from the RAF's Special Investigation Branch (RAF SIB), and they were led by Wing Commander Wilfred Bowes. Aged forty-two, Bowes was a no-nonsense Geordie who had worked his way up through the ranks of the RAF Police, and had a reputation for being a 'tenacious, if unorthodox, interrogator, with an unconcealed contempt for civilian detective procedures'.[3] Although Bowes may not have cared for his counterparts, he chose as his lead investigator Flight Lieutenant Frank McKenna, who had been a detective sergeant in Blackpool before serving as a second pilot in a

Lancaster of 622 Squadron. As well as being suitably qualified, McKenna also knew two of the murdered men, which meant that for him the appointment was more than simply a professional assignment.[4] However, because McKenna was so experienced, he was also aware of quite how ambitious a task it was to hunt down the perpetrators. When he had heard Eden's speech on 23 June, McKenna expressed his doubts with a certain Lancastrian bluntness. 'He doesn't know what he's talking about,' he said. 'Track them down to the last man, in war-busted Germany, when they'll have the best sets of false papers the Gestapo can provide?'[5]

On 3 September 1945, McKenna flew to Germany accompanied by Flying Officer H. J. Williams, who had served in the Portsmouth police before joining the RAF.[6] The only significant lead McKenna had was a list of names which had been assembled from the evidence given to the Court of Inquiry, interrogations of German POWs, and statements made by repatriated Kriegies. The files also revealed that the urns of the dead men bore the names of the towns in which they had been cremated. Shortly after arriving in Germany, McKenna realised that the job was even tougher than he had anticipated, and over the next few weeks, at his request, his team of two was supplemented by two more officers and three sergeants. The relative ease with which the SIB managed to swell its ranks is indicative of the importance that was attached to the investigation. By December, the team grew to five officers, sixteen NCOs and sixteen interpreters, which therefore made it similar in size to a regular war crimes investigation unit, the likes of which were struggling to find manpower.[7]

Nevertheless, as with the regular units, the RAF SIB was afflicted by internal politics. Among the new arrivals was Squadron Leader William Thomas, who only had a few months left to serve in the RAF.[8] McKenna had specifically requested that someone with a higher rank than his own was required out in Germany in order to exert more influence when dealing with senior officers.[9] On paper, the appointment of Thomas seemed like a good one – he had served for twenty-eight years at Scotland Yard, and was the Senior Instructor to CID. However, although Thomas would be senior to McKenna, his role was not clearly defined, and there was some issue as to why the Great Escape inquiry was not passing to the main RAF SIB Command. According to Thomas, when he arrived at the SIB's headquarters in Rinteln, 35 miles southwest of Hanover and near the British war crimes team in Bad Oeynhausen, he found the atmosphere not to his liking. 'It was soon evident that adverse feeling existed,' he wrote, 'for I was casually questioned as to why I had been sent to Germany in sole charge of the enquiry and why it had not been passed to the Command.' Thomas tried to explain that the decision was not of his making, and he stressed that the Great Escape inquiry was 'a common purpose for all and that my team had been sent in order not to interfere with the general work of investigation'.[10]

Thomas found there were other issues as well. One of his greatest problems was the lack of professionalism exhibited by some of the NCOs. On one occasion, Thomas learned about the arrest of two important suspects only through a casual conversation, and was irked that he had received no official notification.[11] Another gripe was transport, a problem that was common to nearly every Allied unit. 'In this I regret to state, I and my team have been treated as absolute outsiders,' Thomas complained. 'It has been disgraceful considering the responsibilities I have had.' Despite repeated requests for cars, Thomas found that the only vehicle that could be supplied to him was a Jeep, which was inadequate for long journeys. Thomas was so incensed that he even considered approaching the Commander-in-Chief, although it is not clear whether he ever did so.[12] Thomas also took exception to what he described as a 'party spirit' in the RAF Police, and at one point even peevishly listed what he regarded as a gluttonous consumption of locally acquired poultry, which he viewed as 'disgraceful considering the food situation in Germany'. Clearly not a popular man, in a complaint he filed to the Director of Personal Services at the Air Ministry that December, Thomas unwittingly revealed how he was perceived by his fellow officers. 'I have not been invited to any parties,' he wrote, 'and one evening was left to eat alone in the Mess, as others had been invited to a party, where I understand about 30 RAF officers sat down to a meal.'[13]

Nevertheless, by the time Thomas came up for his release date on 18 December, he was eager to continue with the investigation:

I have a firm grip on the enquiry, have personal knowledge and good co-operation with all useful contacts and a strong conviction that every criminal concerned with these murders can be arrested or

accounted for by death; and further that the relatives of
those murdered and the British Public are entitled to a
proper enquiry for these dastardly crimes.

Thomas also commented that members of the team,
such as McKenna, Williams and the Dutch interpreters,
had done 'splendid work', although he observed that 'if
it were not for the difficulties the enquiry would be
much further advanced, if not nearly completed'.[14]
Unfortunately for the squadron leader, his request fell
on the stoniest of ground, not least because he had also
insisted that he should be promoted to Wing
Commander. For the Air Ministry, this was 'the milk in
the coconut', and as far as the Director of Personal
Services was concerned, Thomas's release date was 'a
most refreshing anticipation'.[15] Thomas was not to get
his way, and upon his release, he was replaced in
Germany by Bowes himself, who was a much more
popular figure.

The notion that the inquiry could have been nearly
completed in just four months was something of an
exaggeration. Thousands of Germans and other
nationals held in internment camps needed to be interrogated just in order to establish the names of the
several hundred officials who had served in the towns in
which the men had been killed. Journeys of hundreds of
miles had to be undertaken in the worst possible conditions, sometimes, in the words of Bowes, 'to follow
some slender clue which very often proved negative'.[16]
By the time Thomas left, just four suspects had been
transferred to the London District Cage, an interrogation centre at 8 Kensington Palace Gardens in west

London. These included SS-Obersturmbannführer Dr
Ernst Kah, the head of the SD in Warsaw; Lieutenant
General Walter Grosch; Colonel Ernst Wälde; and
General Richard Hoffman, who was the officer in
charge of the Luftwaffe's POW section.[17] As none of
these men were directly responsible for the murders, it
is inconceivable that had Thomas got everything he had
wished for – including his promotion – the Cage would
have been stuffed by Christmas 1945 with the killers
themselves. In fact, the active hunt for the perpetrators
would last for the best part of two years.

In the early stages of the investigation, McKenna and
his colleagues found that one name kept being
mentioned: that of Günther Absalon. After establishing
that he came from Düsseldorf, McKenna and Williams
visited his wife, Gerdha, at Brunnenstrasse 42 and his
parents, Paul and Martha, at Kribbenstrasse 20 in the
suburb of Heerdt. All three family members were
closely interrogated, but they claimed that the last time
they had heard from Absalon was on 7 February 1945,
when he was in Breslau. McKenna and Williams carried
out a full search of both properties, from where they
obtained photographs of Absalon with one of his
children, and also in his SS uniform. The investigators
also visited the home of Absalon's mistress, Hildegarde
Deutz, at Peter-Schnellbach-Strasse 3 in Neckargemünd,
some 200 miles south of Düsseldorf, but she had neither
seen nor heard from her lover since January 1945.[18] A
dispirited McKenna and Williams returned to Rinteln,
where they had a piece of good fortune. During the
Russian advance, many civilians who had fled Breslau
had ended up in Rinteln, including the town's

Bürgermeister, who was able to supply McKenna with a list of former residents. Among them was a former army lieutenant called Klaus Lonsky, who told McKenna that the fanatical Scharpwinkel had formed an eponymous unit consisting of some 150 Gestapo and Kripo men, and most had died while defending the town against the Russians.[19]

The name of Scharpwinkel clearly excited the British investigators, as by then, in early October 1945, they knew him to be a major perpetrator of the killings. When questioned about Scharpwinkel, Lonsky said that he had heard from another former Breslau resident, a former Oberleutnant Hubertus Zembrodt, that Scharpwinkel had admitted himself into hospital in Breslau as a 'Lieutenant Hagamann'. Zembrodt had been in the bed opposite Hagamann, and one day a woman escorted by a group of Russian military police entered the ward and accused Hagamann of being Scharpwinkel. The former Gestapo chief did not deny the charge, and he was taken away.[20] With strong grounds to believe that both Absalon and Scharpwinkel were being held by the Soviets, the onus on finding the two men now fell to the Foreign Office. The following February, the British Ambassador in Moscow, Sir Frank Roberts, presented a list of those wanted by the British in connection with the murders. By the end of March, the Russians had not replied, and Sir Frank sent another letter and another list.[21] It would be the end of August 1946 before the British were able to interview Scharpwinkel and, despite the most concerted diplomatic efforts, the Soviets were never to hand him over to the British for trial. When Scharpwinkel was interviewed in Moscow by a London District Cage officer, Captain Maurice Cornish, he told his interrogator that he hoped 'whoever is judging the matter will take into account the conditions in Germany, and the fact that soldiers and officials in Germany who had taken the oath had to obey every order'. To have disobeyed, he added, 'would have resulted in court-martial proceedings'.[22]

Two years later, the Soviets reported that Scharpwinkel had died following an illness, a claim of which some were sceptical. 'Those of us who worked on the Sagan case were disposed to doubt it,' wrote Lieutenant-Colonel Alexander Scotland, the head of the Prisoner of War Interrogation Section of the Intelligence Corps, in 1957. 'Even to this day I am inclined to put the question: Is Scharpwinkel still alive?'[23] Of Absalon there would be little concrete news from the Soviets, and he is supposed to have died in a Russian prison in May 1948, or in a POW camp in Kursk on 15 July 1947.[24] It is quite possible that the deaths of the two men, especially that of Absalon, were faked by the Russians. At the end of the war, Absalon was just thirty-three, and he was an intelligent and resourceful figure, whose charm and obvious ability might have come to the attention of the Soviet intelligence services. Faking the deaths of war criminals – and it should be stressed that Absalon was almost certainly not guilty in regard to the Great Escape murders – was something that even the British did, to the extent of deceiving their own war crimes units.[25]

As with Scharpwinkel, many of the murderers and their accomplices were never to be apprehended by the

RAF. Of those who escaped justice, several had died. A few, such as Martin Schermer of the Munich Gestapo, had killed themselves. Others, including many members of the Breslau Gestapo, had died in action, or had been obliterated, like Leopold Spann, in air raids. Some, such as Friedrich Kiowsky, were wanted for other crimes elsewhere, and executed by nations such as Czechoslovakia.[26] The instigators of the murders, including Hitler, Himmler, Göring, Kaltenbrunner, Keitel, Nebe and Müller, were all dead, dispatched by the hangman at Nuremberg or by their own hands.[27] And then there were those who had simply disappeared, such as Danzig's Julius Hug and Brno's Adolf Knippelberg. Nevertheless, Bowes and his team did manage to track down around thirty of the wanted men, although even then, some escaped justice by killing themselves while in captivity. Franz Schmidt from Kiel hanged himself on 27 October 1946, and Strasbourg's Max Diessner opted for the same form of suicide on 11 May 1948.[28]

However, it was with much grim satisfaction for the likes of Bowes and McKenna that some of the more repugnant murderers were brought to justice. Among them were Erich Zacharias and Johannes Post, to whom killing came easily. The hunt for Zacharias and his Brno Gestapo colleagues was a *prima facie* example of good detective work, and, like all manhunts, it involved a certain amount of luck, which in this instance came in the form of a mural on a hotel wall. The first lead given to the team regarding the murders of Gordon Kidder and Thomas Kirby-Green came in mid-January 1946 from a Dr F. V. van der Bijl, who had written to the

British Embassy in Prague recounting his compre-
hensive interrogation of Friedrich Kiowsky, who had
driven the two men to their deaths. Van der Bijl provided much detail concerning not only the murders but
also the cover-up, and, more helpfully still, he listed the
names of the perpetrators. Van der Bijl ended his letter
by stating that he was 'deeply interested' in the fate of
Kirby-Green as he had served with him in the RAF.[29]

On Tuesday 12 February, Bowes flew to Prague
accompanied by Flight Lieutenant Arthur Lyon, a former station inspector for the Metropolitan Police and a
fluent German speaker.[30] After holding various meetings, on 19 February the two men were escorted by a
Czech liaison officer on a train to Brno, where they
made contact with the Czech Third Army Intelligence,
which was holding over one hundred members of the
Brno Gestapo. Over the next two days, Bowes and Lyon
interrogated all of them, and found that only five had
any information on the killings. Of these, the most useful was former Kriminalkommissar Franz Schauschütz,
a 33-year-old Austrian who had taken part in organising the cover-up of the murders, and provided much
useful information concerning how the killings had
been ordered, as well as confirming that Adolf
Knippelberg had been involved. 'Schauschütz is a very
intelligent person,' Bowes commented, 'and should
prove to be a good witness.'[31] Schauschütz's eagerness
was not entirely sincere, as he was awaiting trial for
committing war crimes in Czechoslovakia, and by helping the British, he hoped that he might be transferred
into their custody. Such hopes were in vain.

After two days of solid interrogations, Bowes and

Lyon eventually accepted their hosts' offer of a dinner and drinks at a hotel in central Brno. During the war, the premises had been frequented by the Gestapo, and on the walls, Bowes could not help but notice a risqué painting of some lustful satyrs carrying off a group of naked young women, who were reputed to be caricatures of the Gestapo's secretaries. After staring at the mural for a while, Bowes realised that one of the satyrs was a representation of Schauschütz, and he told his host as much. The Czech officer looked at the painting and then pointed to another satyr, saying, 'And this is Knippelberg.' Bowes was delighted. 'Can I have that painting photographed?' he asked. 'This is the first mug-shot of a murderer I have got my hands on in this case.'[32]

On the morning of 22 February, Bowes and Lyon travelled 50 miles east to Uherské Hradiště, where they interrogated Friedrich Kiowsky. After being shown a selection of photographs, including those taken of the mural, Kiowsky was able to identify Knippelberg and several other Gestapo men, including Otto Kozlowski, Hans Ziegler and Erich Zacharias. Two days later, Kiowsky showed Bowes and Lyon the actual scene of the murders, which Bowes immediately identified as being a completely unlikely spot from which Kirby-Green and Kidder might have chosen to escape, as it was situated in open country.[33] The murders were then reconstructed, with Bowes, Lyon and two Czechs posing as the murderers and their victims.[34] As well as interviewing Kiowsky, the investigators spoke to a Gestapo man called Urbanek, who was to provide crucial information concerning the whereabouts of Zacharias. At the end of the war, Urbanek and Zacharias had managed to wangle some papers off the Americans that stated they were 'harmless persons' and former customs officials, and both men had lain low by working on a farm in Mittenwald in the far south of Bavaria, and had lived with a Frau Holshauer on Innsbruckstrasse 34. Urbanek revealed that Zacharias had subsequently moved to Wesermünde, which was essentially part of Bremerhaven in northwest Germany. Much to the delight of Bowes and Lyon, Urbanek was even able to supply the addresses of Zacharias's parents and one of his brothers.[35] These addresses were confirmed a few days later by none other than Zacharias's wife, who was living in Zlin. Frau Zacharias appeared to have little affection for her husband, and even wished Bowes good luck in finding him. Nevertheless, fearing that she might change her mind, the Czechs interned her in case she decided to warn her husband that the RAF was on to him.[36]

The man tasked with finding Zacharias in Bremerhaven was Frank McKenna. On 11 March, he and Lieutenant Vreugdenhil of the Netherlands Military Mission travelled to Wesermünde. Although he had been provided with the two addresses, McKenna had no wish to alert his quarry, and instead contacted the US Army's Public Safety Officer, Lieutenant Freshour.[37] The Americans checked their paperwork recording the movements of German nationals, but the name of Zacharias did not appear. McKenna then tried the Civil Administration Officer, Captain Leather, who checked his files, and swiftly found an entry for Zacharias, which stated that he had come to Wesermünde in

September 1945, and was working as a clerk at the No. 256 US Army Refrigeration Plant on the docks.[38] At 2.15 p.m., McKenna, Vreugdenhil and Freshour visited the plant, and entered a large basement office. At the end of a long row of desks, they found their man, and after Zacharias had produced his identity papers, McKenna searched him while Vreugdenhil and Freshour covered him with their automatics. Zacharias was then taken to the US Army's Counterintelligence Corps Interrogation Centre on Hohenzollernstrasse, where he was given a full body search for concealed poisons and weapons. Neither was found, and Zacharias was placed into custody at a local prison.[39]

What followed next was the result of another obstacle that often hampered the war crimes teams in their manhunts: bureaucracy. McKenna applied to take Zacharias to 'Tomato', the British War Criminals Holding Centre at Minden, but the Americans said that any move would need to be cleared with the Counterintelligence Corps (CIC) in Frankfurt, which would possibly entail a wait of a few days.[40] McKenna was frustrated, not least because he was worried that the prison was staffed by German warders. The following morning, McKenna interviewed Zacharias at the CIC offices, after which he sent him back to the prison at lunchtime. As the prison van drove slowly through the gaol's gateway, Zacharias seized his moment. He broke away from his guards, jumped out of the vehicle and dashed towards a bombed-out building. One of the guards tried to take a shot, but a woman walked into view, and Zacharias was able to get free.[41]

A general alarm was raised, and roadblocks were

mounted, but the resourceful former Gestapo officer appeared to make good his escape. Every address associated with the fugitive was searched, but there was no trace. The only remaining option was to intercept the mail going to and from these addresses, and a disappointed McKenna was forced to resume his search for other quarries.[42]

Towards the end of the month, the Americans finally had a breakthrough. A friend of Zacharias received a letter from a person in Fallersleben, some 45 miles east of Hanover, 135 miles southeast of Wesermünde, and, most significantly, just a few miles from the border with the Soviet Zone of Occupation. One line in the letter read, 'Erich has been ill but is improving, and will soon be on his way.' At 1 a.m. on 31 March, the Americans raided the address in Fallersleben, where they found a fully clothed Zacharias in a bedroom, seemingly ready to go out.[43] After he was transferred back to Wesermünde, the Americans quickly allowed the British to take control of their troublesome prisoner, and by 5 April, McKenna had personally delivered Zacharias into the care of Lieutenant Colonel Scotland in Kensington Park Gardens.[44]

It was to Scotland that Zacharias would recount the story of raping and killing the young Czech woman.[45] The interrogator found Zacharias loathsome. 'What impressed me from the start . . . was the clear delight he took in telling of his bestial activities,' Scotland later wrote. What concerned Scotland most was the question of whether Zacharias had tortured Kirby-Green and Kidder, and although the murderer seemed content to admit that he had taken part in the killings, he would not confirm or deny whether he had abused his two victims. Scotland even tried to recreate the scene in the interrogation room in Zlin, in the hope that the show-man in Zacharias would 'disclose rather more of the truth than had gone into his written statement'.[46] However, the attempt failed, and shortly afterwards, Zacharias was dispatched to the POW camp on Kempton Park racecourse.

Once again, Zacharias found imprisonment not to his liking, and a few weeks later, he made yet another great escape of his own. At one o'clock one morning, he cut around the lock of his prison door with a tool made from a tin plate, and climbed up on the roof of a 12-foot-high outhouse.[47] He then used a crowbar to break through two barbed-wire barriers, but lost a shoe in the process. After dropping into the brightly lit guard walk that ran inside the length of the camp's perimeter, Zacharias climbed a large tree adjacent to the fence and jumped 10 feet down on to the Staines Road and to his freedom. Since he was wearing only one brown shoe and a blue prison uniform, and was unable to speak English, the chances of Zacharias getting far were slim. 'Unless he can steal clothes and shoes,' said one police official, 'the man must be so conspicuous that he cannot be seen by anyone without being spotted.'[48] The official was right, because a little later that day, Zacharias was spotted less than a mile away from the racecourse, hiding in some shrubbery along the riverbank near the Weir Hotel at Sunbury Lock. Three hundred troops from the camp descended upon the area, and RAF planes flew at treetop level helping to coordinate the search. With a cordon established on both sides of the river, Zacharias's recapture was inevitable.[49] As he was taken back to his cell that afternoon, the killer might have reflected that he was lucky not to have been shot while trying to escape.

As with so many manhunts, one method the RAF investigators adopted was *chercher la femme*. This tactic was used to great reward in the hunt for Johannes Post of the Kiel Gestapo, who would be found through his theatre-going mistress Marianne Heidt.[50] During the investigation, McKenna and Lyon had searched her flat, and the only lead they had found was a photograph of the couple on a skiing trip in the Harz Mountains.[51] For many months, Post's trail ran cold, until one day in late May 1947, McKenna decided to visit the Holding Centre in Minden to check over any new arrivals. The commandant informed McKenna that a man called 'Johannes Pohlmann' had been detained on 19 May in connection with some three hundred deaths at the Nordmark Workers Educational Camp in the southern Kiel suburb of Hassee.[52] McKenna peered at Pohlmann through the cell's peephole, and although his face was familiar, he could not place it. After going for a walk and mulling it over, McKenna then realised that Pohlmann bore a strong similarity to Post and he returned to 'Tomato' with the photograph. Under McKenna's questioning, the prisoner continued to assert that he really was called Pohlmann, and that he was a haulage contractor from Celle, some 130 miles south of Kiel. McKenna said that he did not believe him, and that he was in fact Johannes Post, formerly of the Gestapo. Pohlmann denied the accusation, but then McKenna played his trump and brought out the picture of the happy couple.

'Where did you get that?' asked Pohlmann.

'There is no reason why I should tell you,' McKenna replied.

'Well, that's me. I am Post.'[53]

Just over six weeks later, at 10 a.m. on Tuesday 1 July 1947, Johannes Post found himself in the dock at the No. 1 Courtroom of the Curiohaus in Hamburg. Alongside him were seventeen other suspects, who included Roger Bushell's killer, Emil Schulz; Max Wielen of the Breslau Kripo; Emil Weil; Zacharias; and Alfred Schimmel. Presiding over the court was Major General H. L. Longden, and the prosecutor was the experienced Colonel R. C. Halse. The defendants were represented by no fewer than ten counsel, none of whom Lieutenant Colonel Scotland liked the look of. 'I had an unaccountable feeling that there might be trouble ahead,' he wrote. 'I watched that cheerful sadist, the insolent Johannes Post of the Kiel Gestapo, grinning as he whispered in the ear of the woman counsel.'[54]

All the men in the dock were accused of directly taking part in the murders, with the exception of Max Wielen, who was accused of participating in the conspiracy to murder.[55] Although none denied their roles in the killings, all pleaded not guilty, on the predictable grounds that they were following orders, and that they had no power to prevent the shootings. This stance was perhaps best summed up by Oskar Schmidt in a letter he had written to his father, Ernst, that January. 'If at the time I had not obeyed I should have been shot,' he wrote, 'today they want to punish us for having obeyed.'[56] The defence argued that the defendants,

under paragraph 47 of the German Military Penal
Code, were only legally entitled to disobey an order if
they 'knew that the order of the Commanding Officer
concerned an action, the purpose of which was to
commit a general or a military crime or misdemeanour'.
Therefore, the argument went, the defendants could
only refuse to shoot unarmed men in the back of the
head at the side of a road if they knew that to do so was
a crime.[57] In order to build such a case, the German
lawyers had to show that none of the defendants were
in fact aware that the men they were ordered to kill
were escaping POWs, and that they thought them to be
saboteurs or spies – the type of people who, in Nazi
Germany, might lawfully be summarily shot.

This line of defence was presented repeatedly, and at
times, seemingly effectively. The counsel for Emil
Schulz, Dr Adolf Meyer-Labastille, contended that his
client had heard of neither the breakout from Stalag
Luft III nor the *Grossfahndung*, and believed that
Bushell and Scheidhauer were in fact enemy agents.
Furthermore, Schulz believed the order to be legal as it
had come from Hitler, and he had no reason to doubt
the words of his chief, Dr Spann, who told him that the
executions were lawful. In addition, Meyer-Labastille
stated that Schulz had not actually killed anybody when
he pulled the trigger, because the two men had already
been mortally wounded by the shots fired by Spann.[58]
Schimmel's counsel, Dr Motz, similarly argued that the
fact the order emanated from Hitler made it legal, and
therefore Schimmel had no grounds on which to disobey it. Had he done so, he would have been either sent
to a concentration camp and been shot, or put on trial

and shot.[59] Johannes Post argued that he was in no position to refuse an order from Hitler, a fact that was apparently reiterated by his chief, Fritz Schmidt, who had told his men that 'any lack of discipline committed by any one of you in the course of the carrying out of this case will be very severely punished'.[60] When Post was asked by one of the defence counsel whether it was possible for someone like Walter Jacobs to ask not to take part in the killings, an apparently exasperated Post replied that it was 'quite unimaginable'.

> It shows me that you really have no idea about these matters at all. We have heard quite a lot here in this court about how these orders are issued. I just cannot understand all that here. In North Germany you listen to an order and then the order is carried out; no sort of explanations or questions are being asked.[61]

Even Colonel von Lindeiner, who appeared as a witness, concurred that refusing to obey an order from Hitler could only lead to one thing. 'Failure to carry out a Führer order would mean that the best thing for the person . . . would be to shoot a bullet through his own head,' he told the court. When asked whether an officer or an official could have resisted an order on the grounds of immorality or illegality, von Lindeiner replied: 'I discussed this point in 1943 with my senior officers, namely, the possibility that we could be given certain inhuman orders by way of reprisals and I said that in the case of such orders I would take my own life.'[62]

As we have seen, such an attitude was not widely held among members of the Gestapo.

In constructing their case, the defence had to convince the court that there really had been examples of
Gestapo men, or their equivalents, being shot for
refusing to obey similar orders. Unfortunately for the
defendants, their counsel were unable to come up with
any convincing examples, for the simple reason that
there were none. In his summing up, Colonel Halse used
this absence to devastating effect.

> You will remember that questions were asked of all the
> witnesses that I called before you as to whether they had
> heard of *Sippenhaft* ... or whether people who dis-
> obeyed orders could expect to be killed either outright
> or after trial by the SS and Police Courts or immediately
> to go to a concentration camp. Everybody said they had
> heard of it but nobody was able to give us an example.
> Despite all the efforts of counsel not a single example
> has been given of a case where a man was punished for
> disobeying a lawful order; not a single case was given of
> a man who was sent to a concentration camp for
> refusing to do something that he was told to do by his
> superior in the Gestapo; not a single case was produced
> of a wife or family being put in a concentration camp
> under this principle of collective responsibility.[63]

Contrary to popular belief, there is no evidence that
any Germans were ever shot, physically harmed or
sent to a concentration camp for refusing to carry out
orders to murder civilians or Russian POWs. In the
archives of the Central Office for the Investigation of
National Socialist Crimes in Ludwigsburg, there are at
least eighty-five documented cases of individuals who

refused to carry out such orders, including officers and men in the Waffen-SS and the *Einsatzgruppen*. In not one of these cases did those who refused come to any harm, and in forty-nine of the cases, there were no negative consequences whatsoever, with several of the men even later being promoted.[64]

Ironically, one defendant, in the form of Alfred Schimmel, even appeared to admit to the Judge Advocate that had one of his men refused to shoot somebody then the consequences would not have been severe.

Q. What would you have done if you had asked a subordinate to shoot somebody and he had felt exactly like you did, that he had not got the nerve to do it? What would you have done to the subordinate?

A. I would have tried to understand him.

Q. And picked another member?

A. Probably.[65]

At no point during the questioning did Schimmel indicate that he would have punished the man by sending him to trial or a concentration camp.

In arguing its case that citing superior orders provides no excuse in international law, the prosecution quoted the *Llandovery Castle* case, which was used to devastating effect in many other war crimes trials. The case was tried before a German Supreme Court in Leipzig in July 1921, and concerned the sinking in June 1918 of a British hospital ship – the *Llandovery Castle* – by a German submarine, after which the commander had given orders to fire on the lifeboats. Although the commander was not brought to trial, his two lieutenants were, and the German court found that obedience was not considered a defence, and ruled that the two men 'should certainly have refused to obey the order'. The court acknowledged that to have done so would have required 'a specially high degree of resolution', but it nevertheless sentenced the two men to four years in prison. By citing this case, the prosecution in the Sagan case showed that German law was therefore in line with international law.[66] In short, obeying orders was not considered a defence.

At 11.30 a.m. on Wednesday 3 September 1947, the court handed down its sentences. Erich Zacharias, Emil Schulz, Alfred Schimmel, Josef Gmeiner, Walter Herberg, Otto Preiss, Heinrich Boschert, Emil Weil, Eduard Geith, Johann Schneider, Johannes Post, Hans Kähler, Oskar Schmidt and Walter Jacobs were all sentenced to death. Max Wielen and Walter Breithaupt were sentenced to life imprisonment, and Artur Denkmann and Wilhelm Struve to ten years. Back in Britain, the result was warmly welcomed – here at last was 'exemplary justice' – but there were some dissenting voices. Among them was P. E. Roberts, the Vice-Provost of Worcester College, Oxford, who wrote to *The Times* expressing his surprise that no protest had been made at the sentences.

It is agreed that these men acted on direct orders from Hitler, and it is acknowledged that a refusal to obey would have meant their own execution and almost certainly the persecution of their relatives and dependents. The act was a dreadful one, but it was not theirs, it was the High Command's.[67]

Others wrote to the authorities urging clemency. 'The Germans for whom I am begging mercy are young men who could have useful lives before them,' wrote A. B. Chittick from Hammersmith, west London, to the Judge Advocate General. 'I feel that too many young men have been hanged in our name.'[68] Some, such as D. R. Stokes, thought there was an equivalence between the British officers who would have to carry out the executions and the guilty men. 'I find on visiting British Camps with British Commandants when I complain about the sentences I am merely told that they hold the bodies and carry out instructions from higher authority, whether they consider them just or not,' Stokes wrote to Lord Pakenham at the Foreign Office. 'This is just the argument that the Germans always advance.'[69]

Naturally, the families of the guilty men did all they could to reverse the sentences. The wife and daughter of Emil Schulz wrote to Queen Mary, begging her to ask for clemency.[70] The appeal failed. The family of Josef Gmeiner petitioned the Bishop of Osnabrück to enlist the support of Cardinal Bernard Griffin, the Archbishop of Westminster. The Cardinal wrote to the Judge Advocate General stating that he supported the appeal for clemency.[71] As with the Schulz family, the Cardinal's appeal was not successful. Some of the guilty, such as Johann Schneider, who had gunned down Gouws and Stevens, wrote on their own behalf. 'The sentence is very hard,' Schneider wrote to Lieutenant Colonel Scotland, 'and strikes with especial severity my dearly loved children and wife, my aged father and sick mother, who is almost at death's door. I therefore beg you, Sir, to put in a word with the Supreme Court on my behalf.' Scotland was unimpressed, and sent a copy of the letter to the Judge Advocate General with a covering note that read, 'Here is the wail of the strong man who showed Herr Weil how they did it in Russia.'[72]

By the end of January 1948, all but one of the sentences had been confirmed, with Heinrich Boschert having his sentence reduced to life imprisonment. The only letters that the murderers could now write were those of farewell. On 2 February, Hans Ziegler wrote to his mother, stating that 'everybody who had known me knows what I was like', before fatally cutting his throat the following day.[73] Just before he was executed, Emil Schulz wrote to his wife and two daughters:

Dear Angela, dear Ingeborg, dear Helga, you dears of mine, I am here as a prisoner because I carried out an official order in the Spring of 1944. I never on my own initiative acted against the laws of humanity. You must believe me. I'm not guilty. I couldn't lie to you children if I carried such guilt.[74]

On 26 February, Schulz and twelve of his fellow killers were hanged at Hamelin gaol. Over the years, more trials would follow, and on each occasion, the severity of the sentences diminished. On 11 October, a second Sagan trial took place in Hamburg, in which Erwin Wieczorek, Richard Hänsel and Reinhold Bruchardt were in the dock. Although Wieczorek and Bruchardt were sentenced to death, both escaped the hangman on review. Hänsel was acquitted. In October 1950, Oswald Schäfer was found in the British Zone and the RAF urged prosecution. He would never be brought to account, and the case against him would be eventually thrown out eighteen years later.[75] In 1952, Dr Günther Venediger of the Danzig Gestapo entered West Germany from the Russian Zone, and he was arrested and brought to trial. On 4 September of that year a German court acquitted him. The prosecution appealed, and in a new trial, Venediger was sentenced to two years. Finally, after an appeal by Venediger, the former Gestapo chief had his sentence confirmed in February.[76] In January 1967, Fritz Schmidt, the head of the Kiel Gestapo, was brought to trial, during which he pleaded a defence of acting on superior orders. In May the following year, he received the same sentence as Günther Venediger.[77]

Epilogue

The Legacy

ON 23 AUGUST 1945, Sydney Dowse wrote to Eberhard Hesse to thank him for the help the German corporal had given to the Kriegies in Stalag Luft III. 'I had not forgotten you in the slightest,' Dowse stated, 'nor all your invaluable work, such as putting me on to Peenemünde in April 1943, as well as a heap of other things.' Dowse promised Hesse that he would do all he could to help, including being present at his interrogation, but this was turned down. Hesse was, after all, associated with an atrocity that had resonated very deeply, and Dowse was not so blinkered that he did not realise his relationship with the German might be seen with some suspicion. Dowse wrote:

I am afraid 'things' changed in a big way in this country after the 'Mass Escape' from Luft 3, as no doubt you can understand, with the result that there is a very big combing-out process going on. Still, don't lose heart, Hesse, I shall do all in my endeavour to get life back to normal for you.[1]

Dowse's words were fine indeed, but for those associated with the Great Escape, life would never get back to normal. Some, such as the family of Bob Vanderstok, would suffer terribly because of the break-out. After Vanderstok had escaped, his father was arrested by the Gestapo and interrogated. 'They questioned him, torturing him with bright lights in his eyes and physical exhaustion,' wrote Vanderstok. By the time the Gestapo released him, Vanderstok's father had been blinded. His sight returned after three months, but only partially. The family's misery was later compounded by the deaths of Vanderstok's brothers, Felix and Hans, who had worked for the Resistance.[2]

Thanks to the Great Escape, many families would feel similar grief. After learning of her husband's death in May 1944, Maria Kirby-Green visited their son, Colin, at his prep school, and took him out to tea.

She had actually come down to tell me about my father but she just couldn't bring herself to do it. She was always very tearful when she greeted me or said good-bye to me in railway stations, so I didn't think of it as then she kissed me goodbye and went on her way, crying as she always did.

It was left to Colin's headmaster to break the news. 'He said: "I'm sorry to have to tell you your father has been killed." He said it quite quickly. Everyone was very stiff upper lip in those days so the following day it wasn't mentioned again.'³

Tragically, many of the families, including the Bushells, found it hard to accept that their men had died. What had given the likes of Dorothy Bushell so much false hope was an ill-judged article written by either Jens Müller or Per Bergsland in *Collier's Magazine* in September 1944 under the name of 'Lieutenant Per Fjell'. In the piece, 'Fjell' claimed to have talked to some of the repatriated POWs from Sagan.

> During the two days after our flight, they saw those 50 men returned to the camp. Later, they saw them simply manacled and driven away in trucks. To me, this suggests that the 50 men were removed to another camp and announced as shot with the intention of frightening the remaining prisoners.⁴

This article raised many groundless hopes, and it attracted the ire of many POWs.

To make matters worse, the Bushells had to endure their son's reputation being denigrated by his old enemy from Dulag Luft – Railton Freeman. After surrendering himself to US forces near the Bavarian town of Lenggries on 9 May 1945,⁵ Freeman was flown back to Britain on 15 May, where he was interrogated at the Endsleigh Hotel in Euston in London by two MI5 officers.⁶ During the questioning, Freeman claimed that he had a clear conscience regarding his actions in Germany, which had included broadcasting for the

Nazis and joining the Waffen-SS. Freeman then claimed that although he was no traitor, there were some British officers who he had met in Germany who most certainly were. Among them were Paddy Byrne, and 'an RAF officer named Bushell, who I think was shot in Germany, was also a collaborator'.[7] After making his statement, Freeman checked through the transcript and signed it, stating that it was a 'fair summary of the conversation'.[8] Freeman was unable to offer any proof that Bushell was a traitor, because of course there was none, and there can be little doubt that Freeman was sullying the memory of a man who he hated.

In September that year, Freeman was brought before a general court martial in Uxbridge, where he was charged with – among other offences – voluntarily serving with the enemy. On the opening day of the trial, which was heard in public, Freeman's claim about Bushell's supposed treachery was read out in court, and was reported in the newspapers the following day, much to the irritation of the Judge Advocate.[9] However, when Freeman was subsequently examined by his defending counsel, he had a change of mind and withdrew the allegation, stating that it was 'ridiculous', and unconvincingly claimed that the error was owing to a mistranscription.[10] It is possible that Freeman's counsel had convinced his client to change his mind, as the claim that Bushell was a traitor hardly endeared him to a court staffed by RAF officers. 'Incidentally, such an allegation by Freeman,' said the defending counsel in his closing address, 'if he had made it, which he didn't, would be bound to have resulted in anyone who knew Squadron Leader Bushell finding himself unable to conduct this officer's case.'[11]

Although Bushell's reputation remained intact, the families of those shot in the Great Escape must have wondered whether the breakout was worth so much loss. Perhaps for them it was best left unanswered, for fear of augmenting the grief with bitterness. But such questions need to be asked if we are to look beyond the jingoistic representation of the breakout. The word 'great' does, after all, denote not just scale, but also esteem, and there is no doubt that the escape is a source of national pride. Thanks to the efforts of Paul Brickhill and his fellow Kriegie-cum-journalist, Robert Kee, after the war the event immediately took on the air of something out of *The Boy's Own Paper*, a presentation that was solidified when the film *The Great Escape* was released in 1963.[12] Since then, in the many tellings of the story, the emphasis has been too much on glory rather than guts.

Unsurprisingly, most of the former Kriegies held at Stalag Luft III view the Great Escape in a similarly positive light. To question the enterprise would of course seem disrespectful to their murdered comrades, but occasionally, a cooler opinion surfaces. 'I sometimes think it wasn't worth it,' says Alfie 'Bill' Fripp. 'Fifty men's lives it cost to tie up those Germans. Inevitably, they would have lost the war, and fifty people would have been alive today.'[13] Fripp's point is very telling, and captures the fatal flaw at the heart of the enterprise: the breakout was simply pointless and, ultimately, a failure. Only three men escaped, fifty were shot, and the whole purpose of the action – to hamper the German war effort – backfired. Furthermore, in early 1944, the

Kriegies had a very good idea that the Allies would soon be invading, thereby making a mass escape even more superfluous. Thanks to knowledge gleaned from recently captured pilots, the POWs were among the best-informed people in Germany about the approximate timing and scale of the second front. Alan Bryett recalled:

> The news filtered through very quickly, specifically that the invasion was getting very close. There was no doubt about it. We had fighter pilots being shot down, and Bomber Command people, and we could tell from the targets they were getting that there was a huge build up of armament two or three miles from the coast, from Portsmouth right through to Ramsgate. It was quite obvious the invasion was imminent.'[14]

Those who defend the escape suggest that the break-out was great for morale. 'It did bring the Kriegies together more so than before,' says Fripp, although it can hardly be said that the murders did much for the mood of the camp. But the question of morale is worth considering. Although the escape was an act of folly, it is unreasonable to expect hundreds of intelligent and resourceful young men to sit behind barbed wire and accept their lot, to concentrate sensibly on, say, gaining their accountancy qualifications or learning how to speak a foreign language. Escaping not only appeared to be a duty, but it was also patriotic, and, perhaps most important of all, it was enjoyable. 'You might as well have some fun doing something that you should be doing anyway,' observed Richard Churchill.[15] However, escaping was not the only element of camp life that boosted morale, and plenty of Kriegies were able to keep themselves occupied by giving and listening to lectures, playing sport, performing on the stage, building model boats, chatting, reading and the like. But for a certain type of man, indulging only in such activities would have seemed somewhat fey. Escaping was *the* alpha-male activity, and any senior officer ordering it to be banned in the first years of the war might have suffered a mutiny.

Ultimately, the problem with the Great Escape was its scale. The prisoners were repeatedly warned by the likes of Pieber and von Schilling that while more modest escapes would not incur much wrath, the result of a mass escape might indeed be horrific.[16] But, as we have seen, the leading Kriegies were adamant that such warnings were bluff, and the likes of Bushell, Day and Massey were unlikely to order the POWs to down tools after many months of Herculean effort because of an implied threat from the enemy. In truth, the attempt had passed a point of no return, and the collective will of the escapers was always going to outweigh a cool-headed assessment of risk. If the notion of using the tunnel to trickle out a few prisoners on a nightly basis was discussed, it is likely to have been dismissed. The whole point of the escape was that it was a grand gesture, and it was designed more to annoy the Germans than serve as a means by which men could rejoin their units. There were voices, such as those of George Harsh, who regarded the escape as 'an act of typical military madness, a futile, empty gesture and a needless sacrifice of fifty lives',[17] but these voices were rare or simply silent.

It is worth remembering that escaping was a minority sport, and the majority of Kriegies who could not and would not escape kept their opinions of 'tally-ho' activities to themselves.

The Great Escape may have indeed been 'great', but, in the words of Hermann Glemnitz, it was also 'a silly idea'.[18] It is perfectly possible – and indeed desirable – to hold both those notions in our collective consciousness. Historical revisionism does not necessitate a complete demolition, and it can often act as a much-needed correction. In short, we should see the Great Escape as another of our glorious failures.

Such an appraisal might be dismissed as that of an historian born over a quarter of a century after the events, who cannot possibly know what it was like to have 'been there'. Perhaps. But similar views are expressed by men with similar – and indeed worse – experiences to the Kriegies. One of those is Merritt E. Lawlis, who was imprisoned by the Japanese for five months, during which time he was starved and beaten. In the eyes of Lawlis, the Great Escape was only 'great' because 'it involved a large number of men'. 'Every time I see a reference to that event I have the same re-action: I wish those 76 men had stayed in their cells a few more months, until the war was over. What all did they forfeit in their one-day adventure?'[19] Lawlis even raises the idea of commending those who stayed behind, and suggests that deciding not to escape can be honourable. 'Some of them may at least be commended for the admirable quality of common sense,' Lawlis writes. 'One word to describe those who attempted escape is "foolhardy".'[20]

Roger Bushell might not have approved of such an analysis, and regarded it as being somewhat bolshie. After all, he was indeed a hero, but in the Shakespearean sense, with faults and all. It comes as no surprise that Georgie quoted Robert Browning's poem 'Epilogue' when she placed an 'In Memoriam' notice in *The Times* on 30 August 1946.

In proud and ever-treasured memory, on this his birth-day, of my beloved ROGER, who was murdered by the Gestapo after escaping from Stalag Luft III in March 1944.

'One who never turned his back but marched breast forward,
Never doubted clouds would break,
Never dreamed, though right were worsted, wrong would triumph,
Held we fall to rise, are baffled to fight better,
Sleep to wake.'

Love is immortal. Until we meet again – GEORGIE.

Georgie would continue to place notices in *The Times* until 1956.[21] In November the following year, she married again, but it seems that she never found peace. At some point in the 1970s, she was committed to The Retreat in York, a specialist mental health care provider, where she died by her own hand on 11 January 1976.[22] She was buried three days later at the Holy Trinity Church in Penn Street village in Buckinghamshire.[23] Her gravestone carries two lines of verse taken from 'Break, Break, Break' by Alfred, Lord Tennyson:

> Oh for the touch of a vanished hand,
> And the sound of a voice that is still.[24]

It is tempting to suppose that the lines refer to the man who lies in the Old Garrison Cemetery in Poznan in Poland. Placed between those of Gordon Brettell and James Catanach, the gravestone of Roger Bushell reads:

> A leader of men.
> He achieved much.
> Loved England
> And served her to the end.

Georgie and Roger lie 750 miles apart. Even in death, they cannot be together.

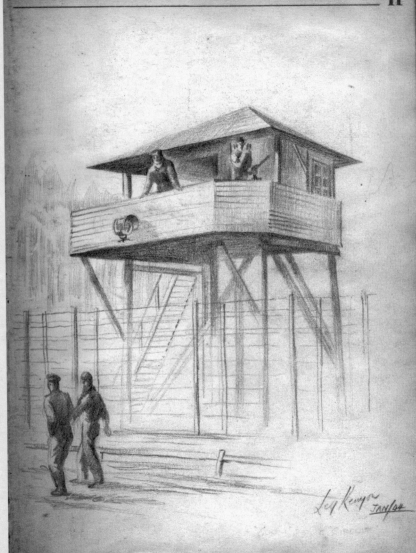

Appendices

THE ESCAPERS

Exit number	Name and rank († = murdered)	Method of travel	Location of capture	Time and date of capture or of gaining freedom	Distance from camp (miles travelled)	Hours on run
1	† Bull, Lester 'Johnny' G., Flight Lieutenant	Train, hard-arse	Mountains near Boberrohrsdorf, Poland	25 March?	50	16?
2	Marshall, Johnny, Flight Lieutenant	Hard-arse	Country lane near Tiefenfurt, Poland	04:00 26 March	16	30
3	† Valenta, Ernst, Flight Lieutenant	Hard-arse	Country lane near Tiefenfurt, Poland	04:00 26 March	16	30
4	Bushell, Roger J., Squadron Leader	Train	Saarbrücken railway station, Germany	14:30 26 March	400 (700?)	39.5
5	† Scheidhauer, Bernard W. M., Pilot Officer	Train	Saarbrücken railway station, Germany	14:30 26 March	400 (700?)	39.5
6	† Gouws, Johannes S., Flight Lieutenant	Train	Near Munich, Germany	18:00? 28 March	275	91
7	† Stevens, Rupert J., Flight Lieutenant	Train	Near Munich, Germany	18:00? 28 March	275	91
8	† Fugelsang, Nils, Flight Lieutenant	Train	Marienhölzungsweg, Flensburg, Germany	22:00? 26 March	330	46
9	† Espelid, Hallada, Flight Lieutenant	Train	Marienhölzungsweg, Flensburg, Germany	22:00? 26 March	330	46
10	† Marcinkus, Romas, Flight Lieutenant	Train	Near Danzig, Germany	28 March?	235	80?
11	† Walenn, Gilbert 'Tim' W., Flight Lieutenant	Train	Near Danzig, Germany	28 March?	235	80?
12	† Langford, Patrick W., Flight Lieutenant	Train?	Not known	Before 31 March	Not known	Not known
13	Plunkett, Desmond, Flight Lieutenant	Train, hard-arse	Klattau station, Czechoslovakia	8 April	177 (803)	345
14	Dvorak, Bedrich, Flight Lieutenant	Train, hard-arse	Klattau station, Czechoslovakia	8 April	177 (803)	345
15	† Picard, Henri A., Flight Lieutenant	Train	Near Danzig, Germany	28 March?	235	80?
16	† Birkland, Gordon E., Flight Lieutenant	Train	Near Danzig, Germany	28 March?	235	80?

Exit number	Name and rank († = murdered)	Method of travel	Location of capture	Time and date of capture or of gaining freedom	Distance from camp (miles travelled)	Hours on run
17	† Kirby-Green, Thomas G., Squadron Leader	Train, hard-arse	Wood near Vsetín, Czechoslovakia	09:00? 28 March	196 (280)	80
18	† Kidder, Gordon A., Flying Officer	Train, hard-arse	Wood near Vsetín, Czechoslovakia	09:00? 28 March	196 (280)	80
19	Vanderstok, Robert, Flight Lieutenant	Train, hard-arse	HOME RUN to Canejan, Spain	18 June	912 (1,800)	>2,000
20	Van Wymeersch, Raymond, 2nd Lieutenant	Train	Metz railway station, France	26 March	440 (775)	40
21	Dowse, Sydney, Flight Lieutenant	Hard-arse	Barn 2½ miles west of Kempen, Poland	16:00 6 April	115 (140)	303
22	† Krol, Stanislaw Z., Flying Officer	Hard-arse	Barn 2½ miles west of Kempen, Poland	16:00 6 April	115 (140)	303
23	† Catanach, James, Squadron Leader	Train	Holm, Flensburg, Germany	22:00? 26 March	330	45
24	† Christensen, Arnold D., Flight Lieutenant	Train	Holm, Flensburg, Germany	22:00? 26 March	330	45
25	Tonder, Ivo, Flight Lieutenant	Hard-arse, train	Train near Zittau, Germany	17:00? 27 March	53 (80)	63
26	† Stower, John G., Flying Officer	Hard-arse, train	Train near Zittau, Germany	17:00? 27 March	53 (80)	63
27	† Cochran, Dennis H., Flying Officer	Train	Lörrach, Germany	26 March?	440	40?
28	Neely, Alexander, Lieutenant	Train	On train between Berlin and Munich	19:00? 29 March	290 (680)	90
29	Dodge, John B., Major	Train, hard-arse	On train at Hirschberg station, Poland	16:00 25 March	52	13.5
30	† Mondschein, Jerzy T., Flying Officer	Train, hard-arse	Mountains near Boberrohrsdorf, Poland	25 March?	50	16?
31	Poynter, Douglas A., Lieutenant	Train, hard-arse	On train between Polaun, Poland, and Hammersdorf, Czechoslovakia	21:00 25 March	56	19.5
32	† Williams, John E. A., Squadron Leader	Train, hard-arse	Mountains near Boberrohrsdorf, Poland	25 March?	50	16?

Exit number	Name and rank († = murdered)	Method of travel	Location of capture	Time and date of capture or of gaining freedom	Distance from camp (miles travelled)	Hours on run
33	† Pawluk, Kazimierz, Flying Officer	Train, hard-arse	Centre of Hirschberg, Poland	p.m. of 25 March	52	15?
34	† Wernham, James G., Flight Lieutenant	Train, hard-arse	On train at Hirschberg station, Poland	16:00 25 March	52	13.5
35	† Kierath, Reginald V., Flight Lieutenant	Train, hard-arse	Mountains near Boberrohrsdorf, Poland	25 March?	50	16?
36	Day, Harry M. A., Wing Commander	Train	Disused factory in Stettin, Poland	10:30 29 March	130 (225)	104
37	† Tobolski, Pawel W., Flying Officer	Train	Disused factory in Stettin, Poland	10:30 29 March	130 (225)	104
38	Green, Bernard, Flight Lieutenant	Train, hard-arse	Boberrohrsdorf, Poland	15:00 25 March	49	14
39	James, Bertram 'Jimmy', Flight Lieutenant	Train, hard-arse	Hirschberg west station, Poland	17:30 25 March	51	16
40	† Skanziklas, Sotiris, Pilot Officer	Train, hard-arse	Hirschberg west station, Poland	17:30 25 March	51	16
41	† Kiewnarski, Antoni, Flight Lieutenant	Train, hard-arse	Centre of Hirschberg, Poland	p.m. of 25 March	52	15?
42	Thompson, A. B., Flight Lieutenant	Hard-arse	Near Halbau, Poland	07:00? 26 March	8	27
43	Müller, Jens, Flight Lieutenant	Train, boat	HOME RUN to Gothenburg, Sweden	23:00 29 March	440 (475)	118
44	Bergsland, Per, Sergeant	Train, boat	HOME RUN to Gothenburg, Sweden	23:00 29 March	440 (475)	118
45	† Grisman, William J., Flight Lieutenant	Hard-arse	Near Görlitz?	Not known	<40?	<72?
46	† Kolanowski, Włodzimierz, Flying Officer	Hard-arse	Near Sagan, Poland?	Not known	<15?	<48?
47	Armstrong, Albert, Flight Lieutenant	Hard-arse	Road near Tiefenfurt, Poland	02:00 26 March	16	24
48	Churchill, Richard, Flight Lieutenant	Hard-arse	Halbau, Poland	12:00 27 March	8	57
49	† Humphreys, Edgar S., Flight Lieutenant	Hard-arse	Near Tiefenfurt, Poland	02:30 26 March	16	24
50	Boyle, Paul G., Flight Lieutenant	Hard-arse	Near Tiefenfurt, Poland	02:30 26 March	16	24

Exit number	Name and rank († = murdered)	Method of travel	Location of capture	Time and date of capture or of gaining freedom	Distance from camp (miles travelled)	Hours on run
51	† Birkland, Henry J., Flying Officer	Hard-arse	Kalkbrugh [Klików?], Poland	06:00 27 March	10?	50
52	Brodrick, Leslie, Flight Lieutenant	Hard-arse	Kalkbrugh [Klików?], Poland	06:00 27 March	10?	50
53	† Street, Denys O., Flying Officer	Hard-arse	Kalkbrugh [Klików?], Poland	06:00 27 March	10?	50
54	McDonald, A. T., Flight Lieutenant	Hard-arse	Near Sagan, Poland?	Not known	<15?	<48?
55	† McGarr, Clement A. N., Lieutenant	Hard-arse	Near Sagan, Poland?	Not known	<15?	<48?
56	† McGill, George E., Flight Lieutenant	Hard-arse	Near Sagan, Poland?	Not known	<15?	<48?
57	† Hall, Charles P., Flight Lieutenant	Hard-arse	Near Sagan, Poland?	Not known	<15?	<48?
58	† Hayter, Anthony R. H., Flight Lieutenant	Train, hard-arse	Between Mulhouse and Altkirch, France	08:30 27 March	440	52
59	† Evans, Brian H., Flight Lieutenant	Hard-arse	Near Halbau, Poland	07:00? 26 March	8	26
60	† Stewart, Robert C., Flying Officer	Hard-arse	Near Sagan, Poland?	Not known	<15?	<48?
61	† Long, James L. R., Flight Lieutenant	Hard-arse	Benau, Poland	14:00 28 March	11	82
62	Langlois, Roy B., Flight Lieutenant	Hard-arse	Wood near tunnel exit	05:00 25 March	0	1
63	† Swain, Cyril D., Flight Lieutenant	Hard-arse	Near Görlitz?	Not known	<40?	<72?
64	Nelson, Thomas, Squadron Leader	Hard-arse	Halbau, Poland	12:00 27 March	8	57
65	Bethell, Anthony, Flight Lieutenant	Hard-arse	Benau, Poland	14:00 28 March	11	82
66	† Milford, Harold J., Flight Lieutenant	Hard-arse	Near Sagan, Poland?	Not known	<15?	<48?
67	† Williams, John F., Flight Lieutenant	Hard-arse	Near Sagan, Poland?	Not known	<15?	<48?
68	† Gunn, Alastair D. M., Flight Lieutenant	Hard-arse	Near Görlitz?	Not known	<40?	<72?
69	Cameron, W. T., Flight Lieutenant	Hard-arse	Near Halbau, Poland	06:00? 26 March	8	26
70	† Hake, Albert H., Flight Lieutenant	Hard-arse	Near Görlitz?	Not known	<40?	<72?

Exit number	Name and rank († = murdered)	Method of travel	Location of capture	Time and date of capture or of gaining freedom	Distance from camp (miles travelled)	Hours on run
71	† Casey, Michael J., Flight Lieutenant	Hard-arse	Near Görlitz?	Not known	<40?	80?
72	† Wiley, George W., Flight Lieutenant	Hard-arse	Near Görlitz?	Not known	<40?	<72?
73	† Leigh, Thomas B., Flight Lieutenant	Hard-arse	Near Sagan, Poland?	Not known	<15?	<48?
74	† Pohé, John 'P. P.', Flying Officer	Hard-arse	Near Görlitz?	Not known	<40?	<72?
75	† Cross, Ian K. P., Squadron Leader	Hard-arse	Near Görlitz?	Not known	<40?	<72?
76	Reavell-Carter, Laurence, Squadron Leader	Hard-arse	Tunnel exit	05:00 25 March	0	0
77	Ogilvie, Alfred, Flight Lieutenant	Hard-arse	Near Halbau, Poland	06:00 26 March	8	25
78	Shand, Michael, Flight Lieutenant	Hard-arse	Kohlfurt railway station, Poland	09:00 29 March	22	100
79	Trent, Len, Squadron Leader	Hard-arse	Tunnel exit	05:00 25 March	0	0
80	McBride, Robert, Squadron Leader	Hard-arse	Tunnel exit	05:00 25 March	0	0

NB: The exit numbers are approximate. It is impossible to be definitive, as so many accounts conflict.

Name and rank	Air Force	Died	Age	Murderers	Location
Birkland, Henry J., Flying Officer	RCAF	31/03/44	26	Breslau Gestapo	Halfway between Breslau and Sagan, Poland
Brettell, Gordon E., Flight Lieutenant	RAF	29/03/44	29	Danzig Gestapo	Wood near Gross Trampken, Poland
Bull, Lester 'Johnny' G., Flight Lieutenant	RAF	29/03/44	27	Reichenberg Gestapo	Unknown, presumed near Reichenberg, Poland
Bushell, Roger J., Squadron Leader	RAF	29/03/44	33	Saarbrücken Gestapo	Between Kaiserslautern and Mannheim, Germany
Casey, Michael J., Flight Lieutenant	RAF	30/03/44	26	Breslau Gestapo	Wooded road 3 miles south of Sagan, Poland
Catanach, James, Squadron Leader	RAAF	29/03/44	22	Kiel Gestapo	Field 6 miles SSW of Kiel, Germany
Christensen, Arnold D., Flight Lieutenant	RNZAF	29/03/44	22	Kiel Gestapo	Field 6 miles SSW of Kiel, Germany
Cochran, Dennis H., Flying Officer	RAF	31/03/44	22	Karlsruhe Gestapo	Road south of Natzweiler concentration camp, France
Cross, Ian K. P., Squadron Leader	RAF	30/03/44	25	Breslau Gestapo	Wooded road 3 miles south of Sagan, Poland
Espelid, Hallada, Lieutenant	RNAF	29/03/44	23	Kiel Gestapo	Field 6 miles SSW of Kiel, Germany
Evans, Brian H., Flight Lieutenant	RAF	31/03/44	24	Breslau Gestapo	Halfway between Breslau and Sagan, Poland
Fugelsang, Nils, Lieutenant	RNAF	29/03/44	24	Kiel Gestapo	Field 6 miles SSW of Kiel, Germany
Gouws, Johannes S., Lieutenant	SAAF	29/03/44	24	Munich Gestapo	Meadow 25 miles north of Munich, Germany
Grisman, William J., Flight Lieutenant	RAF	c. 06/04/44	29	Breslau Gestapo	Unknown, presumed between Görlitz and Sagan, Poland
Gunn, Alastair D. M., Flight Lieutenant	RAF	c. 06/04/44	24	Breslau Gestapo	Unknown, presumed between Görlitz and Sagan, Poland
Hake, Albert H., Flight Lieutenant	RAAF	30/03/44	27	Breslau Gestapo	Wooded road 3 miles south of Sagan, Poland
Hall, Charles P., Flight Lieutenant	RAF	31/03/44	25	Breslau Gestapo	Halfway between Breslau and Sagan, Poland

Name and rank	Air Force	Died	Age	Murderers	Location
Hayter, Anthony R. H., Flight Lieutenant	RAF	06/04/44	23	Strasbourg Gestapo	Just south of Natzweiler concentration camp, France
Humphreys, Edgar S., Flight Lieutenant	RAF	31/03/44	29	Breslau Gestapo	Halfway between Breslau and Sagan, Poland
Kidder, Gordon A., Flying Officer	RCAF	29/03/44	29	Brno and Zlin Gestapo	Road 5 miles south of Moravská Ostrava, Czechoslovakia
Kierath, Reginald V., Flight Lieutenant	RAAF	29/03/44	29	Reichenberg Gestapo	Unknown, presumed near Reichenberg, Poland
Kiewnarski, Antoni, Flight Lieutenant	PAF	c. 31/03/44	45	Breslau Gestapo	Approx. 15 miles northwest of Hirschberg, Poland
Kirby-Green, Thomas G., Squadron Leader	RAF	29/03/44	26	Brno and Zlin Gestapo	Road 5 miles south of Moravská Ostrava, Czechoslovakia
Kolanowski, Włodzimierz, Flying Officer	PAF	31/03/44	30	Breslau Gestapo	Halfway between Breslau and Sagan, Poland
Krol, Stanislaw Z., Flying Officer	PAF	c. 12/04/44	28	Breslau Gestapo	Unknown, presumed between Oels and Sagan, Poland
Langford, Patrick W., Flight Lieutenant	RCAF	31/03/44	24	Breslau Gestapo	Halfway between Breslau and Sagan, Poland
Leigh, Thomas B., Flight Lieutenant	RAF	30/03/44	25	Breslau Gestapo	Wooded road 3 miles south of Sagan, Poland
Long, James L. R., Flight Lieutenant	RAF	c. 12/04/44	29	Breslau Gestapo	Unknown, presumed between Görlitz and Sagan, Poland
McGarr, Clement A. N., Lieutenant	SAAF	c. 06/04/44	26	Breslau Gestapo	Unknown, presumed between Görlitz and Sagan, Poland
McGill, George E., Flight Lieutenant	RCAF	31/03/44	25	Breslau Gestapo	Halfway between Breslau and Sagan, Poland
Marcinkus, Romas, Flight Lieutenant	RAF	29/03/44	33	Danzig Gestapo	Wood near Gross Trampken, Poland
Milford, Harold J., Flight Lieutenant	RAF	c. 06/04/44	29	Breslau Gestapo	Unknown, presumed between Görlitz and Sagan, Poland

Name and rank	Air Force	Died	Age	Murderers	Location
Mondschein, Jerzy T., Flying Officer	PAF	29/03/44	35	Reichenberg Gestapo	Unknown, presumed near Reichenberg, Poland
Pawluk, Kazimierz, Flying Officer	PAF	c. 31/03/44	27	Breslau Gestapo	Approx. 15 miles northwest of Hirschberg, Poland
Picard, Henri A., Flight Lieutenant	RAF (Belg.)	29/03/44	27	Danzig Gestapo	Wood near Gross Trampken, Poland
Pohé, John 'P. P.', Flying Officer	RNZAF	30/03/44	22	Breslau Gestapo	Wooded road 3 miles south of Sagan, Poland
Scheidhauer, Bernard W. M., Pilot Officer	FAF	29/03/44	22	Saarbrücken Gestapo	Between Kaiserslautern and Mannheim, Germany
Skanziklas, Sotiris, Pilot Officer	RHAF	c. 31/03/44	22	Breslau Gestapo	Approx. 15 miles northwest of Hirschberg, Poland
Stevens, Rupert J., Lieutenant	SAAF	29/03/44	25	Munich Gestapo	Meadow 25 miles north of Munich, Germany
Stewart, Robert C., Flying Officer	RAF	31/03/44	32	Breslau Gestapo	Halfway between Breslau and Sagan, Poland
Stower, John G., Flying Officer	RAF	31/03/44	27	Reichenberg Gestapo	Unknown, presumed near Reichenberg, Poland
Street, Denys O., Flying Officer	RAF	c. 06/04/44	21	Breslau Gestapo	Unknown, presumed between Görlitz and Sagan, Poland
Swain, Cyril D., Flight Lieutenant	RAF	31/03/44	32	Breslau Gestapo	Halfway between Breslau and Sagan, Poland
Tobolski, Pawel W., Flying Officer	PAF	c. 02/04/44	38	Breslau Gestapo	Unknown, perhaps near Breslau, Poland
Valenta, Ernst, Flight Lieutenant	RAF (Cz.)	31/03/44	31	Breslau Gestapo	Halfway between Breslau and Sagan, Poland
Walem, Gilbert 'Tim' W., Flight Lieutenant	RAF	29/03/44	28	Danzig Gestapo	Wood near Gross Trampken, Poland
Wernham, James G., Flight Lieutenant	RCAF	c. 31/03/44	29	Breslau Gestapo	Approx. 15 miles northwest of Hirschberg, Poland
Wiley, George W., Flight Lieutenant	RCAF	30/03/44	22	Breslau Gestapo	Wooded road 3 miles south of Sagan, Poland
Williams, John E. A., Squadron Leader	RAAF	29/03/44	24	Reichenberg Gestapo	Unknown, presumed near Reichenberg, Poland
Williams, John F., Flight Lieutenant	RAF	c. 06/04/44	26	Breslau Gestapo	Unknown, presumed between Görlitz and Sagan, Poland

THE MURDERERS

Organisation	Employee	Involvement	Fate	Victims
Alsace Gestapo	Diessner, Max	Murder	Committed suicide on 11/05/48	Hayter (shot by Hilker)
	Hässle	Driver; accessory to murder	Not traced	
	Hilker, Heinrich	Murder	Charged, but case dismissed 11/04/68	
	Isselhorst, Erich (BdS)	Murder	Executed for other crimes on 23/02/48	
	Schimmel, Alfred (chief)	Murder	Executed by British, 27/02/48	
Breslau Gestapo	Dankert	Suspected murder	Unknown	Birkland
	Hampel, Walter	Suspected murder	Arrested 01/09/48; not charged	Casey
	Hänsel, Richard	Suspected murder	Acquitted 06/11/48	Cross
	Kiske, Paul	Suspected murder	Killed in action in Breslau, 1945	Evans
	Knappe	Suspected murder	Killed in action in Breslau, 1945	Grisman
	Kreuzer	Suspected murder	Unknown	Gunn
	Kühnel	Driver; accessory to murder	Killed in action in Breslau, 1945	Hake
	Lang	Suspected murder	Unknown	Hall
	Läuffer	Suspected murder	Unconfirmed suicide, 1945	Humphreys
	Lux, Walter	Murder	Killed in action in Breslau, 1945	Kiewnarksi
	Pattke, Walter	Suspected murder	Killed in action in Breslau, 1945?	Kolanowski
	Prosse	Suspected murder	Died of natural causes, 1944	Krol?
	Schampera	Suspected murder	Unknown	Langford
	Scharpwinkel, Wilhelm (chief)	Murder	Captured by Russians in Breslau; reputed to have died in custody on 17/10/47	Leigh
				Long
				McGarr
				McGill
				Milford
				Pawluk
				Pohé
				Skanziklas
				Stewart
				Street

Organisation	Employee	Involvement	Fate	Victims
	Schmauser, Ernst	Conspiracy to murder	Captured by Russians	Swain Tobolski Valenta Wernham Wiley Williams, J. F.
	Schröder, Robert	Driver; accessory to murder	Material witness, granted immunity	
	Seetzen	Conspiracy to murder	Captured in Hamburg; committed suicide on 28/09/45	
	Tögel	Suspected murder	Unknown	
	Wieczorek, Erwin	Murder	Sentenced to death, 06/12/48; sentence later quashed	
Breslau Kripo	Wielen, Max	Conspiracy to murder	Sentenced to life imprisonment, 03/09/47	All 50 victims
Brno and Zlín Gestapo	Kiowsky, Friedrich	Driver; accessory to murder	Executed for other crimes in Czechoslovakia in 1947	Kidder (shot by Zacharias) Kirby-Green (shot by Knippelberg)
	Knippelberg, Adolf	Murder	Never traced after being released by the Russians in 1945	
	Schauschütz, Franz	Accessory to murder	Executed for other crimes in Czechoslovakia in 1947	
	Schwarzer, Friedrich	Driver; accessory to murder	Executed for other crimes in Czechoslovakia in 1947	
	Zacharias, Erich	Murder	Executed by British 27/02/48	
	Ziegler, Hans (Zlín chief)	Murder	Sentenced to death; committed suicide on 03/02/48	
Danzig Gestapo	Achterberg (deputy chief)	Suspected accessory to murder?	No trace	Brettell Marcinkus Picard Walenn
	Asal	Suspected murder	No trace	
	Bachs, Gerhard	Suspected accessory to murder	No trace	
	Bontenbroich, Peter	Driver	Interned; not charged	
	Bruchardt, Reinhold	Murder	Sentenced to death, 06/11/48; commuted to life imprisonment	
	Fels	Suspected murder	No trace	
	Hug, Julius	Suspected accessory to murder	No trace	

Organisation	Employee	Involvement	Fate	Victims
	Kilpe, Max	Suspected accessory to murder	Arrested on 27/08/48; not charged	
	Reimer, Willi	Driver	Interned; not charged	
	Rörer	Suspected murder	No trace	
	Sasse, Walter	Suspected accessory to murder	Escaped from internment camp	
	Venediger, Günther (chief)	Murder	Sentenced to two years in prison on 17/12/57 after several appeals	
	Völz, Walter	Suspected accessory to murder	No trace, possibly killed in action	
	Wenzler, Herbert	Suspected accessory to murder	Arrested in 1948; not charged	
	Witt, Harry	Suspected accessory to murder	Arrested in September 1948; not charged	
Karlsruhe Gestapo	Boschert, Heinrich	Murder	Sentenced to death 03/09/47; commuted to life imprisonment	Cochran
	Ganninger, Otto	Suspected accessory to murder	Committed suicide on 26/04/46	
	Gmeiner, Josef (chief)	Murder	Executed by British, 27/02/48	
	Herberg, Walter	Murder	Executed by British, 27/02/48	
	Preiss, Otto	Murder	Executed by British, 27/02/48	
Kiel Gestapo	Denkmann, Artur	Driver; accessory to murder	Sentenced to ten years in prison on 03/09/47	Catanach (shot by Post)
	Jacobs, Walter	Murder	Executed by British, 27/02/48	Christensen (shot by Jacobs)
	Kähler, Hans	Murder	Executed by British, 27/02/48	

Organisation	Employee	Involvement	Fate	Victims
	Post, Johannes	Murder	Executed by British, 27/02/48	Espelid (shot by Oskar Schmidt)
	Schmidt, Franz	Murder	Committed suicide on 27/10/46	Fugelsang (shot by Franz Schmidt)
	Schmidt, Fritz (chief)	Murder	Sentenced to two years in prison in May 1968	
	Schmidt, Oskar	Murder	Executed by British, 27/02/48	
	Struve, Wilhelm	Driver; accessory to murder	Sentenced to ten years in prison on 03/09/47	
Luftwaffe	Göring, Hermann	Murder	Committed suicide at Nuremberg on 15/10/46	All 50 victims
Munich Gestapo	Geith, Eduard	Murder	Executed by British, 27/02/48	Gouws
	Schäfer, Oswald (chief)	Murder	Charges dropped on 11/12/68	Stevens (both shot by Schneider)
	Schermer, Martin	Murder	Committed suicide on 25/04/45	
	Schneider, Johann	Murder	Executed by British, 27/02/48	
	Weil, Emil	Murder	Executed by British, 27/02/48	
NSDAP	Hitler, Adolf	Murder	Committed suicide in Berlin on 30/04/45	All 50 victims
OKW	Keitel, Wilhelm	Murder	Executed at Nuremberg, 16/10/46	All 50 victims
Reichenberg Gestapo	Baatz, Bernard	Murder	Released by Russians in 1946	Bull
	Weissman, Robert	Murder	No trace after being captured by French	Kierath
	Weyland, Robert	Murder	Disappeared into Russian Zone of Germany	Mondschein
				Stower?
				Williams, J. E.
RSHA	Kaltenbrunner, Ernst (chief)	Murder	Hanged at Nuremberg, 16/10/46	All 50 victims
	Müller, Heinrich (head of Gestapo)	Murder	Committed suicide in Berlin?	
	Nebe, Artur (head of Kripo)	Murder	Executed by Gestapo in March 1945	

Organisation	Employee	Involvement	Fate	Victims
Saarbrücken Gestapo	Breithaupt, Walter	Driver; accessory to murder	Sentenced to life on 03/09/47	Bushell (shot by Schulz)
	Schulz, Emil	Murder	Executed by British, 27/02/48	Scheidhauer (shot by Spann)
	Spann, Leopold (chief)	Murder	Killed in air raid on Linz, 25/04/45	
SS	Himmler, Heinrich (chief)	Murder	Committed suicide on 23/05/45	All 50 victims

SIPO-SD RANKS AND EQUIVALENTS

Sipo-SD rank	Equivalent SS rank	Equivalent German army rank	Equivalent British army rank	Equivalent Metropolitan Police CID rank (2012)
Kriminalassistent (on probation)	Staffelmann to Unterscharführer	Unteroffizier	Private	Constable
Kriminalassistent	Oberscharführer	Feldwebel	Staff Sergeant	Detective Sergeant
Kriminaloberassistent	Hauptscharführer	Oberfeldwebel	Sergeant Major	Detective Sergeant
Kriminalsekretär	Untersturmführer	Leutnant	2nd Lieutenant	—
Kriminalobersekretär	Untersturmführer	Leutnant	2nd Lieutenant	—
Kriminalinspektor	Obersturmführer	Oberleutnant	Lieutenant	—
Kriminalkommissar	Obersturmführer	Oberleutnant	Lieutenant	—
Kriminalrat	Hauptsturmführer	Hauptmann	Captain	Detective Inspector
Kriminaldirektor	Sturmbannführer	Major	Major	Detective Inspector
Regierungs- und Kriminalrat	Sturmbannführer	Major	Major	Detective Inspector
Oberregierungs- und Kriminalrat	Obersturmbannführer	Oberstleutnant	Lieutenant Colonel	Detective Chief Inspector
Regierungs- und Kriminaldirektor	Standartenführer	Oberst	Colonel	Superintendent
Reichskriminaldirektor und Ministerialrat	Standartenführer	Oberst	Colonel	Superintendent
Oberst der Polizei	Oberführer	Oberst	Brigadier	Chief Constable
Generalmajor der Polizei	Brigadeführer	Generalmajor	—	Deputy Assistant Commissioner
Generalleutnant der Polizei	Gruppenführer	Generalleutnant	Major General	Assistant Commissioner
General der Polizei	Obergruppenführer	—	Lieutenant General	—

(Sources: WO 309/529; GWDN: 1524–1525)

Sources

As with my previous books, I am very happy to send jpeg files of documents I have photographed to bona fide researchers. Simply email me at guy@guywalters.com, including the reference numbers as denoted by the letters GWDN in the endnotes. Please be aware that I am unable to send hard copies of these documents.

UNPUBLISHED SOURCES

(a) Archives
NB: Item numbers of folders consulted at these archives are contained in the endnotes.
Bundesarchiv, Berlin and Freiburg, Germany (BA)
  Series: N 54 (Keitel, Wilhelm); MSG 2; MSG 194; NS 19; RL 23

Imperial War Museum Collections, London, UK (IWM)
National Archives, Kew, UK (UKNA)
    Series: AIR 40; CAB 66; DEFE 2; FO 371; FO 916;
    HW 16; KV 2; TS 26; WO 208; WO 216; WO 224;
    WO 235; WO 258; WO 309; WO 311
Royal Air Force Museum, Hendon, UK (RAFM)
United States Air Force Academy, McDermott Library,
    Colorado, USA (USAFA)

(b) Interviews
Imperial War Museum Sound Archive (with accession number)

Acquier, John Francis, 6091
Atkinson, George Arthur, 6176
Birbeck, John, 31698
Bracken, Hugo, 11337
Brickhill, Paul Chester Jerome, 28977
Bryett, Alan, 27051
Burns, Ken, 31718
Cairns, Peter, 28920
Cassie, Alex, 26558
Chapman, Edward Frederick, 11194
Churchill, John Malcolm Thorpe Fleming 'Jack', 9231
Churchill, Richard Sydney Albion, 13296
Clark, Bud, 30046
Cole, Arthur Westcombe, 15558
Cornish, Geoffrey, 23327
Deans, James Alexander Graham 'Dixie', 6142
Dowse, Sydney Hastings, 27731
Driver, Maurice, 27064
Foinette, Eric Norman, 6095
Fox, Peter Hutton, 28569

Hall, Edgar Louis Graham, 6075
Hall, Leonard, 27271
Hill, James, 9541
Ingle, Alec, 11338
James, Bertram Arthur 'Jimmy', 4987
Lamb, Robert Lionel, 4809
Leng, Maurice Equity, 12217
Lyon, Jack, 28532
Marshall, Bernard Willis, 15337
Morison, Walter, 25030 & 29175
Nelson, Thomas Robert, 8276
Parkhouse, Rupert Charles Langridge, 15476
Pearman, Leonard Lawrence, 11191
Philpot, Oliver Lawrence Spurling, 9938
Rae, Jack, 27813
Rees, Ken, 25029 & 28755
Royle, Paul Gordon, 26605
Waddington, Frank Ogden, 17365
Webster, Roy, 28877
Welch, Patrick Palles Lorne Elphinstone, 10643

United States Air Force Academy

Hermann Glemnitz, interviewed by Lieutenant General
  A. P. Clark & Col E. F. Schrupp, 9–10 April 1984
  (SMS 329)

Conducted by the author
Fripp, Alfie 'Bill', 9 September 2011

(c) Diaries, memoirs and letters
Imperial War Museum Document Archive (with box number)
Private papers of R. A. Bethell (05/4/1)

Private papers of C. N. S. Campbell (86/35/1)
Private papers of G. H. F. Carter (96/41/1)
Private papers of Flight Lieutenant Alexander Cassie (04/03/1)
Papers of Flight Lieutenant David A. Codd (06/117/1)
Private papers of A. G. Edwards (99/82/1)
Private papers of H. E. C. Elliott (88/20/1)
Private papers of N. Flekser (99/82/1)
Papers of Flight Lieutenant C. E. L. Grant (05/68/1)
Private papers of Flight Officer L. G. Hall (06/51/1)
Papers of C. G. King (85/50/1)
Papers of A. G. Lees (06/51/1)
Private papers of Squadron Leader T. R. Nelson (84/45/1)
Private papers of H. Picard (01/25/1)

United States Air Force Academy
Gustav Simoleit, *Prisoner of War Camps of the Air Force in World War II* (SMS 699)

Royal Air Force Museum, Hendon
Prisoner-of-war diary of Squadron Leader W. H. D. Chapple (MF10062/11)
Notebook kept by Flight Lieutenant Tommy Guest whilst a POW, n.d. (X-003-6188)
Wartime log of Flight Lieutenant Bennett Ley Kenyon, 1943–1946 (X-001-2316)
Prisoner-of-war notes on making false German identity documents, *c.* 1943 (X-002-5582)

Bundesarchiv, Freiburg
Colonel Friedrich von Lindeiner, *Im Dienst der Deutschen Luftwaffe, 1938 bis 1944* (MSG 2/1517)

Private collections

Diary of Flight Lieutenant William E. Koch, 301st Bombardment Group, Fifteenth Air Force, Fifth Bombardment Wing, Foggia, Italy

---

PUBLISHED SOURCES

(a) Printed
(i) Biographies and memoirs

Aitken Kidd, Janet, *The Beaverbrook Girl* (London: Collins, 1987)

Ash, William, *Under the Wire* (London: Bantam, 2006)

Bartley, Tony, *Smoke Trails in the Sky* (Wilmslow: Crécy, 1997)

Calnan, T. D., *Free as a Running Fox* (New York: Dial Press, 1970)

Clark, Albert P., *33 Months as a POW in Stalag Luft III* (Colorado: Fulcrum Publishing, 2004)

Codd, David, *Blue Job – Brown Job* (Bradford on Avon: ELSP, 2000)

Forrester, Larry, *Fly for Your Life* (London: The Companion Book Club, 1958)

Harsh, George, *Lonesome Road* (London: Sphere Books, 1976)

James, B. A. 'Jimmy', *Moonless Night* (Barnsley: Pen and Sword Military Kindle Edition, 2010)

Johnson, Stephen P. L., *A Kriegie's Log* (Tunbridge Wells: Parapress Ltd, 1995)

Kee, Robert, *A Crowd is Not a Company* (London: Phoenix, 2000)

Keitel, Wilhelm, *In the Service of the Reich* (London: Focal Point Publications Electronic Edition, 2003)

Lawlis, Merritt E., *Winking at Death: Memoir of a World War II POW* (AuthorHouse, 2008)

Lucas, Laddie, *Voices in the Air 1939–1945: A Unique Collection of Stories from the Great Aerial Campaigns of the Second World War* (London: Random House, 2003)

Morison, Walter, *Flak and Ferrets* (London: Sentinel Publishing, 1995)

Müller, Jens, *Tre Kom Tilbake* (Oslo: Gyldendal, 1946)

Passmore, Richard, *Moving Tent* (London: Thomas Harmsworth, 1982)

Plunkett, Desmond L., & Pletts, The Reverend R., *The Man Who Would Not Die* (Durham: Pentland Press, 2000)

Rees, Ken, *Lie in the Dark and Listen* (London: Grub Street, 2009)

Sage, Jerry, *Sage* (Pennsylvania: Miles Standish Press, 1985)

'Scangriff', *Spotlight on Stalag Luft III* (privately published, 1947)

Smith, Martin, *What a Bloody Arrival* (Lewes: Book Guild, 1997)

Smith, Sydney, *'Wings' Day* (London: Pan, 1968)

Tonder, Ivo, & Sitensky, Ladislav, *Na nebi i v pekle* (Czech Republic: Edice Pilot, 1997)

Vanderstok, Bob, *War Pilot of Orange* (Missoula, Montana: Pictorial Histories Publishing, 1987)

Wellum, Geoffrey, *First Light* (London: Penguin, 2003)

(ii) Histories

Andrews, Allen, *Exemplary Justice* (London: Corgi, 1978)

Brickhill, Paul, *The Great Escape* (London: Faber and Faber, 1951)

Brickhill, Paul, & Norton, Conrad, *Escape to Danger* (London: Faber and Faber, 1949)

Burgess, Alan, *The Longest Tunnel* (London: Bloomsbury, 1991)

Carroll, Tim, *The Great Escape from Stalag Luft III* (New York: Pocket Books, 2005)

Clutton-Brock, Oliver, *Footprints on the Sands of Time* (London: Grub Street, 2003)

Davies, Stephen R., *RAF Police: The 'Great Escape' Murders* (Bognor Regis: Woodfield, 2009)

Dominy, John, *The Sergeant Escapers* (London: Ian Allan, 1974)

Durand, Arthur A., *Stalag Luft III: The Secret Story* (New York: Touchstone, 1989)

Foot, M. R. D., & Langley, J. M., *MI9: Escape and Evasion 1939–1945* (London: Book Club Associates, 1979)

Gill, Anton, *The Great Escape* (London: Review, 2002)

Harris, Whitney R., *Tyranny on Trial* (Dallas: Southern Methodist University Press, 1954)

Holland, James, *The Battle of Britain* (London: Bantam Press, 2010)

Holland, James, *Italy's Sorrow: A Year of War, 1944–1945* (London: HarperPress, 2008)

Kershaw, Ian, *Hitler 1936–1945: Nemesis* (London: Allen Lane, 2000)

Kirk, Tim, *Nazi Germany* (Basingstoke: Palgrave Macmillan, 2007)

Maas, Ad, & Hooijmaijers, Hans, *Scientific Research in*

World War II: What Scientists Did in the War (Abingdon: Routledge, 2009)

MacKenzie, S. P., *The Colditz Myth* (OUP, 2004)

McKinstry, Leo, *Spitfire: Portrait of a Legend* (London: John Murray, 2008)

Macnab, Geoffrey, *Searching for Stars: Stardom and Screen Acting in British Cinema* (Continuum, 2000)

Moulson, Tom, *The Flying Sword: The Story of 601 Squadron* (London: Macdonald, 1964)

Otto, Reinhard, *Wehrmacht, Gestapo und sowjetische Kriegsgefangene im deutschen Reichsgebiet 1941/42* (Oldenbourg Wissenschaftsverlag, 1998)

Reitlinger, Gerald, *The SS: Alibi of a Nation* (New York: Viking, 1957)

Scotland, A. P., *The London Cage* (London: Evans Brothers, 1957)

Sutton, Denise H., *Globalizing Ideal Beauty: How Female Copywriters of the J. Walter Thompson Advertising Agency Redefined Beauty for the Twentieth Century* (Basingstoke: Palgrave Macmillan, 2009)

Toman, Prokop, *Nový slovník československých výtvarných umělců* (Ostrava: Výtvarné Centrum Chagall, 1994)

Vance, Jonathan F., *A Gallant Company* (New York: iBooks, 2000)

Walters, Guy, *Hunting Evil* (London: Bantam Books, 2010)

Weale, Adrian, *Renegades: Hitler's Englishmen* (London: Warner Books, 1995)

(iii) Bulletins, journals, newspapers and magazines

Aeroplane

The British Ski Year Book of the Ski Club of Great Britain and the Alpine Ski Club, No. 25, Vol. XI

Central European History

Chicago Sunday Tribune

Collier's Magazine

Daily Mail

Daily Mirror

Daily Telegraph

Empire News

Evening News

Evening Standard

German Studies Review

Illustrated London News

The London Gazette

The New Yorker

The Prisoner of War

Skiing Heritage Journal

The Straits Times

Sunday Dispatch

Sunday Express

The Times

Völkischer Beobachter

(iv) Reports

Hansard

Law Reports of the Trials of War Criminals, Volume XI, selected and prepared by the United Nations War Crimes Commission (London: HMSO, 1949)

(b) TV and film

The Great Escape (1963), directed by John Sturges

The Great Escape: The Reckoning (2009), produced by Channel 4 Television et al.; http://www.channel4.com/programmes/the-great-escape-the-reckoning

The Great Escape: The Untold Story (2001), produced by Granada Productions

For Which I Am Prepared to Die (2009), directed and written by Lindy Wilson, screened on BBC4 on 24 April 2012 as The Real Great Escape

(c) Electronic

NB: All URLs were successfully accessed at time of publication. If any of the links are dead, then try pasting the URL in the search box at www.archive.org

(i) Histories

Clarke, James, Stoep Talk: Filling in the Gaps in Park Town's History . . . at http://www.iol.co.za/filling-in-the-gaps-in-park-town-s-history-1.627798

Gedenkstätte Gestapo-Lager Neue Bremm by Initiative Neue Bremm at http://www.gestapo-lager-neue-bremm.de/front_content.php

Hickman, Mark, Squadron Leader Roger Joyce Bushell at http://www.pegasusarchive.org/pow/roger_bushell.htm

RAF Bomber Command Campaign Diary, March 1944, at http://www.raf.mod.uk/bombercommand/mar44.html

(ii) Memoirs

Smale, Major John, *Dieppe and Captivity* at
http://www.war-experience.org/collections/land/
alliedbrit/smale/pagetwo.asp

(iii) Film

Ironside, Hugh, interviewed by dewARTvideo (*c*. 2008)
at http://www.youtube.com/watchv=6Qko_e0TLKA
Weir, John, interviewed by MacleansMagazine at
http://www.youtube.com/watchv=J18RMQupsu0
Woehrle, Charles, interviewed by Woehrle, John and
Woehrle, Louise (*c*. 2011), at
http://www.youtube.com/ watchv=DKv280IA4cI&
http://www.youtube.com/watchv=LXThZB-IOac

(iv) Minutes, testimonies, affidavits, legal proceedings

Kugel Erlass ('Bullet Decree') at
http://www.ess.uwe.ac.uk/genocide/kugel.htm
Nuremberg Trial Proceedings at
http://avalon.law.yale.edu/subject_menus/imt.asp

Acknowledgements

For ten years, Tif Loehnis at Janklow & Nesbit represented me superbly and, like all her authors, I was immensely sorry when we lost her to the world of editing. Nevertheless, her successor, Will Francis, is an estimable replacement, and I am very grateful for both his efforts, and for those of Luke Janklow in New York. All members of the Janklow & Nesbit agency are equally capable, and I'd like to thank Claire Dippel, Rebecca Folland, Tim Glister and Kirsty Gordon for their assistance.

Equally deserving of the highest praise is the team at Transworld, which includes the ever-capable Lynsey Dalladay, Philip Lord and Vivien Garrett. However, special thanks should be extended to my editor, Simon Thorogood, who has been uniquely patient in handling a project that took almost as long to complete as a

344-foot tunnel, although, unlike Harry, this was a project that significantly overran. I am extremely appreciative of his forbearance and shrewd suggestions.

Several friends were also on hand for much-needed advice. In alphabetical order, these included Charles Cumming, Jeremy Duns, James Holland, Tobias Jones, James Owen, Boris Starling and Adrian Weale, all of whom, incidentally, have written books that are well worth buying.

I have also benefited from the valuable assistance offered by countless experts. At the National Archives, the admirable Julie Ash was always on hand to answer my queries with her usual charm. Gordon Leith kindly steered me around the archives at the RAF Museum in Hendon, and at the Imperial War Museum, Terry Charman and Nigel Steel were equally helpful. At Cranfield, I was delighted to have drawn on the impressive knowledge contained in the heads of Peter Caddick-Adams and David Turns. At the USAFA, I was grateful to Richard Muller, Sandhya Malladi, M. Douglas Johnson and Mary Ruwell for sending me just what I needed, and once again, I am very lucky to have had the help of Michelle Miles, who gathered and dispatched much archival matter from Germany. In Norway, Ingrid Ryvarden helped me ferret out Jens Müller's memoir, and I was delighted when my good friend George Pendle unearthed in the New York Public Library a copy of Ivo Tonder's book, parts of which were elegantly translated by Chris Rance. From Ostrava in the Czech Republic, Dr Petr Pavliňák kindly sent me the entry for Blažena Zeithammelová from the somewhat hard-to-source *Nový slovník československých výtvarných umělců*. In Poland, Michał Czajka photographed the grave of Roger Bushell, and in Buckinghamshire, my parents, Martin and Angela Walters, located that of Georgie Kidston. If you ever need to know about cars, then do get in contact with Mike Worthy-Williams – he is an automotive encyclopaedia. James Lofthouse of 55 Temple Chambers was kind enough to dispense much legal advice. I still owe him a decent bottle. For historical meteorology, then go no further than the impressive Simon Keeling, who provided much useful data. Jane Fluckiger displayed a similar level of expertise concerning the police. Darius Kacprzak at the Szczecin Museum was a great help in unearthing old maps of that city. For permission to use the beautiful drawings and paintings by Sandy Cassie and Ley Kenyon, I am indebted to Adrian Cassie, Ros Postance and June Barnett. At Cambridge, Rebecca Coombs and Jayne Ringrose kindly unearthed the details of Bushell's degree, and I am grateful to Andrew Scott at White's for a similar piece of digging.

Of course, the greatest thanks of all must go to my family, whose daily mantra – 'Have you finished your book yet?' – I hope I never again give them cause to repeat. Annabel, William and Alice, here is my book, finally finished, and I could not have done it without your love and support.

Notes

Abbreviations
BA Bundesarchiv, Berlin and Freiburg
GWDN Guy Walters's Document Number/Name
IWM Imperial War Museum, London, UK
RAFM Royal Air Force Museum, Hendon, UK
UKNA National Archives, Kew, London, UK
USAFA United States Air Force Academy, McDermott
  Library, Colorado, USA

Chapter One: 'A man of fate'
1   History of Springs at
    http://www.springsoflife.co.za/index.php/springs-
    overview/further-history
2   James Clarke, *Stoep Talk: Filling in the Gaps in Park
    Town's History*, 21 September 2006,
    http://www.iol.co.za/filling-in-the-gaps-in-park-town-
    s-history-1.627798

3   Paul Brickhill, *The Great Escape* (London: Faber and Faber, 1951), p. 18

4   Correspondence between Donald Edwards [?] and Wellington College, 19 May 1994, supplied by Ben Lewsley of Wellington College.

5   Honour roll report supplied by Ben Lewsley at Wellington College.

6   Pembroke College Cambridge Application for Admission form supplied by Ben Lewsley at Wellington College.

7   Arnold Lunn (ed.), *The British Ski Year Book of the Ski Club of Great Britain and the Alpine Ski Club. No. 25, Vol. XI* (London, 1944)

8   *Skiing Heritage Journal*, March 2005, p. 6

9   *The Times* (London), 22 January 1931, 'Skiing – The British Championships'

10   Lunn, *The British Ski Year Book*

11   Paul Brickhill quoted by E. D. O'Brien in *Illustrated London News*, 12 May 1951

12   Kindly supplied by Jayne Ringrose at Cambridge University Library and Rebecca Coombs at Pembroke College, Cambridge.

13   *The Times* (London), 28 June 1938, 'Three Troopers on Trial'

14   *The Times* (London), 29 July 1939, 'Test Pilot Committed for Trial'

15   *Daily Mirror*, 10 June 1938

16   *Empire News*, 12 December 1937

17   Anton Gill, *The Great Escape* (London: Review, 2002), p. 12

18   *The Times* (London), 19 May 1944, 'Personal Tribute – Squadron Leader R. Bushell' by G. D. Roberts, KC

19   See *The Times* (London), 26 November 2011,

'Dashing, daring pilot who was loved and lost by three women' by Simon Pearson at http://www.thetimes.co.uk/tto/news/uk/article323907 6.ece (paysite) in which it is claimed that Max Aitken invited Bushell to join the squadron.

20 Author's correspondence with Andrew Scott of White's. It is often assumed that Bushell was a member.

21 *Daily Telegraph*, 2 March 2009, obituary of Hercules Bellville, http://www.telegraph.co.uk/news/obituaries/ 4928752/Hercules-Bellville.html

22 See http://www.601squadron.com/The_Real_601_ Archival_ Photo.php

23 Laddie Lucas, *Voices in the Air 1939–1945: A Unique Collection of Stories from the Great Aerial Campaigns of the Second World War* (London: Random House, 2003), p. 14

24 Tom Moulson, *The Flying Sword: The Story of 601 Squadron* (London: Macdonald, 1964), p. 41

25 Ibid., p. 41

26 Ibid., p. 42

27 Ibid., p. 46

28 *Daily Mirror*, 17 August 1936

29 Moulson, p. 46

30 *The Times* (London), 11 July 1935, Christenings; GWDN: RBTT110735

31 *The Times* (London), 17 May 1935, Marriages, p. 19. Although the list of attendees includes Georgie, it does not include Bushell. It does, however, feature a 'Miss Bushell', who may have been Bushell's older sister, Rosemary. This makes it more likely Bushell was indeed there. Such lists in *The Times* are not exhaustive.

32 See profile at http://www.500race.org/Men/Howe.htm

33   See http://thepeerage.com/p1066.htm#i10654

34   *The Times* (London), 9 July 1928, Dances, p. 19

35   Geoffrey Macnab, *Searching for Stars: Stardom and
       Screen Acting in British Cinema* (Continuum, 2000),
       p. 62

36   *The New Yorker*, 12 September 1931, p. 81

37   See, for example, Chicago *Sunday Tribune*,
       15 February 1931, p. 10, at
       http://archive.lib.msu.edu/DMC/tribune/trib02151931
       /trib02151931010.pdf

38   *The Straits Times*, 18 December 1931, p. 17, at
       http://newspapers.nl.sg/Digitised/Article/
       straitstimes19311218.2.123.2.aspx

39   Denise H. Sutton, *Globalizing Ideal Beauty*
       (Basingstoke: Palgrave Macmillan, 2009), p. 165

40   *The Times* (London), 26 November 2011 at
       http://www.the times.co.uk/tto/news/uk/
       article3239076.ece (paysite)

41   UKNA: J 77/3967, Records of the Supreme Court of
       Judicature and related courts, Court for Divorce and
       Matrimonial Causes, later Supreme Court of
       Judicature: Divorce and Matrimonial Causes Files,
       Kidston G M & R A, letter from Kidston to Georgie,
       30 November 1941; GWDN: 5379

42   Ibid.; GWDN: 5380

43   Footage of the wedding can be seen at
       http://www.itnsource.com/shotlist//BHC_RTV/1935/1
       1/28/BGU407200943/

44   Moulson, p. 56

45   Janet Aitken Kidd, *The Beaverbrook Girl* (London:
       Collins, 1987), pp. 167–8

Chapter Two: 'I'd left the camp without asking'

1 Moulson, p. 42

2 Ibid., p. 43

3 Leo McKinstry, *Spitfire: Portrait of a Legend* (London: John Murray, 2008), pp. 137–8

4 http://www.telegraph.co.uk/news/newstopics/world-war-2/battle-of-britain/7851060/Battle-of-Britain-the-spitfire-envy-of-the-enemy.html

5 Jonathan F. Vance, *A Gallant Company* (New York: iBooks, 2000), p. 12

6 Tony Bartley, *Smoke Trails in the Sky* (Wilmslow: Crécy, 1997) p. 7

7 Geoffrey Wellum, *First Light* (London: Penguin, 2003)

8 See http://www.pegasusarchive.org/pow/roger_bushell.htm

9 Bartley, *Smoke Trails*, p. 12

10 James Holland, *The Battle of Britain* (London: Bantam Press, 2010), pp. 188–90. Many accounts, such as those of Brickhill and Vance, suggest that Bushell shot down one, perhaps two, enemy aircraft. The squadron's records do not support this.

11 Geoffrey Wellum, quoted in *The Times* (London), 26 November 2011

12 See http://www.epibreren.com/ww2/raf/85_squadron.html for details on Peacock.

13 IWM: Sound Archive recording 13296, Interview with Richard Churchill, Reels 2 & 4

14 IWM: Sound Archive recording 27731, Interview with Sydney Dowse, Reel 4

15 *The London Gazette*, Issue 31112, 7 January 1919, pp. 363–4, at http://www.londongazette.co.uk/issues/31112/pages/363

16 IWM: Sound Archive recording 26558, Interview with Alex Cassie, Reel 15

17 Tim Carroll, *The Great Escape from Stalag Luft III* (New York: Pocket Books, 2005), p. 18

18 UKNA: KV 2/631, Security Service: Personal (PF Series) Files, Renegades and Suspected Renegades, Benson Railton Metcalfe FREEMAN, alias P. ROYSTON, f. 124a; GWDN: 6820

19 Sydney Smith, *'Wings' Day* (London: Pan, 1968), p. 43

20 Carroll, *The Great Escape*, p. 23

21 Vance, *A Gallant Company*, pp. 13–14

22 http://en.wikipedia.org/wiki/Mile_End_ (UK_Parliament_ constituency)

23 Vance, *A Gallant Company*, p. 14

24 Carroll, *The Great Escape*, p. 28

25 Ibid., p. 25

26 UKNA: AIR 18/28, Judge Advocate General's Office: Royal Air Force Courts Martial Proceedings; P/O Freeman, B.R.M. Offence: Aiding the enemy whilst P.O.W.; GWDN: 6736

27 UKNA: AIR 18/28; GWDN: 6724

28 UKNA: AIR 18/28; GWDN: 6755

29 Adrian Weale, *Renegades: Hitler's Englishmen* (London: Warner Books, 1995), p. 145

30 UKNA: AIR 18/28; GWDN: 6691

31 UKNA: KV 2/631; GWDN: 6821

32 UKNA: AIR 18/28; GWDN: 6729

33 UKNA: AIR 18/28; GWDN: 6707

34 Weale, *Renegades*, p. 149

35 Brickhill, *The Great Escape*, p. 20. Other accounts, such as those of Carroll and Vance, place the starting point at the latrine block.

36 UKNA: KV 2/631; GWDN: 6821 & UKNA: AIR 18/28; GWDN: 6740

37   Brickhill, *The Great Escape*, p. 20

38   Smith, *'Wings' Day*, p. 70

39   UKNA: AIR 18/28; GWDN: 6740

40   UKNA: AIR 18/28; GWDN: 6708

41   Ibid.

42   UKNA: AIR 18/28; GWDN: 6743

43   UKNA: AIR 18/28; GWDN: 6707

44   UKNA: AIR 18/28; GWDN: 6741

45   UKNA: AIR 18/28; GWDN: 6744

46   UKNA: AIR 18/28; GWDN: 6708

47   UKNA: KV 2/631; GWDN: 6822

48   Ibid.

49   Smith, *'Wings' Day*, p. 71

50   Ibid., p. 72

51   UKNA: KV 2/631; GWDN: 6822

52   Dulag Luft lay at 50.13 N, 08.34 E, 300 yards north of the Frankfurt to Bad Homburg road. The nearest station to the camp was Niedernhausen.

53   Carroll, *The Great Escape*, p. 28. Brickhill writes that Bushell was shot at by a guard, but this is likely to be an elaboration typical of that author.

54   *The Times* (London), 19 May 1944, 'Personal Tribute – Squadron Leader R. Bushell' by G. D. Roberts, KC

55   Smith, *'Wings' Day*, p. 77

56   Vance, *A Gallant Company*, p. 34

57   See résumé at http://starbacks.ca/~orion47/WEHRMACHT/LUFTWAFFE/Generalleutnant/MASSOW_GERD.html

58   Smith, *'Wings' Day*, p. 79. Throughout 1941 the camp at Barth was called Stalag Luft II, but I have referred to it as Luft I to avoid confusion.

59   Vance, *A Gallant Company*, p. 35

60   See http://fcafa.wordpress.com/2011/10/23/not-forgotten-holland/

61   In *The Times* (London), 26 November 2011, the family are incorrectly called the Zeithammies.

62   For biographical information concerning the Zeithammel family, see http://www.cemetery.cz/english/. For details of Blažena, see Prokop Toman, *Nový slovník československých výtvarných umělců* (Ostrava: Výtvarné Centrum Chagall, 1994).

63   The block still stands, and bears a plaque dedicated to the memory of the Zeithammel family.

64   Brickhill, *The Great Escape*, p. 22

65   *The Times* (London), 26 November 2011

66   See http://www.cemetery.cz/english/

67   Vance, *A Gallant Company*, p. 55

68   Moulson, p. 156. Moulson writes that Bushell was captured with Blažena while in the cinema. 'Marshall' may have in fact been Paddy Byrne.

69   Private information

70   UKNA: J 77/3967, op. cit.; GWDN: 5347

71   Ibid.; Letter from Kidston to Georgie, 30 October 1941; GWDN: 5377

72   Ibid.; Letter from Kidston to Georgie, 30 November 1941; GWDN: 5380

73   *The Times* (London), 17 July 1942; value of £5,000 computed by Officer and Williamson, 'Purchasing Power of British Pounds', MeasuringWorth, 2011 at http://www.measuringworth.com/ppoweruk/using RPI as comparison

74   IWM: 99/82/1, Private papers of N. Flekser, 'Operations: Memoirs of the Great Escape', p. 34

75   *The Times* (London), 19 May 1944, 'Personal Tribute – Squadron Leader R. Bushell' by G. D. Roberts, KC

76   Brickhill, *The Great Escape*, p. 33

77   George Harsh, *Lonesome Road* (London: Sphere
      Books, 1976), p. 165

Chapter Three: Surrounded by Pines

1   Bob Vanderstok, *War Pilot of Orange* (Missoula,
      Montana: Pictorial Histories Publishing, 1987),
      p. 110

2   BA: MSG 2/1517, Militärgeschichtliche Sammlung
      (Lindeiner gen. von Wildau: *Im Dienst der Deutschen
      Luftwaffe*), p. 66

3   USAFAL: The Historical Collection of Stalag Luft III,
      MS 699 (Spivey), A Report by Professor Dr Gustav
      Simoleit, p. 8

4   The outlines of the camp are visible on Google Earth
      at 51.599152 N, 15.307645 E. Breslau is today called
      Wrocław.

5   BA: MSG 2/1517, Lindeiner, *Im Dienst*, p. 69

6   UKNA: WO 208/2901; GWDN: 1116.

7   Arthur A. Durand, *Stalag Luft III: The Secret Story*
      (New York: Touchstone, 1989), p. 103

8   UKNA: WO 208/2901; GWDN: 1117

9   Brickhill, *The Great Escape*, pp. 40–2; Vance, *A
      Gallant Company*, pp. 106–7

10   Stephen P. L. Johnson, *A Kriegie's Log* (Tunbridge
      Wells: Parapress Ltd, 1995), pp. 135–6

11   Jerry Sage, *Sage* (Pennsylvania: Miles Standish Press,
      1985), p. 112

12   Ibid., p. 113

13   William Ash, *Under the Wire* (London: Bantam,
      2006), pp. 155–6. Ash refers to the foodstuff as
      klipfish.

14   B. A. 'Jimmy' James, *Moonless Night* (Barnsley: Pen
      and Sword Military Kindle Edition, 2010), location
      1448

15   Interview with Charles Woehrle at http://www.youtube.com/watchv=DKv280IA4cI

16   Vance, *A Gallant Gompany*, p. 104

17   T. D. Calnan, *Free as a Running Fox* (New York: Dial Press, 1970), p. 153

18   IWM: 99/82/1, Flekser, 'Operations', p. 28

19   Brickhill, *The Great Escape*, p. 40

20   IWM: 85/50/1, Papers of C. G. King

21   Author interview with Alfie 'Bill' Fripp, 9 September 2011

22   Johnson, *A Kriegie's Log*, pp. 123–4

23   IWM: 05/68/1, Private papers of F/O L. G. Hall, 'Prisoner of War' (unpublished m/s), p. 6

24   IWM: Sound Archive recording 4809, Interview with Robert Lionel Lamb, Reel 2 ('cabbages') & Reel 3 ('introspective')

25   Johnson, *A Kriegie's Log*, p. 139

26   RAFM: X002-5428, Extract from *The Prisoner of War* magazine, February 1944, p. 3, 'Our Life as I See It'; GWDN: 5338

27   IWM: 05/68/1, Hall, 'Prisoner of War', p. 17

28   Brickhill, *The Great Escape*, p. 50

29   Interview with Charles Woehrle at http://www.youtube.com/watchv=DKv280IA4cI

30   USAFAL: MS 699 (Spivey), Simoleit, p. 16

31   Ibid., pp. 16–17

32   Johnson, *A Kriegie's Log*, p. 141

33   Vance, *A Gallant Company*, pp. 247–8

34   Johnson, *A Kriegie's Log*, p. 156–7

35   Martin Smith, *What a Bloody Arrival* (Lewes: Book Guild, 1997), p. 118

36   USAFAL: MS 699 (Spivey), Simoleit, p. 16

37   Richard Passmore, *Moving Tent* (London: Thomas Harmsworth, 1982), p. 161

38   IWM: Sound Archive recording 27064, Interview with Maurice Driver, Reel 12

39   IWM: 85/50/1, Papers of C. G. King

40   IWM: 99/82/1, Flekser, 'Operations', p. 58

41   The full list of productions can be seen in BA: MSG 2/1517, Lindeiner, *Im Dienst*, p. 111

42   USAFAL: MS 699 (Spivey), Simoleit, p. 17

43   Author interview with Alfie 'Bill' Fripp, 9 September 2011

44   Ash, *Under the Wire*, p. 154

45   For an exemplary appraisal of the relationship between the POWs and those who guarded them, see S. P. MacKenzie, *The Colditz Myth* (OUP, 2004), Chapter 3, 'Compounds and Commandants'.

46   RAFM: X002-5428, *The Prisoner of War*, p. 3; GWDN: 5338

47   The best summations of von Lindeiner's career can be found in Durand, *Stalag Luft III*, pp. 125–7, and http://en.wikipedia.org/wiki/Friedrich_Wilhelm_von_Lindeiner-Wildau

48   USAFAL: MS 699 (Spivey), Simoleit, pp. 8–9. I have modified the punctuation for clarity.

49   Author interview with Alfie 'Bill' Fripp, 9 September 2011

50   Albert P. Clark, *33 Months as a POW in Stalag Luft III* (Colorado: Fulcrum Publishing, 2004), p. 55

51   USAFAL: MS 699 (Spivey), Simoleit, p. 9

52   Ibid., p. 14

53   Ibid., pp. 15–16

54   Ibid., p. 3

55   RAFM: X001-2316/009/012, Wartime Log of Flt Lt Bennett Ley Kenyon, 1943–1946

56   IWM: 99/82/1, Flekser, 'Operations', p. 58

57   Walter Morison, *Flak and Ferrets* (London: Sentinel
      Publishing, 1995), p. 84
58   Ibid., p. 138
59   Ibid., p. 136
60   IWM: 26558, Cassie, Reel 22
61   Morison, *Flak and Ferrets*, p. 138
62   Brickhill, *The Great Escape*, p. 34
63   Carroll, *The Great Escape*, p. 39. It is unlikely that
      Pieber won the Blood Order for participating in the
      Munich 'Beer Hall' Putsch of 1923. According to a
      post-war investigation contained in UKNA: AIR
      40/2488, Air Ministry, Directorate of Intelligence and
      related bodies: Intelligence Reports and Papers;
      GWDN: 9580, Pieber only held the War Service Cross
      Class 2 with Swords and was an engineer by trade, and
      not involved in education.
64   IWM: 99/82/1, Flekser, 'Operations', p. 58
65   See pp. 86–7.
66   USAFAL: MS 699 (Spivey), Simoleit, p. 11
67   USAFAL: MS 329 (Clark), Oral History Interview
      with Hermann Glemnitz 9 & 10 April 1984, pp. 3–8
68   UKNA: AIR 40/2488, Air Ministry, Directorate of
      Intelligence and related bodies: Intelligence Reports
      and Papers; GWDN: 9562; USAFAL: MS 329
      (Clark), Glemnitz, p. 14. Peschl was transferred to
      Heydekrug in June 1943.
69   John Dominy, *The Sergeant Escapers* (London: Ian
      Allan, 1974), p. 46
70   IWM: 26558; Cassie, Reel 12
71   Author interview with Alfie 'Bill' Fripp, 9 September
      2011
72   Vanderstok, *War Pilot*, p. 120
73   IWM: 26558, Cassie, Reel 22
74   Brickhill, *The Great Escape*, p. 44

75   USAFAL: MS 329 (Clark), Glemnitz, p. 35

76   IWM: Sound Archive recording 23327, Interview
     with Geoffrey Cornish, Reel 4

77   USAFAL: MS 329 (Clark), Glemnitz, pp. 25–6

78   BA: MSG 2/1517, Lindeiner, *Im Dienst*, p. 122

79   USAFAL: MS 329 (Clark), Glemnitz, p. 22

80   UKNA: AIR 2/10121, Air Ministry and Ministry of
     Defence: Registered Files, COURTS OF INQUIRY
     AND INQUESTS (Code B, 29): Court of Inquiry:
     killing of fifty R.A.F. officers from Stalag Luft III,
     Testimony of Flying Officer P. E. Thomas, p. 19;
     GWDN: 9625

81   IWM: 26558, Cassie, Reel 22

82   Author interview with Alfie 'Bill' Fripp, 9 September
     2011

83   IWM: Sound Archive recording 27271, Interview
     with Leonard Hall, Reel 4

84   IWM: Sound Archive recording 27051, Interview
     with Alan Bryett, Reel 11

85   Vanderstok, *War Pilot*, p. 120

Chapter Four: 'Escaping was a real objective'

1   Many accounts, such as those of Smith, Carroll and
     Brickhill, refer to Day as the SBO. This is contradicted
     by the recollections of von Lindeiner in BA: MSG
     2/1517, *Im Dienst*, p. 73. Day was only to be SBO of
     the north compound from June to September 1943. See
     UKNA: AIR 40/2645; Air Ministry, Directorate of
     Intelligence and related bodies: Intelligence Reports and
     Papers; GWDN: 9335

2   Smith, '*Wings' Day*, p. 116; Brickhill, *The Great
     Escape*, p. 28

3   IWM: Sound Archive recording 6095, Interview with
     Eric Foinette, Reel 3

4   Carroll, *The Great Escape*, pp. 84–6

5   Smith, *'Wings' Day*, pp. 116–17

6   Brickhill, *The Great Escape*, p. 30

7   Ivo Tonder & Ladislav Sitensky, *Na nebi i v pekle* (Czech Republic: Edice Pilot, 1997), p. 35. The tunnel Tonder was referring to was Harry, but I have inserted the anecdote here for thematic reasons.

8   IWM: 99/82/1, Flekser, 'Operations', p. 41

9   Smith, *'Wings' Day*, p. 119

10   Brickhill, *The Great Escape*, p. 31. Brickhill claims the tunnel was blown up, but Smith states it was flooded, which is more likely.

11   UKNA: AIR 40/2275, Air Ministry, Directorate of Intelligence and related bodies: Intelligence Reports and Papers, Statements by ex P.O.Ws who took part in the mass escape from Stalag Luft III; GWDN: 9319

12   Brickhill, *The Great Escape*, p. 31

13   USAFAL: MS 699 (Spivey), Simoleit, p. 10

14   Clark, *33 Months*, pp. 70–1

15   IWM: Sound Archive recording 31698, Interview with John Birbeck, Reel 7

16   Harsh, *Lonesome Road*, p. 16

17   Ibid., p. 95

18   Carroll, *The Great Escape*, p. 90

19   Harsh, *Lonesome Road*, p. 172

20   Ibid., p. 160

21   IWM: 27731, Dowse, Reel 5; IWM: Sound Archive recording 30046, Interview with Bud Clark, Reel 1

22   IWM: 26558, Cassie, Reel 15

23   Ibid.

24   IWM: 26558, Cassie, Reel 11

25   *The Times* (London), 24 May 1946, In Memoriam column

26   IWM: 26558, Cassie, Reel 15

27   Harsh, *Lonesome Road*, pp. 168–9

28   Vance, *A Gallant Company*, p. 96

29   Harsh, *Lonesome Road*, p. 169

30   Morison, *Flak and Ferrets*, p. 83

31   IWM: 99/82/1, Flekser, 'Operations', p. 40

32   IWM: 27051, Bryett, Reel 12

33   IWM: 99/82/1, Flekser, 'Operations', p. 45

34   IWM: 27064, Driver, Reel 8

35   IWM: Sound Archive recording 27813, Interview
      with Jack Rae, Reel 6

36   IWM: Sound Archive recording 10643, Interview
      with Patrick Palles Lorne Elphinstone Welch

37   IWM: 13296, Churchill, Reel 4

38   IWM: 27731, Dowse, Reel 4

39   IWM: 27731, Dowse, Reel 2

40   USAFAL: MS 329 (Clark), Glemnitz, p. 36

41   Mail Online, 1 July 2011,
      http://www.dailymail.co.uk/news/
      article-2010014/Great-Escape-veterans-letter-edition-
      book-Oxfam.html

42   Ash, *Under the Wire*, p. 153

43   Ken Rees, *Lie in the Dark and Listen* (London: Grub
      Street, 2009), p. 140

44   Harsh, *Lonesome Road*, p. 166

45   IWM: 06/51/1, Papers of F/Lt J. Hall

46   Johnson, *A Kriegie's Log*, p. 124

47   Clark, *33 Months*, pp. 58–9

48   IWM: Sound Archive recording 6176, Interview with
      George Arthur Atkinson, Reel 2

49   Passmore, *Moving Tent*, p. 165

50   IWM: Sound Archive recording 6142, Interview with
      James Alexander Graham 'Dixie' Deans, Reel 3

51   IWM: 6176, Atkinson, Reel 2

52   IWM: Sound Archive recording 4987, Interview with

Jimmy James, Reel 6. James estimates that some 500 were active escapers. Richard Churchill in IWM: 13296, Churchill, Reel 2, puts the number at around 600 to 700. The 1 to 2 ratio between escapers and stayers seems correct.

53   IWM: 99/82/1, Flekser, 'Operations', p. 40
54   Interview with Brigadier Hugh Ironside at http://www.youtube.com/watchv=6Qko_e0TLKA
55   IWM: 05/4/1, Private Papers of R. A. Bethell
56   IWM: Sound Archive recording 25030, Interview with Walter Morison, Reel 1
57   Mail Online, 1 July 2011, http://www.dailymail.co.uk/news/article-2010014/Great-Escape-veterans-letter-edition-book-Oxfam.html
58   IWM: 6095, Foinette, Reel 3
59   IWM: 27731, Dowse, Reel 5
60   IWM: 31698, Birbeck, Reel 7; IWM: Sound Archive recording 26605, Interview with Paul Gordon Royle, Reel 5
61   IWM: 13296, Churchill, Reel 2
62   UKNA: AIR 40/2488; GWDN: 9547–9548
63   IWM: Sound Archive recording 15558, Interview with Arthur Westcombe Cole, Reel 3
64   IWM: 25030, Morison, Reel 1
65   RAFM: AP 1548, *The Responsibilities of a Prisoner of War*
66   Correspondence with David Turns of Cranfield University, 12 November 2010
67   IWM: 6176, Atkinson, Reel 2
68   IWM: 26605, Royle, Reel 5
69   IWM: 99/82/1, Flekser, 'Operations', p. 75
70   USAFAL: MS 329 (Clark), Glemnitz, p. 26

Chapter Five: Tom, Dick and Harry

1 Rees, *Lie in the Dark*, p. 127
2 Ibid., pp. 128-9
3 MacKenzie, *The Colditz Myth*, p. 105
4 Ibid., pp. 99-100
5 UKNA: AIR 40/2645, Air Ministry, Directorate of Intelligence and related bodies: Intelligence Reports and Papers; GWDN: 9363
6 UKNA: AIR 40/2645; GWDN: 9364
7 Ibid.; Brickhill, *The Great Escape*, p. 47
8 UKNA: AIR 40/2645; GWDN: 9364
9 Brickhill, *The Great Escape*, p. 46
10 IWM: Sound Archive recording 8276, Interview with Thomas Robert Nelson, Reel 1. The Nelson interview has been transcribed and is also held by the IWM.
11 IWM: 8276, Nelson, Reel 1
12 UKNA: AIR 40/2645; GWDN: 9365
13 Brickhill, *The Great Escape*, p. 48
14 IWM: 05/68/1, Hall, 'Prisoner of War', p. 8
15 *Aeroplane* magazine, August 2007, pp. 22-7; http://www.flyingmarines.com/History/Documents/Skua_Article.pdf
16 IWM: 05/68/1, Hall, 'Prisoner of War', p. 9
17 UKNA: AIR 40/2645; GWDN: 9369
18 UKNA: AIR 40/2645; GWDN: 9370
19 UKNA: AIR 40/2645; GWDN: 9371
20 UKNA: AIR 40/2645; GWDN: 9372
21 IWM: 25030, Morison, Reel 1
22 IWM: 99/82/1, Flekser, 'Operations', pp. 52-3
23 IWM: Sound Archive recording 25029, Interview with Ken Rees, Reel 2
24 IWM: Sound Archive recording 28532, Interview with Jack Lyon, Reel 7
25 Rees, *Lie in the Dark*, p. 124

26　　Ibid., p. 122

27　　IWM: 25029, Rees, Reel 2

28　　Ibid.

29　　Rees, *Lie in the Dark*, p. 154

30　　Ibid.

31　　BA: MSG 2/1517, Lindeiner, *Im Dienst*, p. 165

32　　UKNA: AIR 40/170, Air Ministry, Directorate of
　　　Intelligence and related bodies: Intelligence Reports
　　　and Papers; GWDN: 0396

33　　Brickhill, *The Great Escape*, pp. 94-5

34　　UKNA: AIR 40/2273, Air Ministry, Directorate of
　　　Intelligence and related bodies: Intelligence Reports
　　　and Papers, Progress reports, general information and
　　　instructions from Judge Advocate General's Office;
　　　GWDN: 0166

35　　UKNA: FO 916/840, Foreign Office: Consular (War)
　　　Department, later Prisoners of War Department:
　　　Registered Files, Stalag Luft III; GWDN: 1278

36　　UKNA: AIR 40/2491; Air Ministry, Directorate of
　　　Intelligence and related bodies: Intelligence Reports
　　　and Papers, Reports Nos 181-240, Statement by
　　　Wing Commander H. M. A. Day; GWDN: 9782

37　　UKNA: WO 311/997; Judge Advocate General's
　　　Office, Military Deputy's Department, and War
　　　Office, Directorates of Army Legal Services and
　　　Personal Services: War Crimes Files (MO/JAG/FS and
　　　other series), Shooting of 50 RAF officers at Stalag
　　　Luft III, Sagan, Poland, March 1944: original
　　　statements; GWDN: 0773

38　　Ibid.

39　　Ibid.

40　　See p. 147.

41　　UKNA: AIR 40/2275, Statement by Wing
　　　Commander H. M. A. Day; GWDN: 9318

42   James, *Moonless Night*, location 1629

43   UKNA: AIR 40/2275; GWDN: 9324

44   UKNA: WO 311/759, Judge Advocate General's Office, Military Deputy's Department, and War Office, Directorates of Army Legal Services and Personal Services: War Crimes Files (MO/JAG/FS and other series), Escape from Stalag 357, Fallingbostel, Germany, Stalag Luft III, Sagan, Poland, and Stalag Luft VI, Heydekrug, Lithuania; GWDN: 1579

45   USAFAL: MS 329 (Clark); Glemnitz, p. 26

46   UKNA: AIR 40/2274; Air Ministry, Directorate of Intelligence and related bodies: Intelligence Reports and Papers, SPECIAL INVESTIGATION BRANCH, BRITISH AIR FORCES OF OCCUPATION, Prisoners of War: killing of 50 R.A.F. and other officers from Stalag Luft III, R.S.H.A. (Reichssicherheitshauptamt (Main Office for the Security of the Reich)) Amt V (Kriminal Polizei) central organisation and centrally directed activities: E.D.S. (Evaluation and Dissemination Section) reports; GWDN: 0169–0174

47   See p. 131 and for Pieber, see p. 181.

48   Harsh, *Lonesome Road*, pp. 178–9

49   IWM: 26605, Royle, Reel 4

50   Ibid.

51   IWM: 27051, Bryett, Reel 12

52   IWM: 27051, Bryett, Reel 13

53   UKNA: AIR 2/10121; GWDN: 9654

54   See p. 128.

55   IWM: 13296, Churchill, Reel 2. I have tidied up the quote for clarity. The actual interview reads: 'There was always going to be some risk if you were outside the wire and there were people with guns who could shoot at you. I suppose that for most of us the feeling

was nevertheless there . . . One had a certain comfort in the feeling that there was a Red Cross Convention that it was laid down it was an officer's duty to escape and one didn't expect too severe treatment if one was caught having done so.'

56 IWM: 8276, Nelson, Reel 3
57 USAFAL: MS 699 (Spivey), Simoleit, p. 22

Chapter Six: An Anglo-German Affair

1 UKNA: AIR 40/2645; GWDN: 9366
2 Clark, *33 Months*, p. 91
3 Brickhill, *The Great Escape*, pp. 112–13. Carroll, *The Great Escape*, p. 138, states that Tom was within 10 feet of the woods.
4 For involvement of microphones in detecting Tom, see UKNA: AIR 40/170; GWDN: 0396
5 Brickhill, *The Great Escape*, p. 113
6 Ibid., p. 114
7 Ibid., p. 115
8 UKNA: AIR 40/2645; GWDN: 9366
9 Brickhill, *The Great Escape*, p. 115. Brickhill states that it was Glemnitz himself who discovered the tunnel, whereas Glemnitz in USAFAL: MS 329 (Clark), p. 26, says that it was one of his men.
10 IWM: 99/82/1, Flekser, 'Operations', p. 54. Flekser's memory may be at fault – there are numerous POW memoirs from many different camps which feature a variation on these words uttered by a hapless German. The more popular variant is '. . . fuck nothing/fuck all . . .' See MacKenzie, *The Colditz Myth*.
11 BA: MSG 2/1517, Lindeiner, *Im Dienst*, pp. 172–7
12 Brickhill, *The Great Escape*, p. 116
13 Ibid., p. 117; Carroll, *The Great Escape*, p. 139. For

the length of tunnel, see UKNA: AIR 40/2645; GWDN: 9366

14 UKNA: AIR 40/2645; GWDN: 9366

15 Brickhill, *The Great Escape*, p. 117

16 IWM: 13296, Churchill, Reel 4

17 IWM: 26558, Cassie, Reel 15

18 IWM: 26558, Cassie, Reel 21

19 IWM: 27731, Dowse, Reel 4

20 IWM: 26558, Cassie, Reel 15

21 UKNA: WO 311/759; GWDN: 1575

22 UKNA: WO 311/759; GWDN: 1578

23 Ibid.

24 WM: 27731, Dowse, Reel 5

25 Ibid.

26 Calnan, *Free*, p. 233

27 UKNA: WO 311/759; GWDN: 1578

28 Vanderstok, *War Pilot*, p. 124

29 Ibid.

30 IWM: 27731, Dowse, Reel 5; for radio parts, Reel 6; for money, maps and ration cards, Reel 3

31 UKNA: WO 311/171, Judge Advocate General's Office, Military Deputy's Department, and War Office, Directorates of Army Legal Services and Personal Services: War Crimes Files (MO/JAG/FS and other series), Stalag Luft 3, Sagan, Germany: escape, recapture and killing of RAF officers; GWDN: 0411. For mention of Hesse's brother, see UKNA: WO 311/759; GWDN: 1581

32 Calnan, *Free*, p. 248

33 UKNA: WO 311/759; GWDN: 1579

34 In his memoirs Calnan claims that the idea for the escape was his, and that he only enlisted Hesse to help purloin armbands and provide a typewriter. See Calnan, *Free*, pp. 247-54.

35   Calnan, *Free*, p. 249

36   UKNA: WO 311/759; GWDN: 1580 & 1581. For
      the date, see Calnan, *Free*, p. 252.

37   Calnan, *Free*, p. 248

38   UKNA: WO 311/759; GWDN: 1581

39   M. R. D. Foot & J. M. Langley, *MI9: Escape and
      Evasion 1939–1945* (London: Book Club Associates,
      1979), pp. 178–9

40   IWM: 26558, Cassie, Reels 18–19. For Fischer, see
      UKNA: AIR 40/2645; GWDN: 9350. For details on
      how jelly presses work, see http://en.wikipedia.org/
      wiki/Hectograph, and to create a press using Turkish
      delight, see http://www.fell.demon.co.uk/steve/jelly.
      html

41   UKNA: AIR 2/10121; GWDN: 9607

42   UKNA: AIR 40/2645; GWDN: 9357

43   UKNA: WO 311/759; GWDN: 1579

44   UKNA: WO 311/759; GWDN: 1580

45   Ibid.

46   See Epilogue

47   UKNA: WO 311/759; GWDN: 1580

48   UKNA: AIR 40/285, Air Ministry, Directorate of
      Intelligence and related bodies: Intelligence Reports
      and Papers, DEPUTY DIRECTORATE OF
      INTELLIGENCE (ORGANISATION) AIR
      INTELLIGENCE 1 (a) P/W, Stalag Luft III (Sagan):
      report 'X' compiled by members of escape
      organisations; GWDN: 9474

49   IWM: 27813, Rae, Reel 5

50   USAFAL: MS 699 (Spivey), Simoleit, p. 12

51   UKNA: AIR 40/285, Testimony of R. G. Walker;
      GWDN: 9460–9461; and see USAFAL: MS 699
      (Spivey), Simoleit, p. 21.

52   UKNA: WO 208/3628, War Office: Directorate of

Military Operations and Intelligence, and Directorate of Military Intelligence, Ministry of Defence, Defence Intelligence Staff, Prisoner of War Interrogation Section (Home) Kempton Park: interrogation reports, K.P. 636 (Lengnick, Franz); GWDN: 1100

53 UKNA: WO 208/2901; GWDN: 1127

54 I immodestly present this as Walters's Law.

55 UKNA: AIR 40/170; GWDN: 0400

56 UKNA: AIR 40/170; GWDN: 0398

57 UKNA: AIR 40/170; GWDN: 0401

58 Ibid.

59 UKNA: WO 311/993, Judge Advocate General's Office, Military Deputy's Department, and War Office, Directorates of Army Legal Services and Personal Services: War Crimes Files, Shooting of 50 RAF officers at Stalag Luft III, Sagan, Poland, March 1944: witness statements; GWDN: 0699

60 See p. 127.

61 USAFAL: MS 329 (Clark), Glemnitz, p. 36

62 UKNA: AIR 40/170; GWDN: 0401

63 See p. 140.

64 UKNA: AIR 40/170; GWDN: 0396

65 UKNA: AIR 40/170; GWDN: 0402

66 IWM: 23327, Cornish, Reel 3

67 IWM: 31698, Birbeck, Reel 7

68 IWM: 27731, Dowse, Reel 5

69 UKNA: AIR 40/170; GWDN: 0399

70 UKNA: AIR 40/170; GWDN: 0400

71 UKNA: AIR 40/2645; GWDN: 9352 & 9353

72 Ibid.

73 See p. 90.

74 IWM: 99/82/1, Flekser, 'Operations', p. 59

75 See p. 154–5.

Chapter Seven: Harry Reawakens

1   Yes, the Kripo rank is a mouthful. Wielen's rank roughly equates to the British police rank of Detective Chief Inspector – see table in appendices, p. 441.

2   UKNA: AIR 40/2292, Air Ministry, Directorate of Intelligence and related bodies: Intelligence Reports and Papers, SPECIAL INVESTIGATION BRANCH, BRITISH AIR FORCES OF OCCUPATION, Prisoners of War: killing of 50 R.A.F. and other officers from Stalag Luft III, Interrogation reports and statements: documents re SIB/1084/45; GWDN: 9513

3   BA: N 54/36, Keitel, Wilhelm; Generalmajor Westhoff, interviews with Lindeiner; Scharpwinkel; Wielen; Absalon; etc; GWDN: 099

4   UKNA: WO 311/1000, Judge Advocate General's Office, Military Deputy's Department, and War Office, Directorates of Army Legal Services and Personal Services: War Crimes Files (MO/JAG/FS and other series), Shooting of 50 RAF officers at Stalag Luft III, Sagan, Poland, March 1944: working papers; GWDN: 1606

5   Durand, *Stalag Luft III*, pp. 310–11

6   UKNA: WO 311/1000; GWDN: 1622

7   Ibid.

8   UKNA: AIR 40/2488; GWDN: 9564

9   Rees, *Lie in the Dark*, p. 168

10   Johnson, *A Kriegie's Log*, p. 162

11   UKNA: WO 224/63B, War Office: International Red Cross and Protecting Powers (Geneva): Reports concerning Prisoner of War Camps in Europe and the Far East, Unnumbered Reports, Stalag Luft III (after move to Nuremburg); GWDN: 1676–1677

12   Ibid.

13   Rees, *Lie in the Dark*, p. 168

14 UKNA: AIR 40/2645; GWDN: 9367

15 Carroll, *The Great Escape*, p. 169

16 UKNA: AIR 40/2645; GWDN: 9372

17 IWM: 26558, Cassie, Reel 18

18 IWM: 28532, Lyon, Reel 7

19 UKNA: AIR 40/2491, Testimony made by Peter Mohr; GWDN: 9813. For the error, see UKNA: WO 311/177, Judge Advocate General's Office, Military Deputy's Department, and War Office, Directorates of Army Legal Services and Personal Services: War Crimes Files (MO/JAG/FS and other series), Stalag Luft 3, Sagan, Germany: escape, recapture and killing of RAF officers; GWDN: 0588. For a similar error, see Foot & Langley, *MI9*, p. 132. Sorau is now called Zary.

20 Vanderstok, *War Pilot*, pp. 109–110

21 IWM: 26558, Cassie, Reel 18

22 UKNA: AIR 40/2645; GWDN: 9353

23 Vanderstok, *War Pilot*, p. 109

24 UKNA: AIR 40/2645; GWDN: 9354

25 IWM: 26558, Cassie, Reel 19

26 IWM: 26558, Cassie, Reel 18

27 IWM: 26558, Cassie, Reel 15

28 IWM: 26558, Cassie, Reel 19

29 RAFM: X003-6188/002, Notebook kept by Flt Lt Tommy Guest whilst a POW, n.d.

30 UKNA: AIR 40/2645; GWDN: 9347

31 RAFM: X003-6188/002

32 Ibid.

33 UKNA: AIR 40/2645; GWDN: 9348–9349

34 RAFM: X003-6188/002

35 UKNA: AIR 40/2645; GWDN: 9355. During the war, MI9 was also referred to as IS9.

36 Foot & Langley, *MI9*, p. 131

37 UKNA: AIR 40/2645; GWDN: 9355

38 UKNA: AIR 40/2645; GWDN: 9361

39 UKNA: AIR 40/2645; GWDN: 9362

40 Brickhill, *The Great Escape*, p. 151

41 Rees, *Lie in the Dark*, p. 171

42 Johnson, *A Kriegie's Log*, p. 126

43 BA: MSG 2/1517, Lindeiner, *Im Dienst*, p. 178

44 USAFAL: MS 329 (Clark), Glemnitz, p. 36

Chapter Eight: The Warnings

1 BA: MSG 2/1517, Lindeiner, *Im Dienst,* p. 179;
Durand, *Stalag Luft III*, p. 311

2 UKNA: AIR 40/2489, Air Ministry, Directorate of
Intelligence and related bodies: Intelligence Reports
and Papers, SAGAN, STALAG LUFT III CAMP:
MURDER OF 50 RAF OFFICERS, Reports Nos
61–120; GWDN: 9687

3 Durand, *Stalag Luft III*, p. 311

4 IWM: 4987, James, Reel 6

5 James, *Moonless Night*, location 1796

6 UKNA: AIR 40/2275, Statement of Flight Lieutenant
H. C. Marshall; GWDN: 9323

7 UKNA: WO 311/993; GWDN: 0699–0700

8 UKNA: WO 208/2901; GWDN: 1128

9 UKNA: AIR 2/10121; GWDN: 9649

10 For the full text of the *Kugel Erlass*, visit
http://www.ess.uwe.ac.uk/genocide/kugel.htm

11 For this analysis, see UKNA: AIR 40/2273; GWDN:
0167

12 UKNA: AIR 40/2488; GWDN: 9563

13 IWM: 4987, James, Reel 6

14 Ibid.

15 BA: MSG 2/1517, Lindeiner, *Im Dienst*, p. 185

16 Ibid.

17   See, for example, Carroll, *The Great Escape*, p. 181
18   UKNA: WO 311/759; GWDN: 1585
19   UKNA: WO 311/1000; GWDN: 1631
20   Brickhill, *The Great Escape*, p. 158; UKNA: AIR
      40/2645; GWDN: 9367 states a similar length of 345
      feet.
21   Ibid.
22   Rees, *Lie in the Dark*, p. 172
23   IWM: 05/4/1, Private papers of R. A. Bethell
24   Rees, *Lie in the Dark*, p. 172
25   IWM: 99/82/1, Flekser, 'Operations', p. 63
26   UKNA: AIR 40/2488; GWDN: 9562–9573
27   UKNA: AIR 40/2488; GWDN: 9577
28   See p. 130–1.
29   It is not clear from the minutes whether Brünner's
      figure only included escaping POWs. See UKNA: AIR
      40/2488; GWDN: 9574
30   UKNA: AIR 40/2488; GWDN: 9573–9575
31   Brickhill, *The Great Escape*, p. 160
32   Rees, *Lie in the Dark*, p. 172
33   IWM: 4987, James, Reel 6. The new moon rose on
      the afternoon (CET) of the 24th. See
      http://eclipse.gsfc.nasa.gov/phase/phases1901.html
34   Ibid.
35   IWM: 99/82/1, Flekser, 'Operations', pp. 44–5
36   IWM: 26558, Cassie, Reel 20
37   Ibid.
38   UKNA: AIR 40/2275; GWDN: 9328–9330
39   IWM: 4987, James, Reel 3
40   UKNA: WO 311/1000; GWDN: 1632
41   UKNA: WO 311/1000; GWDN: 1633
42   UKNA: AIR 40/2645; GWDN: 9382. There are many
      versions of how the draw was conducted. I have used
      the official RAF report.

43   IWM: 26558, Cassie, Reel 20

44   UKNA: AIR 40/2645; GWDN: 9382

45   Rees, *Lie in the Dark*, p. 175

46   Gill, *The Great Escape*, p. 171

47   UKNA: AIR 40/2645; GWDN: 9382; Carroll, *The Great Escape*, p. 193

48   Brickhill, *The Great Escape*, p. 163

49   IWM: 27731, Dowse, Reel 7

50   Carroll, *The Great Escape*, p. 194

51   Brickhill, *The Great Escape*, p. 166

52   IWM: 05/68/1, Hall, 'Prisoner of War', pp. 9–10

53   Historical weather maps can be found at www. wetterzentrale.de

54   IWM: 05/68/1, Hall, 'Prisoner of War', p. 10

Chapter Nine: The Great Escape

1   IWM: Sound Archive recording 17365, Interview with Frank Ogden Waddington, Reel 5

2   Rees, *Lie in the Dark*, p. 176

3   IWM: 26558, Cassie, Reel 21

4   IWM: 28532, Lyon, Reel 7

5   UKNA: WO 309/529, War Office: Judge Advocate General's Office, British Army of the Rhine War Crimes Group (North West Europe) and predecessors: Registered Files (BAOR and other series), Stalag Luft 3, Sagan, Germany: escape, recapture and killing of RAF officers; GWDN: 1527

6   Vanderstok, *War Pilot*, p. 147

7   Rees, *Lie in the Dark*, p. 177

8   Les Brodrick quoted in Gill, *The Great Escape*, p. 177

9   IWM: 27051, Bryett, Reel 14

10   IWM: 99/82/1, Flekser, 'Operations', p. 68

11   Carroll, *The Great Escape*, pp. 190–1; Stephen R.

Davies, *RAF Police: The 'Great Escape' Murders* (Bognor Regis: Woodfield, 2009), p. 51

12   Jens Müller, *Tre Kom Tilbake* (Oslo: Gyldendal, 1946), p. 112. Müller's book is often overlooked, mainly because it is written in Norwegian and is also out of print. Researchers wishing to consult it are welcome to email me requesting an electronic copy. Please note: I cannot supply an English translation.

13   UKNA: AIR 40/2645; GWDN: 9368. For Marshall's account see UKNA: AIR 40/2490, Air Ministry, Directorate of Intelligence and related bodies: Intelligence Reports and Papers, SAGAN, STALAG LUFT III CAMP: MURDER OF 50 RAF OFFICERS, Reports Nos 121–180; GWDN: 9755

14   Brickhill, *The Great Escape*, p. 177

15   IWM: 27731, Dowse, Reel 7

16   UKNA: AIR 40/2645; GWDN: 9355

17   Interview with John Weir at http://www.youtube.com/watchv=J18RMQupsu0

18   Ibid.

19   RAFM: X001-2316/009/048, Log of Flt Lt Bennett Ley Kenyon

20   UKNA: WO 208/2901; GWDN: 1115–1118

21   RAFM: AL00057 (also listed as 306/0404/00004), photo album 'Tunnel to Freedom'

22   See testimonies contained in UKNA: AIR 40/2645.

23   UKNA: AIR 40/2645; GWDN: 9458

24   See p. 186. Brickhill, *The Great Escape*, p. 158, states 348 feet.

25   See, for example, Brickhill, *The Great Escape*, p. 177; Vanderstok, *War Pilot*, p. 147; IWM: 27051, Bryett, Reel 14; IWM: 27731, Dowse, Reel 3; IWM: 8276, Nelson, Reel 2

26   IWM: 8276, Nelson, Reel 2

27   See UKNA: AIR 40/2645; GWDN: 9384, which
       mentions the problems of the blanket carriers and the
       dislodged timber.

28   Brickhill, *The Great Escape*, p. 180. According to
       other sources, the rope system was not employed, at
       least not for the first several escapers. The RAF
       report (UKNA: AIR 40/2645; GWDN: 9383) states
       that Johnny Bull simply lay on a blanket at the top of
       the shaft and pressed down on an escaper's head until
       it was safe for him to emerge. It seems unlikely,
       despite the darkness, that Bull would have risked
       being quite so exposed. In his interview with the
       Imperial War Museum, Sydney Dowse claims that no
       rope was used, and that it was 'up and out' and that
       every man looked out for himself: 'They climbed up
       the ladder, very carefully looked around first, and
       when it seemed clear, and the guard in the sentry
       tower had his back to them, they would go out.'
       (IWM: 27731, Dowse, Reel 3)

29   Mittelwalde is today called Międzylesie.

30   UKNA: AIR 40/2490, Air Ministry, Directorate of
       Intelligence and related bodies: Intelligence Reports
       and Papers, SAGAN, STALAG LUFT III CAMP:
       MURDER OF 50 RAF OFFICERS, Reports Nos
       121–180; GWDN: 9754–9759; UKNA: WO 309/529;
       GWDN: 1526–1528

31   UKNA: AIR 40/2490; GWDN: 9758. Marshall made
       at least three testimonies after the war, and it is
       unclear whether ten men assembled in the woods, or
       twenty. As Bob Vanderstok was in the first twenty
       and does not mention meeting the group in the
       woods, I have assumed that some ten to twelve men
       gathered at this point.

32   UKNA: AIR 40/2275; GWDN: 9320

33   UKNA: AIR 40/2490; GWDN: 9758

34   Desmond L. Plunkett & The Reverend R. Pletts, *The Man Who Would Not Die* (Durham: Pentland Press, 2000), pp. 40–1

35   UKNA: AIR 40/2490; GWDN: 9736

36   UKNA: WO 311/993; GWDN: 0695

37   RAFM: X001-3886, Account of escape of Bram van der Stok given to MI9, 11–12 July 1944; GWDN: 5236

38   Vanderstok, *War Pilot*, p. 149

39   Ibid., p. 150

40   RAFM: X001-3886; GWDN: 5235–5236

41   RAFM: X001-3886; GWDN: 5236; Vanderstok, *War Pilot*, p. 151. Once again, the two accounts do not tally, but there is less discrepancy in this instance than there is with the previous two episodes.

42   Vanderstok, *War Pilot*, p. 151

43   Brickhill, *The Great Escape*, p. 186

44   IWM: 27051, Bryett, Reel 14

45   Royal Air Force Bomber Command 60th Anniversary, Campaign Diary, March 1944, http://www.raf.mod.uk/bombercommand/mar44.html

46   Rees, *Lie in the Dark*, p. 178

47   IWM: 27051, Bryett, Reel 14

48   UKNA: AIR 40/2275; GWDN: 9315

49   IWM: 27731, Dowse, Reel 3

50   Ibid.

51   UKNA: AIR 40/2275; GWDN: 9315

52   IWM: 8276, Nelson, Reel 3

53   IWM: 27051, Bryett, Reel 14

54   IWM: 25029, Rees, Reel 2

55   Tonder & Sitensky, *Na nebi i v pekle*, p. 36

56   Harsh, *Lonesome Road*, p. 176

57 Ibid., p. 177

58 Harsh claims in his book to have been sent to Belaria after the Great Escape, which is untrue. Harsh was no doubt lax with his recall of the order of events in order to satisfy his readers and publisher.

59 UKNA: AIR 40/2490; GWDN: 9740

60 Carroll, *The Great Escape*, pp. 208 & 211

61 IWM: 27051, Bryett, Reel 14

62 UKNA: AIR 40/2645; GWDN: 9392

63 Ibid.

64 Müller, *Tre Kom Tilbake*, p. 119

65 UKNA: AIR 40/2645; GWDN: 9384. See IWM: 25029, Rees, Reel 2, for Rees's assertion that he was to be the last man out.

66 Brickhill, *The Great Escape*, pp. 191–2

67 UKNA: AIR 40/2645; GWDN: 9388

68 UKNA: AIR 40/2490; GWDN: 9761

69 UKNA: AIR 40/2490; GWDN: 9753

70 UKNA: AIR 40/2645; GWDN: 9388

71 For the guard noticing movement, see the Charge Sheet made against Lindeiner and others in UKNA: AIR 40/170; GWDN: 0395

72 Ibid.

73 UKNA: AIR 40/2490; GWDN: 9713

74 Rees, *Lie in the Dark*, p. 179. There is no evidence at all for this story.

75 UKNA: AIR 40/2490; GWDN: 9753

76 IWM: 25029, Rees, Reel 2. Rees incorrectly states that he went back to Piccadilly in this interview, although in his book he would correctly state that it was Leicester Square.

77 Rees, *Lie in the Dark*, p. 179

78 Ibid.

79 Ibid.

80 IWM: 25029, Rees, Reel 2
81 IWM: 27051, Bryett, Reel 14
82 Brickhill, *The Great Escape*, p. 198
83 IWM: 15558, Cole, Reel 3
84 Rees, *Lie in the Dark*, p. 180
85 UKNA: WO 208/2901; GWDN: 1118
86 UKNA: AIR 40/2645; GWDN: 9389
87 BA: N 54/36; GWDN: 113. Many of the times recorded in German-produced documents are an hour earlier than those produced by Allies. I have used the Allied times, not least because they tally with the time of sunrise.
88 UKNA: AIR 40/2645; GWDN: 9389
89 UKNA: WO 208/2901; GWDN: 1118
90 UKNA: AIR 40/2645; GWDN: 9385
91 Rees, *Lie in the Dark*, p. 180
92 IWM: 27051, Bryett, Reel 14
93 Rees, *Lie in the Dark*, p. 180
94 IWM: 25029, Rees, Reel 2
95 IWM: 25029, Rees, Reel 3
96 UKNA: AIR 40/2645; GWDN: 9385
97 IWM: 99/82/1, Flekser, 'Operations', p. 74
98 Durand, *Stalag Luft III*, p. 312
99 Brickhill, *The Great Escape*, pp. 200–201; UKNA: AIR 40/2645, op. cit.; GWDN: 9385
100 BA: N 54/36; GWDN: 113
101 UKNA: HW 16/14, Government Code and Cypher School: German Police Section: Decrypts of German Police Communications during Second World War, 1944 Mar–1945 Mar; GWDN: 0827. The cable is dated 22.3.44, which is clearly an error. I believe it more likely to have been sent on the morning of 25 March.
102 UKNA: WO 235/425, Judge Advocate General's

Office: War Crimes Case Files, Second World War, Stalag Luft III Case, Defendant: Proceedings Place of Trial: Hamburg, 1947 July; GWDN: 1766–1767. In his testimony to the court Wielen claims that he heard immediately that 81 officers had escaped, a figure that was impossible for him to have known until after the *Appell* had taken place later that morning.

103 UKNA: WO 311/1000; GWDN: 1613

104 UKNA: AIR 40/2488; GWDN: 9551

105 UKNA: WO 208/3659, War Office: Directorate of Military Operations and Intelligence, and Directorate of Military Intelligence, Ministry of Defence, Defence Intelligence Staff: File, Prisoner of War Interrogation Section (Home) London District Cage: interrogation reports, L.D.C. 774; GWDN: 1103

106 UKNA: AIR 40/2488; GWDN: 9545

107 James Taylor & Warren Shaw, *The Penguin Dictionary of the Third Reich* (Penguin Books: London, 1997), p. 203

108 UKNA: AIR 40/2645; GWDN: 9386

109 IWM: 27051, Bryett, Reel 15

110 IWM: 28532, Lyon, Reel 7

111 BA: N 54/36; GWDN: 113

112 BA: MSG 2/1517, Lindeiner, *Im Dienst*, pp. 185–90

Chapter Ten: Early Fallers

1 IWM: 4987, James, Reel 6

2 UKNA: AIR 40/2490; GWDN: 9718 & 9726

3 Today, the village is called Trzebów.

4 James, *Moonless Night*, location 1874

5 Today, the towns are called Siedlęcin and Jelenia Góra respectively.

6 UKNA: AIR 40/2490; GWDN: 9724

7 Today, the town is called Polubny.

8   Today, the town is called Piechowice. In his testimony
    in UKNA: AIR 40/2490; GWDN: 9724, Poynter
    thinks he caught a train at Hammersdorf
    (Harrachov), but as this is 15½ miles from
    Boberrohrsdorf, it is unlikely.

9   Today, the town is called Harrachov and is in the
    Czech Republic.

10 UKNA: AIR 40/2490; GWDN: 9724

11 Today, the town is called Szklarska Poręba.

12 UKNA: AIR 40/2645; GWDN: 9395–9396. See also
    UKNA: WO 311/993; GWDN: 0702

13 Carroll, *The Great Escape*, p. 233

14 UKNA: AIR 40/2491; GWDN: 9771

15 James, *Moonless Night*, location 1925

16 UKNA: AIR 40/2645; GWDN: 9401

17 UKNA: AIR 40/2645; GWDN: 9399–9400

18 Carroll, *The Great Escape*, p. 239. See UKNA: WO
    311/993; GWDN: 0702, in which it is established
    that the interrogator is not the chief of the Hirschberg
    Gestapo.

19 UKNA: AIR 40/2491; GWDN: 9771

20 James, *Moonless Night*, location 2072

21 UKNA: WO 311/993; GWDN: 0702

22 UKNA: AIR 40/2490; GWDN: 9724–9725

23 UKNA: WO 311/993; GWDN: 0702

24 UKNA: AIR 40/2490; GWDN: 9719

25 See, for example, UKNA: KV 2/1722, the
    interrogation of SD agent Osmar Hellmuth by
    Lieutenant Colonel Robert 'Tin Eye' Stephens;
    GWDN: HE1804–1806. 'I shall tell you something
    about your future treatment in this prison. You are
    absolutely alone. You are incommunicado. You will
    never get a letter out of this place and you will never
    receive a letter . . . Now you will be sent for

investigation, and that investigation will be carried out by the officer on my left, together with a number of assistants. Our determination is to obtain the entire truth from you, the whole truth, and when you lie, we shall know instantly. And day by day I shall call you for reports; and day by day, if those reports are not satisfactory, you will suffer. Now for your information, some three hundred men have been stood where you are standing now. Some of the men have obstructed, and because they have obstructed they have been hanged. All the spies that have been hanged in this country have gone from this room, from the place where you are actually standing now.'

26   Carroll, *The Great Escape*, p. 240
27   BA: N 54/36; GWDN: 113
28   IWM: 6176, Atkinson, Reel 3
29   UKNA: WO 311/997; GWDN: 0774
30   UKNA: AIR 40/170; GWDN: 0395
31   UKNA: AIR 40/2488; GWDN: 9564
32   Durand, *Stalag Luft III*, p. 312
33   UKNA: WO 311/1000; GWDN: 1606
34   Durand, *Stalag Luft III*, pp. 312–13
35   UKNA: AIR 40/2488; GWDN: 9564
36   Ian Kershaw, *Hitler 1936–1945: Nemesis* (London: Allen Lane, 2000), pp. 628–9
37   Ibid., p. 631
38   James Holland, *Italy's Sorrow: A Year of War, 1944–1945* (London: HarperPress, 2008), p. xliii. The ensuing reprisal was reduced to a ratio of 10 to 1, and 335 were murdered in the Ardeatine Caves on 24 March, the morning of the Great Escape. Rome was left untouched.
39   See Sir David Maxwell-Fyfe's cross-examination of Göring on the eighty-sixth day of the trial,

Wednesday 20 March 1946:
http://avalon.law.yale.edu/imt/03-20-46.asp; Whitney
R. Harris, *Tyranny on Trial* (Dallas: Southern
Methodist University Press, 1954), pp. 232–5.

40   UKNA: WO 235/425; GWDN: 1812–1813

41   UKNA: WO 235/425; GWDN: 1812

42   Brickhill, *The Great Escape*, p. 211

43   See, for example, Carroll, *The Great Escape*, p. 243

44   Nuremberg Trial Proceedings, hundredth day, Friday
5 April 1946, Morning Session, found at
http://avalon.law.yale.edu/imt/04-05-46.asp

45   Ibid.

46   UKNA: WO 235/425; GWDN: 1813

47   See, for example, the commentary by Walter Görlitz
in Wilhelm Keitel, *In the Service of the Reich*
(London: Focal Point Publications, Electronic Edition,
2003), edited by Walter Görlitz and translated by
David Irving.

48   UKNA: AIR 40/2728, Air Ministry, Directorate of
Intelligence and related bodies: Intelligence Reports
and Papers, War Crimes, Stalag Luft III: murder of 50
RAF officers, investigation correspondence; GWDN:
9943

49   Ibid.

50   UKNA: AIR 40/2268, Air Ministry, Directorate of
Intelligence and related bodies: Intelligence Reports
and Papers, SPECIAL INVESTIGATION BRANCH,
BRITISH AIR FORCES OF OCCUPATION,
Prisoners of War: killing of 50 R.A.F. and other
officers from Stalag Luft III, Interrogation reports and
associated papers, Voluntary statement by Peter
Mohr; GWDN: 0040. In his statement, Mohr
declares that he is uncertain whether Hitler was
mentioned in the order.

51   UKNA: AIR 40/2489; GWDN: 9682

52   UKNA: AIR 40/2489; GWDN: 9688

53   UKNA: WO 311/176, Judge Advocate General's
     Office, Military Deputy's Department, and War
     Office, Directorates of Army Legal Services and
     Personal Services: War Crimes Files (MO/JAG/FS and
     other series), Stalag Luft 3, Sagan, Germany: escape,
     recapture and killing of RAF officers; GWDN: 0570.
     For red leather sofa and bomb damage, see UKNA:
     AIR 40/2488; GWDN: 9548–9549

54   UKNA: AIR 40/2488; GWDN: 9546

55   UKNA: AIR 40/2488; GWDN: 9556

56   UKNA: AIR 40/2488; GWDN: 9546

57   UKNA: WO 235/425, Judge Advocate General's
     Office: War Crimes Case Files, Second World War,
     Stalag Luft III case, Defendant: Max Wielen, Place of
     Trial: Hamburg; GWDN: 1745

58   UKNA: WO 235/425; GWDN: 1746

59   UKNA: WO 311/176; GWDN: 0570

60   UKNA: AIR 40/2488; GWDN: 9547

61   UKNA: WO 235/424, Judge Advocate General's
     Office: War Crimes Case Files, Second World War,
     Stalag Luft III case, Defendant: Max Wielen, Place of
     Trial: Hamburg; GWDN: 1216

62   UKNA: WO 235/426, Judge Advocate General's
     Office: War Crimes Case Files, Second World War,
     Stalag Luft III case, Defendant: Max Wielen, Place of
     Trial: Hamburg; GWDN: 1823

63   UKNA: WO 311/176; GWDN: 0571

64   UKNA: WO 235/575, Judge Advocate General's
     Office: War Crimes Case Files, Second World War,
     Stalag Luft III Case No. 2, Defendant: Exhibits: 1–30;
     GWDN: 0834

65   IWM: 26605, Royle, Reel 4

66   Today, the village is called Parowa.
67   IWM: 26605, Royle, Reel 4
68   UKNA: AIR 40/2275; GWDN: 9328
69   UKNA: AIR 40/2490; GWDN: 9741
70   UKNA: AIR 40/2490; GWDN: 9758
71   UKNA: AIR 40/2490; GWDN: 9741
72   UKNA: WO 208/3659; GWDN: 1103
73   UKNA: AIR 40/2275; GWDN: 9328
74   UKNA: AIR 40/2490; GWDN: 9761. Today, Halbau
      town is called Iłowa.
75   UKNA: AIR 40/2645; GWDN: 9412
76   Today, Kohlfurt is called Gmina Węgliniec.
77   UKNA: AIR 40/2490; GWDN: 9753
78   IWM: 13296, Churchill, Reel 2
79   Ibid.
80   IWM: 8276, Nelson, Reel 3
81   IWM: 13296, Churchill, Reel 2
82   IWM: 8276, Nelson, Reel 3
83   UKNA: AIR 40/2490; GWDN: 9748
84   IWM: 13284 05/4/1, Private papers of R. A. Bethell,
      'My Story of the Tunnel "Harry" and of Subsequent
      Events', p. 2. In his interview given to IS9 on 23 May
      1945, Bethell does not mention hearing the sound of
      the shot and merely states that the group split up
      after walking west through the woods for 2 km (1½
      miles). See UKNA: AIR 40/2490; GWDN: 9744
85   Today, Benau is called Bieniów. In his IS9 interview,
      Bethell states the distance was some 30 km, but the
      figure is nearer to 16 km, which is 10 miles. Clearly
      progress was slower than Bethell had appreciated,
      and his misjudgement is surely forgivable.
86   IWM: 13284 05/4/1, Bethell, 'My Story', p. 3
87   Ibid. The sequence of events in Bethell's IS9 interview
      and his reminiscences contained at the IWM conflict.

As the IWM material was written some fifty years after the escape, I have chosen to follow the sequence in the IS9 interview.

88 UKNA: AIR 40/2490; GWDN: 9744

89 Gill, *The Great Escape*, p. 200

90 Ibid., p. 201

91 UKNA: AIR 40/2490; GWDN: 9746

92 Gill, *The Great Escape*, p. 201. In UKNA: AIR 40/2490; GWDN: 9746, Brodrick says that the cottage may have been near 'Kalkbrugh', but I have been unable to locate this village.

93 Ibid.

94 Today, Rothwasser is called Czerwona Woda. I have been unable to locate Stolzenberg.

95 UKNA: AIR 40/2490; GWDN: 9738. Today, Reichenberg is the Czech town of Liberec.

96 Carroll, *The Great Escape*, p. 236

97 Tonder & Sitensky, *Na nebi i v pekle*, p. 38

98 Today, the town is called Szczecin.

99 UKNA: AIR 40/2275; GWDN: 9315

100 Smith, *'Wings' Day*, p. 168

101 Today, the station is Berlin's Ostbahnhof.

102 Smith, *'Wings' Day*, p. 174

103 Ibid., p. 162. Smith calls Boyd Carpenter 'Fitz-Boyd'.

104 UKNA: AIR 40/2295; Air Ministry, Directorate of Intelligence and related bodies: Intelligence Reports and Papers, SPECIAL INVESTIGATION BRANCH, ROYAL AIR FORCE, Prisoners of War suspected of aiding the enemy, Statement of Raymond Hughes; GWDN: 0217 & 0226

105 UKNA: AIR 40/2295, GWDN: 0223; Smith, *'Wings' Day*, p. 161

106 Smith, *'Wings' Day*, p. 162

107 Ibid., p. 179

108   Ibid., pp. 180-2
109   Ibid., p. 184
110   UKNA: AIR 40/2275; GWDN: 9316
111   UKNA: AIR 40/2279; Air Ministry, Directorate of
      Intelligence and related bodies: Intelligence Reports
      and Papers, SPECIAL INVESTIGATION BRANCH,
      BRITISH AIR FORCES OF OCCUPATION,
      Prisoners of War: killing of 50 R.A.F. and other
      officers from Stalag Luft III, The Kiel murders:
      enquiries and interrogation of persons involved;
      GWDN: 0183
112   UKNA: AIR 40/2279; GWDN: 0189
113   UKNA: AIR 40/2491; GWDN: 9774
114   Today, the town is called Leszno.
115   UKNA: WO 311/175; Judge Advocate General's
      Office, Military Deputy's Department, and War
      Office, Directorates of Army Legal Services and
      Personal Services: War Crimes Files (MO/JAG/FS and
      other series), Stalag Luft 3, Sagan, Germany: escape,
      recapture and killing of RAF officers; GWDN: 0532
116   UKNA: AIR 40/2278; Air Ministry, Directorate of
      Intelligence and related bodies: Intelligence Reports
      and Papers, SPECIAL INVESTIGATION BRANCH,
      BRITISH AIR FORCES OF OCCUPATION,
      Prisoners of War: killing of 50 R.A.F. and other
      officers from Stalag Luft III, Murder of Fg. Off [sic].
      Hayter: interrogation of associated German
      personnel; GWDN: 0180
117   UKNA: Air Ministry, Directorate of Intelligence and
      related bodies: Intelligence Reports and Papers,
      SPECIAL INVESTIGATION BRANCH, BRITISH
      AIR FORCES OF OCCUPATION, Prisoners of War:
      killing of 50 R.A.F. and other officers from Stalag
      Luft III, French Zone: enquiries and statements of

German internees in Civilian Internment Camps; GWDN: 1691

118 UKNA: AIR 40/2284; GWDN: 1690

119 UKNA: AIR 40/2489; GWDN: 9696

120 See, for example, Carroll, *The Great Escape*, p. 240

121 UKNA: AIR 40/2266, Air Ministry, Directorate of Intelligence and related bodies: Intelligence Reports and Papers, SPECIAL INVESTIGATION BRANCH, BRITISH AIR FORCES OF OCCUPATION, Prisoners of War: killing of 50 R.A.F. and other officers from Stalag Luft III, Interrogation reports and associated papers, Interrogation of Jakob Hartz, 30/7/46; GWDN: 9960

122 UKNA: AIR 40/2284; GWDN: 1688

123 UKNA: WO 309/1368, War Office: Judge Advocate General's Office, British Army of the Rhine War Crimes Group (North West Europe) and predecessors: Registered Files (BAOR and other series), Stalag Luft 3, Sagan, Germany: killing of 50 escaped British officers, Statement of Theodor Trost; GWDN: 1556

124 UKNA: AIR 40/2284; GWDN: 1688

125 UKNA: AIR 40/2493, Air Ministry, Directorate of Intelligence and related bodies: Intelligence Reports and Papers, SAGAN, STALAG LUFT III CAMP: MURDER OF 50 RAF OFFICERS, Report No. 325; GWDN: 9889

126 *Daily Mail*, 24 October 2009, 'He shot the hero of the Great Escape in cold blood. But was this one Nazi who DIDN'T deserve to hang?' by Phil Craig; http://www.dailymail.co.uk/news/article-1222565/He-shot-hero-Great-Escape-cold-blood-But-Nazi-DIDNT-deserve-hang.html

127 UKNA: AIR 40/2493; GWDN: 9889

128 UKNA: AIR 40/2493; GWDN: 9890

129 UKNA: WO 235/426; GWDN: 1830

130 UKNA: WO 309/530, War Office: Judge Advocate
General's Office, British Army of the Rhine War
Crimes Group (North West Europe) and predecessors:
Registered Files (BAOR and other series), Stalag Luft
3, Sagan, Germany: escape, recapture and killing of
RAF officers, Voluntary Statement by Walter
Breithaupt; GWDN: 1529

131 UKNA: WO 309/530; GWDN: 1530

132 UKNA: AIR 40/2493; GWDN: 9890

Chapter Eleven: 'This dirty work'

1 UKNA: AIR 40/2268; GWDN: 0031

2 UKNA: AIR 40/2268; GWDN: 0032

3 Ibid.

4 UKNA: AIR 40/2268; GWDN: 0033

5 Gerald Reitlinger, *The SS: Alibi of a Nation* (New
York: Viking, 1957), pp. 182–3

6 See p. 226.

7 UKNA: AIR 40/2491, 236B, Statement made by
Erich Zacharias; GWDN: 9824

8 UKNA: AIR 40/2490; GWDN: 9708. Today,
Moravská Ostrava is simply called Ostrava.

9 Ibid. Gordon Kidder was brought up at 105 Queen
Street, St Catharines.

10 UKNA: AIR 40/2491, 236B, Statement made by
Erich Zacharias; GWDN: 9824

11 UKNA: AIR 40/2491, 236B, Statement made by
Erich Zacharias; GWDN: 9823

12 UKNA: AIR 40/2270, Air Ministry, Directorate of
Intelligence and related bodies: Intelligence Reports
and Papers, SPECIAL INVESTIGATION BRANCH,
BRITISH AIR FORCES OF OCCUPATION,
Prisoners of War: killing of 50 R.A.F. and other

officers from Stalag Luft III, Enquiries in British Zone: miscellaneous correspondence in respect of whereabouts and detention of wanted personnel; GWDN: 0111

13 A. P. Scotland, *The London Cage* (London: Evans Brothers, 1957), p. 148

14 UKNA: AIR 40/2491; GWDN: 9795

15 UKNA: AIR 40/2491, 236B, Statement made by Erich Zacharias; GWDN: 9824

16 UKNA: AIR 40/2490; GWDN: 9702

17 UKNA: AIR 40/2491, 236B, Statement made by Erich Zacharias; GWDN: 9826

18 UKNA: AIR 40/2491; GWDN: 9788

19 UKNA: AIR 40/2490; GWDN: 9702

20 UKNA: AIR 40/2491; GWDN: 9788

21 UKNA: AIR 40/2281, Air Ministry, Directorate of Intelligence and related bodies: Intelligence Reports and Papers, SPECIAL INVESTIGATION BRANCH, BRITISH AIR FORCES OF OCCUPATION, Prisoners of War: killing of 50 R.A.F. and other officers from Stalag Luft III, Czechoslovakia: reports of information received and statements by various German nationals, Statement of Anton Liebert, 13B; GWDN: 1307

22 UKNA: AIR 40/2491, 236B, Statement made by Erich Zacharias; GWDN: 9827

23 UKNA: AIR 40/2491; GWDN: 9789

24 Ibid; UKNA: AIR 40/2491, 236B, Statement made by Erich Zacharias; GWDN: 9827. Friedeck is now called Frýdek-Místek.

25 UKNA: AIR 40/2491; GWDN: 9789

26 Photographs of the reconstruction of the murder can be seen in the plates; also see UKNA: WO 311/173, Judge Advocate General's Office, Military Deputy's

Department, and War Office, Directorates of Army
Legal Services and Personal Services: War Crimes
Files (MO/JAG/FS and other series), Stalag Luft 3,
Sagan, Germany: escape, recapture and killing of
RAF officers; GWDN: 0443–0470

27 UKNA: AIR 40/2491, 236B, Statement made by
Erich Zacharias; GWDN: 9827

28 Ibid; and for the position of Kidder's cuffed hands,
see Kiowsky's statement at UKNA: AIR 40/2491;
GWDN: 9789

29 UKNA: AIR 40/2491, 193 'G', Statement of Emil
Schreier; GWDN: 9791

30 UKNA: AIR 40/2491, 236B, Statement made by
Erich Zacharias; GWDN: 9827

31 UKNA: AIR 40/2491; GWDN: 9789

32 UKNA: AIR 40/2490; GWDN: 9705

33 UKNA: AIR 40/2491, 236B, Statement made by
Erich Zacharias; GWDN: 9827

34 UKNA: AIR 40/2491, 193 'G', Statement of Emil
Schreier; GWDN: 9791

35 UKNA: AIR 40/2491, 193 'H', Statement of
Frantisek Krupa; GWDN: 9792

36 UKNA: AIR 40/2491, 236B, Statement made by
Erich Zacharias; GWDN: 9828

37 UKNA: AIR 40/2491, 193 'H', Statement of
Frantisek Krupa; GWDN: 9792

38 UKNA: AIR 40/2269, Air Ministry, Directorate of
Intelligence and related bodies: Intelligence Reports
and Papers, SPECIAL INVESTIGATION BRANCH,
BRITISH AIR FORCES OF OCCUPATION,
Prisoners of War: killing of 50 R.A.F. and other
officers from Stalag Luft III, Statement of Karl Raska;
GWDN: 0062

39 UKNA: AIR 40/2490; GWDN: 9707

40   UKNA: AIR 40/2491, 193 'H', Statement of
      Frantisek Krupa; GWDN: 9792

41   See p. 179.

42   Unpublished memoir by William E. Koch; GWDN:
      8217

43   For more on 'community of fate' (*Schickalsgemeinschaft*),
      see Tim Kirk, *Nazi Germany* (Basingstoke: Palgrave
      Macmillan, 2007), p. 214

44   UKNA: WO 208/2901; GWDN: 1168

45   The location of the killings is approximate.

46   UKNA: AIR 40/2492, Air Ministry, Directorate of
      Intelligence and related bodies: Intelligence Reports
      and Papers, SAGAN, STALAG LUFT III CAMP:
      MURDER OF 50 RAF OFFICERS, Reports No. 296,
      Statement of Johann Schneider; GWDN: 9836. The
      Wittelsbach Palace is today called the Munich
      Residenz.

47   UKNA: WO 311/178, Judge Advocate General's
      Office, Military Deputy's Department, and War
      Office, Directorates of Army Legal Services and
      Personal Services: War Crimes Files (MO/JAG/FS and
      other series), Stalag Luft 3, Sagan, Germany: escape,
      recapture and killing of RAF officers, Statement by
      Emil Weil; GWDN: 0609. For Weil's background, see
      UKNA: AIR 40/2492, No. 297, Statement of Emil
      Weil.

48   UKNA: AIR 40/2265. Air Ministry, Directorate of
      Intelligence and related bodies: Intelligence Reports
      and Papers, SPECIAL INVESTIGATION BRANCH,
      BRITISH AIR FORCES OF OCCUPATION,
      Prisoners of War: killing of 50 R.A.F. and other offi-
      cers from Stalag Luft III, Judge Advocate General's
      interim report: interrogation reports and associated
      papers, Statement by Eduard Geith; GWDN: 9950.

More information about Martin Schermer's activities can be found in Reinhard Otto, *Wehrmacht, Gestapo und sowjetische Kriegsgefangene im deutschen Reichsgebiet 1941/42* (Oldenbourg Wissenschaftsverlag, 1998).

49 UKNA: WO 235/427, Judge Advocate General's Office: War Crimes Case Files, Second World War, Stalag Luft III Case, Defendant: Proceedings Place of Trial: Hamburg, p. 26; GWDN: 5350

50 UKNA: WO 235/427; GWDN: 5351

51 UKNA: WO 235/427; GWDN: 5347 & 5355

52 UKNA: AIR 40/2265; GWDN: 9950

53 GWDN: 9951. For Schneider's service in Russia, see Colonel Scotland's observation in UKNA WO 311/180, Judge Advocate General's Office, Military Deputy's Department, and War Office, Directorates of Army Legal Services and Personal Services: War Crimes Files (MO/JAG/FS and other series), Stalag Luft 3, Sagan, Germany: escape, recapture and killing of RAF officers; GWDN: 0646.

54 UKNA: AIR 40/2265; GWDN: 9951

55 UKNA: AIR 40/2265; GWDN: 9952

56 UKNA: WO 311/176, Statement of Johann Schneider; GWDN: 0579

57 UKNA: AIR 40/2492; GWDN: 9837

58 UKNA: AIR 40/2265; GWDN: 9954

59 UKNA: AIR 40/2265; GWDN: 9955

60 UKNA: WO 235/427; GWDN: 5340

61 UKNA: AIR 40/2265; GWDN: 9955

62 UKNA: AIR 40/2265; GWDN: 9956

63 UKNA: WO 311/994, Judge Advocate General's Office, Military Deputy's Department, and War Office, Directorates of Army Legal Services and Personal Services: War Crimes Files (MO/JAG/FS and

other series), Shooting of 50 RAF officers at Stalag Luft III, Sagan, Poland, March 1944: sundry exhibits and photographs; GWDN: 0708

64 UKNA: AIR 40/2491, Testimony made by Peter Mohr; GWDN: 9812

65 Tonder & Sitensky, *Na nebi i v pekle*, p. 39

66 UKNA: AIR 40/2270; GWDN: 0114

67 UKNA: AIR 40/2292; GWDN: 9534. Today, Brüx is the Czech town of Most.

68 See p. 200.

69 Today, Gross Trampken is the Polish village of Trąbki Wielkie.

70 UKNA: AIR 40/2292; GWDN: 9497.

71 Today, Elbing is the Polish town of Elblàg.

72 Today, Opava in the Czech Republic and Radom and Szczecin in Poland respectively. For Post's career, see UKNA, AIR 40/2269, Statement by Johannes Post; GWDN: 0057

73 UKNA: AIR 40/2279; GWDN: 0187. For fear of Post and his sadism, see UKNA, AIR 40/2269, Statement of Wilhelm Struve; GWDN: 0083

74 UKNA, AIR 40/2269, Statement by Johannes Post; GWDN: 0057. Today, the site of the murders is largely covered by a factory making maritime radio equipment.

75 UKNA: AIR 40/2493, Interrogation of Oskar Schmidt; GWDN: 9918

76 UKNA: AIR 40/2269, Statement of Wilhelm Struve; GWDN: 0080

77 UKNA: AIR 40/2493, Interrogation of Hans Kähler; GWDN: 9907

78 UKNA: WO 311/177, Statement of Artur Denkmann; GWDN: 0591

79 UKNA: AIR 40/2269, Statement by Johannes Post; GWDN: 0059

80 UKNA: WO 235/427; GWDN: 5386

81 UKNA: AIR 40/2493, Interrogation of Walter Jacobs; GWDN: 9912

82 UKNA: AIR 40/2493, Interrogation of Hans Kähler; GWDN: 9908

83 UKNA: WO 311/177, Statement of Artur Denkmann; GWDN: 0591

84 UKNA: AIR 40/2493, Interrogation of Hans Kähler; GWDN: 9908. According to his examination by Colonel Halse during his trial, Post claimed to have spoken to Catanach before he killed him. 'I have orders to shoot you,' Post said, to which Catanach is supposed to have replied, 'Why?' Post then answered, 'I do not know,' and pulled the trigger. As this conversation was not seemingly noticed by Kähler, it is unlikely to have taken place, and may have been part of the effort made by Post to give the impression to the court that the killing was a legitimate execution rather than a murder. See UKNA, WO 235/427; GWDN: 5407

85 UKNA: AIR 40/2493, Interrogation of Oskar Schmidt; GWDN: 9900

86 UKNA: AIR 40/2493, Interrogation of Hans Kähler; GWDN: 9909

87 UKNA: AIR 40/2269, Statement of Oskar Schmidt; GWDN: 0078. It is hard to establish definitively who killed each of the prisoners, but it appears likely that Franz Schmidt killed Fugelsang, Oskar Schmidt shot and wounded Espelid, Walter Jacobs killed Christensen, and Post killed Catanach and administered the *coup de grâce* to Espelid. See Post's testimony during his trial in UKNA: WO 235/427; GWDN: 5388

88   UKNA: AIR 40/2493, Bowes to Lyon, 30 October
      1946, fo. 341; GWDN: 9898
89   The building no longer stands.
90   UKNA: AIR 40/2493, Statement of Walter
      Breithaupt; GWDN: 9894
91   UKNA: AIR 40/2493, Statement by Emil Schulz;
      GWDN: 9890
92   The exact location of the murders is unclear.
      Breithaupt's statement appears to indicate that the
      deaths took place to the east of Kaiserslautern,
      whereas a statement given by Olga Braun, a
      shorthand typist at Neue Bremm *Straflager*, suggests
      that the location was between Kaiserslautern and
      Landstuhl, which is to the west of Kaiserslautern. For
      Braun's statement, see UKNA: WO 235/430, Judge
      Advocate General's Office: War Crimes Case Files,
      Second World War, Stalag Luft III Case, Defendant:
      Exhibits: 1–3 Place of Trial: Hamburg; GWDN:
      1703
93   UKNA: AIR 40/2493, Statement of Walter
      Breithaupt; GWDN: 9894
94   Ibid.
95   UKNA: AIR 40/2493, Statement by Emil Schulz;
      GWDN: 9890
96   UKNA: AIR 40/2493, Statement of Walter
      Breithaupt; GWDN: 9895
97   UKNA: AIR 40/2493, Statement by Emil Schulz;
      GWDN: 9890–9891
98   UKNA: WO 235/426; GWDN: 1855. An informative
      website about Neue Bremm can be found at
      http://www.gestapo-lager-neue-bremm.de
99   UKNA: WO 235/430; Statement of Olga Braun;
      GWDN: 1703
100   Ibid.

101   The firm is still in business. See http://www.laubach-bestattungen.de

102   UKNA: AIR 40/2489; GWDN: 9698

103   UKNA: AIR 40/2489; GWDN: 9699

104   UKNA: AIR 40/2489; GWDN: 9695

105   See p. 131.

106   See p. 132.

107   See The Empire Club of Canada Addresses, 6 Feb 1947, 188–199 found at http://speeches.empireclub.org/60666/datan=12; *The Times* (London), 7 October 2008, Obituary of Brigadier Hugo Ironside, at http://www.timesonline.co.uk/tol/comment/obituaries/article4893797.ece, and interview with Ironside at http://www.youtube.com/watchv= 6Qko_e0TLKA

108   Recollections of Major John Smale at The Second World War Experience Centre at http://www.war-experience.org/collections/land/alliedbrit/smale/pagetwo.asp

109   UKNA: AIR 40/2493, Statement of Otto Preiss; GWDN: 9877

Chapter Twelve: An 'atmosphere of sudden death'

1   See p. 251.

2   IWM: 8276, Nelson, Reel 3

3   UKNA: AIR 40/2493, Statement of Richard Max Hänsel; GWDN: 9866

4   IWM: 13296, Churchill, Reel 3

5   IWM: 8276, Nelson, Reel 3

6   IWM: 13296, Churchill, Reel 3

7   UKNA: WO 208/2901; GWDN: 1136

8   UKNA: WO 208/2901; GWDN: 1135

9   UKNA: AIR 40/2493, Statement of Richard Max Hänsel; GWDN: 9867

10   IWM: 13296, Churchill, Reel 3

11   IWM: 8276, Nelson, Reel 3

12   UKNA: WO 208/2901; GWDN: 1136–1137. The POWs left Görlitz in the following parties: 1st party, 30 March: Casey, Wiley, Cross, Leigh, Pohé, Hake (with the latter two supposedly going to hospital, but this is unlikely); 2nd party, 31 March: Humphreys, McGill, Swain, Valenta, Hall, Kolanowski, Stewart, Birkland, Langford, Evans; 3rd party, 1 April: Ogilvie, McDonald, Thompson, Royle; 4th party, 6 April: Grisman, Street, McGarr, Gunn, Milford, J. F. Williams; 5th party, 6 April: Shand, Armstrong, Marshall, Churchill, Bethell, Nelson, Cameron, Brodrick; 6th party, c. 12 April: Long. Only the men in the 3rd and 5th parties were spared. The rest were shot.

13   IWM: 8276, Nelson, Reel 3

14   The Görlitz Gestapo was incorporated into the Breslau Gestapo, and as such, Scharpwinkel was responsible for both offices.

15   Many secondary sources, such as Allen Andrews, *Exemplary Justice* (London: Corgi, 1978), state that these men were killed on 31 March, but UKNA: WO 208/2901; GWDN: 1136–1137; and IWM: 13296, Churchill, Reel 3, contradict this.

16   Today, Pieńsk, Ruszów and Iłowa respectively.

17   UKNA: AIR 40/2493, Statement of Richard Max Hänsel; GWDN: 9867

18   See p. 187.

19   UKNA: AIR 40/2493, Interrogation of Richard Max Hänsel; GWDN: 9873

20   UKNA: AIR 40/2493, Statement of Richard Max Hänsel; GWDN: 9867

21   UKNA: AIR 40/2493, Interrogation of Richard Max Hänsel; GWDN: 9873

22   UKNA: AIR 40/2493, Statement of Richard Max Hänsel; GWDN: 9868

23   UKNA: AIR 40/2269, Statement by Erwin Wieczorek; GWDN: 0089. It is still not known for certain on what day Wernham, Kiewnarski, Skanziklas and Pawluk were shot. According to Andrews, *Exemplary Justice*, p. 240, the SIB established that the Hirschberg killings took place before the first of the Görlitz killings. However, Andrews states that 'this was never satisfactorily cleared up', especially as Hänsel, a relatively reliable witness, recalled Lux stating the imminent visit to Hirschberg at the scene of the first Görlitz killings. Unfortunately, Dodge's testimony is of no assistance, as he left Hirschberg before the four victims. Poynter's testimony muddies the pool still further, as he claims that Dodge, Skanziklas, Pawluk and Kiewnarski were all taken on 27 March and Wernham on the 28th. This contradicts Dodge, who says he was the first to leave Hirschberg. However, Jimmy James states that the four victims left on 30 March, which coincides with the conclusion reached by the SIB, but still contradicts Hänsel's testimony. It is possible that the four men were in fact transferred to Hirschberg's Gestapo HQ on the 30th – which is where Wieczorek states they were interrogated by Scharpwinkel – and were shot the following day. Trying to establish the precise day of death may seem like nitpicking, but it is illustrative of the problems faced by the investigation teams, and indeed by historians.

24   UKNA: AIR 40/2269, Statement by Erwin Wieczorek; GWDN: 0091

25   Ibid.

26   UKNA: AIR 40/2269, Statement by Erwin Wieczorek; GWDN: 0092

27   Andrews, *Exemplary Justice*, p. 241

28   UKNA: AIR 40/2313, Air Ministry, Directorate of Intelligence and related bodies: Intelligence Reports and Papers, PROVOST MARSHAL, AIR MINISTRY, War Crimes – killing of 50 R.A.F. officers who escaped from Stalag Luft III: correspondence and statements made by Germans accused of complicity, Voluntary Statement of Robert Schröder; GWDN: 9488

29   See p. 261–2 for Hayter's capture. Schimmel is often incorrectly described as the head of the Gestapo only in Strasbourg, but his geographical remit was far broader. See UKNA: WO 235/426, Judge Advocate to Schimmel, 22 July 1947, p. 41; GWDN: 1899

30   UKNA: AIR 40/2269, Statement by Alfred Schimmel; GWDN: 0071

31   UKNA: WO 235/426, Schimmel testimony, 22 July 1947, p. 21; GWDN: 1878

32   UKNA: WO 235/426, Schimmel testimony, 22 July 1947, p. 21; GWDN: 1880

33   UKNA: WO 235/426, Schimmel testimony, 22 July 1947, p. 21; GWDN: 1879

34   Today, the street is called Rue Séllénick and the building houses the Lycée ORT.

35   UKNA: WO 235/426, Schimmel testimony, 22 July 1947, p. 21; GWDN: 1881–1882

36   UKNA: WO 235/426, Schimmel testimony, 22 July 1947, p. 21; GWDN: 1882

37   UKNA: WO 235/426, Schimmel testimony, 22 July 1947, p. 21; GWDN: 1883

38   UKNA: WO 235/426, Schimmel testimony, 22 July 1947, p. 21; GWDN: 1884

39   See http://forum.axishistory.com/viewtopic.phpf=
     38&t=34260 for biographical data on Isselhorst.
     Information concerning the post-war fate of this
     unappealing character can be found in UKNA: WO
     235/682 and WO 309/22

40   UKNA: WO 235/426, Schimmel testimony, 22 July
     1947, p. 21; GWDN: 1884

41   UKNA: AIR 40/2269, Statement by Alfred Schimmel;
     GWDN: 0073

42   Ibid.

43   UKNA: WO 235/426; Schimmel testimony, 22 July
     1947, p. 21; GWDN: 1884 & 1887

44   Ibid.

45   UKNA: WO 235/426, Schimmel testimony, 22 July
     1947, p. 21; GWDN: 1885

46   UKNA: AIR 40/2272, Air Ministry, Directorate of
     Intelligence and related bodies: Intelligence Reports
     and Papers, SPECIAL INVESTIGATION BRANCH,
     BRITISH AIR FORCES OF OCCUPATION,
     Prisoners of War: killing of 50 R.A.F. and other
     officers from Stalag Luft III, Progress reports in
     respect of Stalag Luft III investigation: results of
     effort to trace wanted German personnel, McKenna
     to Provost Marshal, 22 March 1947; GWDN:
     0132. And see UKNA: AIR 40/2278, Linssen to
     Deputy Provost Marshal, 21 March 1947; GWDN:
     0177

47   UKNA: WO 235/426, Schimmel testimony, 22 July
     1947, p. 21; GWDN: 1885

48   Andrews, *Exemplary Justice*, p. 250

49   UKNA: AIR 40/2269, Statement by Alfred Schimmel;
     GWDN: 0073

50   UKNA: AIR 40/2269, Statement by Alfred Schimmel;
     GWDN: 0073–0074

51   See Berg's statement in WO 311/175; GWDN:
       0528–0531. Berg was sentenced to death at the
       Natzweiler trial and executed in October 1946.

52   UKNA: AIR 40/2269, Statement by Alfred Schimmel;
       GWDN: 0074

Chapter Thirteen: 'No one *wounded*?'

1   Paul Brickhill & Conrad Norton, *Escape to Danger*
       (London: Faber and Faber, 1949), p. 326

2   IWM: 05/68/1, Hall, 'Prisoner of War', p. 11

3   IWM: 99/82/1, Flekser, 'Operations', p. 76

4   IWM: 27051, Bryett, Reel 15

5   IWM: 27813; Rae, Reel 7

6   UKNA: AIR 40/2275; GWDN: 9324. Some accounts,
       such as Brickhill's, state that the Commandant at this
       time was Oberst Braune. This is incorrect, as Braune
       was not appointed until either May or July. See WO
       208/2901; GWDN: 1145 for confirmation that the
       replacement Commandant was a Lieutenant Colonel,
       and therefore the same rank as Cordes.

7   Murray's nickname was 'Wank', a name used
       throughout many accounts of the Great Escape. For
       contemporary readers, such a name would detract
       from the gravity of the episode, so I have chosen not
       to use it.

8   UKNA: AIR 2/10121, Testimony of Flying Officer
       P. E. Thomas, p. 25; GWDN: 9631

9   UKNA: AIR 40/2645; GWDN: 9415

10   Brickhill, *The Great Escape*, p. 226

11   Ibid., p. 227

12   Ibid.

13   Ibid., p. 229

14   IWM: 15558, Cole, Reel 3

15   IWM: Sound Archive recording 11194, Interview
      with Edward Chapman, Reel 3

16   IWM: Sound Archive recording 6091, Interview with
      John Acquier, Reel 2

17   UKNA: AIR 40/2269, Statement of Johann Franz
      Pieber; GWDN: 0055

18   UKNA: WO 311/811, Judge Advocate General's
      Office, Military Deputy's Department, and War
      Office, Directorates of Army Legal Services and
      Personal Services: War Crimes Files (MO/JAG/FS and
      other series), Shooting of RAF officers at Stalag Luft
      III (Sagan, Poland): enemy personnel and organisation,
      Massey to Kommandant 6 April 1944; GWDN: 1595

19   UKNA: WO 311/811; GWDN: 1596–1597

20   IWM: 17365, Waddington, Reel 5

21   Brickhill, *The Great Escape*, p. 228

22   UKNA: AIR 40/2313; GWDN: 9480

23   UKNA: AIR 40/2275; GWDN: 9325

24   Ibid. Today, Bunzlau is called Bolesławiec, Siegersdorf
      is called Zebrzydowa.

25   See p. 152.

26   UKNA: WO 311/993; GWDN: 0701

27   IWM: 05/68/1; Papers of Cy Grant, 'The War
      Experiences of Flight Lieutenant C. E. L. (Cy) Grant
      from Guyana (then British Guiana) in the Royal Air
      Force, 1941–1945', p. 17. Grant's was almost
      certainly the only black face in the north compound
      of Stalag Luft III.

28   David Codd, *Blue Job – Brown Job* (Bradford on
      Avon: ELSP, 2000), p. 160, found in IWM: 06/117/1,
      Papers of F/L David A. Codd. According to Codd, the
      memorial service took place on 18 April.

29   IWM: 05/68/1, Grant, 'War Experiences', pp. 17–18

30   Codd, *Blue Job – Brown* Job, p. 160
31   UKNA: AIR 40/2313; GWDN: 9480
32   Brickhill, *The Great Escape*, p. 229
33   IWM: 25029, Rees, Reel 3. I have tidied up Rees's words for clarity.
34   UKNA: AIR 40/2313; GWDN: 9480
35   IWM: 26605, Royle, Reel 5

Chapter Fourteen: Later Fallers and Finishers
 1   UKNA: WO 311/177; GWDN: 0589
 2   UKNA: WO 311/177; GWDN: 0588. For details of the errors on the passes, see p. 173.
 3   UKNA: HW 16/14; GWDN: 0828. The cable itself states seventy had been recaptured, but this is incorrect.
 4   UKNA: AIR 40/2645; GWDN: 9396. The coupons were likely to have been supplied by Corporal Hesse.
 5   UKNA: AIR 40/2491; GWDN: 9768
 6   IWM: 27731, Dowse, Reel 7
 7   UKNA: AIR 40/2491; GWDN: 9768; IWM: 27731, Dowse, Reel 7. In his post-war statements, Dowse claims to have teamed up in the woods with Krol and to have never entered Sagan station. Today, Liegnitz is called Legnica.
 8   IWM: 27731, Dowse, Reel 7. Dowse's interview does, however, contradict two testimonies he made shortly after the war, in which he says that he and Krol walked by night. See AIR 40/2645; GWDN: 9396 and UKNA: AIR 40/2490; GWDN: 9732. However, in UKNA: AIR 40/2491; GWDN: 9768, Dowse talks of walking for '12 days'.
 9   IWM: 27731, Dowse, Reel 7
10   Ibid.
11   Ibid., Reel 8

12 Ibid.
13 Today, Olesnica and Kępno respectively.
14 IWM: 27731, Dowse, Reel 8
15 UKNA: AIR 40/2490; GWDN: 9732
16 IWM: 27731, Dowse, Reel 8
17 Ibid.
18 UKNA: AIR 40/2491; GWDN: 9768
19 Ibid.
20 UKNA: AIR 40/2491; GWDN: 9769
21 IWM: 27731, Dowse, Reel 8
22 UKNA: AIR 40/2491; GWDN: 9769
23 For accounts of the escaping activities of these men while imprisoned in Sachsenhausen, see Carroll, *The Great Escape*, pp. 264–78; James, *Moonless Night*; Smith, *'Wings' Day*.
24 Today, Pardubitz is called Pardubice.
25 See p. 210.
26 UKNA: WO 235/575; GWDN: 0836
27 UKNA: WO 311/993; GWDN: 0695
28 Plunkett & Pletts, *The Man Who Would Not Die*, p. 42
29 UKNA: AIR 40/2490; GWDN: 9736
30 Plunkett & Pletts, *The Man Who Would Not Die*, p. 42
31 Today, Glatz is called K3odzko.
32 Plunkett & Pletts, *The Man Who Would Not Die*, p. 43
33 UKNA: WO 311/993; GWDN: 0695
34 Plunkett & Pletts, *The Man Who Would Not Die*, p. 44
35 Today, the town is called Duszniki-Zdrój.
36 UKNA: WO 311/993; GWDN: 0695; Plunkett & Pletts, *The Man Who Would Not Die*, p. 46
37 Plunkett & Pletts, *The Man Who Would Not Die*, p. 46

38   Ibid.

39   UKNA: WO 311/993; GWDN: 0695. I am unable to locate 'Güsshübel', which is also called 'Grunneshubel' in Plunkett & Pletts, *The Man Who Would Not Die*, p. 46.

40   Today, Nový Hrádek.

41   UKNA: WO 311/993; GWDN: 0696

42   Plunkett & Pletts, *The Man Who Would Not Die*, p. 47

43   UKNA: WO 311/993; GWDN: 0696. Today, Neustadt is called Nové Město nad Metují.

44   Plunkett & Pletts, *The Man Who Would Not Die*, p. 49

45   Ibid., p. 50, and see UKNA: WO 311/993; GWDN: 0696

46   Plunkett & Pletts, *The Man Who Would Not Die*, p. 51

47   Ibid., p. 52

48   UKNA: WO 311/993; GWDN: 0696. Today, Jungbunzlau is called Mladá Boleslav.

49   UKNA: AIR 40/2490; GWDN: 9736; Plunkett & Pletts, *The Man Who Would Not Die,* p. 52

50   Today, Taus is called Domažlice.

51   Plunkett & Pletts, *The Man Who Would Not Die*, p. 54

52   Today, Klattau is called Klatovy.

53   Plunkett & Pletts, *The Man Who Would Not Die*, p. 55 states that their leave passes were out of date, yet the Kripo report in UKNA: WO 235/57; GWDN: 0836 suggests that the men did not actually possess such documentation.

54   UKNA: WO 311/993; GWDN: 0696; Plunkett & Pletts, *The Man Who Would Not Die*, pp. 54–5

55   UKNA: AIR 40/2490; GWDN: 9736

56   Plunkett & Pletts, *The Man Who Would Not Die*,
      pp. 56–9
57   UKNA: AIR 40/2490; GWDN: 9736
58   UKNA: WO 311/993; GWDN: 0696
59   Plunkett & Pletts, *The Man Who Would Not Die*,
      p. 71
60   UKNA: AIR 40/2490; GWDN: 9738–9739
61   Tonder & Sitensky, *Na nebi i v pekle*, p. 39
62   UKNA: AIR 40/2490; GWDN: 9739
63   UKNA: WO 311/993; GWDN: 0697
64   UKNA: WO 311/993; GWDN: 0698; Plunkett
      & Pletts, *The Man Who Would Not Die*, pp. 80–1
65   Plunkett lived at 19 Mill Hill Close, Haywards
      Heath, Sussex, England.
66   See plates.
67   See p. 217.
68   RAFM: X001-3886, Collection of MI9 escape and
      evasion reports, 1943–1944, Statement of Per
      Bergsland, p. 4; GWDN: 5244; and see Jens Müller,
      Tre Kom Tilbake, p. 110
69   Müller, *Tre Kom Tilbake*, p. 110
70   RAFM: X001-3886, Statement of Jens Müller;
      GWDN: 5238 (and Bergsland, GWDN: 5244)
71   Müller, *Tre Kom Tilbake*, p. 110
72   Ibid., p. 120. Today, Küstrin is called Kostrzyn nad
      Odrą.
73   Müller, *Tre Kom Tilbake*, p. 121. It is unclear who
      these two fellow POWs were. Müller on page 123 of
      his memoir states that the two men had 'presumably'
      made it to Danzig, and that he had heard a story of
      two stowaways who had sneaked on board a boat at
      that port. After setting sail, the two men declared
      themselves to the captain, who was sufficiently
      incensed to turn the boat round and to hand the

stowaways back to the Germans, who promptly shot them. It is unlikely that these stowaways were from Sagan. However, it is possible that the two men at the Küstrin station café were two of Romas Marcinkus, Tim Walenn, Gordon Brettell and Henri Picard, all of whom were travelling to Danzig. Of these, Walenn was well known to both Norwegians, and Müller would have named him in his memoir. This author hazards that the two men were Brettell and Marcinkus.

74 Müller, *Tre Kom Tilbake*, pp. 121–2
75 RAFM: X001-3886; GWDN: 5244
76 Müller, *Tre Kom Tilbake*, p. 122
77 Ibid., p. 124
78 The street no longer exists. The location of the brothel was approximately at 53.425508 N, 14.563148 E. A 1936 map of Stettin can be found at http://sedina.pl/wpfb_dl=248, on which Klein Oder Strasse can be seen leading in a northeasterly direction away from the red '3'. I am grateful to Darius Kacprzak at the Szczecin Museum for his help.
79 RAFM: X001-3886, Statement of Jens Müller; GWDN: 5239. Müller never knew how the X Organisation had heard of the brothel.
80 Müller, *Tre Kom Tilbake*, p. 124
81 Ibid. Grüne Schanze is now called Dworcowa. For pictures of Grüne Schanze before the war, see http://sedina.pl/galeria/thumbnails.phpalbum=574
82 Müller, *Tre Kom Tilbake*, p. 125
83 For pictures of Klein Oder Strasse before the war, see http://sedina.pl/galeria/thumbnails.php album=539
84 Müller, *Tre Kom Tilbake*, p. 125

85 Ibid., p. 126, and see RAFM: X001-3886; GWDN: 5244

86 Müller, *Tre Kom Tilbake*, p. 126

87 Ibid., p. 127

88 RAFM: X001-3886, Statement of Jens Müller;
GWDN: 5239

89 Müller, *Tre Kom Tilbake*, pp. 127–8

90 Ibid., p. 128

91 Ibid.

92 Ibid., p. 130

93 Ibid.

94 Ibid., p. 132

95 Ibid., pp. 132–3

96 RAFM: X001-3886, Statement of Jens Müller;
GWDN: 5240. Today, Parnitz is called Parnica.

97 Müller, *Tre Kom Tilbake*, p. 133

98 Ibid., p. 134

99 Ibid., p. 136

100 Ibid., p. 138

101 Ibid., p. 139

102 Ibid., pp. 140–1

103 RAFM: X001-3886, Statement of Jens Müller;
GWDN: 5240

104 Müller, *Tre Kom Tilbake*, p. 142

105 Ibid., p. 143, and see RAFM: X001-3886, Statement
of Jens Müller; GWDN: 5237. It is not clear whether
the two Mosquitoes flew in formation. In his memoir,
Müller gives the impression that he flew alone, but
Bergsland's MI9 report shows that he landed in
Leuchars on the same day as Müller. As the operation
presumably took place at night, Bergsland could not
have been that far behind.

106 Smith, '*Wings' Day*, p. 184

107 RAFM: X001-3886, Statement of F/Lt Bram van der
Stok; GWDN: 5236

108 Vanderstok, *War Pilot*, p. 152

109 UKNA: AIR 2/10121; GWDN: 9676

110 Vanderstok, *War Pilot*, p. 152

111 Ibid., p. 153

112 Ibid., plate opposite p. 168

113 Ibid., p. 154. The sequence of Vanderstok's journey to Holland in his memoir differs from that he gave to MI9 in July 1944 (see endnote 96). I have relied more on the interview than the memoir.

114 Ibid., p. 155

115 For an account of Jongbloed's wartime activities, see Ad Maas & Hans Hooijmaijers, *Scientific Research in World War II: What Scientists Did in the War* (Abingdon: Routledge, 2009), pp. 98–100

116 In his memoir, Vanderstok claims to have stayed for one night; in the MI9 interview, it is three nights.

117 Vanderstok, *War Pilot*, p. 156

118 Ibid., p. 155

119 Ibid., p. 156

120 Ibid., p. 157

121 Ibid. Once again, the sequences in the memoir and the MI9 interview are contradictory, and I have followed the timeline laid out in the latter.

122 Ibid., p. 206

123 Ibid., p. 158

124 The sequences between memoir and interview are wildly at variance. Vanderstok seems keen to present himself as being highly proactive in his odyssey across Europe, whereas his MI9 interview shows him to be far more of a passenger.

125 Vanderstok, *War Pilot*, p. 160. As is evident from satellite imagery, the tennis court is still in existence.

126 Ibid., and see RAFM: X001-3886, Statement of F/Lt Bram van der Stok; GWDN: 5236 for date.

127 Vanderstok, *War Pilot*, p. 162

128 Ibid.

129 UKNA: AIR 40/2645; GWDN: 9439. Once again, Vanderstok's memoir is remarkably at odds with his wartime testimony. In *War Pilot of Orange*, Vanderstok does not stay in Toulouse, but instead goes to the small town of Saint-Gaudens, which lies just 17 miles from the border with Spain, and some 60 miles southwest of Toulouse.

130 Vanderstok, *War Pilot*, pp. 164–5

131 UKNA: AIR 40/2645; GWDN: 9439. It is at this point that Vanderstok's memoir seems to enter into the realm of fantasy. Vanderstok supplements the group with a party of thirteen German Jews, which features a truculent 14-year-old and a menstruating woman prone to fainting, and who complain when the members of the Resistance ask to be paid for helping them across the mountains. It seems unlikely that such a large party of Jews could have fled Germany so late in the war, and have successfully crossed half of Europe without being caught or separated from each other. Vanderstok also refers to Stonebarger as 'Barrel' in his book.

132 Ibid. In his memoir, Vanderstok claims to witness this shooting, but this would appear to be unlikely.

133 Vanderstok, *War Pilot*, p. 166. On p. 207, Vanderstok identifies Felix as a man called Leon Estrade, which may or may not be correct. Who knows?

134 Ibid., p. 166

135 Ibid., p. 167. For an idea of the nature of the terrain, see http://www.grpdesbf.nl/esfr-html-markers-411-419.html and http://www.grpdesbf.nl/esfr-html-trips-20060830.html

136 Ibid.

137 Ibid.

138 Ibid., p. 168

139 UKNA: AIR 40/2645, op. cit.; GWDN: 9440

140 Vanderstok, *War Pilot*, p. 170

141 Ibid., p. 171. In his memoirs, Vanderstok claims to have been given the news of the murders by Sir Arthur Street, the Permanent Under Secretary of the Air Ministry, and the father of the murdered Denys Street. I have yet to find any confirmation that Sir Arthur was in Madrid during this period, but it is not inconceivable.

142 Ibid., p. 172

143 RAFM: X001-3886, Statement of F/Lt Bram van der Stok; GWDN: 5234. Whitchurch Airport no longer exists – see http://www.chew76.fsnet.co.uk/whitchurch/whitchurch.html for a brief history. In his memoirs, Vanderstok gives the impression that he returned to Britain before D-Day on 6 June, which is quite simply untrue.

144 Vanderstok, *War Pilot,* p. 173

Chapter Fifteen: Helpless Outrage and Cover-up

1 UKNA: AIR 40/2313; GWDN: 9480

2 UKNA: AIR 40/2269, Statement of Johann Franz Pieber; GWDN: 0055

3 IWM: 99/82/1, Flekser, 'Operations', p. 79. According to UKNA: AIR 40/2313; GWDN: 9480, there were forty-six urns and four boxes.

4 See, for example, the logbook in IWM: 88/20/1, Private papers of H. E. C. Elliott.

5 UKNA: AIR 40/2313; GWDN: 9480

6 IWM: 17365, Waddington, Reel 5. £25 was indeed a ridiculous price for a silk scarf. At the time of

writing, such a figure is equivalent to £2,500 in terms of average earnings (Lawrence H. Officer, 'Five Ways to Compute the Relative Value of a UK Pound Amount, 1830 to Present', MeasuringWorth, 2011).

7   IWM: 26558, Cassie, Reel 22

8   UKNA: AIR 2/10121; GWDN: 9591

9   UKNA: AIR 40/170; GWDN: 0404

10 UKNA: AIR 2/10121; GWDN: 9591

11 UKNA: AIR 2/10121; GWDN: 9592

12 UKNA: AIR 2/10121; GWDN: 9591–9592

13 HC Deb 19 May 1944 vol 400 cc 437–9 at http://hansard.millbanksystems.com/commons/1944/may/19/officer-prisoners-of-war-germany-shooting

14 *Daily Express*, 23 May 1944, p. 1; UKNA WO 208/2901; GWDN: 1174

15 UKNA WO 208/2901; GWDN: 1169

16 UKNA WO 208/2901; GWDN: 1171

17 Ibid.

18 UKNA WO 208/2901; GWDN: 1169

19 UKNA WO 208/2901, Challen to Anthony Eden, 1 June 1944; GWDN: 1159-1163

20 UKNA WO 208/2901; GWDN: 1175

21 Foot & Langley, *MI9*, p. 36

22 UKNA WO 208/2901; GWDN: 1164

23 UKNA: AIR 40/2268; GWDN: 0047

24 Ibid.

25 UKNA: WO 311/172, Judge Advocate General's Office, Military Deputy's Department, and War Office, Directorates of Army Legal Services and Personal Services: War Crimes Files (MO/JAG/FS and other series), Stalag Luft 3, Sagan, Germany: escape, recapture and killing of RAF officers, f. 39, Statement of Walter Schellenberg; GWDN: 0420

26   UKNA: AIR 40/2268, Statement of Peter Mohr;
        GWDN: 0043

27   UKNA: AIR 40/2491, Testimony made by Peter
        Mohr; GWDN: 9815

28   UKNA: AIR 40/2491, Testimony made by Peter
        Mohr; GWDN: 9816

29   See p. 301–2.

30   UKNA: AIR 40/2493; GWDN: 9883

31   UKNA: AIR 40/2269, Statement by Alfred Schimmel;
        GWDN: 0074

32   UKNA: WO 311/177, Statement of Artur Denkmann;
        GWDN: 0592

33   Ibid. According to Walter Jacobs, in the new report,
        Jacobs 'was not included in the execution squad',
        which makes it more likely that Denkmann was. See
        UKNA: AIR 40/2268; GWDN: 0014

34   UKNA: WO 311/178; GWDN: 0611

35   UKNA: WO 208/2901; GWDN: 1114

36   Ibid.

37   UKNA: AIR 2/10121; GWDN: 9598

38   UKNA: AIR 2/10121; GWDN: 9611

39   *Manchester Guardian*, 21 June 1944

40   Wisdom of Solomon, 3.2–4. The order of service can
        be found in UKNA: AIR 2/10121; GWDN:
        9659–9663

41   *Manchester Guardian*, 21 June 1944

42   *The Times*, 21 June 1944

43   HC Deb 23 June 1944 vol 401 cc 477–82 at
        http://hansard.millbanksystems.com/commons/ 1944/
        jun/23/ officer-prisoners-of-war-germany-shooting

44   UKNA: AIR 2/10121; W. M. Catanach to Eden,
        f. 61B; GWDN: 9665

45   Extract from *Völkischer Beobachter*, 23 July 1944,
        contained in UKNA: WO 311/997; GWDN: 0790

46   UKNA: AIR 40/2268, Statement of Peter Mohr;
      GWDN: 0050

47   See p. 238.

48   UKNA: WO 311/1000; GWDN: 1630. For blue
      notebook, see UKNA: AIR 40/2491, Statement of
      Bode Struck; GWDN: 9804

49   See King James Bible, 2 Samuel 19.4: 'But the king
      covered his face, and the king cried with a loud
      voice, O my son Absalom, O Absalom, my son,
      my son!'

50   UKNA, AIR 40/2728, Statement of Edgar Lewerentz;
      GWDN: 9940

51   UKNA: AIR 40/170; GWDN: 0395

52   See p. 147.

53   UKNA, AIR 40/2728, Statement of Joachim
      Ziegenhorn; GWDN: 9939

54   USAFAL: MS 699 (Spivey), Simoleit, p. 24

55   UKNA: WO 311/997; GWDN: 0774

56   BA: MSG 2/1517, Lindeiner, *Im Dienst*,
      pp. 190/195

57   UKNA: AIR 40/170; GWDN: 0393 & 0394

58   UKNA, AIR 40/2728, Statement of Edgar Lewerentz;
      GWDN: 9940

59   Durand, *Stalag Luft III*, p. 314

60   UKNA: AIR 40/2488; GWDN: 9560 & 9561

61   Durand, *Stalag Luft III*, p. 315

62   UKNA: FO 916/840; GWDN: 1299

63   Interview with Charles Woehrle at
      http://www.youtube.com/watchv=LXThZB-IOac

64   UKNA: AIR 40/2645; GWDN: 9344

65   Brickhill, *The Great Escape*, p. 244

66   Stephen Robb, 'By George! Fourth Great Escape
      tunnel to be excavated', BBC News, 19 January 2001,
      http://www.bbc.co.uk/news/uk-12226521

67   Brickhill, *The Great Escape*, p. 245

68   UKNA: AIR 40/2645; GWDN: 9348 & 9350

69   UKNA: AIR 40/2645; GWDN: 9344

70   A copy of the poster can be seen at http://www. harrogate-scene.com/vintagegames/pdfs/colditz.pdf

71   UKNA: AIR 40/2270; GWDN: 0117 & 0118. The ashes were returned to the new location of Oflag 8F in Brunswick.

72   UKNA: WO 311/997. Statement of Erwin Kutath; GWDN: 0770

73   Vance, *A Gallant Company*, p. 306 for Lindeiner's donation; for the involvement of the YMCA see UKNA: AIR 2/6807, Air Ministry and Ministry of Defence: Registered Files, MEMORIALS (Code B, 49): Stockholm monument to R.A.F. personnel shot by Germans at Stalag Luft III; GWDN: 9581–9590

74   Vance, *A Gallant Company*, p. 306

Chapter Sixteen: Exemplary Justice?

1   UKNA: AIR 40/2492, Voluntary Statement by Emil Weil; GWDN: 9840–9841

2   See Guy Walters, *Hunting Evil* (London: Bantam Books, 2010), Chapter 2, for a full account of the failures of the war crimes investigation teams and bodies such as the UNWCC and CROWCASS.

3   Andrews, *Exemplary Justice*, p. 33

4   Ibid., pp. 33–4

5   Ibid., p. 34

6   UKNA: AIR 40/2492; GWDN: 9844

7   Walters, *Hunting Evil*, pp. 283–9

8   Andrews, *Exemplary Justice*, p. 93, and Davies, *RAF Police*, p. 76

9   Davies, *RAF Police*, p. 76

10   UKNA: WO 208/5633, War Office: Directorate of

Military Operations and Intelligence, and Directorate of Military Intelligence, Ministry of Defence, Defence Intelligence Staff: Stalag Luft III, RAF Special Investigation Branch progress reports and statements, f. 33b; GWDN: 0861

11   UKNA: WO 208/5633; GWDN: 0863

12   Ibid.

13   UKNA: WO 208/5633; GWDN: 0864

14   UKNA: WO 208/5633; GWDN: 0866–0867

15   UKNA: WO 208/5633; f. 34A; GWDN: 0869

16   UKNA: AIR 40/2313; GWDN: 9491

17   UKNA: AIR 40/2492; GWDN: 9845

18   Ibid.

19   Davies, *RAF Police*, p. 77; and see UKNA: AIR 40/2272; GWDN: 0160

20   UKNA: AIR 40/2272; GWDN: 0160–0161

21   UKNA: FO 371/57595, Foreign Office: Political Departments: General Correspondence from 1906–1966, POLITICAL: RECONSTRUCTION (U): War Crimes (73), Sagan murder case: interrogation of Dr. Scharpwinkel in Moscow; GWDN: 1264–1265

22   UKNA, AIR 40/2269, Statement by Scharpwinkel 19/9/46; GWDN: 0067

23   Scotland, *The London Cage*, p. 135

24   Andrews, *Exemplary Justice*, p. 288; and see http://forum.axishistory.com/viewtopic.phpf=38&t=84576 for claims of Absalon's death in Kursk.

25   See the case of Horst Kopkow in Walters, *Hunting Evil*, pp. 321–7.

26   Andrews, *Exemplary Justice*, p. 276–9

27   The death of Heinrich Müller has never been definitely established.

28   Andrews, *Exemplary Justice*, pp. 276–9

29   Ibid., pp. 121–3

30   UKNA: WO 311/173; GWDN: 0422; Andrews,
      Exemplary Justice, pp. 34–5. The regal combination
      of Bowes and Lyon is not lost on the author.
31   UKNA: WO 311/173; GWDN: 0422
32   Andrews, *Exemplary Justice*, pp. 127–8
33   UKNA: WO 311/173; GWDN: 0424
34   See plates and GWDN: 0447 & 0454. The cars are a
      Czech-built 1939 Aero Type 50 and a 1939 DKW
      Meisterklasse. With thanks to Mike Worthy-Williams
      for his staggering expertise.
35   UKNA: WO 311/173; GWDN: 0423
36   Andrews, *Exemplary Justice*, p. 135
37   UKNA: WO 311/174; Judge Advocate General's
      Office, Military Deputy's Department, and War
      Office, Directorates of Army Legal Services and
      Personal Services: War Crimes Files (MO/JAG/FS and
      other series), Stalag Luft 3, Sagan, Germany: escape,
      recapture and killing of RAF officers, McKenna to
      Bowes, 4 April 1946; GWDN: 0504
38   Andrews, *Exemplary Justice*, pp. 138–9. Andrews
      grossly exaggerates the timescale in which
      Zacharias was tracked down, presumably for
      dramatic effect.
39   UKNA: WO 311/174; GWDN: 0504
40   Ibid.
41   Andrews, *Exemplary Justice*, p. 141
42   Ibid.
43   Ibid., p. 142
44   UKNA: WO 311/174; GWDN: 0505
45   See p. 191.
46   Scotland, *The London Cage*, pp. 148–9
47   Andrews, *Exemplary Justice*, p. 143
48   Undated *Evening Standard* cutting in UKNA: AIR
      40/2492; GWDN: 9833

49   Undated *Evening Standard* cutting in UKNA: AIR
40/2492; GWDN: 9832

50   See p. 293.

51   Andrews, *Exemplary Justice*, p. 293

52   The *Arbeitserziehungslager* are often overlooked
components of the Nazi camp system. For more
information on Nordmark, see http://de.wikipedia.
org/wiki/Arbeitserziehungslager_Nordmark

53   Andrews, *Exemplary Justice*, pp. 225–6

54   Scotland, *The London Cage*, pp. 151–2

55   *Law Reports of the Trials of War Criminals, Volume
XI*, selected and prepared by the United Nations War
Crimes Commission (London: HMSO, 1949), p. 35.
All 15 volumes in this series can be downloaded from
http://www.loc.gov/rr/frd/ Military_Law/law-reports-
trials-war-criminals.html

56   UKNA: WO 311/177; GWD: 0603–0605

57   Ibid., p. 46

58   UKNA: WO 235/429, Judge Advocate General's
Office: War Crimes Case Files, Second World War,
Stalag Luft III Case, Defendant: Proceedings Place of
Trial: Hamburg, 26 August 1947; GWDN:
5440–5441

59   UKNA: WO 235/424; GWDN: 1257–1258

60   UKNA: WO 235/427; Post's examination-in-chief by
Dr von Saldern, 6 August 1947; GWDN: 5379

61   UKNA: WO 235/427; Post's cross-examination by Dr
Adler; GWDN: 5394

62   UKNA: WO 235/429; Von Lindeiner cross-examination
by Dr Adler, 25 August 1947; GWDN: 5413

63   UKNA: WO 235/429, p. 40; GWDN: 5461

64   For a full analysis, see David H. Kitterman, 'Those
Who Said "No!": Germans Who Refused to Execute
Civilians during World War II' in *German Studies*

Review, Vol. 11, No. 2 (May 1988), pp. 241–54 at http://www.jstor.org/stable/1429971

65   UKNA: WO 235/426, Judge Advocate to Schimmel, 22 July 1947; GWDN: 1903

66   *Law Reports of the Trials of War Criminals, Volume XI*, pp. 47–50

67   *The Times* (London), 18 September 1949. Cutting found in UKNA: WO 311/179, Judge Advocate General's Office, Military Deputy's Department, and War Office, Directorates of Army Legal Services and Personal Services: War Crimes Files (MO/JAG/FS and other series), Stalag Luft 3, Sagan, Germany: escape, recapture and killing of RAF officers; GWDN: 0625

68   UKNA: WO 311/179; GWDN: 0628

69   UKNA: WO 311/180; GWDN: 0643

70   UKNA: WO 311/180; GWDN: 0649–0651

71   UKNA: WO 311/180; GWDN: 0648

72   UKNA: WO 311/180; GWDN: 0646–0647

73   UKNA: WO 311/180; GWDN: 0640

74   *Daily Mail*, 24 October 2009; http://www.dailymail.co.uk/news/article-1222565/He-shot-hero-Great-Escape-cold-blood-But-Nazi-DIDNT-deserve-hang.html

75   Andrews, *Exemplary Justice*, pp. 288–9

76   Davies, *RAF Police*, p. 167

77   Andrews, *Exemplary Justice*, p. 289

Epilogue: The Legacy

1   WO 311/171; GWDN: 0411–0412

2   Vanderstok, *War Pilot*, pp. 193–4

3   'The love story that inspired the Great Escape', *Daily Telegraph*, 26 September 2004, http://www.telegraph.co.uk/news/ uknews/1472657/The-love-story-that-inspired-The-Great-Escape.html

4   *Collier's Magazine*, 2 September 1944

5   Weale, *Renegades*, p. 150

6   UKNA: AIR 18/28; GWDN: 6681

7   UKNA: AIR 18/28; GWDN: 6682

8   UKNA: AIR 18/28; GWDN: 6683

9   UKNA: AIR 18/28; GWDN: 6705

10   UKNA: AIR 18/28; GWDN: 6757

11   UKNA: AIR 18/28; GWDN: 6783

12   See, for example, Paul Brickhill, *Sunday Express*, 'Dramatic night of the break-out', 7 October 1945; Robert Kee, *Sunday Dispatch*, 'The Escape Machine', 30 September 1945. Both cuttings can be found in UKNA: WO 311/599.

13   Author interview with Alfie 'Bill' Fripp, 9 September 2011

14   IWM: 27051, Bryett, Reel 13

15   IWM: 13296, Churchill, Reel 4

16   See p. 179.

17   See p. 133.

18   See p. 116.

19   Merritt E. Lawlis, *Winking at Death: Memoir of a World War II POW* (AuthorHouse, 2008), p. 234. Here Lawlis uses 'all' as a synonym for 'future' ('What all did they forfeit . . .').

20   Ibid., p. 235

21   *The Times* (London), 26 November 2011

22   Information supplied privately.

23   *The Times* (London), 14 January 1976, p. 26

24   Tennyson devotees will realise that the words on the gravestone are a little different to those of the poem itself.

Picture Acknowledgements

Every effort has been made to trace copyright holders; those overlooked are invited to get in touch with the publishers.

The sketch of a watchtower on p. 426 is by Ley Kenyon/ RAF Museum.

The photographs in the picture section were kindly supplied by the author except for the following:

First section
Bushell with shotgun: Georgina Thynne and 601 Squadron Re-created/601 Squadron OCA.

Bushell at wedding: © Illustrated London News Ltd/ Mary Evans; Georgiana and Glen Kidston: Dorothy

Wilding © William Hustler and Georgina Hustler/ National Portrait Gallery, London.

Caricature of Pieber: © Estate of Ley Kenyon/RAF Museum.

Alfie Fripp: courtesy of Alfie Fripp; Bobby Laumans and drawings: Alex Cassie/Imperial War Museum; Cooking cartoon: © Estate of Ley Kenyon/RAF Museum.

Cassie self-portrait: Alex Cassie/Imperial War Museum.

Second Section
'London Underground' cartoon: © Estate of Ley Kenyon/RAF Museum.

Forgery templates: RAF Museum (Object number: X002-5582).

Tunnelling paintings: © Estate of Ley Kenyon/RAF Museum.

'Exodus of Room 4': Alex Cassie and © Estate of Ley Kenyon/RAF Museum; Escapers: The National Archives, Kew.

Third Section
Escapers: The National Archives, Kew.

Gestapo officers and reconstructions: The National Archives, Kew.

Sketch by Breithaupt: The National Archives, Kew.

Bushell gravestone: Michał Czajka; Georgie gravestone: Angela Walters.

INDEX

The Leader

GREAT BRITAIN, 1937:
Edward VIII will not abdicate. He and his new bride, Wallis Simpson, are preparing for their coronation.

Winston Churchill is a prisoner on the Isle of Man.

The Prime Minister, Oswald Mosley consults the new Chancellor of Germany, and his close ally, Adolf Hitler on a more 'permanent' solution to the 'Jewish problem'.

The secret police have Britain in an iron grip.

But one man, James Armstrong, a hero of the Great War, is organizing the resistance against the government. While 'the leader' is determined to see him hang, Armstrong, constantly on the run, is every bit as clever and resolute as his enemy.

In the tradition of Robert Harris's *Fatherland*, Guy Walters has writen a compelling, page-turning what-if thriller that imagines a nightmare vision of a Britain that could have been, if history had gone the other way.

The Occupation

FEBRUARY 1945. IN his bunker in Berlin, Hitler makes a desperate decision. He will deploy the V3 – a weapon so secret that its lethal nature is unclear even to the slave labourers constructing it deep beneath the Channel Island of Alderney.

June 1990. Workmen on Alderney mysteriously start to fall sick. Journalist Robert Lebonneur believes he knows why. But the closer he gets to the truth, the more he realizes he is up against the same deadly forces that caused so much upheaval nearly half a century ago . . .

The Colditz Legacy

GERMANY 1941. TWO British officers, Hugh Hartley and Malcolm Royce, achieved what many believed to be impossible. They escaped from Oflag IVC, better known as Colditz Castle. But as they are about to cross the border into Switzerland, and within yards of reaching freedom, Royce is shot. He begs Hartley to go on and save himself. Wracked with guilt, Hartley leaves his friend behind.

London, 1973. Thirty years later and Hartley is now a senior MI6 officer. When a shadowy contact tips him off that Royce may still be alive, and still being held in Colditz – now a lunatic asylum – Hartley is desperate to discover what really happened to his friend. He plans a perilous mission to break back into Colditz, but the truth he will find there will be more shocking than he could possibly have imagined.

The Traitor

IT IS 1943. British SOE agent Captain John Lockhart is in Crete, fighting with the Resistance. Captured by the Germans, Lockhart faces a stark choice, between death and betrayal of his country. Concealing his true motives, Lockhart makes a bargain: in return for the life of his imprisoned wife, he will work with the Germans.

When his mission is revealed, Lockhart is stunned. He is to lead a unit of the Waffen SS made up of British fascists and renegades culled from POW camps: the British Free Corps. Lockhart takes command, but he has an audacious plan to free his wife and other innocent victims of the war – whatever the personal cost.

Hunting Evil

Guy Walters

AT THE END of the Second World War some of the highest ranking members of the Nazi party fled from the ruins of the Third Reich. Many are names that have resonated deeply in twentieth-century history – Adolf Eichmann, Josef Mengele, Franz Stangl and Klaus Barbie – not just for the monstrosity of their crimes, but also because of the shadowy nature of their post-war existence.

Guy Walters has travelled the world in pursuit of the real account of how these fugitives escaped, the attempts, sometimes successful, to bring them to justice, and what really happened to those that got away.

He has interviewed Nazi hunters and Nazis alike, former intelligence agents, travelled the escape routes himself, and pored through archives in Germany, Britain, the United States, Austria, and Italy to bring this remarkable period of our recent history to dramatic and vivid life.

'The stuff of thrillers . . . An enthralling book
and a sobering one'
PATRICK BISHOP

'Gripping and well documented, deserves a lasting place
among histories of the war' DAILY TELEGRAPH

'Walters' account of what happened is first-rate'
MAX HASTINGS

'Absorbing and thoroughly gripping . . . Walters proves
emphatically that the reality of Nazi hunting is far more
fascinating than the myth'
JAMES HOLLAND